Boards, Governance and Value Creation

What is the role of boards in corporate governance? How should they be used and developed in order to maximise value creation? This book looks at boards in a variety of countries and contexts, from small firms to large corporations. It explores the working style of boards and how they can best achieve their task expectations. Board effectiveness and value creation are shown to be the results of interactions between owners, managers, board members and other actors. Board behaviour is thus seen to be a result of strategising, norms, board leadership, and the decision-making culture within the boardroom. Combining value creation, behavioural and ethical approaches to the study of boards, this work offers a systematic framework that will be of value to reflective practitioners, graduate students and researchers in the fields of business ethics, strategic management and corporate governance.

Morten Huse is Professor of Innovation and Economic Organisation at the Norwegian School of Management and Visiting Long-Term Research Professor in the Department of Strategy at Bocconi University, Milan.

'This is an extraordinarily insightful book on an important and timely topic: what boards do and how they add value in different organizational settings. Cognizant of the legal and political debates on corporate governance, Morten Huse pays special attention to board dynamics and how they influence the processes directors follow in making their decisions, bringing a fresh perspective on boards as a key instrument of governance. Huse's attention to smaller and privately held companies is an important contribution, as is his discussion of effective ways to revitalize boards. The artful analysis of the various systems of governance worldwide is another contribution. This is an important book with a clear and an important message. Huse reaches the top of his craft, eloquently enriching the debate on the importance and future of boards. This book is a must-read for scholars, managers and public policy-makers.' (Shaker A. Zahra, *Professor and Robert E. Buuck Chair in Entrepreneurship, Co-Director, Center for Entrepreneurial Studies, and Co-Director, Center for Integrative Leadership, University of Minnesota, Minneapolis*)

'At last, a book about the human side of corporate governance. This is a refreshing and intellectually invigorating read for anyone who is serious about understanding the vital role of boards and governance in value creation.' (Andrew Crane, *George R. Gardiner Professor of Business Ethics, Schulich School of Business, York University, Toronto*)

'Morten Huse presents us with a major work in the area of corporate governance, which is the result of not only an in-depth research programme conducted by one of the top-class scholars in the field, but also of twenty years' experience studying boards throughout Europe. Huse provides us with a unique synthesis. This work reflects the kind of wisdom that is acquired only through years of interaction with directors on a both professional and personal level. There is no doubt that it will become a reference work for researchers as well as for practitioners who are involved on a day-to-day basis with boards and questions of governance.' (Pierre-Yves Gomez, *Professor in Strategic Management, Director, Institut Français de Gouvernement des Entreprises, EM Lyon Business School*)

'Prof. Huse's book is based on two key premises, that the main task of a board of directors is to create value for the firm, and that to understand this value creation process one needs to look inside boards and understand how the team of directors works. Both premises are true and important. Thanks to the serious research he and his colleagues have carried out in the past twenty years, this book is a major contribution to our understanding of the realities of the fundamental task of corporate governance. A book every director should read!' (Joan E. Ricart, *President, European Academy of Management and Strategic Management Society, and Carl Schrøder Chair of Strategic Management, IESE Business School, University of Navarra, Barcelona*)

'This book successfully combines the value creation and the behavioural and ethical approaches to the study of boards, offering a systemic framework which contributes both to the practitioner and the academic debate. I'm especially pleased to see that the subject of corporate governance is deployed with reference to all classes of firms and to different stages of their life, whereas most literature is still concentrated on large listed companies. The book suggests a wide range of different views and interpretations of the roles of boards and governance in our society.' (Giuseppe Airoldi, *Professor of Business Administration, Institute of Strategic Management, Bocconi University, Milan*)

Boards, Governance and Value Creation

The Human Side of Corporate Governance

MORTEN HUSE

Norwegian School of Management BI, Oslo, and Bocconi University, Milan

CAMBRIDGE
UNIVERSITY PRESS

CAMBRIDGE UNIVERSITY PRESS
Cambridge, New York, Melbourne, Madrid, Cape Town, Singapore, São Paulo

Cambridge University Press
The Edinburgh Building, Cambridge CB2 8RU, UK

Published in the United States of America by Cambridge University Press, New York

www.cambridge.org
Information on this title: www.cambridge.org/9780521606349

© Morten Huse 2007

First published 2007

Printed in the United Kingdom at the University Press, Cambridge

A catalogue record for this publication is available from the British Library

ISBN   978-0-521-84460-4 hardback
ISBN   978-0-521-60634-9 paperback

Contents

Tables

Preface

A past president of a large multinational corporation recently confronted me with the view that corporate leaders and board members have not learnt anything from research into corporate governance. This observation has at least two aspects to it. The first is that corporate governance research needs to be relevant and actionable. The second is that research-based findings must be communicated. Through this book my aim is to communicate actionable research and knowledge about boards and governance.

My objective is to stimulate thinking, rather than to produce a handbook that purports to present definitive answers to various questions. This is a research-based book that, it is hoped, will help the reader reflect on and gain a deeper understanding of boards and governance. But it is also a book that communicates actionable knowledge with regard to boards of directors. Thoughtful readers are the target group; these may be board members, potential board members, business school students, researchers, or others who may have an interest in boards. The book has an ambitious objective: it is written in a management tradition with an emphasis on strategic decision-making, organisation theory and organisational behaviour. Value creation, including entrepreneurship and corporate social responsibility issues, are used to frame the presentation.

Boards of directors in different countries and contexts
The tasks facing boards of directors have received considerable attention of late, and in a range of countries. The attention has to a considerable extent focused on large corporations following the corporate governance debate, but there is also an increasing emphasis on boards in small and medium-sized enterprises (SMEs), including family businesses. Few business topics seem to be so urgent to explore and understand today as boards and governance.

The focus of this book is boards and some aspects of governance or corporate governance. When I say 'the board' I mean the board of directors – the organisational body that, in most countries, is usually expected to hire, fire and compensate the chief executive officer (CEO) or the top manager, to set objectives for the firm and to ask discerning questions. However, the formal setting may vary between nations. The book has, therefore, been written so as to meet the differing needs of different countries and different firm sizes. Examples are taken from various countries and from firms of various sizes.

Corporate governance systems vary between countries. A delegated system exists in most places in continental Europe, whereas there are no formal delegation requirements in the United States or the United Kingdom. In this book I address both delegated and non-delegated systems, and I put forward the proposition that, in trying to understand value creation and the human side of governance, the similarities may be greater than the differences. When I write about boards I am referring to the supervisory boards to be found in the German and other two-tier board systems. When I write about the CEO and management, in the two-tier board system it will often refer to the executive boards.

Frequently I talk about firms. However, many of the concepts and relationships presented are more general and may also be applied to boards of voluntary or public organisations, or even project teams. Even though I do not always specifically address boards in SMEs, the book is written in the clear understanding that most firms fall into this category. The book is premised on a corporate governance setting, but boards and governance are also important for activities and enterprises other than large corporations.

Value creation and the human side of corporate governance
The title of this book underlines the emphasis on value creation. The value creation concept is introduced for three reasons. First, it is written in a tradition that sees organisations as tools to create value. This book is intended to be a contribution to board effectiveness and accountability. Second, I see value creation as a broad concept, in which different stakeholders may all make a variety of contributions to the value creation concept. Third, the value creation concept focuses on the board's task in creating value throughout the whole value chain and not just in the value distribution phase.

This book has an open system approach to understanding actual board behaviour and the human side of corporate governance. Understanding actual board behaviour means understanding the underlying processes that go on behind boards' public actions and statements. It goes beyond assumptions about what boards are doing, and it explores boards' working style and how closely in practice boards meet their task expectations. An open system approach also means that we may go outside the boardroom, and even the board members, in order to understand how the boards' decision-making is influenced and formed.

The evolution of the book
This book has been in gestation for more than fifteen years. In 1989 I started teaching my first Master of Science class about boards and governance in Norway, at Bodø Graduate School of Business. I had then just started my research agenda on boards of directors. Since then between twenty and thirty research projects on boards and governance have followed, and the results of these projects have been presented in various articles and publications. This book presents the accumulated findings and conclusions resulting from this research, teaching and consulting. Many sections of this book are based on, and make use of, work that was developed with colleagues and published in various articles. I am very grateful for the contributions of these colleagues. The notes found at the end of this volume indicate the articles and the colleagues that various sections draw on. Here I would particularly like to mention Huse and Rindova (2001) in chapter 2, Gabrielsson and Huse (2005) in chapter 4, Van Ees, Gabrielsson and Huse (unpublished) in chapter 6, Huse and Eide (1996) in chapter 6, Huse, Minichilli and Schøning (2005) in chapter 8 and Huse, Minichilli and Gabrielsson (forthcoming) in chapter 10.

The first full textbook based on this teaching and research was published by the Nordland Research Institute, Bodø, in 1993 (in Norwegian). The title then was (in English) *Aunt, Barbarian or Clan: About Boards of Directors*. The Norwegian publisher Fagbokforlaget, based in Bergen, decided to publish a revised version of this book in 1995. A new version, incorporating major revisions, was published in 2003. The title was then changed to *The Board: Aunt, Barbarian or Clan?* Both versions from Fagbokforlaget are in Norwegian.

Boards, Governance and Value Creation: The Human Side of Corporate Governance is based on new and different concepts, and was conceived with a non-Scandinavian audience in mind. The core ideas and the basic framework of the book have been developed and refined in published articles[1] and conference presentations, and through MBA teaching and research seminars at universities in Norway, Sweden, Finland, the Netherlands, France, Switzerland, Italy, Ireland and the United States.

Research projects

This book is not the result of a single research project but, rather, has evolved through experiences gained from many projects. Several of my own projects will be referred to throughout the book, and when referring to them I use certain labels or nicknames. These are listed below.

- The 'distanced closeness' study,[2] which was my doctoral dissertation. It had a deductive-theory-driven empirical design, and in it I tried to solve the paradox of simultaneous independence and interdependence in board–management relationships.
- The 'bankruptcy' study[3] had a matched-pair design. I studied board compositions in small firms that had filed for bankruptcy, and for each of the forty-four bankrupt firms a twin firm was found. A time series approach was used and the findings were supplemented with qualitative data.
- The 'one of the lads' study[4] was designed to explore interactions inside and outside the boardroom. Participant observation methodology was used while I was the board chairperson in three small firms in different life cycle phases. Various illustrations from this study are presented in chapters 5 and 6.
- The 'U'n'I' study[5] was a reconstructive case study based on newspaper articles, reports and interviews with actors and informants. The objective of the study was to explore the power bases and techniques that the CEO in a large financial corporation uses to circumvent the corporate governance mechanisms. An extract of this study is presented in chapter 6.
- The 'board life story' study[6] was based on collecting and analysing the life stories of women corporate directors. The objective was to explore the experiences of women directors and to get a gendered perspective on boards of directors. Illustrations from this study are presented in chapters 6, 7 and 8.

- The 'fly on the wall' study[7] was based on observations over a period of one year in the boardroom of the TINE Group. The objective was to explore boardroom dynamics. Interviews with all the board members and the top management team (TMT) were also conducted. Extracts from this study are presented in chapter 8.
- The 'value-creating board' programme[8] consisted of large-scale data collections in various surveys. The surveys took place in Norway and various other European countries. The survey instrument followed the framework adopted in this book. In Norway the responses were collected from CEOs, board chairs and other board members. The responses were collected at two points in time. Results from this study are presented in chapters 9 and 10.

Other studies have also been conducted, including the subsidiary board study,[9] the environmental reporting studies,[10] the venture capitalist studies[11] and the innovation studies.[12] When referring to the various projects I sometimes use the first person singular, 'I', and sometimes the plural, 'we'. Generally, 'we' is used when the contribution was made in conjunction with colleagues.

Framework and outline

In this book I use a framework for the understanding of behavioural perspectives on boards so as to guide the reader. The framework is presented in chapter 1, and each of the subsequent chapters is devoted to one of the main elements in the framework. Theoretical and practical issues are presented in each chapter. Chapters 4 to 9 include in-depth case studies. These case studies employ and summarise concepts from the preceding presentations, and they are used to investigate certain topics more deeply.

Sometimes the first person plural form, 'we', is used, which denotes that I am including the reader in the presentation. However, sometimes the singular pronoun 'I' is the most natural – in particular when it refers to my own private experience. Books, chapters, sections or tables are considered to be passive objects that cannot say, indicate, present or show anything by themselves; nevertheless, in order to simplify long and difficult sentence constructions, I let these objects constitute the subject of many sentences.

Acknowledgements

There are many people who have supported me in the writing of this book, and they have contributed in various ways. First I would like to express my thanks to my family, who have seen me at work on this book for years; the manuscript has accompanied me all the time! Next I thank Jonas Gabrielsson, my former student, colleague and friend. His thinking has continually stimulated me in my writing, and he has made useful comments not only during the preparatory period but also, in more detail, on late drafts of my manuscript. I would also like to thank Shaker Zahra, for a long-standing friendship and many lengthy and interesting discussions, which led to this manuscript. Then I would like to put on record my gratitude to all those whom I have worked with at the Norwegian School of Management on the 'value-creating board' project. They include Cathrine Hansen, Ping Wenstøp, Margrethe Schøning, Edle Gjøen, Lise Haalien, Jon Erik Svendsen, Elbjørg Gui Standal, Jon Erland Lervik, Ingjerd Jevnaker and Thomas Sellevold. Thanks must also go to the Norwegian Research Council and other sponsors of the project.

In addition, I would like to acknowledge my colleagues at Bocconi University, participants at the three Norefjell workshops on behavioural perspectives on board research, and the colleagues who are carrying out comparable research in other places. I thank all those who have read my manuscripts at various stages along the way, mentioning in particular Hans van Ees, Anita van Gils, Mattias Nordqvist and Alessandro Zattoni, all of whom have given me comments on the final draft. I would also like to mention Inger Marie Hagen, Sabina Tacheva, Luca Gnan, Alessandro Minichilli and Amedeo Pugliese for valuable discussions in the latter stages of the manuscript's preparation, and Anna Grandori, Sven Collin and Giuseppe Airoldi for important insights in the process.

Thanks must also go to co-authors and colleagues on various earlier manuscripts that I am using in this book. They include Dorthe Eide, Halvard Halvorsen, Anne Grethe Solberg, Diana Bilimoria, Bengt Johannisson and Violina Rindova. I am grateful to Tom Keogan for making the English-language corrections to the manuscript and to Bård Hansen for compiling the references. Thanks also to Katy Plowright, Paula Parish and other editors at Cambridge University Press, and also to my Norwegian publisher Fagbokforlaget.

The starting point for this book was my Norwegian textbook *The Board: Aunt, Barbarian or Clan*. Finally, I would like to thank all the colleagues and friends who have invited me to discuss and present the content of this book at faculty seminars and to graduate students. I would particularly like to mention Hans Landström, Martin Lindell, Odd Jarl Borch, Juha Näsi, Guido Corbetta, Winfried Ruigrok, Pierre-Yves Gomez and their students.

Morten Huse

Oslo, 2006

1 | *Investigating boards of directors*

It is my intention in this book to present the human side of corporate governance. A landmark book about boards of directors was written in 1971 by Professor Miles Mace of Harvard Business School, with the title *Directors: Myth and Reality*.[1] His key observation was that there was a disparity between board task expectations (myths) and actual board task performance (realities). Mace placed the human side of corporate governance in this disparity. He recognised that this human side helps us explore the discrepancy between myths and realities. By understanding the human side of corporate governance, in this book we will:

- explore how boards can contribute to value creation;
- highlight behavioural and ethical dimensions of corporate governance; and
- present a coherent and unifying framework for exploring boards.

This book is about boards and value creation. Accountability and creating accountability are key concepts in the discussion about the board and value creation. Accountability is concerned with value creation, and creating accountability is concerned with bridging the gap between board task expectations and performance. The focus in this book is on how boards of directors can contribute to value creation.

Regularly these days, almost on a daily basis, we read in the press about boards and governance issues. Generally we read about mal-governance, cases in which boards are not doing what they are supposed to do. Institutional investors have increasingly turned their attention to corporate governance and boards of directors and their work, and during the 1990s many countries saw a mushrooming of codes of best corporate governance practice. An ethical dimension is often included in these codes. In this book I intend to highlight the behavioural and ethical dimensions of corporate governance. The focus on the human side of corporate governance will help us understand arenas for board ethics.

1

It has been clearly demonstrated in the ongoing debates that many of the actors, including board members, investors, the public in general and even business scholars, have only a limited understanding of the dynamics of boards and their governance. Concepts that are used in one context are, all too often, just copied and implemented in other contexts. Often there is confusion with respect to theories, concepts and contexts. A cohesive, coherent and unifying framework is missing. This makes it necessary to clarify some of the main concepts related to boards and governance, and to position these concepts in a context, and in relation to each other. The presentation of a unifying framework or structure may be considered to be both a strength and a weakness of a book such as this one. It is a strength insofar as it brings together aspects of corporate governance and board literature into a single view, but it may be difficult for the reader to combine all the different concepts and perspectives. I also run the risk of upsetting defenders of 'holy cows' in several different disciplines. Here I have to concede that I am not equally familiar with all the various disciplines and approaches that contribute to the understanding of boards of directors. These challenges have helped provide guidelines for the presentation and outline of the book.

An integrative framework will be used as a presentation guide throughout the book. Practical questions from ongoing debates will be addressed, and concepts, theories and research results will be presented. In this chapter the guiding framework is introduced. It is a framework for exploring the behavioural perspectives of corporate governance. The main contribution of the framework is the focus on actual board behaviour and the board's working style. The so-called 'black box' of actual board behaviour is opened. The book and the framework are concerned with how boards may contribute to value creation. Contingency and evolutionary perspectives are also central to this discussion.

A framework: the value-creating board

Reviews of research articles may give us a framework with which to analyse boards and governance. More than fifteen years have elapsed since Shaker Zahra and John A. Pearce showed in their seminal article that there are needs to use mid-range theories, including measures of a set of board attributes going beyond board composition.[2] However, in practice these needs are rarely met. In their follow-up, state-of-the-art article Jonathan Johnson, Catherine Daily and Allan Ellstrand divided research about board-financial performance links into three research traditions by focusing on various board tasks; control, service and resource dependence.[3] The main differences between the three traditions are the theoretical perspectives employed. The hypothesised relationships may vary, but board composition is generally measured by the same variables, as are most of the financial performance variables. The various tasks are reflected as theoretical board task expectations, and actual board task performance is rarely measured. Johnson, Daily and Ellstrand concluded that it is difficult to find relationships between board composition and financial performance in any of these traditions. For future research they suggested that boards should also be seen as social constructs.

Opening the black box

Actual board behaviour and the dynamics within the boardroom have in most research been considered as something of a 'black box'. Andrew Pettigrew argues in a 1992 article that the work of boards of directors was one of the most under-researched management topics, and because this research was still in its infancy there were few theoretical, empirical and methodological guideposts to assist researchers through this minefield.[4]

Daniel Forbes and Francis Milliken present, in a timely contribution from 1999, the board as a social construct and employ cognitive theories to understand boards.[5] They emphasise the need to open the black box, and they present a model of board processes. They argue that the board should be understood through the attributes of board composition and its members, the board's working style, and the board-level outcomes. They assign attributes to boards in the same way as for any other decision-making group, including preparations and the use of knowledge and skills, effort norms and cognitive conflicts. While Forbes and Milliken argue for understanding and measuring processes inside the boardroom, Pettigrew argues in favour of considering the board as an open system, and suggests that studies of board tasks should not be separated from studies of power in institutions and society, or from studies of the composition and attributes of top management teams.[6] He concludes that various research directions of managerial elites should be integrated, and that we must understand the dynamism in relations both inside and outside the boardroom.

In a review article from 2000 I show the importance of using a contextual approach to understand boards.[7] Research into boards and the development of codes for boards and good governance is more or less based exclusively on research and concepts developed in the United States from Fortune 500 firms with institutional ownership. However, most firms are in fact small, most firms are family businesses, and most firms are located outside the United States.

This brief summary provides the following behavioural input for the evaluation framework:

- a need for mid-range theories and studies to replace input-output research;
- a need to bridge the gap between assumptions from board task theories and actual board task performance;
- a need for cognitive approaches to understanding the board's decision-making and actions;
- a need for research on the interaction among the board members and the larger set of stakeholders inside and outside the boardroom; and
- a need for board research that differs from the contexts of large US corporations.

In this framework, the firm is seen as a bundle of resources and relationships. Moreover, in this framework corporate governance is defined as the interactions between coalitions of internal actors, external actors and the board members in directing a corporation for value creation.

Overall guiding framework for this book

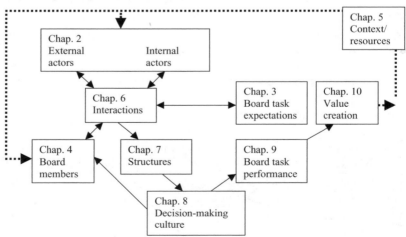

In this book and in the framework I integrate four main approaches to understanding boards and governance. These are:
- the discussion about board effectiveness and value creation;
- the exploration of behavioural perspectives on boards and governance;
- how various types of contextual factors influence boards, governance and value creation; and
- the importance of evolution and learning (these are all illustrated in the framework).

The framework has nine boxes and several arrows. Each box corresponds with a content chapter of this book. The arrows linking the boxes indicate how the content chapters of this book are linked. The framework may appear complex, but it is possible to include more concepts and relationships. I have here, however, tried to keep it as simple as possible. More arrows could have been included, and some of these possibilities will be discussed in the various chapters.

The chapter sequence follows the logic of intermediate steps from input to output. I first present the actors and their board task expectations (chapters 2 to 4). The interactions between the various actors are then presented (chapter 6). The board working style, including structures and processes, follows in chapters 7 and 8. Board task performance and value creation are presented in chapters 9 and 10. Context and resources could equally well have been placed at the beginning or at the end; they feature here as chapter 5. The main concepts from the bulk of board literature have already been presented and defined by then, and it makes sense to present the context in relation to them. Chapter 11 includes cross-chapter summaries.

Main concepts

A large number of concepts are presented in the book, and they are clearly related at many levels. I present them in different chapters, however, and the various chapters build on each other, as indicated above, in chronological order.

In chapter 2 I present concepts about the actors (internal, external and board members) and various corporate governance definitions (managerial, shareholder supremacy, stakeholder and firm definitions). With these different definitions corporate governance may be seen as a struggle between ideologies, and new paradigms for governance are suggested. In chapter 3 I present concepts related to accountability and various board task expectations. A typology of six groups of board tasks relating to control (output and internal), service (networking and advisory) and strategy (decision control and collaboration) follows, and finally in that chapter board task theories are sorted under four different headings (aunt, barbarian, clan and value-creating). Chapter 4 is about the board members. Both the demand side and the supply side are presented. The main concepts in this chapter are the characteristics, competence, compensation and composition of the board members.

The context and resources are presented in chapter 5. The main concepts in this chapter are resources, CEO tenure and characteristics, national and cultural differences, industrial environment, firm size, the firm life cycle, and ownership. In greater detail, these are: resources; CEO tenure, ownership and TMT competence; national, geographical and cultural differences, variations in stakeholder pictures and variations in legislation, including one-tier versus two-tier systems; differences in industries and competitive environments; firm size, including the comparison between large Fortune 500 corporations and SMEs; firm life cycle phases, including start-ups, growth firms, mature firms, firms in crisis and firms at different thresholds – as, for example, with initial public offerings (IPOs); ownership structures, including ownership dispersion and types, different kinds of family firms, institutional investors, venture capitalists (VCs), business angels and corporate ownership (including subsidiaries).

In chapter 6 I present interactions and steps towards a behavioural theory of boards and governance. The main concepts in this chapter are actors and arenas, trust, emotions, power and strategising. The main concepts in chapter 7 are rules, codes, norms, structures and leadership. Also included are concepts such as committees, the CEO work description, board instructions, board evaluations and 'away days'. In chapter 8 I present concepts related to the board as a team. The main concepts are criticality and independence, creativity, cohesiveness, openness and generosity, preparation and involvement, and cognitive conflicts. Various paradoxes and vicious and virtual dynamics are also presented.

Chapter 9 is about actual board task performance. Among the concepts presented are board strategy involvement, output control, quantitative control, behavioural control, qualitative control, reputation building and networking, advice and counsel, and mentoring and collaboration in strategic decision-making. In chapter 10 I present internal and external value creation, and the board's contribution in value creation through the whole value chain. Important concepts include corporate financial performance, corporate social responsibility, mergers, divestments, process innovation, product innovation and organisational innovation, and domestic and international market venturing. The main concepts in the concluding chapter (chapter 11) are board ethics, the 'value-creating board', balancing, and the human side of corporate governance.

Value creation and board effectiveness

The outline of this book is based closely on the framework. Governance, value creation and board effectiveness are the starting points. These concepts are introduced in chapter 2 and discussed at board level (chapters 3 and 9), as well as at corporate level (chapter 10).

Corporate governance and board effectiveness are concerned with accountability and about who and what really count. I present corporate governance definitions in which alternative value creation concepts are discussed. Corporate governance is defined here as the interactions between internal actors, external actors and the board members in directing a corporation for value creation. Accountability thus goes beyond controlling managerial opportunism on behalf of distant shareholders. A broader stakeholder picture is introduced (in chapter 2).

The actors may be categorised in different groups. External actors, internal actors and the various board members constitute such groups. However, the framework does not state clearly who the external and internal actors are, as this may vary depending on the context. The owners in a family business context may, for example, be classified as internal actors.

Firm-level outcomes relate to short- and long-term value creation in the firm as well as to the distribution of the firm's values among various stakeholders. Value creation is, in addition, more than just value distribution. Value creation occurs throughout the whole value chain, and board accountability thus also includes a large set of board tasks.

'Governance' and 'corporate governance' are both used as terms. Here I consider 'governance' in a broader sense than specifically

'corporate governance'. 'Governance' may relate to more levels in the
corporate hierarchy, and it may relate to organisations that are not
corporations. Boards in small firms, medium-sized firms and large
firms, as well as boards in various other types of enterprises, are
addressed in this book. 'Corporate governance' is therefore not a
term that it is correct to employ in all situations. I will, however, still
use it when the presentation relates to the ongoing corporate governance debate. In this book the term 'governance' is used in relation
to boards; 'governance' is used when accountability and effectiveness
are discussed, and the board is one of several tools to provide good
governance.

Actors, behaviour and the human side

In this book I open what is often characterised as the black box of
board behaviour, and I present behavioural perspectives on boards
and governance. Strategic processes are emphasised more than strategic
contents.

This book is about the human side of corporate governance, and
it is based on a behavioural perspective with regard to boards and
governance. A behavioural theory of boards and governance will have
assumptions about the limited rationality of the actors and the fact
that decisions are made by coalitions of individuals.[8] The behavioural
assumptions are different from those that are found in the neoclassical
understandings, and in most of the agency-theory-based input-output
studies of boards of directors.

The framework indicates that there may be a wide disparity between
expectations from traditional theories about board tasks (chapter 3)
and actual board task performance (chapter 9). The behavioural perspectives presented in the chapters about the board's working style
explain why we have this difference. The framework indicates that
the interactions (chapter 6) among various actors or groups of actors
with varying and changing power influence the decision-making and
actions taking place in the boardroom (chapter 8). This influence can
be directed through formal and informal structures (chapter 7), such
as leadership, formal instructions, informal rules of the game, committees, efforts, norms, codes of conduct, etc. The changes and variations
in the power of actors are indicated in the learning loops.

Contexts and resources

A contingency perspective for understanding boards and governance
will have as its starting point the realisation that there is no single best
way of designing boards and governance systems, but that not all ways
are equally good.[9] When designing boards and governance systems we
must take into account the actors and the context. The actors are not
only the board members but also the whole range of internal and external stakeholders or actors. Earlier in this chapter I defined corporate
governance as the interactions among the various actors who have
various stakes and power in a corporation. Their stakes relate to the
value creation and distribution of the values of the corporation. Their
power will vary in nature and intensity in accordance with the variation of contextual factors, as will their knowledge and use of various
governance mechanisms.

The corporate governance discussion has largely been shaped by
the situation and developments in the United States and the United
Kingdom. Much of this discussion has been about the board and how
boards contribute to corporate financial performance – for example,
should a firm have more outside board members, and should the CEO
also be the board chairperson? In continental Europe the discussion
has to a large extent been centred on whether or not a two-tier system
is better than a one-tier system. A two-tier system exists if the board
has to delegate the responsibilities for daily operations to executives
chaired by a CEO or an executive board. The Anglo-American and
the European discussions both concern accountability. Core questions
raised in both discussions include what constitutes effective boards
(including board tasks, board structures and leadership), how independent and knowledgeable board members are, and what the board's
decision-making style is. In this book I concentrate more on the com-
monalities than the differences between the two discussions, but at
the same time I clearly emphasise how boards and governance systems
should fit contingencies and the context.

Since 1995 we have seen a fast-growing number of studies and publications on comparative governance systems, governance in different
countries, and governance under various systems – such as economies
in transition. Recent corporate scandals also lead scholars to use alternative perspectives in understanding governance and to search for

alternative organisational forms. Stakeholder perspectives on corporate governance have received increased attention.[10]

The contextual factors that are most often identified in corporate governance research are:
- the firm's resources;
- the CEO and TMT's tenure, attributes and background;
- national, geographical and cultural differences;
- the industry and environment of the corporation;
- the firm's size;
- life cycle variations, including the importance of crises and the configuration of corporate resources; and
- the ownership dispersion and types, including family ownership.

The contextual factors are more fully described in chapter 5. The various contextual factors may have several aspects. In the firm's production system some of the contextual factors constitute input resources and some are the results of or directly influenced by the firm's outcome. Some of the contextual factors are tools for designing governance systems in addition to shaping the context for corporate governance.

The basic approach in this book is that governance designs must be tailored to the particular situation and needs of each firm. The discretion and thoughtfulness of the actors, and in particular the board members, are thus challenged.

Evolution

Understanding boards involves understanding dynamic processes, including various types of evolution and learning. This dynamism is illustrated in the arrows and loops in the framework diagram.

The dynamism of actual board behaviour and corporate governance is rooted in various learning and influencing loops.[11] These processes and loops exist at various levels:
- societal;
- institutional;
- organisational;
- group; and
- individual.

This evolutionary perspective is illustrated in the framework diagram by means of the arrows. The evolution at a societal level is illustrated through the changing awareness, concepts and rules of corporate governance in society.[12] Institutional learning also takes place through mimetic processes, which occur in social networks at interorganisational levels.[13] The evolutionary perspective may also be illustrated through contextual changes resulting from the performance of the corporation. For example, several studies have shown that there is a negative relationship between the prior performance of a firm and the overall involvement of the board.[14] Literature about organisational and group learning[15] and dynamic capabilities[16] may also contribute to the exploration of the evolutionary processes in the organisation and in the board.[17] Finally, individual learning will contribute to evolution. The learning perspective is rarely used in corporate governance research, and the integration of learning theories may be an important direction for future research into boards and governance to pursue.

Summary

In this chapter I have presented the objective of the book and the guiding framework from which the outline of the book has been developed. The objective of the book is to present:

- the human side of corporate governance, opening the 'black box' of actual board behaviour;
- how boards of directors can contribute to value creation;
- an ethical dimension of boards and governance; and
- a cohesive and coherent framework for exploring boards of directors.

The guiding framework outlining the book has been presented in this chapter. This framework will be displayed as an introduction to each subsequent chapter.

2 | *Internal and external actors*

In this chapter I present concepts about:
- the actors (internal and external); and
- various corporate governance definitions (managerial, shareholder supremacy, stakeholder and firm definitions).

Using these different definitions corporate governance may be seen as a struggle between ideologies, and new paradigms for governance are suggested.

The goal of this chapter is to understand external and internal actors or stakeholders. This is done through a presentation of how the corporate governance debate has developed. Corporate governance is about who and what really count, and the corporate governance debate has seen a shift in focus from management to various groups of stakeholders. The chapter also shows that shareholders and stakeholders are not identical groupings. This is illustrated through various waves of shareholder activism. The more recent crisis in confidence in large corporations also opens up the potential for new paradigms of governance.

A three-group categorisation of actors is presented. The three groups are: the internal actors; the external actors; and the board members.[1] The most important aspect of this classification is not the identification of who the actors are, as they may vary depending on situation, firm and context; rather, it is the realisation that there are various groups of actors, and that the relations between them may empower the board members for special roles.

Definitions of corporate governance based on the positioning of various actors are presented and discussed in this chapter. Agency theory, and other theories influencing and describing corporate governance and board task expectations, are presented in chapter 3.

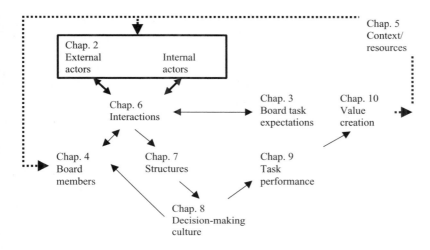

Who and what really count?

'The largest owners are not wanted on the board.'[2] The board of Storebrand, a large Scandinavian insurance company, argued this point when it claimed that the two largest owners of the company would not act in the company's best interests, and that therefore they were not wanted on the corporate board. The arguments from the board chairperson of Fokus Bank in Norway were similar when defending his actions and attitudes against a takeover: 'The company is more than its shareholders, and the board must think holistically.' In both cases, other stakeholders were referred to rather than shareholders. 'Who and what really count?' was a key question in both cases, along with the perception that the shareholders did not necessarily act in the company's best interests.

These illustrations were found in Scandinavian newspapers, but similar examples exist elsewhere. This is a dilemma that board members face in many countries.[3] Recently Fortune 500 companies in the United States have started appointing prominent environmentalists to their corporate boards in addition to individuals drawn from the usual business circles. This has particularly been the case for chemical, oil, and pulp and paper manufacturers – i.e. industries that are under strong public scrutiny for their impact on the environment. For example, the leader of the Conservation Fund, Patrick Noonan, was on the boards of both Ashland Oil and International Paper Co. A former EPA[4] administrator and currently the company's board member advised EI du Pont through its difficult decision to continue making ozone-depleting chlorofluorocarbons (CFCs) upon government request. Including environmentalists as board members is a strategic decision that ensures that companies have access to sophisticated outside views on environmental issues, thus improving the company's 'bottom-line' results. However, focusing on bottom-line results may not be a board task or a criterion of performance from the point of view of every stakeholder group.

This change in the composition of some corporate boards contradicts the conventional theoretical views of corporate directors, that they are either pawns of powerful managers or 'watchdogs' for the company's shareholders. These two theoretical approaches – managerial hegemony and agency theory – have dominated lines of research seeking to resolve the issue of whether boards control managers or incumbent managers control their company's boards.[5] However, boards also perform service tasks, such as giving advice to management and legitimising the corporation in relation to important stakeholders.[6]

What is corporate governance?

A corporation can be defined as bundles of resources and relationships. This definition includes the production and governance aspects of the corporation, or, in broader terms, the enterprise.[7] The purpose of the corporation is value creation that is sustainable in the long term. Value creation takes place through the transformation of resources, and the governance system is about who and what really count in this conversion process.

Why should legislation make allowances for corporations with limited liability? Margaret Blair argues that the reason is the need to undertake large and risky enterprises of major social value.[8] Consequently, it can be argued that the shareholders, or shareowners, own the shares, but they do not own the corporation. They do not have the ownership rights over a corporation – unlike the ownership rights that may exist in relation to other physical objects.

Corporate governance definitions will often be biased and reflect the values of those using them.[9] For example, I heard in a corporate governance presentation given by representatives of Oslo Stock Exchange that they implicitly used three different definitions of corporate governance – 'managerial', 'shareholder supremacy' and 'stakeholder'. A managerial definition was used when relating to their own owners, a shareholder supremacy definition was used in their efforts to develop codes for listed companies, and a stakeholder definition was used when communicating with large corporations and society at large. These three definitions will be discussed later in this chapter.

Corporate governance can be seen as the system by which companies are directed or controlled.[10] The definition of corporate governance that has influenced this book the most is a 'firm' definition. The definition in this book is based on behavioural assumptions, and in it the task of the board is to contribute to value creation. Corporate governance is seen as the interactions between various internal and external actors and the board members in directing a firm for value creation. Accordingly, in this perspective there will not be any a priori assumptions about those for whom the value is created; this is seen purely as a result of the interactions.

Let us turn now to the attributes of the various actors. Corporate governance has been seen as a struggle between ideologies in which the various actors promote their differing conceptions of firms and corporate governance. It is necessary therefore to present various corporate governance definitions.

Internal and external actors

In the framework of this book actors are categorised into three groups: internal actors, external actors and the board members. Another grouping of the actors could have been: capital providers, labour providers and management providers.[11] First I present our distinction between actors and stakeholders, and then I discuss the distinctions between internal and external actors. Then I present the four definitions of corporate governance. Any definition of corporate governance will necessarily be biased, so the various definitions will also be influenced by various ideologies or world-views. From this perspective corporate governance may be considered as a struggle not only between actors but also between ideologies.

Actors and stakeholders
What are the characteristics of corporate stakeholders? Various stakeholder definitions are used to establish these characteristics, and in the

literature we find both wide and narrow stakeholder definitions. One narrow definition includes only actors who have a legitimate stake in the corporation. Another narrow definition includes only those who have contributed something that is at risk with the firm. A wide stakeholder definition will generally include all the actors who may be influenced or who may influence a corporation. Furthermore, the board members are important actors in corporate governance; whether or not they are also stakeholders is arguable. From a behavioural perspective of boards and governance there is a need to understand all actors who may influence the decision-making of a board. These actors do not need to have any stake in the corporation, but they may still be very influential. It may therefore be important to distinguish conceptually between the narrow set of stakeholders and the large group of actors who may influence board decision-making. Corporate governance is, from a behavioural perspective, the interactions among the various actors who may influence the board's decision-making.

The literature on stakeholders often divides actors into three groups. These are equity stakeholders, economic stakeholders and environmental stakeholders.[12] Equity stakeholders are most often discussed in the finance-related literature, and traditionally they have mainly voting power. Economic stakeholders are most often presented in the economic or market literature, and these stakeholders are considered to have economic power through market mechanisms. Examples of economic stakeholders are customers, suppliers, banks and other debt holders. Environmental stakeholders are usually discussed in the political and sociological literature, and usually they are considered to have political power.

Who are internal actors and who are external actors?

We have made a distinction between the various actors because there may be conflicting interests between various groups of actors. Definitions of corporate governance often make a distinction between firm management, which is carried out by internal actors, and owners, who are external actors. A fairly common way to identify who the internal actors are and who the external actors or stakeholders are is to make a distinction based on whether the actors operate within the strategic apex of the corporation. In this view the internal actors are those who make decisions and take actions, and the external actors or stakeholders are those who seek to influence and control decisions.[13]

Shareholders are usually considered to be external actors and the management and employees to be internal actors. The board of directors and the board members are often included as a third group of actors. One of the main discussions in corporate governance is whether board members should be regarded as internal actors or external actors.

However, it is not always easy to identify who or what is inside or outside the corporation. The usual example is the family firm, in which family members are typically considered to be insiders, and the non-family executives to be outsiders. In the United Kingdom a distinction is often made between executives and non-executives. However, a full-time chairperson may be non-executive, but at the same time an insider.[14]

Are employees internal or external actors? Employees may be external to the executives or the management and their decision-making, but internal to the firm. Ruth Aguilera and Gregory Jackson show one way in which stakeholder interactions may be structured.[15] They group the most important actors into three categories of capital providers, labour providers and management providers, and they describe two conflict-of-interest situations; one between classes and another between insiders and outsiders. In the class situation, the employees (the lower class) may be on one side, while the providers of capital and management (the upper class) are on the other side. In the insider–outsider situation, employees may have common interests with the management (the insiders), but have conflicting interest with the capital providers (the outsiders).

The board of directors

The board of directors is just one of several governance mechanisms. Other governance mechanisms include markets for control, auditors, laws and regulations. Board members are typically elected to the board by the owners of the shares, but in some countries and/or in certain enterprises they may be elected by other stakeholders or investors of other kinds of capital – for example, employees, public authorities, suppliers, customers, etc.

The board's role in governance is generally considered to be less important in the United States than in Europe. In the United States corporate laws are generally implemented at state level rather than at federal level, and most large US corporations are incorporated in the state of Delaware as the state laws there are the most flexible. While most countries in Europe have formal requirements to separate the board from the daily operations of the corporation, this is not the case in the United States. One manifestation of this separation is the two-tier board system in some European countries.

In the United States there has traditionally been an attitude that markets will act to control or discipline corporations. The main markets are the markets for corporate control, for product control and for labour control.[16] The main element in the market for corporate control is the threat of hostile takeovers. However, recently we have seen that stock exchanges and various investor groups have been making regulations stressing the need for board independence and the importance of separating supervisory and executive functions. This is also emphasised in the US Sarbanes–Oxley Act, introduced in 2003 as a consequence of governance scandals in large corporations.

Corporate governance definitions

Here I present the four groups of corporate governance definitions that are indicated above. These are the 'managerial', 'shareholder supremacy', 'stakeholder' and 'firm' definitions.

The managerial definition

In this definition it is the perspectives of management and the other internal actors that are emphasised. The board members and external actors are seen simply as instruments for management. From this perspective the accountability of board members is to serve management. Management is often seeking to co-opt external actors who control important resources; this may be achieved by including them on the board of directors.

Corporate governance from the managerial perspective will be to employ or design techniques or systems that can secure the interests and values of the management. During the 1970s and the beginning of the 1980s corporate governance was typically related to how the firm could manage resource dependencies. Resource dependence theory is a theory that is regarded as seeing corporate governance from a managerial perspective.[17] Instrumental stakeholder theory also supports this definition.[18] In instrumental stakeholder theory management is regarded as using the stakeholder relations to support its own objectives and activities.

Table 2.1 *Various anti-takeover defences*

Greenmail 'Someone buys a large stake in the company and if the managers don't like it, they offer to buy the buyer out at a bonus over the market price of the stock.'

Poison pills 'The pill is a doomsday device with such potent wealth-destroying characteristics that no bidder has ever dared proceed to the point of causing a pill to actually become operative. Poison pills are shareholders' rights plans. They usually take the form of rights to shareholders that are worthless unless triggered by a hostile acquisition attempt. If triggered, pills give shareholders the ability to purchase shares from, or sell back to, the target company.'

Fair price provision '[This] requires an acquirer to pay the same price for all shares bought, rather than only paying a premium for a sufficient number of shares to gain control.'

White knights 'This is a friendly third party who agrees to buy a significant portion of the stock to keep it out of the acquirer's hand.'

Crown jewels 'The target company will divest itself of its most valuable assets, its core business for example. The acquirer will then receive a less valuable company.'

PacMan 'In this case the target company will make a bid on the acquirer with the strategy that "I will eat you before you eat me".'

Source: Monks and Minow 2004.

A problem arises with the managerial definition when managerial values and objectives are in conflict with the values and objectives of other stakeholders. This was clearly in evidence in the United States in the 1970s and 1980s. This was considered the era of managerial hegemony, and during this period the salaries of managers skyrocketed, with managers also giving themselves extravagant benefits – at great cost to shareholders.[19] The consequences of this increased expenditure were that, during the 1980s, the United States experienced an era of corporate takeovers. These takeovers were, from a managerial perspective, often considered to be hostile, and they challenged the values of management. Various anti-takeover defences were then influenced, invented and employed by managers. Collectively known as 'shark repellents', they include 'greenmail', 'poison pills', 'fair price provisions', 'white knights', 'crown jewels' and 'PacMan', amongst others;[20] see table 2.1.

The shareholder supremacy definition

The perspectives of shareholders are emphasised in this definition, and management and the board members are seen as instruments for the shareholders. In general terms, shareholder value is considered to be the sum of the dividends plus the market value of the company. There has, however, been a recent move away from focusing on dividends (which were historically the focus) to focusing on market value. The consequences of this refocusing have been a shift from competing for customers to competing for investors. It is a one-dimensional, investor-based definition of shareholder supremacy, which has dominated much of the recent public discussions and research from a financial economics perspective.

In this definition, the board is considered to be accountable to *all* shareholders; such accountability includes the monitoring of managerial opportunism and the potential exploitation of minority shareholders by majority shareholders. In order to avoid managerial opportunism, the shareholder supremacy ideology would argue that shareholders should co-opt board members and managers. This would be achieved by providing them with incentive systems based on shareholding or share options.

This definition has its origin in the separation of the ownership and the leadership of corporations that was discussed in the early 1930s,[21] and agency theory was developed to explain solutions to this separation dilemma.[22] In large corporations with large ownership dispersions, owners were very often collectively too numerous and individually too powerless to be able to control the corporations successfully.[23] The corporate control or governance discussion was concerned with this situation, and a board of directors was seen as a way to overcome or meet these governance challenges. In the United States the need for boards to monitor management to avoid bad managerial behaviour and opportunism was clearly evident in the 1980s. Corporate managers had used their power to circumvent shareholders' interests, and the markets for corporate control were circumvented through various anti-takeover defences (see table 2.1). These defences have, from a shareholder supremacy perspective, been considered as negative.

From a shareholder supremacy perspective, investors are seen as principals, and the firms or their management, including the boards, as the agents.[24] The shareholder supremacy definition became the dominating corporate governance definition during the 1990s. Its importance developed as a reaction to managerial opportunism, and through the evolution of 'heartless' and 'faceless' owners in the new economy.

The main task of the board from a shareholder supremacy perspective is to represent shareholders, and in particular to protect them from managerial opportunism. Following the trends in the new economy, and in particular the emergence of information technology (IT) and the consequent disappearance of geographical constraints, the shareholder supremacy definition continued to develop during the 1990s, and is still developing.

An 'enlightened' version of this definition exists. The enlightened shareholder supremacy definition has a long-term perspective. Maximising shareholder value remains the core in this definition, but it is stressed that attention must also be paid to other stakeholders.

Some general extensions of the shareholder supremacy definition also exist. Stakeholders other than the shareholders may exercise this supremacy, and the boards may be agents for these other stakeholders, who may, for example, be the employees, the state or public authorities. Families may often also have this supremacy, and in many cases we find that the most important family stakeholders may not be formal shareholders in the corporation.

Furthermore, there exist arguments that the shareholder supremacy definition is an ideology used by corporate managers to give them freedom to make interventions in the organisation – for example, through restructuring. With a shareholder supremacy definition managers may not need to pay attention to other stakeholders.

The stakeholder definition

The stakeholder definition, often also called the triangulation or interaction definition, is an action-centred institutional approach.[25] It explains firm-level corporate governance practices in terms of institutional factors that shape how actors' interests are defined and represented. Corporate governance, according to this approach, is, ultimately, the outcome of interactions between multiple stakeholders or actors.

Corporate governance is defined as the relationships between actors who are in the process of decision-making and exercising control over firm resources. Actors will try to develop corporate governance mechanisms in order to control and influence corporate decision-making.

The shareholder supremacy definition and shareholders' rights do not capture the entire complexity of institutional domains. Corporate governance is, from an interaction perspective, defined as the structure of rights and responsibilities between parties with a stake in the firm.[26] It is the relationship between various actors in determining the direction and performance of corporations. The primary actors are usually shareholders, management and the board. Other participants include employees, customers, suppliers, creditors and the community.

This definition relates corporate governance to the national and institutional context it is embedded in. The purpose of the actor-centred model is to specify how the behaviour of each stakeholder towards the firm is shaped by different institutional domains – but, in specifying this, the actor-centred model generates different types of conflicts and coalitions.

The stakeholder or interaction definition thus emphasises that:
• corporate governance is embedded in its institutional context; and
• corporate governance is the interactions among various actors influencing the decision-making of corporations, and social relations are the fundamental unit of analysis.[27]

Board members may experience accountability conflicts, and the accountability of the board in relation to this definition is to balance the interest of various stakeholders. This balance may be achieved through board members being truly independent from all stakeholders, or by balancing stakeholder representation on the board.

The firm definition

The firm is focused on in this definition, bearing in mind that corporate governance is not only about the distribution of value to various actors but also about creating values throughout the whole value chain. The double independence notion is important in this definition and requires that the board members do what is best for the company, and act impartially when representing all stakeholders. The accountability of the board members from this perspective is thus to do what is best for the corporation.

According to this definition, the purpose of corporate governance institutions is to facilitate cooperation – in addition to resolving

Table 2.2 *A comparison of corporate governance definitions*

	Unitary perspectives – discrete – short-term	Balancing perspectives – relational – long-term
External perspectives – *value distribution* *and protection*	**Shareholder definition** 'What is best for the shareholders' – shareholders	**Stakeholder definition** 'What is best for the stakeholders' – stakeholders – triangulation
Internal perspectives – *value creation*	**Managerial definition** 'What is best for the management' – circumventing stakeholder control	**Firm definition** 'What is best for the firm' – value creation throughout the whole value chain

conflicts between stakeholders and monitoring control. A more important purpose may be solving the problems of coordination and engaging in the collective processes of search and discovery. The board's independence is emphasised in this definition, and the board members have to balance the interests of internal and external actors.

A comparison of the definitions

We have presented four main definitions of corporate governance: the managerial definition, the shareholder supremacy definition, the stakeholder definition and the firm definition. These definitions are summarised and sorted in table 2.2. They can be described in two dimensions: internal versus external perspectives, and unitary versus balancing perspectives.

The external perspectives will often focus on value protection or value distribution, while the internal perspectives will more often focus on value creation. The unitary perspective will often be short-term and based on discrete contracts,[28] and the board members will act as agents working for the shareholders or the management. The balancing perspective will more often be long-term and relational. In this perspective the board is not an agent acting on behalf of various principals; it is an independent organisational body positioned at the top tier of the corporation.

The *managerial definition* emphasises what is best for the management. It is about how stakeholder relations can be used and governed. Corporate governance mechanisms will be designed to support management and to protect the management from hostile takeovers and stakeholder control. The *shareholder supremacy* definition focuses on how boards, managers and corporations are instruments for the shareholders. Corporate governance mechanisms will, from this perspective, be there to protect shareholder value. The *interaction or triangulation definition* does not have an a priori definition of who value creation is for, but focuses on the interaction between coalitions of actors. Corporate governance will, from this perspective, be embedded in various national and cultural contexts, and corporate governance mechanisms will be designed for value distribution and protection. The *firm definition* focuses on how the board contributes to value creation throughout the whole value chain.

Corporate governance: a struggle between ideologies

Corporate governance can be seen as a struggle between ideologies. Advanced market economies, led by waves of shareholder activism from the United States over the last twenty years, have been dominated by investor-biased shareholder supremacy definitions supported by agency theory. Investors have been the principals, and the firms or their management, including the boards, have been the agents.

Waves of corporate governance activism

The evolution and changes in emphasis of the different corporate governance definitions have followed various waves of corporate governance and shareholder activism.

The first wave of shareholder activism was led by major long-term institutional investors such as Dale Hansson in the California Public Employees Retirement System (CalPERS). Guided by agency theory reasoning, these shareholders fought for boards and board members to be sufficiently independent to resist managerial dominance or hegemony. According to this perspective, boards should be more than rubber stamps for decisions made by management, or ornaments on the corporate Christmas tree. Boards should instead set objectives, ask discerning questions and hire, fire and compensate the CEO. The task of boards should be to create value for shareholders through value creation in the firm. In the United Kingdom this view was supported by the Cadbury Commission.[29] Headed by Sir Adrian Cadbury, this commission developed a seminal code of best practices in 1992. Recommendations included in this code of best practice included separating the positions of the chairperson and the CEO and having a majority of independent directors.

A second wave of shareholder activism occurred after the emergence of trends such as globalisation, IT and the 'shrinking of the world', and rapid changes in the new economy. Firms became increasingly global, and owners became faceless and heartless. Large corporations were listed on stock exchanges around the world, and private individuals invested in stock saving funds that were administered by portfolio managers who were being evaluated on quarterly earnings. Attention to market prices replaced attention to dividends. These impatient owners or portfolio managers also prescribed remedies rooted in agency theory and financial economics. A key argument was that managerial incentives should always be aligned with shareholders' interests, so managers became residual claimants through shares or stock options. Stock exchanges and various investor groups continued to develop corporate governance codes, and corporate governance was redefined as monitoring by owners.

CSR, family business and psychological ownership

An alternative trend in corporate governance received considerable wind in its sails as a result of the unveiling of the conflicts of interest between stakeholders that became apparent during the large corporate scandals of recent years. These crises, such as those at Enron, WorldCom, Tyco, etc., clearly showed the importance of stakeholders other than the shareholders. Employees, customers, suppliers and local organisations suffered severe losses from managers being motivated by the opportunities to benefit personally through dramatic increases in the market prices of their shares.[30] As a result a broader perspective was reintroduced into corporate governance, and corporations were reminded of their corporate social responsibility (CSR) to national as well as to international bodies, such as the United Nations and the

World Bank. Suggestions to address the problems included CSR reporting and the introduction of various stakeholder representatives (for
example, employee directors) on boards. The US government went so
far as to introduce the Sarbanes–Oxley Act; even though in the United
States it is very unusual for federal laws to be passed to regulate corporate activities.

The ideology behind the corporate governance definitions and codes
developed during the waves of shareholder activism also represented a
conflict of interest in relation to shareholders such as industrial owners, holders of blocks of shares, corporate owners, private investors and
other owners who wish to contribute to value creation through their
own contribution in the boards of corporations. Most firms, and in particular small and medium-sized enterprises, are dominated by owners
who also wish to make such a contribution to value creation. Included
in such businesses are family firms and entrepreneurial firms. These
groups of owners may have objectives for their involvement and ownership other than value creation through dividends or earnings. Their
involvement may be of a strategic nature, and may also be related to
value creation in other arenas.

New paradigms of governance

The recent scandals in corporations have made many commentators
reflect and react, and even the United Nations General Secretary, Kofi
Annan, has presented a vision of corporations being held accountable
for creating sustainable value for shareowners, customers, employees
and communities.[31] Corporate managers have been called crooks and
liars, and unethical corporate behaviour has once again been highlighted. The calls for more ethical and principled leadership have
become louder, and there have been questions about the root causes
and imminent consequences of the crisis in confidence in corporations.
What can be done? A governance revolution seems to be taking place,
'and while many official reforms have already been passed following
Enron's meltdown, boards are going even further, instituting sweeping
changes in their composition, structure, and practices on a scale not
seen since skyrocketing executive pay gave birth to the modern governance movement in the 1980s'.[32] The recent scandals now give us the
opportunity to ask if there is a need for a new paradigm for governance.

Governance reform now ranks high on the priority list of policy-makers and regulators. Governance is not only control, incentive and ownership structure; it is also the allocation of decision rights, as well as normative and value-based control. Governance is not just something 'internal' to the firm; it also cuts across organisations. The governance concept is broader than just corporate governance, as organisations other than 'corporations' face governance challenges.

Understanding and reforming boards and governance

Trust is an important ingredient of the free market capitalist system, and the recent corporate scandals have demonstrated how some corporate managers misuse and breach this trust by circumventing stakeholders' power. Corporate governance is about the use of corporate power and the ability to control this power. The various corporate scandals have highlighted the importance of corporate governance – and underlined the fact that corporate governance deserves exceptional attention.

Scandals such as Enron, WorldCom, Tyco, Royal Aholt and Parmalat were not only executive or board failures – but also governance malfunctions. It was episodes in the late 1980s that initially intensified the need for corporate governance reforms. Various provisions were proposed in order to achieve a better basis for governance. These reforms were aimed at protecting the investors. Board committees and compensation consultants restructured executive contracts so as to align management incentives more closely with investors' interests. Similarly, boards turned to CEOs who could manage relations with the financial community and project an image of confidence.

However, the corporate governance reforms have raised questions about the means to good governance, but not about the ends for which corporations should be responsible. It is not only the providers of capital who invest in corporations and bear the associated risks; shareholder interests are never the *only* relevant interests. The problem of 'short-termism' for many shareholders is an issue highlighted in the present debate.[33] The question of responsibility to longer-term stakeholders deserves to receive more attention. Stakeholders such as employees, customers and communities are also residual risk bearers, and their interests will often be more long-term than what has been in evidence on the part of many stock owners in the recent corporate scandals.[34] Corporations often show a lack of sensitivity towards local concerns and interests, so they should focus more on their human capital as a corporate asset.

There are several options for securing good corporate citizenship and sustainable value creation that also consider the stakes of residual risk bearers other than the stock owners.[35] These options can be realised through regulators, independent board members or board members who represent specific stakeholder groups.

Should it be distant regulators who decide on the most appropriate option or should this be left to the discretion of the board and its directors? Ideally it would not be necessary to place corporate decision-making in the hands of remote regulators. This implies that executives and directors will need not only to defend stock owners' interests but also to be genuinely independent and have the courage to make socially responsible decisions. The directors are there to make decisions based on what is best for the company – and a company is much more than just its stock.

Different stakeholder groups will vary in their expectations of what the board's tasks are.[36] Voting rights on corporate boards have accordingly been suggested for employees and local communities – not only to secure sustainable value creation but also to enhance the creation of value for stakeholders other than the stock owners.[37] Recent scandals have proved that there is a need for independence between the stock owners, the board and management in order to ensure sustainable value creation in the company, and in certain situations voting rights for employees and local communities may provide the necessary checks and balances.

Rethinking management and governance

The recent corporate scandals suggest that there may be a need to rethink management and governance, and even promote a search for alternative paradigms of governance. However, corporate governance reforms and an emphasis on corporate social responsibility are not sufficient remedies in themselves for solving corporations' present governance problems. What is required is more fundamental and holistic thinking, involving alternative paradigms to replace or complement the prevailing shareholder value ideology. Below are some considerations that may be borne in mind when developing alternative paradigms of governance.

Questioning shareholder supremacy

Shareholder dominance should be questioned. In the context of viewing corporate governance as a struggle between various ideologies, it is the shareholder supremacy principle that has been dominant since the late 1980s. Defining an ideology as a set of ideas or a system of meaning that serves the pursuit or maintenance of power makes it clear that the doctrine of shareholder supremacy is not ideology-free.[38] Corporate governance practices should be viewed through the lens of ideological struggle.[39] Since the mid-1980s the shareholder value ideology has clearly replaced the previously prevailing doctrines.[40]

The corporation as a legal entity grew out of its ability to protect not only the shareholders and other investors but also other stakeholders. That was important for the creation and sustainability of institutions during the early development of an industrial economy.[41] For example, we are now moving towards a knowledge-based economy, and many of the underlying assumptions of agency theory can be considered empirically wrong when related to knowledge-based activities and resources.[42] Human capital investors are critical, and employees will often be in the same position as financial capital providers.[43] This calls for the regulation of multiple principals rather than the regulation of the relationship between a single principal and an agent.

Corporate governance assumptions

Agency theory is viewed almost as having divine authority by various actors in the present corporate governance debate, but some of the agency theory assumptions need to be questioned.[44] The assumptions from agency theory and the shareholder supremacy paradigm about human behaviour can have negative consequences. In this context, individuals are perceived as being opportunistic and one-dimensional economic entities, with the legal system taken as the underlying principle for decision-making. Executive contracts are designed accordingly and do not take into account the fact that individuals are social beings, with social obligations such that decision-making may be based on fellowship, and that trust may be the underlying principle.

The first set of assumptions in agency theory easily leads to 'short-termism', while long-term relations are governed most efficiently by social contracts. A primary reason for the recent corporate scandals is the design of executive compensation based on agency theory assumptions.[45] Board committees and compensation consultants restructured executive contracts so as to align management incentives more closely with investor interests. Boards likewise turned to CEOs who could manage relations with the financial community and project an image of confidence.[46] Instead of solving the problems, these assumptions and the resultant governance structures only make things worse. Self-intrinsic motivation is reinforced. Managers become more involved in managing the share price than the company. These compensation contracts may also cultivate corporate leadership that is obsessed *only* with the personal bottom line. As an alternative, less emphasis on variable pay for performance may be suggested. Such an alternative would increase intrinsically motivated virtue and honesty, and, more specifically, would result in managers being selected on the basis of pro-social intrinsic preferences.[47]

The directions in principal–agent relationships

The shareholder supremacy ideology and agency-based hierarchies are challenged in actor-centred institutional analysis.[48] There are various contingent governance arrangements, but it is not self-evident who the agent is and who the principal is in agency-based hierarchies. One example is the relationship between the venture capitalist and the entrepreneur. Another example is the relationship between the headquarters of a multinational corporation and a country hosting a subsidiary of the multinational corporation as part of an international joint venture.[49] As a consequence, codes of corporate governance – and even laws, when inconsistent with equilibria in complementary domains – may be dysfunctional.

Summary

In this chapter I have presented concepts relating to the actors and various corporate governance definitions. With these different definitions corporate governance may be seen as a struggle between ideologies, and new paradigms for governance are suggested.

In this chapter we have seen that corporate governance is concerned with the nature of the interactions and relationships between the firm and its various stakeholders in the process of decision-making and in terms of control over firm resources. Corporate governance is to be understood here, in general, as the interactions between internal actors, external actors and the board members in directing a corporation for value creation. For understanding corporate governance in a specific firm it is necessary to identify and understand the behaviour of the main actors, including the board members, external actors and internal actors, and the context in which governance takes place.

Four different types of corporate governance definitions have been presented: the managerial definition, the shareholder supremacy definition, the stakeholder definition and the firm definition. The shareholder value focus has brought benefits to various corporate stakeholders, but there are also costs associated with it.[50] It is evident that one consequence has been less respect for business in society at large, and there has also been a decline in customer and business loyalty. The current debate focuses too much on control for managerial opportunism and value distribution, and value creation throughout the corporate value chain has been neglected. Bernard Taylor argues that there should be a change from corporate governance to corporate entrepreneurship.[51] By this he means that a key task for the board should be the development of a corporate entrepreneurial mindset and the building of an entrepreneurial company. There should be a move from the established shareholder or stakeholder models towards an entrepreneurial model of corporate governance.

In this chapter the values and ideologies of various internal and external actors have been presented. Corporate governance is about who and what really count, which includes a struggle between the various ideologies. However, a simple shareholder supremacy understanding of corporate governance has been brought into question. This is illustrated through the application of various corporate governance definitions. Corporate governance definitions are biased and reflect the values of those promoting them. In this chapter we have also seen how corporate governance definitions emerge over time, and that practice often precedes theory.

The categorisation of various actors also emphasises the importance of human behaviour and politics in corporate governance. This categorisation is most beneficial in understanding the attributes of the actors and the relationships between them. Corporate governance is about the interactions of coalitions of actors inside and outside the firm and inside and outside the boardroom. The actors have various attributes and objectives, and all have a biased definition of corporate governance. This will also influence board task expectations and their expectations regarding value creation. Board expectations are covered in chapter 3.

3 | *Board task expectations and theories*

In this chapter I present concepts relating to accountability and various board task expectations. A typology of board tasks follows:
- board output control tasks;
- board internal control tasks;
- board advisory tasks;
- board decision control tasks; and
- board collaboration and mentoring tasks.

Various board tasks are also presented in this chapter. They are sorted under the headings:
- aunt theories;
- barbarian theories;
- clan theories; and
- value creation theories.

This chapter is concerned with board task expectations. In chapter 2 we saw how various actors may have different perspectives on corporate governance and board tasks. In this chapter various perspectives on board tasks are presented, and we will see how the various theories contribute to seeing board task expectations from different perspectives and with differing emphases.

I distinguish between board roles and board tasks. In the literature we find concepts such as board roles, board tasks, board functions, board activities and board involvement, and often they are all used as if they have the same meaning. In our use we see the board role concept as being related to board-level outcomes as well as to the board's working style.[1] In this book I employ the term 'board task' as an expression related to board level-outcomes only. Board tasks can be specified in even more detail: they are about task involvement, *not* about the results of task involvement. I use the board task concept in relation to both expectations and actual performance.

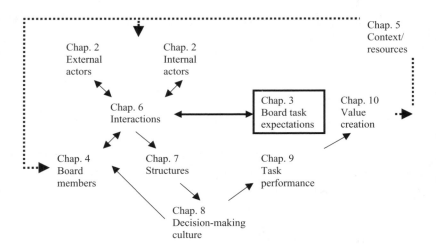

In this chapter I first present the accountability issue. Accountability is about how board task performance measures up to board task expectations. Then I present six theoretically derived sets of board tasks. The rest of the chapter is devoted to describing and categorising various theories that help us understand board tasks. The theories are sorted into four sections based on the underlying assumptions behind the theories.

- Property rights theory, law and managerial hegemony theory are here labelled *aunt theories*. Aunt theories refer to an understanding of the formal roles of boards. From these theories we often find that, in practice, boards function mostly as rubber stamps.
- Agency theory, stewardship theory and stakeholder theory are labelled *barbarian theories*. In this group I have also included paternalism. The main focus in these theories is how boards can be instruments for external actors. The tasks of boards are often related to those of value protection and control. The term 'barbarians' refers to the intrusion of outside actors. These will often have norms and world-views at variance with those inside the organisation. The board members may have contributions to make to firm value creation, but it may be that these are not intended or openly communicated.
- Institutional theories, including social capital theory, social movement theory and interlocking directorates, are here labelled *clan theories*. These theories show that boards are influenced by social relations both inside and outside the boardroom.

- Resource dependence theory and a resource-based view of the firm are here labelled *value creation theories*.[2] These theories argue that boards are strategic resources or instruments for the firm.

Accountability

'Accountability', 'responsibility' and 'liability' are three terms we often meet in the corporate governance debate, and many people are frequently mistaken in their understanding of the three terms in this context. Accountability is about doing what you are supposed to do. In the corporate governance discussion the accountability concept has a focus on board tasks and actors. Accountability is clearly related to understanding, evaluating and balancing various perspectives and interests. Anthony Giddens explains accountability in the following way: '[T]o be accountable for one's activities is to explicate the reasons for them and to supply the normative grounds whereby they may be justified.'[3]

Responsibility and liability are concepts often used interchangeably with accountability. However, in this book I refer to responsibility when there is a focus on the board members individually. Liability represents the legal side and has a focus on enforcement.

Following on from the discussion in chapter 2, a pluralistic accountability definition is used. Therefore, when discussing accountability, I do so in the context of balancing various external and internal perspectives, various board tasks, and various theories.

Accountability and effectiveness

Effectiveness requires not only a mechanism but also standards. The board members are the mechanism and the board task expectations are the standards. Board effectiveness can be gauged by comparing board task expectations with actual board task performance.

The fiduciary duty of directors under most legislative regimes is to do what is best for the company.[4] Defining what is best for a company requires a pluralistic approach. However, from this perspective board effectiveness will be derived from the deployment of knowledge rather than from the reduction in agency costs. Board members contribute to effective governance primarily by using the information and expertise they possess to enhance creativity and coherence in the processes of decision-making and control over firm resources.

Accountability, ideology and stakeholder interactions

Board accountability cannot be understood without understanding whom the board is accountable to. In chapter 2 I presented various definitions of corporate governance. The various definitions arise from a consideration of different ideologies, and the definitions have different implications for accountability. Boards may be accountable to the management, the shareholders, the broader set of stakeholders or the firm.

As I am emphasising a behavioural perspective in this book I do not have any clear *ex ante* definition of whom the board is accountable to. Accountability and board task expectations are results of the interactions between internal actors, external actors and the board members.

The argument has already been made that corporate governance is a struggle between ideologies, and that various and changing coalitions of stakeholders contribute to dynamism in board accountability. Aguilera and Jackson provide an example of this.[5] They make a distinction between three main groups of stakeholders: providers of capital, providers of labour and providers of management. Using these groups of stakeholders they present various coalition formations representing various types of conflicts that have implications for accountability. Class conflict may arise when there is a coalition between capital and management, insider–outsider conflict may arise when there is a coalition between labour and management, and 'accountability conflicts' may arise when there is a coalition between capital and labour. Such coalitions may change over time, but they may also be issue-related and thus coexist.

Issues and perspectives on corporate governance and board tasks

Board tasks may be classified in various ways. Common ways are the cafeteria classification, the empirical classification, the perspective classification, the focus classification and the discipline or theory classification. The cafeteria classification is often found in the board handbook literature. It is usually based on an ad hoc listing without relating the tasks to any overarching logic. In such listings we often find a mix of board tasks, board working styles and board tools such as board evaluations included in lists of board roles. The empirical classification results from statistical analyses and data reduction techniques on empirical observations of various board tasks. The perspectives of different actors – as presented in chapter 2 – provide the background for the perspective classification.

A theory or discipline classification is presented by Humphry Hung.[6] He has made a typology that links board theories to various board tasks. His six board tasks or roles are linking roles, coordination roles, control roles, strategic roles, maintenance roles and support roles. According to Hung these tasks are related to resource dependence theory, stakeholder theory, agency theory, stewardship theory, institutional theory and managerial hegemony theory respectively. Hung's typology is presented in a matrix with perspective and focus dimensions.

In this chapter I introduce the focus classification and the perspective classification. First, I present the focus of various board tasks, and then I present a typology of board tasks based on a combination of the perspective classification and the focus classification. The main part of the chapter, the final part, is a presentation of various board task theories.

Focus on external issues, internal issues and decisions

Board tasks can be sorted depending on orientation or focus. There will be differences according to whether there are orientations towards internal or external efficiency. For example, the board members' concerns for internal factors of cost control, employee relations, organisational structure, employee utilisation and qualitative control have been contrasted with their concerns for external control factors, including services and programmes to meet community needs, relations with governmental agencies, relations with competing firms, relations with community groups and capital investments.[7]

Agency theory has recently become the dominant theory in the literature about boards of directors. Agency theory has an external perspective on board tasks, but it also explains how various focuses or orientations have implications. The board tasks presented in the seminal agency theory contributions by Eugene Fama and Michael Jensen are output control tasks, behavioural control tasks and decision-making control tasks.[8] The output control tasks have an external focus, the behavioural control tasks have an internal focus, and the decision-making control tasks focus on the future or on strategies.

Similar distinctions may also be found in theories and the literature with an internal perspective. Some examples follow. Resource dependence theory has an external focus, and the main associated board tasks are networking, lobbying, legitimacy, etc.[9] The resource-based view of the firm has an internal focus, and the main associated board task is the provision of advice for long-term value creation.[10] Stewardship theory has a strategy focus in practice because the main associated board tasks are mentorship and strategic participation.[11]

External issues will often be related to the environment, markets, competitors and resource providers. Internal issues will be related to managerial behaviour, organisational behaviour, sales development, costs and resources, employees, etc. Strategic issues will be proactive rather than reactive, and they will concentrate on the future rather than the past.

A typology of board tasks

A typology of board tasks from internal and external accountability perspectives is presented table 3.1.[12]

In the board task typology I combine various focuses with the two perspectives. The three focuses used are firm-internal, firm-external and strategic. The board may have a focus on how the firm relates to the external environment, what takes place inside the firm, and it may focus on decisions having impact on the long-term and short-term development of the firm. Six main board tasks are thus displayed in the body of table 3.1.

- *Board output control tasks.* Boards acting on behalf of external stake-holders and having an external focus will most often concentrate on output control. The main interest of these stakeholders will be how firm outcomes meet their needs or objectives. Usually they will either be stakeholders or shareholders who use the markets for control, and the board members will spend a limited amount of time on board commitments. These stakeholders will abandon the firm if the firm outcome is unsatisfactory. Outside evaluators and board members will usually have limited time and access to explore qualitative

Table 3.1 *Typology of board tasks*

	Firm-external perspective (control tasks)	*Firm-internal perspective (service tasks)*
External focus	Board output control tasks	Board networking tasks
Internal focus	Board internal control tasks	Board advisory tasks
Decision/strategy focus	Board decision control tasks	Board collaboration and mentoring tasks

information about the firm. The output control will thus most often be based on quantitative information, usually financial in nature. The output control task also includes how various stakeholders supervise and negotiate the distribution of value from the firm.

- *Board networking tasks.* Boards acting on behalf of internal stake-holders and having an external focus will often have resource dependence tasks.[13] These involve networking, lobbying and legitimacy tasks. People controlling or influencing resources that are important to the firm may be co-opted or selected as board members.
- *Board internal control tasks.* These board tasks take place when external stakeholders use the board members to control top management's behaviour and firm-internal issues. This kind of control is more time-consuming than output control. The focus is on how things are done or performed rather than on the final outcome.[14] The attention is on control routines and on behaviour, including CEO evaluations.
- *Board advisory tasks.* Board members may be consultants to the management, and they may themselves provide various kinds of knowledge and competencies.[15] The inclusion on the board of individual or groups of persons providing such resources may be a way of providing the firm with sustainable competitive advantage. Resources should, however, be valuable, rare, inimitable and non-substitutable. Offering board membership to these persons may be a way of binding resources to the firm.
- *Board decision control tasks.* From a firm-external perspective based on agency theory, the advice is to separate decision management

from decision control.[16] From this perspective boards are expected to ratify and control important decisions and to allocate resources. Strategic control is a major aspect of decision control. By its very nature, strategic control will, in comparison with operational and financial control, be more qualitative and long-term.[17]

- *Board collaboration and mentoring tasks.* From an internal perspective and a decision or strategic focus, board members are expected to collaborate with management in shaping the content, context and conduct of strategy.[18] This may be done through mentoring and supporting the management in strategic decision-making.

Theories about board task expectations

We have seen how various theories contribute to explaining board task expectations. Next I give a systematic presentation of the various theories. Aunts, barbarians and clans are concepts used when describing board members and boards.[19] The aunt, barbarian and clan concepts are, as shown in chapter 2, basically related to various perspectives on accountability and definitions of corporate governance. The descriptions of these concepts relate to various theories.

Aunt theories focus on the formal aspects of board tasks, but the role and tasks of the boards are not questioned. Property rights theory, legalistic perspectives and managerial hegemony have formal requirements or expectations for boards of directors, but the contributions of board members are not questioned. Barbarians are outsiders who are independent of management. They often represent values different from those of management, or even the firm, and decisions are often based on rational choice. Agency theory is the typical theory relating to the barbarian notion, but transaction cost theory, stakeholder theory and even stewardship theory and paternalism have some of the same elements. Clan theories are related to friendships and social network. Class theories, social exchange theories, interlocking directorates and other institutional theories can be found in this category. A fourth group of theories has a focus on value creation in the firm. In this group I have listed resource dependence theory and the resource-based view of the firm.

A contingency perspective on boards and governance may reflect the fact that contextual factors emphasise different perspectives. Different theories should thus be chosen depending on the context.[20]

Table 3.2 *Board task theories and value creations*

Barbarian theories	Value creation theories
Agency theory	Resource dependence theory, resource-/competence-based view of the firm
Stakeholder theory, stewardship theory, paternalistic theory, game theory	
Value creation for external stakeholders	Value creation in the firm
Aunt theories	*Clan theories*
Property rights, law, managerial hegemony	Institutional theories: social network and social movements, interlocking directorates, class hegemony
Value protection, but no value creation	Value creation for internal actors and business elites

There are streams within each main category, and the theories do not all lie at their outer boundaries; many are closer to the centres. External perspectives will often emphasise control tasks, and internal perspectives will often emphasise service tasks. It can also be argued that the control aspects of resource dependence theory and the resource-based view of the firm are missing.

The presentation in this section generally follows the four categories presented in table 3.2. However, I have devoted a separate subsection to agency theory.

Property rights, law and managerial hegemony

These theories focus on the formal side of boards and corporate governance, and in practice this leads to passive 'aunt boards'. The theories come from different disciplinary backgrounds – from economics/organisation, law and sociology. Here I present property rights theory, the legalistic perspective and managerial hegemony theory. Property rights theory is concerned with team production, the legalistic perspective is normative, and managerial hegemony is descriptive. In general, these theories have more to do with board existence and board representation than the actual working of boards.

Property rights theory

Property rights theory has its background in economics, and it considers the role of organisations and corporations to be about team production. Incomplete contracts are assumed in property rights theory.[21] Instead of multilateral contracts among all actors in a joint production, property rights theory argues that a central common party should make bilateral contracts with the various team members or input providers. Property rights theory defines a firm in relation to these rights, or residual claims in relation to team production.[22] In the property rights perspective it is possible to terminate contracts, and long-term contracts are thus not seen as an essential attribute of the firm.

It is the rights holders – including the residual claimants – who observe input behaviour, who constitute the central party common to all contracts with inputs, who alter the membership of the team, and who sell those rights that define the ownership or employer of the classical firm. The residual claimants will most often be those who are willing and able to pay in advance and who can commit sufficient wealth to cover negative results.

Property rights theory makes a distinction between and separates control rights from property rights. In property rights theory it is assumed that the cost of team production will increase if the residual claimant is not also the central party or monitor of the contracts regulating the rights. For example, in large corporations there may be many share owners. Sizeable costs would be incurred if each share owner participated in every decision in a corporation. The shirking of responsibilities might then become a problem. Property rights theory concerns itself with shirking and the monitoring of teams.

With the rise to dominance in the corporate community of the shareholder supremacy perspective, the significance of the contribution of property rights theory has approached that of the contribution in agency theory. Co-determination is a constraint on property rights. The general tasks of boards are to define and safeguard property rights, and output control will be the main board task. However, shareholders are not the same as property rights holders. Board members are expected to represent property rights holders. As property rights theory is a team production theory, proponents of this theory have argued that, instead of solely representing shareholders' interest, *boards should represent those stakeholders who add value, assume unique risk and possess strategic information.*[23] It is argued in property rights theory that, optimally, control is held by those contributing the most to value creation.[24] It is a debatable point as to whether shareholders are those who add the most value, assume the highest unique risks and possess the most strategic information.

One of the shortcomings in traditional property rights theory is that behavioural consequences are not apparent. The main board task is to regulate and safeguard property rights, and – according to property rights theory – board members should, in order to avoid shirking, be the property rights holders. Furthermore, team production theory – as a sub-theory of property rights theory – seems to open up new avenues for studying boards and value creation.

Legalistic perspective
From a legal perspective the main task of the board is defined as the regulation of the firm in society. A legalistic perspective indicates that the board's contribution to corporate performance is to carry out its legally mandated responsibilities. Advocates of this approach posit that corporate laws vest considerable powers in directors so as to enable them to fulfil their roles.[25]

A legalistic perspective often adds financial, systemic and social obligations to corporate governance. Boards are to meet these obligations without interfering in the day-to-day operations of the firms. Financial obligation criteria are often related to creating shareholders' wealth, systemic obligations are to secure the survival of the firm, and social obligations revolve around corporate responses to societal expectations. Often the legal requirements are related only to the existence of boards and the number of board members. In some contexts there are requirements with respect to composition – for example, about outsiders or non-executives, employees, publicly appointed directors, women directors, etc. Recently efforts have also been made to make legal requirements of such issues as a standard minimum number of board meetings per year, the existence of board instructions, various aspects of transparency, etc.[26] Enforcement and liability issues are often included in the legislation.

From a legal perspective the main board task will, to a large extent, be that of acting in crisis. Board members are generally formally elected by shareholders, but the law may also define other criteria for the selection of board members – for example, employees or other stakeholders based on societal considerations.

Laws and corporate governance systems vary between countries. Laws may be made contingent on various contextual factors, such as firm size and ownership. This means that different governance systems may exist in the same country. Three main factors seem to influence national laws. These are, first, the national cultures and contexts; secondly, the mimetic processes across various countries – often guided by investor interests – on corporate governance codes and systems; and, thirdly, cross-national corporate law convergence efforts, such as those within the European Union (EU) or Organisation for Economic Co-operation and Development (OECD) countries.

However, empirical evidence shows that boards are not doing what they are supposed to do according to the law. The legal perspectives do not take into account actual board behaviour, and the processes inside and outside the boardroom influencing actual board task performance. Empirical evidence over five decades has demonstrated that boards are often put together only to meet the formal and legal requirements, and that in reality there are other forces and norms that empower the boards in their active involvement – for example, managerial hegemony or shareholder activism.

Managerial hegemony

The theory of managerial hegemony describes the board as a legal fiction, viewing it as formally but not genuinely the principal governance body of the corporation. Despite the board's formal governing power over management, it is in reality dominated by corporate management. Boards are creatures of the CEO, according to this perspective, and in practice the task of boards is to enhance the welfare of the CEO. There is a lack of independence associated with the board members, the selection of outside board members being controlled by management.

Managerial hegemony is a descriptive theory, and it describes the consequences that have evolved from property rights theory and the legal perspectives. The classic publication in managerial hegemony theory is the seminal contribution of Professor Mace from 1971. His book *Directors: Myth and Reality* demonstrated that it was a myth that boards perform the tasks prescribed in theories mentioned hitherto.[27] Instead, boards are generally passive, although they may serve the management through advice and discipline.

Various other, more recent publications have similar results. Jay Lorsch and Elizabeth MacIver's landmark 1989 book *Pawns or*

Potentates is another major contribution to managerial hegemony theory.[28] Research shows the time constraints that part-time board members labour under in performing their work, with the result that they tend to be passive until a crisis occurs. Managerial hegemony theory is an institutional theory drawing on sociology as well as psychology. The roles of the board are surrounded and influenced by various norms and strategising techniques.[29]

Agency theory

At present agency theory (within the corporate community) is, in practice, regarded as the Bible of corporate governance. Agency theory may be seen as an extension of property rights theory. The contribution of agency theory is to follow the behavioural implications of property rights as specified in the contracts between the owners and the managers.[30] The focus in agency theory is on how principals can reduce agency costs. The key determinant in agency theory is the agency relationship. This is where one party (the principal) delegates work to another party (the agent). There are two main streams in agency theory: a positive and a normative stream. The *positive stream* has a focus on the separation of ownership and control in large corporations, and in this stream the shareholders are the principals while the management is the agent. The *normative stream*, also called common agency theory, considers all principal–agent relationships. In this stream the board may be considered as an agent for the owners as well as the principal for the management. Other principals than shareholders may be included, and the direction of the principal–agent relation may be reversed – for example, in the relationship between an entrepreneur and a venture capitalist.

In recent years agency theory has dominated and guided both the public discussion and research on corporate governance.[31] Agency theory argues that boards should monitor the actions of agents (managers) on behalf of their principals (shareholders).[32] With its roots in financial economics, agency theory was developed to address the conflicting relationships between owners and managers in large corporations.[33] Agency theorists typically take the maximisation of shareholder wealth as the primary standard for evaluating corporate performance, and ask how the board can serve to further corporate performance. Boards maximise shareholder wealth and minimise agency cost. Operationally, they monitor and evaluate a company's performance, its CEO and its strategies.

Agency theory has been adopted by investors. It fits their language and objectives, and it is easy to communicate. Stock exchanges and groups of investors have developed codes and rules based on agency theory reasoning in order to safeguard their interests.

Basic assumptions in agency theory

Some basic assumptions underlie agency theory.[34] The main assumptions are about information asymmetry and opportunism. The firm is seen as a legal entity that serves as a focus for a complete process in which the conflicting goals of individuals are brought into equilibrium within a framework of contractual relationships.[35]

Bounded rationality is assumed, but decision-makers are intendedly rational, they are generally considered to have one goal, and their roles are one-dimensional. Information asymmetry between principals and agents is assumed. This information asymmetry is usually divided into two aspects: adverse selection and moral hazard. Adverse selection is the asymmetry that existed at the time the contract or relationship was established. Moral hazard is the information asymmetry that develops afterwards. The literature about boards and governance has focused on moral hazard in particular, and, more specifically, on the fact that managers may have information not revealed to the owners.

Furthermore, individuals may be self-interest-seeking. This will imply that agents might, when possible, act to serve their own interests rather than the interests of the principals. There has been some discussion about strong and weak opportunism. Strong opportunism exists when individuals try consistently to serve their own interests. Weak opportunism is the assumption that some individuals at some times may seek to further their own interests. Combining the assumptions about information asymmetry and opportunism implies that principals cannot expect agents to perform their tasks without the existence of agency costs of some sort.

Agency costs

The focus in agency theory is on reducing agency costs, and the main remedy is generally that of objective alignment between principals and agents. The focal concern in agency theory is residual loss. One starting point in agency theory is that it is impossible for outside investors (principals) to assure at zero cost that managers (agents) are maximising shareholders' interests. Michael Jensen and William Meckling define agency costs as the sum of monitoring costs, bonding costs and residual costs.[36] Residual costs are a key feature in agency theory, since the other costs are of interest only as long as they give cost-effective reductions of residual costs.

Monitoring costs include the use of rules, having a board of directors and the use of auditors, etc. Bonding costs include constraints to managerial decision-making and behaviour.[37] Contractual arrangements with 'golden parachutes' are considered to be bonding costs.

Objective alignment is a key issue in reducing residual costs. This is achieved through incentive mechanisms such as the allocation of stock ownership and stock options.

Board tasks and independence in agency theory
Various board tasks are identified in the positive agency theory literature. These are output control, behavioural control and strategic control. The separation of distinct roles between management and the board is highlighted by Fama and Jensen, and they illustrate it through the decision process.[38] In broad terms the decision process has four steps. These are:
- initiation;
- ratification;
- implementation; and
- monitoring.

Initiation is the generation and formulation of proposals for resource allocation and the structuring of contracts. Ratification is the choice of the decision initiatives to be implemented. Implementation is the execution of ratified decisions, and monitoring is the measurement of the performance of the decision agents and the implementation of rewards.

Because of information asymmetry and opportunism, agency theory recommends that decision management should be separated from decision control. Management should be in charge of the decision management, while a separate and independent board should have the responsibility for decision control. Decision management includes decision formulation and implementation, while decision control includes decision ratification and monitoring.

Boards should be independent of management in order to avoid managerial opportunism, as just mentioned. The board and at least a majority of its members should be psychologically and financially independent of management. It is thus not enough for there to be different persons or organisational bodies in charge of decision management and decision control; requirements also have to be set for the independent functioning of the board.

There are two main facets to independence in agency theory reasoning. These are independence in incentives and independence in knowledge.[39] The incentive argument is, on the one hand, about the relationship with the management (agents) and, on the other hand, about the relationship with the owners (principals). Individuals with family ties, friendship ties or business ties with the management are not considered to be independent. Incentives should be used, for example through ownership, to align the interest of the board members with the interests of the owners (principals). Agency theory also recognises other kinds of incentives. Incentives through reputation and the markets for boards and directors are also included.[40]

However, independence in incentives alone is not sufficient. Board members also need knowledge and information so that they can independently ratify decision formulation and monitor implementation, including managerial opportunism. Independence is thus related both to the knowledge and competency of the board members, and to the information-gathering processes.

The requirements of the decision control tasks will depend on the context in which the firm is embedded in alternative control mechanisms.[41] Alternative control mechanisms are the various markets for control and objective alignments between owners and managers. It is often difficult to rely on output control mechanisms in complex organisations operating in complex and dynamic environments. The decision control tasks will then be more time-consuming as the need for behavioural control will increase. Ownership types and dispersion will also influence board task involvement and independence.

The consequences of normative agency theory for board practices are, for example, having outsider-dominated boards, avoiding CEO duality and increasing the shareholding of board members. Another consequence is aligning the interests of the managers with those of the owners through ownership or ownership options.

Common agency theory

Common agency theory is another term for the normative principal–agent direction of agency theory. In this direction all principal–agent relationships are included and not only the relationship between owners and managers. Among elaborations from the common agency theory are multiple agency theory[42] and stakeholder agency theory.[43]

Common agency theory may discuss the various principal–agent hierarchies in an organisation. The board is not only a means or tool for shareholders to control or monitor agents; the board is itself an agent for principals as shareholders. In addition, the board is also a principal for the management as agent. Board–management relationships thus constitute only a single level in a larger principal–agent hierarchy.

Multiple agency theory refers to a situation in which there is more than one party in agency relationships – as principals, or agents, or both.[44] This is clearly illustrated in equity joint ventures. Equity joint ventures are characterised by few owners, by owners contributing complementary tangible and intangible assets, and by managers acting as agents for the owners. The various owners usually have their own rationale for entering the alliance and each is sufficiently salient to require its own interests to be respected. Furthermore, the alliance may also have difficulties in surviving if the complementary assets from the alliance partners are withdrawn. The agency role of the managers is often complicated when various alliance partners thrust their own expectations upon the managers.

In the stakeholder agency theory, shareholders are substituted with stakeholders, and the task of the board is to act on behalf of stakeholders. Not only does this elaboration include an increase in the number of principals, it also requires that the principals are of various types, and may have different stakes and types of power. The stakeholder agency theory does not give all stakeholders the same position as shareholders, but instead it focuses on power differentials and market processes, and it points towards ways in which management and stakeholder interests may be aligned.

Among further elaborations is the direction of the principal–agent relationships. This may be illustrated via game theory.[45]

Agency theory in SMEs

The positive agency theory is based on descriptions rather than norms. It has been developed mainly for large open corporations with a separation of ownership and management. Closely held firms and family firms are not included in these arguments. However, when using common agency theory it is easily seen how agency theory also can be applied to closely held firms and small firms. The main arguments for applying agency theory to small and medium-sized firms are the importance of asymmetric information, the importance of principals other than owners, and the fact that SMEs often operate in weak markets for control.

The key role of the entrepreneur as owner-manager, operational flexibility, and the abundant potential for information asymmetry between insiders and outsiders are among the main differences between small and large firms. Another feature of many small firms is ambiguity with respect to reported as well as actual results. Many managerial and even operational tasks may be unprogrammable and difficult to distinguish and measure Small firms are often also more characterised by debt financing than equity financing.[46] The importance of principals other than shareholders – for example, stakeholders such as banks, etc. – thus becomes evident.

Critics of agency theory

Agency theory has been subject to considerable criticism from various sources. A main criticism is related to how it has had a negative impact on society. Another criticism has been that agency theory is wrong in its focus. A third criticism has been to do with the direction of the principal–agent relationship, while a fourth set of criticisms asserts that the underlying assumptions are wrong.

Several prominent scholars have been very negative and critical of agency theory because of its negative impact on society.[47] Sumantra Ghoshal accuses agency theory of being one of the main reasons for some of the corporate scandals in firms such as Enron.[48] He argues that exaggeratedly strong claims of truthfulness have been given, by some, to the extreme assumptions in agency theory, which, as a 'bad' theory, may have had a profound and unfortunate impact on management practice. These affected management practices have produced dysfunctional organisations, which neither serve shareholders well nor provide much by way of a humane and progressive work environment for employees. Ghoshal concludes that our societies are less well off as a result of theories such as agency theory.

Other authors direct their criticism mainly at the wrong focus of agency theory. Agency theory has been criticised by process scholars for not addressing processes,[49] and by transaction cost theory for not addressing governance mechanisms.[50] Agency theory has also been criticised by game theorists for focusing on only one direction of the relationship.[51]

Another area in which agency theory has been criticised is that it embodies incorrect assumptions. These criticisms are also found in the evolution of other theories. Criticisms regarding agency theory's wrong assumptions include:

- opportunism (stewardship theory[52] and altruism[53]);
- shareholder value supremacy (stakeholder theory[54] and property rights theory[55]);
- ownership and separation of roles (paternalism and role integration[56]); and
- time perspective and discrete contracts (relational norms[57]).

These points of criticism are further elaborated in separate sections.

Transaction cost theory

Transaction cost theory could have been presented in a section of its own, but transaction cost theory and agency theory have several similarities, and some argue that transaction cost theory falls within agency theory. Others argue that agency theory is a sub-theory of transaction cost theory. I will not attempt a comprehensive study of transaction cost theory here, but limit the discussion to how transaction cost theory differs from agency theory.

Transaction cost theory is a theory about market failures, and governance alternatives to markets are presented.[58] Transaction cost theory is thus a theory of governance mechanism, while agency theory is a theory about incentives. The focus in transaction cost theory is on exchange transaction, with asset specificity as the driving force.

Asset specificity is an investment that has another value outside, rather than inside, the transaction. Somebody making an investment with a value that depends on the transaction becomes dependent on the transaction. There are six types of asset specificity, connected with spatially bounded sites, physical assets, human assets, brand names and reputation, dedicated assets and time. Asset specificity influences the choice between different governance mechanisms, the general hypothesis being that, with increasing specificity, corporations will move from market-based to hierarchically based governance mechanisms.

Transaction cost theory incorporates assumptions about managerial discretion that diverge somewhat from agency theory. Both assume that human agents are subject to bounded rationality and are given to opportunism. However, authors in agency theory have in practice used an operative rationality assumption and are in an unbounded rationality tradition.[59] Bounded rationality has gradually come to be thought to imply irrationality and satisficing.

The leading difference is in the choice of a basic unit of analysis. In transaction cost theory the transaction is the unit of analysis, whereas in agency theory the individual is the basic unit. The focal concern in agency theory is residual loss; in transaction cost theory it is maladaptation.

Ex ante incentive alignments in agency theory are contrasted with *ex post* costs in transaction cost theory. While agency theory focuses on incentive alignment, the choice of market, hierarchy or hybrid forms of governance structure constitute the remedy according to transaction cost theory.

Transaction cost theory arguments may help define optimal board membership. From a resource perspective the board may be a hybrid governance mechanism, and it should have members who will provide governance and competency that it would be more costly to have in the market place or in the hierarchy.

Stakeholders and stewards

In this section I focus on theories that have similarities with agency theory, but where one or more of the assumptions are changed. In the introductory section I introduced these theories together with agency theory as barbarian theories – as they all have a firm-external perspective. The firm is seen as an instrument by external actors or stakeholders, and the board is there to ensure value creation for these external actors.

Such theories are stakeholder theory, stewardship theory, game theory and paternalistic theory. Stakeholder theory emphasises a broader set of principals, stewardship theory presents alternative assumptions about the agents, game theory questions the directions of the principal–agent relationship, and paternalism focuses on alternative assumptions about the principals.

Stakeholder theory

Stakeholder theory adopts a pluralistic view of organisations, and is concerned with balancing and managing stakeholder interests. This is done by negotiations and compromise. The 'who or what really count?' question is a main issue in the stakeholder perspective literature. In other words: a main task of the board is to define who the most important stakeholders are.

The stakeholder perspective originated more than fifty years ago,[60] but Edward Freeman's landmark book *Strategic Management: A Stakeholder Approach* from 1984 brought the stakeholder concept to prominence in the management literature.[61] There exist various definitions of stakeholders and the stakeholder concept.[62] In narrow definitions of the stakeholder concept the focus is most often on how a company defines relevant groups in term of 'their relevance to the company's core economic interests'. The broad definitions are based on the 'empirical reality that companies can indeed be vitally affected by, or they can vitally affect, almost anyone'.[63] In the context of this book I generally use a broad definition of the concept, and use Freeman's definition of a stakeholder as 'any individual or group who can affect or is affected by the achievement of the organisation's objectives'.[64] Stakeholders with similar interests, claims or rights can be classified as belonging to the same group. Stockholders, employees, communities (the general public) and customers have, in addition to the management, been considered to be the major stakeholder groups in most companies.[65] Stakeholder theory has therefore been seen as common agency theory with multiple principals.[66]

Three main streams of stakeholder literature are generally referred to.[67] There is a normative stream, debating the legitimacy of various stakeholder groups, and a descriptive stream, presenting the stakes and power of these stakeholder groups. There is also an instrumental stream, arguing that a company that attends to the demands of various stakeholders gains both a favourable reputation and easier access to the resources that stakeholders control,[68] and that the attention to stakeholders leads to competitive advantage by reducing opportunism and enhancing trust and cooperation.[69]

Although interest in stakeholder theory continues to grow, the theory has been applied to research into boards of directors infrequently and with few empirical findings. To some extent this lack of integration is due to difficulties in specifying stakeholder variables pertaining to different stakeholder groups. The problem also arises from the pre-occupation of research into boards with the interest of shareholders, to the neglect of other stakeholder interests.

According to stakeholder theorists, the board's tasks will also be to advocate and ensure corporate social responsibility and its interests to a broader set of stakeholders, including the employees and society. In stakeholder theory there is a need to balance and negotiate various perspectives, and to avoid opportunism from certain groups of stake-holders – for example, shareholders or the management. There may also be a need to develop laws or regulations safeguarding the inter-ests of stakeholders. These efforts may also be included in codes of best practice. An alternative approach can be to let various groups of stakeholders appoint the board members.

Stewardship theory

The core concept of stewardship theory is trust. Stewardship the-ory is an alternative to agency theory, and it has gained a foothold among many management scholars.[70] While agency theory builds on the assumption of managerial opportunism, which leads to the need for boards to be active in controlling and monitoring, stewardship theory assumes that managers in general should be trusted as good stewards.[71]

Stewardship theorists accept the assumptions in agency theory about bounded rationality, but not those about opportunism. They argue that there are different kinds of motivation for managers: managers are motivated by non-financial incentives, feeling a need to achieve, and to gain intrinsic rewards and satisfaction through their work. They will take on responsibility and gain recognition by individu-als. Managers should be regarded not as opportunistic actors but as people wanting to do a good job. Stewardship theory disregards the basic assumption of a conflict of interest – just as agency theory does. Instead of seeing managers as individualistic, opportunistic and self-serving, stewardship theory holds that managers are trustworthy and collectivistic.[72]

Stewardship theory has been used as an argument for CEO duality. In the absence of opportunism, it is argued that CEO duality gives greater unity of direction and strong command and control. The emphasis on trust is also related to the board's decision-making culture. Trust in the boardroom is expected to stimulate cohesiveness, openness and generosity as well as creativity and involvement. Based on stewardship theory, it is also argued that the main board tasks should be the various service tasks with a focus on collaborating strategy involvement, including mentorship.[73] The role of boards in stewardship theory is that of guiding management in achieving the missions and objectives of the enterprise.[74]

In sum: stewardship theory employs an external perspective on boards, but, as the core concepts are related to trust, cohesiveness and openness, board tasks will also be those of supporting and mentoring the CEO. Stewardship theory is thus also used to argue for internal perspectives.

Game theory
Game theory first of all questions the directions in the principal–agent relationship in agency theory. Who are principals and who are agents? The directions are the results of ongoing games. The category of 'actors' also includes people other than shareholders and managers. Game theory may incorporate opportunism by the 'principals'.

A much-used example is the prisoner's dilemma situation. The prisoner's dilemma is a well-known metaphor used in psychological, sociological and economic research. The essence of the dilemma is that each individual actor has an incentive to act according to competitive, narrow self-interests even though all actors are collectively better off if they cooperate.[75]

Game theory is not restricted to shareholders and managers, and it may include a game with several actors. Masahiko Aoki has also developed a cooperative game theory of the firm.[76] Corporate governance is here seen as nexuses of various elements such as property rights, control rights, rewards, information and social relationships. A game may be described as an arrangement composed of a set of players, sets of action choices, and a consequence function that links the chosen actions by each player to some consequences.[77]

The inclusion of social relationships also incorporates time perspectives into the games. The time dimension will influence the outcome of the game. There may be outcomes in short-term relations with discrete contracts that are different from long-term relations with relational contracts. In the short term actors may benefit from opportunism, but in the long term the greatest rewards will come from collaboration.

As corporate governance is seen as a game between multiple actors, it is argued in game theory that, in contract relationships, it is not clear who the principals are and who the agents are.

Paternalism

The welfare of the family is the core issue in paternalism. Family businesses have traditionally been governed according to a paternalistic ideology, whereby the care and well-being of the employees and other stakeholders are emphasised.[78] In paternalism there are principals 'with faces and hearts', and paternalism is characterised by role integration. By 'faces' we mean that the identity of the owners is known, and by 'hearts' we mean that the owners may make decisions based on values other than pure profit maximisation for the business. Behavioural assumptions about bounded rationality are implied, and decisions may be taken based on, for example, emotions or routines.

The decision-makers may integrate roles related to the business with other roles, such as roles related to the family. This will imply governance mechanisms in which the various governance roles are integrated. Empirically, this is shown by the manner in which boards in small family businesses not only have control tasks but also may undertake executive or service tasks.[79]

Paternalism as logic and as an ideology has been introduced in various studies. It has been argued that paternalism is the ideology distinguishing a family business from other businesses.

Paternalism as it appears in a business setting presents itself as a clan structure where the hierarchy is structured by seniority and kinship ties ... The meaning of business life is a safe domicile for the family ... In this context everyday life becomes as important as maintaining traditions and building a future for generations to come. The competencies needed for this endeavour are deeply embedded in the personal histories of the family members and of further confidants inside the firm. Keeping the business within the family is the dominant objective within the family.[80]

An organisation is not only an instrument to reach the goals shared by all members of the organisation. It is also an arena for emotions and politics.[81] In a family business there are needs to balance the interests of both the family and the business, which makes this type of company an arena for competing ideologies.

Board members typically are persons in the family, but there may also be some board members from outside the family. Often outside board members have had a long-term relationship with the family, as their lawyer, consultant, etc. Board members in family businesses are rarely independent. The paternalistic logic emphasises that interactions and structures are related to family values and norms.

Institutional theories

'Clan', as referred to in the following discussion, is the term reserved for various institutional theories relating to board tasks.[82] The institutional perspective addresses the questions of how and why organisational processes and structures are taken for granted. The key idea behind institutionalisation is that many organisational actions reflect a pattern of doing things that has evolved, over time becoming legitimised within an organisation. Institutional theories have a system focus rather than a focus on corporate financial performance. The focus is on interactions outside the boardroom.

Institutional theory posits that organisations are constrained by social rules and follow taken-for-granted conventions that shape their form and practice.[83] Firms are embedded in a larger social system, and their existence needs to be legitimised by conforming to social rules. The importance of norms in guiding, constraining and empowering behaviour is emphasised.[84] Boards will have a maintenance role, and organisations will over time reflect rules in their social environment.

Much of the literature on institutionalisation is related to isomorphism. Isomorphism is concerned with how organisations adapt to accepted norms. Institutional isomorphism is how organisations have a propensity to resemble other organisations that operate under similar conditions.[85]

Here I split the discussion of the clan theories into three sections. First, social capital and social networks; second, social movements and class hegemony; and, finally, interlocking directorates. In studies of board tasks, social capital and social networks have an internal perspective; social movements and class hegemony have external perspectives; and interlocking directorates is one practical application of both perspectives.

Social capital and social networks

Board members do not just have knowledge or human capital. They may also have relational or social capital.[86] Social capital is an attribute created between people, whereas human capital is an attribute of individuals. A director's social capital is defined through his or her social relations with peers, managers and friends.[87] Investments that create social capital are therefore different in fundamental ways from the investments that create human capital. Social capital is, for a given actor, an investment in terms of time and energy. Through their social activity, actors develop social structure.

Social capital theory often deals with three distinct levels of analysis.[88] Who do you know? Which are the social mechanisms that incite exchange between parties? What is the social resource exchange between actors? Social capital predicts that returns to intelligence, education, and seniority depend in some part on a person's location in the social structure of a market or hierarchy.[89] Social capital is a dynamic asset. Often *who* you know really is more important than *what* you know – but *who* you know influences *what* you know.

Besides their roles in providing managers with information, directors establish links between firms and provide firms with legitimacy.[90] Social relations ease the negotiations of partnership agreements.

Social network theory shows how social networks facilitate cohesion and the exchange of information.[91] The firm's economic actions are embedded in social networks, where embeddedness refers to the extent that economic actions are informed, influenced and enabled by the network of accumulated stable and preferential social relations.[92] Social network theory suggests that demographic similarities between board members reflect the organisation's emergent inter-organisational networks.[93] The board's composition will, from a social network perspective, reflect the social networks of the principal stakeholders.

Structural holes,[94] the strength of weak ties[95] and the control power of bridging are important concepts in social network theory. Structural hole theory describes how social capital is a function of brokerage opportunities in a network.[96] Controlling the bridging of structural holes may contribute in the form of information benefits and control benefits. The weak ties are the real bridges; weak ties are more likely to link members of different small groups than strong ones – so this can be considered a 'strength of weak ties'.

There are both positive and negative aspects to directors' social relations. For example, social networks enhance social solidarity between directors and managers, social elites develop their influence through participation in different boards, organisations' need for legitimacy results in the homogenisation of organisations, and boards will be ruled by prevailing institutional norms.

Social movements and class hegemony

Modern social movement theory has its background in collective action. Social movement theory holds that corporate control is inherently political, and that politics is accomplished by coalitions of mutually acquainted actors who recognise or construct a common interest.[97] Board tasks and behaviour, like other social actions, are embedded in social structures, which influence whether, when and how collective action is accomplished. Shareholder and investor activism, and the mushrooming of codes of best practice on corporate governance, are results of social movements.

Collective action can be analysed as a function of changing combinations of four elements. There are three primary elements that determine a group's capacity to act. These are interests, social infrastructure and mobilisation processes.[98] A group's interests are defined by the gains and losses resulting from its interaction with other groups. The more homogeneous and the more easily identifiable interests are the more likely it will be that a social movement will develop. Social infrastructure concerns the degree of common identity and social ties linking the individuals or organisations in a group. Corporate elites developed through overlapping directorships are examples of a social infrastructure. Another example is the networks of institutional investors and stock exchanges. Mobilisation is the process by which a group acquires collective control over resources needed for collective action. Homogeneous interests and dense social networks increase a group's capacity to mobilise resources. The fourth element is the political opportunity structure.

Shareholder activism is not the only result of social movement; other results include managerialism and class hegemony. Class hegemony theory has its background in Marxist ideology.[99] A cohesive upper class is identified. Power is shared by an elite group at the head of large corporations. Boards of directors seek to perpetuate this ruling elite group and encourage the strengthening of it through interlocking directorates. There is self-selection of board members. An inner circle – a managerial elite or class elite – controls the selection of board members.

The individuals who form the interlocks are the inner circle, which constitutes a distinct semi-autonomous network, one that transcends company, regional, sectoral and political lines within the corporate community. Class hegemony adopts the view that organisations are agents of individuals, families or a social class. A successful director must also copy the capitalist elite and, through the network, promote legislation favourable to big business.

Interlocking directorates

An interlock exists when a particular person sits on two or more corporate boards. Interlocks may be direct or indirect. An indirect interlock exists when directors of firms A and B do not sit on each other's boards but are linked through their joint membership of a third board. Interlocking directorates can be directional and non-directional. A directional interlock occurs when an inside director or person from the top management team in firm A sits on the board in another firm (B). Although this person may contribute to firm B, the primary employment and loyalty is with firm A.[100]

There are numerous studies of interlocking directorates. Studies of interlocking directorates are characterised by the use of similar methods but a large number of theories – for example, financial control theory, inter-organisational co-optation theory, finance capital theory and management control theory.[101]

Interlocking directorates are important both in the social capital/network and the social movement/class hegemony theories. Interlocking directorates fulfil different tasks.[102] They contribute to inter-organisational linkages, which serve as mechanisms of co-optation or control. Interlocking directorates also have integrative ties that fulfil the functions of class consolidation or elite integration.

A class hegemony perspective focuses on interlocking directorships as instruments of intra-class integration and structural support for a ruling elite.[103] However, board interlocks are also a co-optation mechanism similar to the one described from a resource dependence perspective.[104] For example, a company can reduce risks by horizontal coordination when two or more competitors are linked together through interlocking directorates, by vertical integration when suppliers or customers are invited to be board members, by the personal expertise of the board members, and by the reputation of board members with high prestige. As a class hegemony instrument, interlocking directorates integrate, maintain and support existing power elites.[105] As a co-optation mechanism in inter-organisational relationships, board interlocks ensure financial and managerial control across interdependent organisations.

Strategies and resources

The fourth group of theories are labelled value-creating theories. The main perspective in these theories is value creation in the firm. Value creation theories combine strategies and resources. Two value creation theories are presented: resource dependence theory and the resource-based view of the firm. Resource dependence theory has an external focus, while the resource-based view of the firm has an internal focus. The social or relational capital/resources of the board members are emphasised in resource dependence theory, while the board members' human capital/resources, including competence, knowledge and skills, are emphasised in the resource-based view of the firm.

Resource dependence theory
Resource dependence theory explains how external dependencies are reduced by linking the organisation to its external environment through networking and legitimacy. Boards contribute to financial performance by including directors who have direct or indirect access to, control of or knowledge of important external resources or influential groups. By establishing links to such groups, uncertainty and search costs are greatly reduced for the firms. A linking task of the board emerges from this perspective, and this linking task emphasises the importance of board composition that includes well-networked individuals. Resource dependence theorists argue that large boards are positive for firm performance as a board consisting of a large number of members may provide more links than a board with a small number of members.

The other side of dependence is power. Resource dependence theory views the firm as an open system. It depends on external organisations and environmental contingencies.[106] A resource dependence perspective suggests that boards span the boundary between a company and its environment and serve their company as a legitimising and co-optation mechanism to extract resources.[107] Directors help companies manage environmental interdependencies.[108] This unique boundary-spanning position of directors is associated with two types of benefits for companies: co-optation and connection. Co-optation is a tactic for managing interdependence,[109] and it can be implemented by putting stakeholder representatives on boards.[110] Directors themselves are resources of companies' management, through their contacts or connections with stakeholder groups and through their professional and personal prestige in these groups. Connection is the ability of directors to supply management with timely information and to convey information about the company to its environment. Furthermore, the prestige and reputation of board members in the political or business communities enable boards to legitimise companies' actions and to mobilise external support and resources for them. Thus, by connecting, co-opting and legitimising, boards are expected to contribute positively to companies' achievements and performance.

For many years resource dependence theory was a dominant approach in sociology, strategy and organisation theory, used to motivate the existence of active boards. It provides an external focus from an internal perspective. The board is viewed from a resource dependence perspective as an administrative body linking the organisation with its environment. The board is considered to be a 'boundary spanner' that is able help the corporation acquire important resources from its environment, and thus reduce the corporation's dependence on external stakeholders or protect the corporation from external threats. More recently, resource dependence theory has been supplemented with contributions from social network theory.[111] The important board tasks from this perspective are those of networking, door-opening, legitimacy, and communication in inter-organisational relations. Boards will reflect the environment of the firm.[112]

Resource-based view of the firm

A resource-based view of the firm will view the board as a firm-internal resource of competitive advantage.[113] A resource-based view of the firm has been suggested as a realistic approach for understanding boards of directors.[114] These approaches are more dynamic than what is presented in most other theories, and they are particularly relevant to young firms.[115] Arguments from these theories suggest that the resource and knowledge tasks of boards may be particularly important for increasing strategic flexibility and ensuring long-term growth and survival.

There are two basic assumptions in the resource-based view of the firm:

- resources are distributed heterogeneously across firms; and
- these productive resources cannot be transferred from firm to firm without cost.[116]

Given these assumptions, it is argued that resources are both rare and valuable, and when such resources are also simultaneously not imitable, not substitutable and not transferable they can produce sustainable competitive advantage. It is resources that are simultaneously rare, valuable, inimitable, non-substitutable and non-transferable that will create competitive advantage that will last.

From a resource-based perspective, governance choices may affect the creation of economic rents. There will be a difference in economic rents between boards that have board members who provide access to valuable, rare, costly to imitate and non-substitutable resources and boards that focus only on minimising agency costs.[117]

The service tasks of the board have been described in the literature for several years. The board is considered to be a service resource for the company and its management. More recently this approach has been considered within the framework of the resource-based view of the company and similar theories,[118] and the board has been considered as a strategic resource impacting company performance.

The *knowledge-based view* and the *competence-based view* of the firm are follow-ups and specifications of the resource-based view. Human resources are brought into sharper focus. However, resources, knowledge, competence and capabilities are often used interchangeably in the resource-based view. Often we find that the concepts of a knowledge- or a competence-based approach will better recognise the importance of the context. There will be different needs for knowledge in different contexts.

A capability is a core concept in the resource-based view of the firm. A capability can be considered as the coordinated use of resources in order to respond and act competently when the firm is facing problems and challenges. Capabilities may allow the firm to address and solve a particular issue or problem better than the competitors of the firm. *Dynamic capability* is another concept that is often presented in the literature. The difference between a capability and a dynamic capability is that a capability can be related to the need for a firm to meet just a single problem or challenge, whereas a dynamic capability is related to the need for a firm to meet dynamic and changing problems and challenges.

A dynamic capabilities approach will consider not only the knowledge or competence of the board members but also whether the board has the capability to transform the knowledge into actual task performance.[119] Capabilities and dynamic capabilities will thus be a subset of the resource-based concept of resources. If the board is to contribute to sustainable competitive advantage and value creation it will need to be valuable, scarce, inimitable and difficult to substitute. The following criteria relating to boards can thus be applied from a resource-based perspective.[120]

- Boards are valuable for the whole firm and not only for external actors.
- Good board members who have both knowledge and motivation are scarce.
- The culture and processes within the boardroom are inimitable.
- The services of boards are hard to substitute.

Summary

In this chapter we have looked at concepts related to accountability and various board task expectations. A typology of six groups of board tasks relating to control, service and strategy tasks, as well as various board task theories, has been presented. The board task theories were sorted under four different headings (aunt, barbarian, clan and value creation).

Board effectiveness requires not only a mechanism but also a standard. The board members are the mechanism, and the various board task theories present standards. Board accountability cannot be understood without understanding what it is that boards are accountable to. In this chapter we have seen how various board task theories are influenced by Darwinian competition.[121] Society is a battlefield for individuals, organisations and movements adhering to various theories.

The chapter started with a typology of board task expectations. The following board tasks were presented:
• board output control tasks;
• board networking tasks;
• board internal control tasks;
• board advisory tasks;
• board decision control tasks; and
• board collaboration and mentoring tasks.
Each set of tasks had theoretical rationales.

Various board task theories were presented in the remainder of the chapter. They were sorted in the following categories:
• aunt theories – formal tasks;
• barbarian theories – external perspectives and incentives;
• clan theories – institutional perspectives and norms; and
• value-creating theories – strategies and resources.
A summary of the presentation appears in table 3.3.

The various theories contribute to understanding board task theories and accountability issues. Most theories are clearly rooted in a defined value-creating perspective. Various actors will therefore also tend to favour or avoid identifying themselves with various value-creating consequences. The actors were presented in chapter 2, and value creation is presented in chapter 10. Various board tasks are also extracted from the different theories. Theories and board task expectations have been presented in this chapter, while actual board task performance is presented in chapter 9. Accountability exists when expectations and actual task performance are aligned. The 'board members' column indicates the type of board member recommendation based on the different theories. The 'board structures and processes' column to the right indicates if the theory has implications for board structures and processes.

The first group of theories are those in which, in practice, boards will be passive 'aunt' boards. Property rights theory will emphasise output control and distribution, and the board members will be rights holders. Board tasks in the legalistic perspective will be to carry out legally mandated responsibilities, and the board members will in most cases be elected by shareholders. 'Box-ticking' may be the main board task, as a consequence of the evolution of corporate governance codes.

The second group of theories are those defining a firm as an instrument for external 'barbarian' actors. Various types of control are recommended in agency theory: output control, behavioural control and

Table 3.3 *A summary of board task theories*

	Value creation perspective (chapters 2 and 10)	Board tasks (chapters 3 and 9)	Board members (chapter 4)	Board structures and processes (chapters 6 to 8)
Aunt theories				
Property rights	External: safeguard property rights	Output control and distribution	Rights holders	Existence
Legalistic perspective	External: regulate firm in society	'Box-ticking'	Shareholders	Existence
Managerial hegemony	Internal: welfare of management	Advice and discipline	Insiders, friends and managerial elite	Interactions, structure and norms DM culture[122]
Barbarian theories				
Agency theory	External/ financial: reduce agency cost	Output, behavioural and strategic control	Independent and incentives	Structure and norms DM culture
Stakeholder theory	External/social	Output control	Stakeholders	Interactions, structure and norms
Stewardship theory	Mixed/ financial: collaborative governance	Collaboration and mentoring strategic management	Executives and non-executives	Interactions, structure and norms DM culture

Game theory	Not given, but is result of a game	Cooperation and negotiation	Inter-dependence	Interactions

Game theory	Not given, but is result of a game	Cooperation and negotiation	Inter-dependence	Interactions
Paternalistic theory	Welfare of the family	Task integration	Family and outsiders	Interactions, structure and norms
Clan theories				
Social capital	Mixed	Network	Social capital	Interactions, structure and norms; DM culture
Social movement	Safeguard and protect values of groups of actors	Mixed	Inner circle	Interactions, structure and norms; DM culture
Interlocking directorates	Mixed	Network	Interlocks	Interactions
Value creation theories				
Resource dependence	Internal/financial: resource acquisition	Network	Co-opted	Interactions
Resource- and competence-based theories	Internal: sustainable competitive advantage	Advice	Human capital	DM culture

strategic control. The board member focus is independence and incentives. Stakeholder theory will focus output on control. Stewardship theory will focus on the collaboration and mentoring tasks of boards, and how the board will be involved in strategic management. Cooperation and negotiations are board tasks elaborated from game theory, and there should be interdependence among the board members. A paternalistic theory will imply task integration.

The third group of theories are institutional 'clan' theories. Networking tasks and the social capital of board members are important in social capital and social network theory. Social movement and class hegemony will have boards that safeguard and protect values for the inner circle. The inner circle will keep the boardrooms for themselves.

The fourth group of theories are resource theories in which the purpose is to create value for the firm. Networking, lobbying and legitimacy are important board tasks in resource dependence theory, and the board members will be co-opted to perform these tasks. Resource- or competence-based theories will focus on the advisory tasks and the human capital of the board members.

A first consideration may be that the presentation of the theories can be compared with an extended version of the classical story about the blind men and the elephant. The actors in the corporate governance debate may all find a theory, and all theories may have something right. They may all understand something about board tasks and corporate governance from this theory. However, some of the theories have competing perspectives and assumptions, and the actors may have different objectives. Board task expectation and accountability thus easily becomes a struggle between ideologies, and not all theories lead to value creation for everybody. The overall perspective in this book remains that boards must balance their various tasks in order to be accountable.

4 | *The board members*

'Only an odd number of people can lead a corporation, and three are too many.'[1] This chapter looks at the board members both from the demand side and the supply side. The main concepts are the characteristics, competence, compensation and composition of the board and its members.

As has been said before, this book is about the human side of corporate governance. The board members are, necessarily, core players in this respect, but much of the ongoing debate and research hardly even seems to acknowledge that boards have a human side. In this chapter I present the attributes of boards and their members, focusing in particular on three: characteristics, motivation and composition. I also present the selection process for board members.

Board members can be explored and understood both from a demand and a supply perspective. A demand perspective means that there are firms that have a need for board members. The supply perspective means that there are individuals who are available to act as board members. In this chapter I first present the market place for board members. How are board members recruited? Then I present the board members from supply and demand perspectives.

There are four board member features that have dominated not just research but also the public debate. These features have been called 'the usual suspects',[2] and are the number of board members, the insider/outsider ratio, CEO duality and shareholding by the board members. In this chapter I make a more in-depth study of board member characteristics and compensation[3] and board composition.

In the guiding framework at the start of this chapter there are arrows relevant to this discussion coming from context, interactions and decision-making. The line from decision-making is an indicator of individual- and board-level learning. The lines from context and

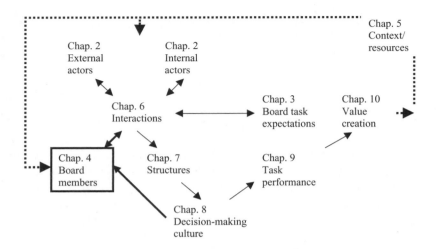

interactions indicate that the identities of the board members are influenced by the context and interactions. The identities of the board members include both the choice of board members and their role expectations.

The market for board members: election or selection?

Board members are rarely elected by shareholders. They are selected. Even though there should be a formal election process, more often than not there is only one candidate. It is very unusual for there to be more than one candidate presented at a shareholder meeting, and thus no real election takes place. Candidates will frequently withdraw their candidature if there is a possibility that they will not be chosen; candidates for either a non-executive board member or a top managerial position often find it detrimental for their professional career to run for such a position and lose.

Who appoints board members?

Most firms have concentrated ownership, and many of them are owned by a limited number of individuals or families. Only a limited number of firms have institutional ownership and dispersed ownership. In most cases the board members are the main shareholders of a firm. In family firms it is typically some kind of formal or informal family council that makes the final decision. The recent corporate governance debate does take this aspect of concentrated ownership into account – but only to a limited extent.

Who appoints board members in firms with separation of ownership and control? In most cases it is the shareholders that are supposed to appoint the board members. However, in some firms and in some countries laws require that board members are also to be appointed by other stakeholders – for example, the employees. Nevertheless, even in firms in which the board members are supposed to be elected by the shareholders, there may be company regulations stipulating that the present board and the CEO should have significant influence both over the process and the results. Even some of the new corporate governance codes include these provisions, with their involvement to be either in the nomination committees or in the final election or selection. Such provisions are made to ensure that board members have a proper understanding of the firm, and so that they can enjoy a good working relationship with the other board members. This provision follows the argument that the CEO and the existing board members are the ones who know best what the firm requires.

Who is appointed?

In chapters 2 and 3 I discussed the ongoing debate about who the board members are meant to represent. Are they to represent the various stakeholders appointing them, or are they representing themselves with the purpose of creating value in the firm?

Despite the various arguments behind the appointment of directors, traditionally board members have been selected from individuals already in the professional networks of the CEO and the other board members. Usually there has been limited consideration as to the qualifications required, and selections often take place without an assessment of the present needs of the board. Changes in boards are often incremental, and the selection of a new board member usually takes place after an existing board member withdraws from the board for some reason. There are, however, variations in why and how members are replaced and selected.

Mechanisms and reforms in appointing board members

As a result of the various ongoing debates – for example, from share-holder activism and the development of codes of best corporate governance practices,[4] and through the discussions about recruiting women to corporate boards – there has been considerably greater emphasis placed on the procedures and mechanisms of director selection. This is also the case in firms with concentrated ownership. More often than heretofore, rational selection processes are now taking place. They include considerations or analyses of the needs of the firm as well as an extensive search to consider a larger set of candidates than just those in the close, existing professional network.

Nomination committees, recruitment agencies, and formal and informal registers of potential candidates of board members are among the existing selection mechanisms. Nomination committees constitute one of the main provisions stemming from the ongoing corporate governance debate and are included in most of the recent codes of good corporate governance. The experience with nomination committees so far is, perhaps, that they have become very influential in the selection of board members in large corporations. It is rare for shareholders (at shareholder meetings) or other governance bodies of large organisations to select board members other than those suggested by the nomination committee. The selection of the nomination committee's members therefore becomes very important.

Various recruitment agencies have recently begun to play a larger role in the selection of directors. They often provide liaison between the pool of potential candidates and firms searching for board members. Some agencies are close to the demand side (for example, the firms that traditionally seek executives), while others are close to the supply side (for example, organisations wanting to increase the number of women directors). Some agencies adopt active approaches while other agencies remain more passive. The most active agencies may, for example, make detailed assessments of the needs of both the firm and the board members before starting the selection process, while other, less active agencies may, for example, require only that the potential board members registered with them self-update their profiles in data registers. Various meeting places and networks are also being developed to facilitate the selection of board members. Formal networks through associations of directors or women networks may supplement the traditional professional and social networks of the CEOs and the board members.

The demand side

Few questions have received more attention in the corporate governance debate than that of who the board members should be. The main considerations in this regard are the competence of the board members, the size and composition of the board and the design of the incentive plans for board members. The discussion about board members' competence has to a large degree been influenced by the resource dependence perspective. Agency theory has made the greatest contribution to the discussion about board composition and incentive plans.[5]

Most of the focus on board members has concerned board demographics. The reason for this is that cognitive bases and values are hard to measure. Most of this focus has been on the 'usual suspects'.[6] They include the number of board members, the insider/outsider ratio, CEO duality and the shareholding of board members.[7] The demographics may be important, but here I also present some of the cognitive bases behind the demographics.

Amy Hillman and Thomas Dalziel combine agency and resource theories by introducing the 'board capital' concept.[8] They define board capital as the human capital and the relational capital of the board members. The human capital is the experience, expertise, reputation, etc. of the board members. The relational capital is the social ties to other firms and external contingencies. Hillman and Dalziel argue that, in order for boards to meet their task expectations from agency theory and resource theories, board capital must be combined with proper incentives. In this section I first present the board capital of the individual board members, then the incentives, and finally I present the aggregated board capital. The subsections are labelled 'characteristics', 'compensation' and 'composition'.

Characteristics

In the discussion about increasing the number of women directors the most commonly heard phrase is that 'the board members *must* be qualified'. With this phrase as a background, the question is then to define the *required* qualifications. We must understand the qualifications or abilities needed to perform the various tasks a board is supposed to perform.

The characteristics of board members may be divided into a variety of sub-groups. Hillman and Dalziel distinguish between human capital and relational capital. I have made a distinction between competence and knowledge, and other characteristics.

Competence and knowledge

The importance of competence and knowledge has its roots in resource theories. Board member competence or knowledge is considered as a resource for the firm. I now present seven types of competence and knowledge. They are motivated from both agency and resource perspectives. The competencies are firm-specific knowledge, general business and functional knowledge, board process knowledge, relational knowledge and competence related to personality. There are also often competency requirements related to negotiation and ownership skills.

The first type of competence is firm-specific knowledge. Such knowledge may come from experience in the same industry as the firm in question, but in general much of this knowledge is attained by membership of the board and through personal investigations. Training programmes for new board members are also a way of acquiring this kind of knowledge. Firm-specific knowledge may, for example, be about the main activities of the firm; the firm's critical technology and core competence; the weak points in the firm and in its products and services; the development of the firm's customers, markets, products and services; the bargaining power of suppliers and customers; threats from new firms or new products or services in the industry; etc. This kind of knowledge may also be important for board members when asking critical questions and participating in strategic decision-making and control.

General and function-oriented competence is the second type of competence. Function-oriented competence may, for example, be in finance, accounting, law, marketing, human resources, organisational behaviour and design, strategy or just general management experience. This kind of knowledge is particularly important for the advisory tasks of boards. An entrepreneur will often see the board and its members as a cheap resource, and as a consequence seek board members with the competence that may be needed.[9] It is important from a resource-based perspective to ask why it is the board members that should contribute this kind of knowledge. Would it not be better to have this resource in the organisational hierarchy?[10] Or perhaps it would be better to source this kind of resource in the market. Transaction cost theory and the resource-based view of the firm will help make such decisions.[11] Board members may be firm-specific investments, and the commitment of board members may help the firm create long-term sustainable value.

There may also be a need for process-oriented competence. This is the third type of competence. Process-oriented competence may include knowledge about how to run a board. Lawyers in small firms are often invited to become board members because of their knowledge of the formal requirements related to board membership. There are now also a growing number of people wanting to make their living from board memberships. These are often individuals with specialised knowledge of the tasks and workings of boards. This kind of process knowledge is often combined with a specialist knowledge in, for example, accounting, strategy or law.

The fourth type of competence is relational competence.[12] Relational competence is the 'sum of actual and potential resources embedded within, available through and derived from the network of relationships possessed by an individual or social unit'.[13] This kind of competence is particularly related to acquiring resources from important elements outside the firm, such as financial capital influence and influence with political bodies or stakeholders outside the firm.[14] Communication and information between the firm and environment may also be facilitated through this competence. Communication with internal actors is also important. Stewardship theory and the board's involvement in strategic decision-making, including mentorship and collaboration, may include relationship-oriented competence. Relational competence has specific requirements for the personal rapport between the CEO and board members. The board members should be able to listen to and support the CEO. Stewardship theory will put much emphasis on the time the board members are willing to spend with the CEO. Involvement in strategic control – and, in particular, strategic leadership – will demand the proactive participation of the directors.

The fifth type of competence is related to the personalities and personal characteristics of the directors. This kind of competence may be the ability to think creatively, to think analytically, to think critically, etc. For many years I have been mentoring women who want to become directors on corporate boards, and in so doing I realised that some of them had a competency as energy mobilisers. They were able to create a good boardroom atmosphere – leading to cohesiveness in the board and active contributions from the other board members.[15]

A sixth type of competence is negotiation skills. Board members, according to agency theory, need to represent outside stakeholders, but most of the focus is on representing shareholders. The board members are the agents of external principals. Therefore, they must have the competence to control and monitor the management to make sure that the management and the board make decisions according to the objectives of the external principals. Two special kinds of competence come from this perspective: integrity competence, and negotiation and specific advocate competence. Integrity competence is highly related to independence. The board members need to know why they are there, namely to take care of the interests of their principals, and thus they may avoid overly close relationships with the CEO. The negotiation and specific advocate competence relates to the requirement that they understand the game in which they are involved. There may be board members representing other groups of shareholders with other and conflicting interests, and there may be various other stakeholders trying to influence the CEO and the board's decision-making. From this perspective, board members need to influence the decision-making in order for it to meet the interests of their principals.

Ownership is the seventh type of 'competence', and it is considered by many to be the ultimate qualification for being a board member. In most firms the shareholders want to be board members themselves. The main qualification will thus be ownership. However, institutional investors will most often not be able to participate as board members, due to, for example, investments in competing firms. The various waves of shareholder activism have paid varying levels of attention to board task expectations, and thus also to the competence requirement of the board members. Long-term institutional investors have often emphasised the need for double independence, and the fact that board members have to be experienced business people. Their task is to monitor managerial behaviour to ensure long-term value creation. They should be able to make the proper checks to make sure that the firm develops in a sound way. When behavioural control is important, it is also important to have board members who are able to spend considerable time with the firm, so full-time directors may be considered. On the other hand, short-term institutional investors are generally not interested in the development of the business; instead, they are more interested in board members being qualified to raise the firm's market price in the short term. Board members who ensure predictability and transparency in investor relations will therefore be important to these investors.

Other characteristics

Qualifications and abilities are not the same as knowledge and competence. Boards may benefit from individuals who may provide prestige and secure reputation and legitimacy tasks.[16] These individuals do not necessarily need to have knowledge or competence with respect to key issues facing the firm and its business. However, board members fulfilling networking and legitimacy tasks will, in general, be highly experienced people with a large network and a good reputation. This requirement has, in practice, resulted in bringing in present or previous CEOs from firms with a high reputation. Individuals representing important stakeholders may also be co-opted. These may be bankers, politicians, bureaucrats, but also people representing employees, customers, suppliers, etc. Tokenism is related to this discussion. This implies the need to have women and other minorities, including regional representatives, as board members. Employee directors may also serve as tokens.

Other board member characteristics may be age, gender, education and school/university attended, position, etc. These characteristics may be mandatory requirements and will contribute to board development and accountability – for example, in relation to networking, legitimacy, etc. However, while knowledge and skills are about doing, other characteristics may, rather, be about being.

Compensation – motivation

Compensation, motivation and incentive issues are hardly discussed at all in the resource literature. In managerial hegemony theory and agency theory, however, these questions have received considerable attention. Dependence or interdependence is probably the incentive that has been most studied in the corporate governance literature. Board members have incentives not to 'rock the boat' and ask critical questions or monitor management. The response from agency theory is to stress independence: board members must not be psychological or financial dependants of the CEO. Board members having family ties, business ties or friendship ties with the CEO are not expected to be sufficiently independent to monitor the CEO and evaluate managerial performance.[17] Another consequence of agency theory is equity compensation for board members. This will align the objectives of the board members with those of the shareholders. However, board members may also be motivated in other ways. Various monetary and non-monetary incentive schemes exist. Board members may also have intrinsic incentives – for example, in relation to liability, private and professional standards, and their own reputation.

Ownership

Most board members are motivated because they themselves or their family are majority shareholders of the firm. In situations with corporate ownership, board members are often members of the top management team of the firm in possession, and their main motivation will be through that firm. Employee-elected directors may have their main motivation through representing those who elected them, and executive directors will also have incentives through the career paths of the firm. In this section I discuss some of the incentive schemes that are designed for recruiting and motivating non-executive directors. However, in many firms all the directors have similar incentive schemes as they are all considered to be a part of the same collegium, with all having the same responsibilities. However, variations do occur, based on differences in board assignments – for example, being chairperson or a member of a committee.

How should external or non-executive board members be remunerated? There is an ongoing debate about incentive plans for board members. Should their remuneration be fixed or should it vary? Should the varying part be based on activities, performance or results? And who should design this incentive scheme? It may also be that other schemes are needed to motivate the directors actually to *work* on the board rather than just to *sit* on the board. The general thinking is that high fixed compensation is an incentive to be a board member, while performance- or activity-based compensation serves as an impetus for working on the board.

Fixed compensation

Traditionally compensation paid to external board members has been fairly low, the argument being that board remuneration should be low so that board members are not dependent on receiving this income. Most board members earn the major parts of their income from other sources, and being a board member is often considered to be a sign of status. However, board members also often receive other direct and indirect benefits or compensation from firms where they are board members. Some of these may be monetary. It is common for board members to develop business relations with the firms of which they are board members, and the remuneration from the business relationship can be more important than the remuneration from being a board member. There are numerous examples of how a major part of board involvement has been categorised as consultancy work – and paid accordingly. External stakeholders, among them in particular the shareholders, may not always even be aware of such agreements made by the management. When such incentive schemes do exist it is likely that it is the management that will be considered to be the dominant factor for the board members. The board members will then probably avoid offending or criticising the management because of the risk of losing this compensation.

High fixed compensation will also have similar effects. If the compensation for being on the board in one firm becomes a major source of income for a board member, it is likely that the person will avoid losing this source of income. He or she will then be more dependent on the company than on the shareholders. When CEOs have major influence on the replacement and choice of board members, the person will then also avoid being critical of the CEO.

Compensation based on firm performance

Arguments based on agency theory have secured a strong foothold in the corporate governance literature. Board members may be considered to be agents for the shareholders. According to this assumption, the board members represent the shareholders and have the task of monitoring management. It is important therefore that it is not the management that fixes the remuneration of the board members. As the board may have its own agenda, the remuneration should also be designed such that the interests of its members are aligned with the interests of the shareholders. However, the potential value of this kind of remuneration needs to pass a certain threshold before it becomes an incentive to act on behalf of the shareholders.[18] There are many incentives for board members not to be critical of the CEO.

Generally, in the case of long-term institutional investors being in the ascendant, board members should be remunerated in accordance with the long-term dividends that are paid from the company. Similarly, in the case of short-term institutional investors being predominant, it is likely that they will remunerate board members based on developments in the market price of the shares. Remuneration in shares or stock options would thus be prescribed.

I have already pointed out that there are stakeholders in a firm other than shareholders, and that the predominance of institutional investors is to a large extent a phenomenon in large US corporations.[19] Other stakeholders may have stakes that are not fully aligned with the interests of the dominant shareholders. We experienced some of this situation in the recent large corporate scandals. As, for instance, with Enron. Shareholder, managerial and director incentives were aligned, but the incentives that had been put in place did not take sufficient heed of the interests of stakeholders such as employees, customers, suppliers and society in general. The incentives for corporate managers and directors were so high that formal and informal accountability to other stakeholders was circumvented.[20]

Activity-based compensation and liability

It is often argued that the task of boards is of particular importance when firms are in crisis situations.[21] Then boards often need to be more active. Board members may be replaced in order to help the firm recover from stressful financial situations, and the odds may be high that the outcome will not be positive – even though the recovery operation will have much time at its disposal.

Board members recruited in situations of crisis will probably have a particular awareness of their legal responsibilities, and they will also be motivated by professional standards. These criteria may be important incentives for board members to try their utmost to perform well in that capacity.[22]

The argument is often put that recourse should be had to activity-based compensation when there is much work to be done and little prestige or similar benefits to be gained. Activity-based compensation is frequently a function of three elements. These are the time spent working on the board, the responsibility and liability involved and the compensation provided. The estimation on the time spent working on the board will often include time spent during ordinary board meetings, time spent on preparations, time set aside for availability between board meetings (including work on board committees) and time for extraordinary board activities (including work to solve crises). The second element, the responsibility and liability involved, will be reflected in the qualifications and competence of the board members, who will set rate standards. Consultancy rates will often be used, as board members in many such situations are already consultants or lawyers who are making board membership a part of their business approach. The third element of activity-based compensation is the compensation for the risk involved, including any liability for which responsibility is taken. A liability insurance can partly replace the risk compensation.

Professional standards, the market for board members and intrinsic motivation

Board members are evaluated by their peers, and a motivating factor for many board members is to meet the private and professional standards set by peers or the norms in the culture in which the board members are acting.

Several authors have also argued that a major motivating factor for board members is the fact that they are candidates in the market for board members and top executives. The board members are, more than anybody else, the group of people selecting candidates for boards and top management positions in society. People doing a good job and performing well on one board will be good candidates for board and top management positions in other firms. Awareness of this market is thus considered to be one of the main motivations for board members. In particular, this is important for those aspiring to further their career on other boards. Furthermore, having a reputation as a top-level decision-maker and board member is important in business society.[23]

Private and professional standards, including reputation and awareness of liability, have in various studies been labelled intrinsic motivation. In these studies, measures of intrinsic motivation have been a more accurate predictor of effective board behaviour than extrinsic or monetary incentives.

Composition

Board composition is defined here as the number and configuration of members on the board. It is, essentially, about how a board should be assembled so that, as a group, it can successfully carry out its tasks. In international research and debate, board composition has to a great extent been about how large the board should be, and how many outside members the board should have. A related question is CEO duality. CEO duality is about board leadership, and issues related to CEO duality are tackled in chapter 7.

There are at least three main board composition dimensions. These are concerned with independence, competence and processes. Board composition is, however, broader than just finding a proper mix of outside and inside directors. The board composition question is mainly related to finding a proper balance between involvement and distance. It is a question about dependence versus independence. Board composition is also about finding proper balances of competence. Finally, board composition is about finding a group of people who can work together.

The number of board members
How many members should boards have? This is a question that is raised in various codes of practice as well as in research into boards and governance. The general conclusion is that boards should not be excessively large: seven or eight board members is often considered to be the ideal number.[24] The number of board members in large US corporations is now decreasing, and it is now normal to have ten to twelve members. Some research has indicated that there is a negative relation between the number of board members and corporate financial performance. On the other hand, it is also argued that, if the number of board members is too low, the board will not have sufficient competency to tackle its various tasks.

There are advantages with both large and small boards. Resource theories have been used to argue for a positive relationship between board size and corporate financial performance. Resource dependence theory argues that boards form environmental links in order to secure resources, and a large board will be better able to do so than a small board. It is argued that, the greater the need for external linkages, the larger the board should be.[25] Interlocking directorates are expected to facilitate communication and inter-organisational coordination. From this perspective it can also be argued that a larger board will be associated with positive corporate performance.[26] Finally, it can also be assumed that there will be a positive relationship between the existence of knowledge and competence among board members and the boards' advisory contributions. A positive relationship between a large board and company performance is therefore to be expected.

On the other hand, there are also various advantages to be gained from small boards. The main argument for small boards is related to board working processes: it is argued that smaller boards will have greater focus and participation, and genuine boardroom interaction and debate.[27] The advantages bestowed by large size may be overwhelmed by poor internal communication and decision-making processes.[28] Larger boards may also develop fractions and coalitions that lead to group conflict. Large boards may have a tendency to react slowly and indecisively in a crisis.[29] Furthermore, the argument has been advanced that larger and diverse boards may be more easily manipulated than smaller boards, on the grounds that it will be easier for the CEO to gain dominance over the board through various manipulation techniques such as coalition building. However, the opposing stance is adopted by some authors, who argue that larger boards have more ways of avoiding managerial dominance.

When making comparisons between countries, and even between firms, we should make a distinction between the number of people with voting rights and the actual number of people attending the board meetings. In some places, such as the Scandinavian countries, the number of formal board members tends to be small. However, there may be various other persons permanently attending the board meetings, but without voting rights. Some of the arguments for large and small boards may vary as much for the actual number of attendees as for the ordinary board members with voting rights.

Insiders or outsiders?

The insider or outsider ratio has become one of the classical concepts in understanding, designing and researching boards of directors. The underlying concept is that of independence, which comes from a managerial hegemony background in which the board members, in practice, are dependent on management and are thus unable to fulfil their tasks as monitors of managerial opportunism. The insider/outsider discussion comes from the Anglo-American governance tradition, in which boards were usually dependent on the management and most of the board members were individuals from the TMT. In the continental European governance tradition – which has a two-tier system – most, if not all, board members are typically supposed to be outsiders.

The business press and the corporate community, and in particular institutional investors, show near-consensus in their promotion of a majority of outside directors onto corporate boards. This preference for outsider-dominated boards has its background in agency theory. Agency theory assumes managerial opportunism and focuses on the control tasks of boards. According to agency theory, effective boards will consist of outside directors. However, even in agency theory, there are arguments that independence is not only a matter of being financially and psychologically independent. Board members also need independence in relation to time, knowledge and information. This is particularly imperative in complex organisations where behavioural control is important.

Furthermore, we have stewardship theory to contend with. In this theory it is argued that managers are trustworthy and good stewards of the corporation. The external control task and independence is thus not as important, and the discussion of insiders or outsiders in the context of stewardship theory is related to board members collaborating with the management. The insider/outsider ratio discussion is about finding a balance between distance and closeness. To be able to achieve behavioural control there may be a need for involvement and information that only insiders can have, but it may be difficult for insiders to monitor a CEO they themselves are heavily dependent on.

Dan Dalton, together with colleagues Catherine Daily, Alan Ellstrand and Jonathan Johnson, has conducted meta-analytical reviews of the relationship between board composition and financial performance.[30] They report that no relationship at a meaningful level exists between the insider or outsider ratio and financial performance. There are a considerable number of ways to define independence and that of being an outsider. The traditional understanding of an outsider is an individual who is not a part of the TMT of the firm. This definition can be expanded in different directions. To be independent, an outsider should also be financially and psychologically independent of the CEO and the TMT.

Individuals who have family ties, friendship ties or business ties with the firm or the CEO are not considered to be independent.[31] This is a very static definition, as both friendship and business ties are likely to develop during a period of board membership. Another concept is quasi-outsiders.[32] Quasi-outsiders are non-executive outside board members recruited to the board to support and provide advice to management. They will often be consultants who want to make a living from having a number of board memberships.

Being an insider or outsider is usually defined in relation to the executive leadership of the firm. Owners are typically considered to be outsiders. This definition may be somewhat problematic in family firms. With an ownership definition of a family firm we may consider family owners on boards to be insiders even though they are not a part of the executive leadership of the firm. Non-family executives, even the CEO, may be considered to be outsiders. In family firms, non-executive family members use the board as a way to monitor executive family members.

Another question concerns employee-elected directors.[33] In most cases they are employees of the firm, and therefore they may have a financial dependence, but in many cases the CEO and the shareholder-elected board members seem to be united, while the employee-elected directors will be the ones with an alternative perspective. In systems with employee-elected directors on the board there seems to be a triangulation of interests.

There does not seem to be any research support regarding the outsider dominance of corporate boards from the Anglo-American tradition. Practice in the United States and the United Kingdom has developed in two divergent directions as to what is best: to have mostly insiders or outsiders on the board. In the United States there is now a majority of outside directors, while most directors in the United Kingdom are executives or insiders. However, the question of CEO duality is strongly related to the insider/outsider ratio. CEO duality is the situation in which the CEO is also the chairperson. This used to be the case in both the United States and the United Kingdom. However, the situation is now different. In the United States boards seem to retain the CEO duality, while in the United Kingdom in most cases there is a separation of the positions. The chairperson position in the United Kingdom is often a full-time position, and thus both the chairperson and the CEO may be considered as insiders.[34]

The continental European alternative to finding a balance between insiders and outsiders on the board is to have one executive board with insiders and one supervisory board containing individuals most often representing various external stakeholders, including employees. In this situation the executive board will be able to exercise behavioural control, while the supervisory boards will exercise output control.

Diversity

Corporate directors are considered to be a homogeneous group of people. The usual pattern is for them to be men, and often they are in the later stages of their careers. They have had considerable experience in top management positions, they come from the same schools and they belong to the same kinds of social networks. This will often mean that they have similar kinds of interests, points of reference, language and competence. When attending board meetings they are expected to know the informal rules of the game, and thus they rarely challenge the way things are done. They have the advantage of being quickly able to grasp how board and corporate issues should be dealt with and decided on. By being in the same or similar social and professional networks they will also easily find arenas to discuss and decide on board issues outside the formal board meetings.

Diversity and pluralism will involve board members with varied backgrounds and competences – for example, diversity with respect to educational and social background, business and professional experiences, age, gender, etc.[35] Diversity may also relate to differences in personalities. Directors with alternative or varied backgrounds may have alternative networks, see the firm from complementary perspectives, bring different competences to the board, and challenge the rules of the game on the board.

The diversity question has, to a large extent, been linked to increasing the number of women or minority directors on corporate boards. The arguments come from resource theories indicating that diversity among board members contributes to superior company performance through resource provision, network and advisory tasks. Diversity may relate to the various combinations of competences and backgrounds among the board members. However, there are also some downsides to diversity. Diverse boards are more likely to experience coordination and communication difficulties than homogeneous boards.[36] They may need more time for preparation and ask more questions during board meetings, and communication may be more involved or time-consuming as a common language may not exist. Diverse board members may have difficulties understanding each other because of differences in jargon and terminology. Boards with members with diverse backgrounds are likely to be less cohesive.

The main question relates to whether it will benefit a firm more to have diverse backgrounds or competences among the board members or to opt for homogeneity. Are some kinds of diversity more important than other kinds of diversity, and when is diversity of particular importance? One important question relevant in many firms – but in particular in small and medium-sized firms – is whether the board members should have a competence and background that, for the most part, supplements those of the firm and the management team. Or should the board members have a competence covering all aspects of the firm?

Diversity is at present the main business argument for increasing the number of women on corporate boards.[37] For many years now women have been considered to be important 'tokens' in the boardroom. They may contribute to the reputation of the firm in relation to various stakeholder groups. Women on corporate boards may also serve as role models for women in business, and for women in general. There may also be a need to show that women can rise above the 'glass ceiling' in the corporate hierarchy.

The diversity argument concerns two main issues. These may relate directly to firm performance, or to board processes. The firm performance contribution is that women may have a competence and networks that male board members do not have, and this competence and these networks may have a direct contribution to product, process, organisational and market development. One of the most frequently cited examples is that of Nike Corporation, which started to produce a new line of shoes made for women as a result of having women directors. Women are also expected, in general, to have or to embody values different from those that men have. Women are expected to be more egalitarian and caring than most men, and therefore it is also expected that women on corporate boards will contribute to emphasising caring tasks in the firm, both internally – for example, in relation to upgrading human resource management – and externally, by giving corporate social responsibility greater attention. Women may also devote more attention to behavioural control than their male counterparts.

The other main firm contribution issue of women directors is their contribution to the board's working style and board processes.[38] Anecdotal evidence indicates that boards and the male board members may alter their behaviour when women are introduced to male-dominated boards. Preparations and involvement may increase, more discerning questions may be asked, and the boardroom atmosphere may change.[39]

The supply side

Why should anybody want to become a board member? In this section I describe the supply side of setting up a board. I put forward reasons for wanting to become a board member, suggestions on how to become a board member, presentations of the kinds of boards that are the most attractive and, lastly, some issues to look for before accepting an invitation to become a board member. Finally, I present some thoughts on time spent at meetings, and numbers of board memberships.

Reasons for becoming a board member

There are a variety of reasons that people have for being or wanting to be board members. The main reason is, clearly, that of ownership. Those investing in a firm want to become board members to make sure that their investments are properly taken care of. Other major reasons are a desire for power, the possibility of gaining influence, prestige, the potential for learning, increased possibilities in the labour market and the ability to develop networks.[40] The boardroom may be an exhibition window for people who want to have a career in various arenas. Some also want to make a living from being a professional board member. The reasons for becoming a board member are very individual, and so is the choice of firms that people want to become a board member of.

Generally, large firms with a good reputation, a solid economic position and good leadership are the most attractive.[41] For some individuals it is more important, however, to find boards where it is possible to make a contribution. Others will prefer boards in interesting firms, where they can find something to learn. The learning part may also be related to who the other board members are. Monetary incentives are rarely mentioned as a major reason when priorities are listed in connection with what constitutes the most attractive boards.

How to become a board member

Various theories may be helpful in explaining the board member selection process. These theories include decision-making theories, signalling theory, tournament theory, similarity attracts theory and social network theory. These theories can also provide guidance on how to become a board member. Agency theory can also be included in this list, as ownership or representing ownership is definitely the most important reason for becoming a board member.

It is important to signal interest in a board position (signalling theory), to gain experience from boards in less prestigious organisations (tournament theory), find mentors (similarity attracts theory) and be involved in the social and professional network (social network theory) of those influencing board decisions. Board members will often be included in a net of interlocking directorates. Novices who perform well on one board will therefore find it easier to make a smooth transition to other boards.

Many women have recently shown considerable interest in becoming board members. They have been supported by many private and public initiatives that have the aim of getting more women on corporate boards. Another group of potential board members that is growing rapidly at present consists of those wanting to make board memberships their living. In this group initiatives are taken to professionalise board memberships, through certification and membership in associations for board members. Such organisations are established and expanding in most countries, and they provide networking and discussion arenas, courses and teaching about board practices, registers and selection aids for finding board members, etc.

What to look for before accepting

There exist checklists to be adhered to before accepting a board membership, but, in general, one of the main questions to be considered is the amount of time required to serve as a member of that board, and how this time requirement fits in with other time commitments.

How much time does it take to be a board member and how many board memberships can one person support? Some codes of corporate governance set down limits as to the maximum number of board memberships one person can support. There is, however, no clear answer to this question. Board membership in some firms demands a lot of time and energy, while other boards are less time-consuming. It is also obvious that some people are more capable of handling a sizeable number of simultaneous board memberships than others. This depends on experience, other commitments and the kinds of positions that the individuals have on the boards of which they are members. There are several examples of people working effectively on more than 100 boards at once, very often also serving as the chairperson. Such examples usually have something to do with the kinds of firms involved. Most often such a board member will be a lawyer doing the paperwork for a large number of more or less equal real estate boards. Here I indicate two individual factors that may be of importance, namely availability and experience.

To be a board member is not only a matter of the total hours spent on the board. It is also a question of when these hours are spent, and it requires the flexibility to spend the necessary time on board work when it is urgent. It is, therefore, not just a matter of summing the number of hours expected to be spent on each board. Sometimes board work requires meetings and other kinds of work at very irregular hours, and sometimes board work requires that the board member be present at certain places at certain times. To be a board member sets major demands on availability and flexibility. This may make it difficult to combine many simultaneous board commitments. Board membership may also require flexibility in relation to other commitments – for example, in relation to ordinary job commitments or in relation to the family.

Experienced board members may have many advantages. Experience may relate to tenure on the board, as a board member in general, or simply knowledge of business practices. Experience and tenure may be advantageous not only in relation to time being used effectively in the preparation of board tasks but also in relation to power.

Checklists for those considering board membership often include recommendations to study the following points:
- the regulations of the firm;
- the expectations the shareholders and other important stakeholders have of the board;
- the working style of the board, including formal and informal structures;
- the other board members;

- potential conflicts of interest the applicant may have, and whether they are acceptable to the other board members;
- protocols from earlier board meetings, and in particular if there are earlier decisions that will bind the board and the firm in a way that is not desired;
- the annual reports and results;
- the quality of board preparations;
- the monetary and non-monetary remuneration; and
- the existence of board liability insurance.

Several of these points are tackled at length in other places in this book.

The case of women directors

This in-depth summarising case concerns the Norwegian law designed to increase the number of women on corporate boards. Norway has received attention in the international corporate governance debate because of the introduction in 2006 of a law requiring at least 40 per cent of the board members in corporations to be women.

Background

Norway has been at the forefront of moves to include employees in the governance of corporations. Laws regulating co-determination have been enacted as a result of wide-ranging discussions that took place in the 1960s. One of the debates centred on the question of what corporations are and what they are for. The other area of discussion concerned the workers' role in business development.[42] The outcome of the debate was that employees received the legal right to be represented on corporate boards at the beginning of the 1970s. The Company Act of 1976 was a result of joint Nordic efforts and cooperation.

In 1988 the Nordic Council of Ministers issued a statement to the effect that Nordic cooperation with respect to company law should continue. As the need for a new Company Act became apparent at the beginning of the 1990s, there was also a desire to make adjustments and to harmonise this Act with company laws and regulations in the European Union. At that time Denmark was a member of the EU but the other Nordic countries were not; as a result it was difficult to achieve the same kind of inter-Nordic harmonisation and cooperation as there had been in 1976, as Denmark had also to obey EU law.

There were several features in the development of Norwegian society that made it urgent to have a new company law. One core aspect was the adjustments to EU regulations. This adjustment led, as expected, to a separation between big 'public' companies and small 'private' firms. Another aspect was the development of economic crime and the misuse of the corporate form. This was significantly more extensive at the beginning of the 1990s than it had been in the 1970s: the extent of bankruptcies, including 'black' bankruptcies, had increased considerably.

Proposals for new company laws were given to the Ministry of Police and Justice in March 1996, and the laws were ratified in June 1997, coming into force in January 1999. There were two laws: one dealt with private companies, with the suffix AS, and the other with public companies, ASA.[43] The major advance in these laws compared to earlier laws was that they spelt out the responsibilities of the board. This led to renewed discussions about liability insurance for board members, and concerns that in the future it would be difficult to get qualified board members.

The laws also had other concrete stipulations, including requirements for CEO working descriptions, board instructions, voting rules and financial reporting to the board. The requirement for board instructions was only for companies with employee representatives on the boards. The intention of the board instruction stipulation was to ensure that employee-elected board members had real – rather than only nominal – influence on board decision-making.

Women on corporate boards

One aspect of the laws that created considerable debate was the proposal to have a quota of women on corporate boards. The subject of having quotas of women on boards was originally an equal opportunity issue, and rules concerning gender representation on boards were introduced in 1981 in the Act about Equal Opportunity. Becoming effective in 1988, paragraph 21 of the Act of Equal Opportunity had the following wording: 'When a public body appoints a committee, board or council, etc. with four members or more, then each gender must be represented with at least 40 per cent of the members. Both genders must be represented in committees with two or three members. These rules are also valid for subsidiary members.'

The requirement concerning gender representation was motivated by social justice and a societal need. It was also argued that the particular interests of women would be better taken care of by women than by men, and that women had different background experiences from men. The objective was to accelerate this development by a quota system. This regulation had major effects. Between 1979 and 1987 the ratio of women board members in public boards and councils increased from 22 per cent to 40 per cent; since then this figure has been constant.

In 1992 there were 764 board member positions in the companies listed on the Oslo Stock Exchange. Only twenty-six of these positions, or 3.4 per cent, were held by women. In some industries there were no women at all as board members. In 1996 the ratio of women board members increased to 7.5 per cent, but the increase was mainly due to the acceptance of new types of firms on the Oslo Stock Exchange: savings banks were now allowed to enter. Around this time, however, attention became focused on this issue once more, input to the discussion coming from the NHO (the Confederation of Norwegian Enterprise), the government's Equality Centre, various feminist groups and the debates in other countries, in particular Sweden. The motivation for increasing the number of women directors changed from an equality and societal issue to a firm profitability issue, as newspapers started to report research findings about positive relationships between the ratio of women on boards and board performance.

Programmes to increase the number of women directors started to mushroom. Various programmes designed to train women as board members were introduced, mentorship programmes and women's networks were established, and databanks, registers or archives of women board candidates were launched.

Since the mid-1990s the political situation in Norway has been quite volatile, with frequent changes of government between a social democratic Labour administration and one headed by a Christian Democratic or Christian People's Party Prime Minister, Kjell Magne Bondevik. In 1999 the Equality Department in the Ministry of Children and Families in Bondevik's first Cabinet submitted for hearing a proposed reform to have at least 25 per cent female board membership in all companies – private and public alike. The proposal involved a change in the Equality Act between the genders, and it led to a strong reaction from men as well as from women. In 2000 the ratio of female board members fell to 6.4 per cent in the companies listed on the Oslo

Stock Exchange. In 2002 the ratio of women board members in all public companies (ASA) was also reported to be 6.4 per cent.

This proposal, which had originated with the first Bondevik Cabinet, was acted on by the first administration headed by Jens Stoltenberg (Norwegian Labour Party). The changes in the Act of Equality were implemented without the requirements for board representation, but a new proposal for quotas for women on corporate boards in public companies was submitted in 2001. In the hearing, it was suggested that the ratio of women to men could be as high as 40 per cent in public companies (ASA companies). The proposal received only mixed support, however, with the NHO and the financial community the most negative in their reaction.

In 2002 the Minister of Industry in the second Bondevik administration presented a law proposal, derived from the two previous hearings, to the effect that each gender should have at least 40 per cent representation in all public companies. There were no exceptions to this rule for board members elected by employees; the gender representation rule was to apply to the whole board. The law proposal was ratified by the Norwegian Parliament in 2003. However, the implementation rules for the Act dictated that the law did not need to be enforced if the mandatory 40 per cent representation for each gender had been achieved on a voluntary basis before 1 July 2005. As this was not achieved, the law requiring 40 per cent of corporate board members to be women was put into effect in January 2006 – by which time the actual figure had increased to around 13 per cent. However, the representation of women on boards in corporations with more than 5000 employees had risen to more than 20 per cent by then. All companies were given two additional years' grace before any sanctions would be imposed.

The Norwegian debate about women directors was characterised by many simplistic and partially wrong arguments. Nevertheless, the discussion and the law proposal have probably had a greater impact on the development of good board practice than was suggested in the public discussions themselves. In the Norwegian corporate community, probably no single event has contributed as much to a thorough rethinking of the contribution of boards, board tasks and board composition as the debate regarding women directors – probably more so even than the waves of shareholder activism and the evolution of codes of best practice. The contribution from these discussions has been that board member selection has, by and large, moved from being an informal and often unconscious search through professional and social networks to a professional and rational search process containing specifications of competence and qualification requirements of board members.

Summary

This chapter has looked at board members' characteristics and compensation and board composition, which constitute the core concepts of the chapter. I relate characteristics to each individual board member, whereas compensation refers to the individual board member's incentive structure and composition is a description of the board members as a group. It is important to identify the three concepts and to distinguish between them. However, characteristics, compensation and composition should not be viewed separately from each other when exploring boards and value creation, as the three attributes interact. Both competence and motivation are needed at the individual level, and the composition of the board should reflect the need to balance the various task expectations.

Board member characteristics is a broad term. A sub-group is competence. Seven types of board member competence criteria were presented based on arguments from theory and board task expectations.

- Firm-specific knowledge may, for example, be about the main activities of the firm, the firm's critical technology and core competence, the weak points in the firm and in its products and services, the development of the firm's customers, markets, products and services, the bargaining power of suppliers and customers, threats from new firms or new products or services in the industry, etc.
- General and function-oriented competence may, for example, be in finance, accounting, law, marketing, human resources, organisational behaviour and design, strategy or just general management experience.
- Process-oriented competence may include knowledge about how to run a board.
- Relational competence includes the abilities the board members have to build relationships with internal and external actors.
- Competence is related to the personalities and personal characteristics of the directors.
- Negotiation skills.
- Ownership.

Characteristics are also related to who the board members are, where they live, their age, etc.

We have used the term 'compensation' to describe the board members' incentives and motivation. Included are internal as well as external incentives, and the incentives go beyond independence and shareholding. Motivation arising from liability, reputation and personal and professional standards were also introduced. Composition is about the size and configuration of the board with respect to the board members' competence, characteristics and compensation. Board size, outsider ratio and diversity were the main types presented. The discussion and arguments about compensation and composition were also based on competing theoretical perspectives and board task expectations.

5 | *Contexts and resources*

The context and resources are presented in this chapter. The main concepts are:

- resources;
- the CEO tenure and characteristics;
- national and cultural differences;
- the industrial environment;
- the firm size;
- the firm life cycle; and
- the ownership.

The objective of this chapter is to present contextual factors that influence actual board and governance behaviour. The factors are both firm-internal and firm-external. The logic in contingency theory adapted to boards and governance is that there is no single best design of corporate governance but that, in addition, not all designs are equally good. A corporate governance design needs to fit both the context and the actors. In the previous chapters I have presented the actors and their board task expectations; in this chapter I present some of the contextual variables that have received the most attention in the corporate governance literature.

Contextual variables are often divided into internal and external contexts.[1] The internal context often includes:

- the management, including style, ownership and corporate tenure;
- resources, including types and configuration;
- the firm's size;
- the firm's life cycle;
- the type of business, including foundation, voluntary organisation and not-for-profit organisation;
- the ownership; and
- strategies, including growth, product, price and market.

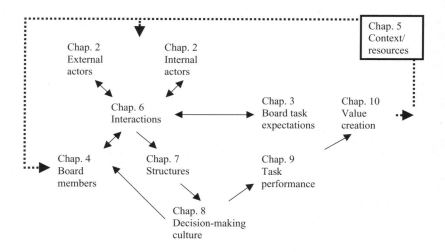

The external context often includes:
- the industry – such as finance or high-tech;
- the cultural, legal and geographical, stakeholder power and legal system; and
- the competitive environment, including technological opportunities, hostility, heterogeneity and dynamism.

There is some debate, however, as to what an internal context is and what an external context is, with different outcomes depending on what the context is internal or external to – i.e. internal or external to the board, to the firm or to the owners. Some of the contextual variables also have attributes that clearly are both internal and external. The ownership structure will, for example, definitely be related to the industry. For this reason I deliberately do not make a clear distinction between internal and external contexts.

It is apparent in the guiding framework that context and resources may have a direct effect on the actors – who they are and their relative power. The framework also illustrates that corporate performance and value creation may influence the context. Even though the context and resources may be considered permanent in the short term, over a longer time-frame they will vary. Changes in context and resources will to a large extent be influenced not only by the firm's performance but also by decisions taken by the board of directors. Some of the contextual variables I present here – for example, ownership – can also be considered as corporate governance mechanisms or tools. Even though not shown in the framework illustration, we also find that various contextual variables may have direct effects on most of the concepts in the framework, and to a large extent we expect that they will moderate the relationships.

In this chapter I present the context under the following headings: (a) resources; (b) CEO tenure and other characteristics; (c) national, geographic and cultural differences; (d) industry and a competitive environment; (e) firm size; (f) firm life cycle; and (g) ownership. It needs to be borne in mind, however, that not only do resources and some other contextual variables represent the context in which the board operates – they may also be the outcome of corporate governance, and they may be important mechanisms and tools in a corporate governance design. In the final section of this chapter an in-depth summarising case of 'outside' directors in small firms is presented.

Resources

A firm may have different kinds of resources and resource configurations. Resources are often categorised as human resources (such as the leadership, and the education and experience of the employees), social resources (such as networks and relational capabilities), organisational resources (such as the firm's structure), technological resources, financial resources and locational resources.[2]

Resources can be considered as contextual variables, but the definition of resources varies. The whole list of the most-used contextual variables may be considered as resources. This list includes organisational, process- and product-related resources; CEO characteristics; the national, geographic and cultural location; the industry and the industrial environment; the firm size; the firm life cycle; and ownership. These variables are each of a different nature, and they are interrelated. Even though they all can be considered as contextual variables, some of them will also be:

• resources and input;
• results and output; and
• governance design variables and tools.

Some of the variables may be considered solely as resources and used as such, while others can also be considered as output or results. Some of them may also be considered to be design parameters.

Resources and results

Some of the contextual variables are used in various ways in studies of boards of directors. Therefore, in the framework used in this book, context is positioned not only as an input to understanding stakeholder relations and board roles but *also* as something influenced by the outcome of board activities and corporate performance.

There are also relations between resource configurations and competitive strategies.[3] Resources therefore shape the context for the strategic orientation of the firm.[4] The resource situation of a firm also shapes stakeholder relations and the relative importance of various stakeholders. Typical directions for the strategic orientation of a firm relate to whether it is growth-, profit- or stability-oriented.

Resources and resource configurations change over time and often as a result of board behaviour. Thus, the strategic orientation may change as a consequence of a changing resource configuration, and board tasks and accountability may change as a consequence of changes in power relations between stakeholders. The strategic orientation therefore also becomes an important contextual variable influencing board tasks, and the use or empowerment of a board of directors may thus be a result of strategic decisions. On the other hand, it is also evident that the strategic orientation and resource acquisitions are results of board decision-making.

The strategic orientation is one example of the complexity of categorising resources as contextual variables. The ownership and CEO characteristics are similar examples. The ownership, for instance, will influence board tasks. Furthermore, the ownership may also be the result of firm performance: well-performing firms will generally have more flexibility regarding ownership than poorly performing firms.

Design parameters

We have just seen how the resource configuration, and resources such as the ownership and CEO characteristics, may be input variables, output variables, and even design variables. The ownership structure, CEO characteristics and strategic orientations are among the main design variables in corporate governance. A main task of the board is to make decisions about and to implement the most appropriate ownership structure.

CEO tenure and other characteristics

The CEO is an actor. However, I have also made the point that the CEO may be regarded as a resource as well as a contextual variable. Board tasks will vary depending on attributes of the CEO – for example, the CEO's tenure, ownership and competence.

Tenure

Tenure is often seen as an indication of expert power. A CEO has tenure in the firm as well as in the actual position. Board tasks may vary depending on his or her tenure as CEO, as well as on his or her tenure in the organisation prior to being appointed to the CEO position. Board tasks may also vary depending on the CEO's tenure relative to the tenure of the board chairperson.

The power of the board may vary with the tenure of the CEO and the relative tenure of the CEO and the board chairperson. In an article on the dynamics of CEO–board relationships Wei Shen shows how boards with a newly recruited CEO should focus on supporting and mentoring the CEO.[5] Research on executive leadership shows that CEOs who are recently recruited spend considerable time trying to understand and get to know the organisation. They need to learn and adjust to their new role. They need to find out how to work with the board, the other members of the management team and important stakeholders. This adjustment situation is greater for externally recruited CEOs than for those recruited internally. Shen argues that the board in this situation, based on stewardship theory, should focus on a mentoring approach. However, the general observation is that CEO power increases over time. New CEOs normally need a few years to acquire the necessary task knowledge before they can take major actions to reshape the organisation. Once CEOs have exceeded the expectations of the board and important stakeholders, they may be more susceptible to opportunism. The board's task should then change from mentoring to monitoring.

The relative tenure of the CEO and the board members is also considered to be important for understanding boards. The selection of board members is often influenced by the CEO, and board members who are selected after the CEO is appointed are often considered to be dependent on the CEO. The corollary of this is when we find examples of new board chairpersons – particularly if the person is not recruited from the existing board members – who may be inclined to position themselves strongly and to take an independent stand in relation to the CEO and what has been done before.

CEO ownership

Furthermore, boards will relate in a different way to CEOs representing majority ownership – for example, through a family firm – from when the CEO is independent of owners. The discussion of the separation of ownership and control relates to the situation when the CEO only has a minor (if any) ownership stake.[6] When the CEO is also an important owner, the board's task will to a large extent be the service tasks of advice and networking activities. Such situations typically arise in owner-manager firms or when the CEO is also the founder of the firm.

Executive ownership is one of the most studied topics in corporate governance. In this debate it is argued that CEO ownership facilitates objective alignments. The CEO will then have the same objectives as the shareholder. The need for boards to perform control tasks will then be reduced.

Top management team competence

Boards of directors are important sources for direct and indirect resource provision. However, there is an ongoing debate about whether the board and its members should have a general knowledge that may be relevant for the firm, or just knowledge that supplements that of the CEO and the TMT. The supplementary knowledge is important from a service perspective, but the general knowledge is important from a control perspective.

National, geographic and cultural differences

There are variations between countries with respect to culture, laws and economic development, and these variations influence corporate governance. Corporate governance is influenced by legal systems. A common-law system operates in both the United States and the United Kingdom, and a civil-law system operates in continental Europe. In a common-law system, laws and regulations evolve from practice. This may be characterised as a type of 'bottom-up' approach, while the civil-law system may be characterised as a 'top-down' approach. Formal regulations are more important in the civil-law system, and this also relates to corporate governance and boards of directors.

Comparison between countries

The recent corporate governance debate and the spread of agency theory have both been based on the separation of ownership and control as it was described by Adolf Berle and Gardiner Means in 1932 in large US corporations.[7] But does this describe the situation of firms in a range of countries today? Considerable evidence indicates that this is not the case.[8] The United States is a special case, and the situation there today is not the same as it was seventy years ago.

There is general agreement in the literature that a distinction can be made between the Anglo-American and the continental European models of corporate governance. Most international comparisons of corporate governance systems are stylised comparisons of the Anglo-American and the continental European systems. The Anglo-American system represents dispersed ownership, active markets for corporate control and flexible labour markets, and it is based on a common-law system. The Anglo-American corporate governance system is considered to be market-based. The continental European system represents long-term debt financing, ownership by holders of large blocks of shares, weak markets for corporate control, and rigid labour markets. The continental European system is generally based on a civil-law system, and is considered to be control-based. Differences in corporate governance across countries are illustrated in table 5.1, where ownership dispersion, ownership identity, the identity of board members, the power of shareholders, potential takeover threat, and the financing of corporations are displayed. These corporate governance attributes vary between the countries listed.

Ownership dispersion is very high in the United States and low in Canada and Germany. In the United States and the United Kingdom the main owners are pension and mutual funds. Board composition also varies. Board composition in the Anglo-American system is generally a mix of insiders and outsiders. The insiders are the CEO and other executive members of the TMT. Shareholders are rarely represented – as

Table 5.1 *Cross-national comparison of corporate governance*

	United States	United Kingdom	Canada	France	Germany
Ownership dispersion	Very high	High	Low	Medium	Low
Ownership identity	Individuals Pension and mutual funds	Pension and mutual funds	Family Corporate	Corporate State	Banks Corporate
Board members	Executives Outsiders	Executives Outsiders	Shareholders Executives Outsiders	Shareholders Employees	Shareholders Employees
Shareholder power	Low	Low	Moderate	High	High
Takeover	High	High	Moderate	Low	Low
Financing	Equity	Equity	Equity/debt	Debt/equity	Debt

Source: Gedajlovic and Shapiro 1998.

the ownership in these countries is widely dispersed and institutional. Such shareholders will, for various reasons, avoid having direct representation on the board. Shareholders in the United States will generally avoid board involvement as board members will obtain inside information, and that will limit the shareholders' ability to trade shares. In the continental European model, ownership concentration is strong, and owners will have a more active involvement with the board. The stakeholder emphasis in these countries has also resulted in employee representation on boards.

The stakeholder picture

Aguilera and Jackson have developed a model to describe and explain variations in corporate governance.[9] The model identifies the social relations and institutional arrangements that determine who controls corporations, what interests corporations serve, and the allocation of rights and responsibilities among corporate stakeholders.[10] Their model is based on an analysis of three stakeholder groups; capital, labour and management.

Their starting point is the premise that corporate governance is the outcome of interactions among multiple stakeholders, and that corporate governance needs to be understood in the context of a wider range of institutional domains. This means that corporate governance designs and conceptualisations should be understood in terms of how they are embedded in different social contexts and institutional environments. Furthermore, institutions shape the processes of how stakeholders' interests are defined, and institutional environments are nationally distinct.

National variations in the stakeholder picture include variations in attributes associated with capital, labour and management. Various types of capital possess different identities, interests, time horizons and strategies. Table 5.1 shows comparisons of corporate governance between nations. One distinction may be between the financial and strategic interests associated with capital. Strategic interests will be related to the shareholders' control of power in an organisation. A second distinction is concerned with the degree of liquidity or commitment. The liquidity or commitment dimension is often related to ownership dispersion or concentration. A third dimension is the distinction between debt and equity. Debt holders will generally be more risk averse than equity holders.

Among important attributes relating to labour we find participation in the organisation versus control of the organisation, and portable skills versus firm-specific skills. These attributes vary across countries and cultures with respect to, for example, representation rights, union organisation and skill formation. The management attributes described by Aguilera and Jackson are autonomous versus committed, and financial versus functional. Across countries and cultures these attributes vary with respect to managerial ideology and careers.

Variations in national institutional configurations may have importance for the understanding of various stakeholder coalitions and power structures, and thus also for the role and accountability of boards of directors.

Tiers and delegation

Board systems vary between countries as well as within countries. In several countries – for example, the Netherlands, France and Finland – various board systems exist within the same country.

Table 5.2 *Two-tier systems*

	Delegation/two tiers	*No delegation/one tier*
One-board system	Scandinavian	Anglo-American
Two-board system	Continental European	

However, in large corporations there are two main sets of distinctions; whether there is a one-board system or a two-board system, and whether there is a compulsory delegation of the daily operations from the board to management.

In the *Anglo-American* model there is one board, which also has direct responsibility for the day-to-day running of the firm. The board typically consists of the CEO, members of the top management team and a few non-executives. The non-executives are traditionally added to provide external resources and manage resource dependencies.

In the typical *Continental European* two-board system there is one supervisory board and one executive board. The supervisory board consists of non-executives, often representing shareholders and various other stakeholder groups. The executive board has the day-to-day tasks delegated to it. The executive board consists of the TMT, and the CEO is usually the chairperson of the executive board. It is the supervisory board that – in this book and in most other comparative descriptions – is called the 'board'.

In the *Scandinavian* model there is a one-board system, but the board members are generally non-executives elected by the shareholders. It is compulsory to delegate the day-to-day running to a CEO, and is therefore a two-tier system. The CEO can be replaced by an executive board, but in practice this hardly ever happens.

Employee board representation and co-determination are features often emphasised in European corporate governance models. There are various models of employee representation. In some countries employee representation is a voluntary system. In other countries, such as Norway, the employees can require board-level representation. There the employee representatives are elected by employees. In Sweden the employee representatives are elected by the unions, and in Germany and some other countries the employee representatives do not even have to be employees of the firm.

How laws are applied in practice may vary from how they appear in theory. The relationship between the formal legal system and institutional forces must be understood when comparing corporate governance between nations. For example, the two-tier systems in the Netherlands and Germany are formally similar, but they are embedded in two very different corporate cultures.[11] In Germany there is a corporate governance culture such that boards may be described through stakeholder agency theory. Board members are elected to represent certain stakeholders. In the Netherlands the corporate governance culture can best be described by resource dependence theory, and board members are selected rather than elected. They are put in place to function as resource providers for the firm. These examples illustrate how the national context has to be taken into account in order to understand boards and governance.

Industry and a competitive environment

Industry and a competitive environment are among the factors that, in general, are presumed to influence corporate governance.

Different industries

Cross-industry comparisons of corporate governance are found in some studies, while other studies restrict themselves to exploring just a single industry.

Often there are correlations between the industry of a corporation and its competitive environment, but industries can also be described in terms of, for example, technological sophistication, knowledge intensity, capital intensity, stakeholder sensitivity and international orientation. Governance in emerging industries may also vary from governance in established industries or declining industries.[12] Some industries will have many firms that can be compared (for example, the hotel industry, the food production industry, the construction industry, etc.), while other industries (for example, those characterised by technological sophistication and knowledge intensity) will have firms that may be difficult to compare. In the first group it may be possible for board members to rely on output control, while behavioural control may be more essential in the second group.

Governance systems may vary significantly between knowledge-intensive firms and capital-intensive firms.[13] Some of these differences may also relate to variations in property rights, and there may be resemblances to partnerships in consultancies and the faculty's role in university boards.[14] In stakeholder-sensitive industries there may be particular emphasis on transparency and accountability. Boards in such industries will, more than boards in other industries, be related to various stakeholder concerns such as corporate social responsibility.[15] This is the case, for example, in highly polluting industries, the energy sector, the health care sector, etc.

Competitive environment

The industrial environment is often characterised in terms of heterogeneity, dynamism, hostility and technological opportunities.[16] When the environment is complex or characterised by heterogeneity there will normally be a need for a broad scope of knowledge in the firm and among board members. Diversity among board members may be important, and giving advice to the CEO and executives will be a main task for the board. Fast decision-making may be needed in environments characterised by dynamism and rapid changes. Board members may be needed who can swiftly assess a situation and ratify suggestions presented by the management. Board members with the same background and cognitive framework as the CEO may meet such requirements more readily than people with alternative modes of thinking. Homogeneity among board members may be preferable to diversity when the industrial environment is characterised by dynamism. Hostility relates both to the competitive climate as well as to the relationships between various stakeholders, such as municipalities etc. Fierce or hostile competition may require participative board members who are involved in strategic leadership, while a hostile attitude from other stakeholders may benefit from board members who can contribute to making the environment friendlier. The legitimacy task will therefore be important. Corporations in industrial environments characterised by technological opportunities may in particular benefit from entrepreneurial orientation and the creativity of board members. This creativity may include innovative use of the network of the board members.

The competitive environment may also vary geographically. International activities may be a contextual variable but also a result of board involvement and decisions. Traditionally there is a distinction between domestic and foreign markets, and the contextual impact of international activities may vary depending on whether the international activities are related to sales or exports, production, research and development, or various headquarter functions. Distinctions between international, transnational, multinational and global activities may also be important.

Firm size

Some authors consider firm size to be the contextual factor with the greatest impact on boards and governance. Most of the literature and research on boards is on firms in large corporations, but now there is growing attention being focused on boards in SMEs – both in research and in practice.[17] Boards in small firms are often considered to be 'aunt' boards, intended to have no role other than the formal role given by law.

There are many ways to measure firm size. The commonest measures of firm size are the number of employees or the volume of sales, though sometimes firm size is also gauged by a combination of both these measures. Another common measure is the value of the share capital, but complexity and impact, in addition to measures relative to markets and countries, are also often used. What is considered to be a small or medium-sized firm in Europe is thus quite often very different from what it is in, for example, the United States. The size measures to be used will depend on the issues to be explored, and often we find variations in pieces of legislation that are linked to various size measures – for example, the share capital or the number of employees. In this book I generally consider all firms that are not Fortune 500 firms to be either small or medium-sized firms. Firms with fewer than fifty employees are considered to be small, but even in the case of Norway we have found that firms with fewer than fifty employees have been listed among Fortune 500 firms based on sales figures.

Small and medium-sized firms

As mentioned above, there are various kinds of small firm, and they are often characterised by ownership concentration and the presence of values of importance for the shareholders other than return. Small firms will frequently be characterised by a lack of basic resources, and the various service tasks will therefore often be more highly valued in small firms than in large firms. The service tasks are enforced by the empowerment of boards in such firms, as it will to a large extent be based on the CEO's trust in the board members. The board members in small firms are often a pool of helpers, playing roles such as providing a sounding board, a shoulder to cry on or a source of advice in decision-making.[18] This pool of helpers may include 'professional' board members and business angels.

The traditional shareholder-initiated control tasks may be of less importance in small firms, as the manager is often the main owner in such firms. However, there are certain forces in small firms that also lead to an emphasis on the control tasks. In small firms, stakeholders other than shareholders may play important roles.[19] Banks, customers, suppliers, employees and local societies may be important actors with both stakes and power in the firms, and significant evidence exists as to how banks empower boards with external directors.

Markets for control vary between small and large firms, and the substitution effects arguments predict an emphasis on the board control tasks. External stakeholders in small firms often have a difficult control task, as reliable information and accounting practices may be lacking. This may cause significant information asymmetry. Small firms often lack the resources to prepare reliable information about the firm, and accounting and management systems often rely on one person, the CEO, with the prime source of data storage and processing being the CEO's own head. Incentives for board membership may also vary between small and large firms. In large firms monetary awards and status are often included as incentives, while in small firms board membership often results in hard work and may be taken on as an altruistic gesture towards a small business manager, in many cases a friend needing help.

Firm life cycle

The importance of the firm life cycle for board roles is illustrated in table 5.3. This table is reproduced from the 'one of the lads' study – a study in which three small firms in different life cycle phases were examined.[20]

The differences in table 5.3 may also be attributed to differences between industries, but the stakeholder picture, the extent of

Table 5.3 *Board life cycle*

Life cycle phase	Start-up	Growth	Crisis
Industry	Constructor	Food production	Car retailing
Stakeholder picture	Bank	Owners (family)	Bank
	Regulating authorities		Employees
	Management		Suppliers
			Customers
Stakeholders' power	Moderate	Low	High
Main theoretical perspective	Resource dependence	Resource-based view	Stakeholder/agency theory
Main board tasks	Legitimacy	Advice	Control

stakeholders' power, the main theoretical perspectives and the main board tasks clearly differ across the three firms that were examined. Resource dependence theory and the legitimacy tasks were the most important in the start-up firm, the resource-based view and the advisory tasks were the most important in the growth-phase firm, and agency theory and control tasks were the most important in the firm in crisis.

Crisis

Much of the recent corporate governance debate has been related to situations of crisis. We may think of Enron, Royal Aholt or Parmalat in this context. Board tasks will be different in times of crisis from what they would be in normal times. Many scholars have carefully studied the board's tasks in situations of crisis.[21] However, there are various kinds of crises, and each of the different kinds may require different kinds of actions.

- Internal versus external origin of crisis
- Internal versus external pressures to respond to crisis
- Sudden versus gradual development of crisis
- Financial versus managerial crisis
- Firm or board crisis
- Crisis in different markets for control
- Severity of crisis

An internal crisis usually refers to a crisis that has an internal origin, while an external crisis has an external origin. In Enron the origin of the crisis was internal, while hurricane Katrina was an external source of crisis for many companies. However, there may be external *and* internal pressure to respond to the crisis regardless of its origin. Fraudulent or corrupt employees or management may be responsible, but the strongest pressure to act may come from owners, customers or society in general.

A crisis may have developed gradually – for example, due to negative market trends – but the situation may have appeared suddenly – for example, due to a sudden and unforeseeable rise in oil prices. A negative relationship between the CEO and the TMT may have built up over a period of time, but the untimely death of a key officer would be a sudden event. A situation of crisis may be due to short-term financial problems – for example, related to liquidity – but it may also be a managerial or a leadership problem – for example, emotional conflicts or unethical behaviour in the TMT.

We may find board-level crises that do not have a direct impact at the firm level, and there may be crises in the corporation that have only a limited impact on the board. It is also a different kind of crisis when shareholders are fighting for corporate control and board dominance from when the firm is threatened in its product markets.

The severity of a crisis situation will also impact boards and governance. A situation of stress may have different consequences from a situation calling for immediate and urgent action. The various kinds of crises change the stakes, power and activities of various actors, and there will be pressures to change board tasks – for example, in times of financial distress banks and other stakeholders often take over the tasks usually performed by shareholders.

Life cycle phases

Firms' evolution through the corporate life cycle may be supported by changes in the corporate governance system. Some empirical studies have been carried out on the role of boards in different life cycle phases, and a growing body of literature shows how the theoretical rationale for boards varies with the life cycle stage of the firm.[22] Traditionally, according to Max Weber, a firm's life cycle typically consisted of an entrepreneurial phase with charismatic authority, an institutional phase with traditional authority and a professional phase with legal authority.[23] Firms may be forced to move from one phase to another, or to cross a certain threshold, due to various crisis situations. Board tasks when crossing various thresholds are presented below; first I present board tasks in various life cycle phases.

Board tasks in the three phases of start-up, growth and crisis were illustrated above in the discussion about the three small firms used in the 'one of the lads' study. However, contributions on the firm life cycle summarise the stages somewhat differently, as typically consisting of an entrepreneurial stage, a collectivist stage, a formalisation and control stage and an elaboration of structure stage.[24] The entrepreneurial stage is the phase in which the firm is seeking to achieve a certain threshold to survive. This phase will be characterised by flexibility, an abundance of ideas, the marshalling of resources and the formation of a niche. Mentoring and legitimacy may be important board tasks in this phase. The collectivist stage is usually related to growth, and is often characterised by continued innovation, informal communication, a sense of collectivism, a sense of mission and high commitment. The board advisory tasks may be of particular importance in this phase. The formalisation and control stage is the phase in which procedures are institutionalised. It is characterised by the formalisation of rules, stable structures and an emphasis on efficiency and maintenance. Strategic control and decision ratification may be important tasks in this phase. The elaboration of structure stage is the phase during which firms mature. This phase is characterised by the elaboration of structures, adaptations, decentralisation and renewal. This is a stage with strong cash flows, but with fewer attractive investment opportunities. Behavioural as well as output control may be the main board tasks in this phase.

Board task expectations are likely to vary across the different stages, and board composition should reflect the board tasks that are important in the various life cycle phases. However, there may be a lagged relationship between board task expectations and board composition. Matthew Lynall, Brian Golden and Amy Hillman propose that board composition may reflect the relative power of internal and external actors at the time the board members are selected.[25] They propose that (a) boards established in the entrepreneurial stage reflect the social network of either the CEO or the external financier depending on who has the dominant power; (b) boards established in the collectivist stage reflect the resource needs of the firm if the CEO has the dominant power, but reflect the requirement of the institutional environment if the external financier has the dominant power; and (c) boards established in the formalisation and control stage reflect the resource needs of the firm if the CEO has the dominant power, but reflect an agency perspective if external financiers have the dominant power.

Thresholds and IPOs

The corporate governance system may help the firm overcome strategic thresholds. Firms may experience various thresholds – for example, from the founder-managed firm to the professional-managed firm, the initial public offering, public to private, etc. Boards should be understood not only from the perspective of the various life cycle phases but also from the perspective of the specific needs when crossing the thresholds between the phases.

Successful founder-managed firms are evolving towards thresholds at which the capabilities that brought them success in the past are insufficient to carry them forward. The inclusion of outside directors may help the founder-managed firm overcome such thresholds and become a professional-managed firm.[26] The founder-managed firm may also need to secure access to external financial resources. This may result in an opening up of the board for external investors, such as venture capital firms and business angels. When this happens the firm is no longer a closely knit group of founder-managers and family investors. Another threshold is crossed when the firm needs access to the stock market.

The main arguments for boards in threshold firms are to do with knowledge and competence,[27] signalling[28] and governance.[29]

Ownership

Ownership is presented here as a part of the context, but ownership is also a governance design parameter as well as an important input to stakeholder power. Ownership may impact boards and governance in a variety of ways. Important characteristics of ownership are ownership structure, ownership types, the location of owners and the time perspective of owners. Ownership types and structures vary between countries, and we have also seen that they are changing rapidly. Foreign ownership is also increasing.

In this book I usually use the term 'ownership' to refer the ownership of shares, but ownership can also be considered in a much wider context than just shareholding. For example, earlier in this book ownership has also been referred to in relation to the ownership of human resources,[30] and I have also made a distinction between owning the shares of a firm and owning a firm. The ownership of intellectual property rights is among topics that have been receiving increased attention in recent years. Socio-symbolic ownership is also being addressed.[31] Socio-symbolic ownership is about how ownership is created and acted out in practice. It has in particular been used in relation to family firms. Included in the socio-symbolic understanding of ownership is ownership at the personal, psychological level.

Ownership structure

Variation in ownership has traditionally been studied in relation to ownership dispersion. Other aspects of ownership structure are the role of pyramids and group ownership, cross-shareholding and common equity.

It is important, however, to understand the different kinds of ownership.[32] Both the type and dispersion of ownership vary greatly between countries and between different industries. In earlier chapters I have presented the corporate governance debate in relation to various types of ownership, including institutional ownership.[33] Institutional owners are often reluctant to have direct representation on boards due to simultaneous involvement in multiple companies that may have competing interests. Individual, corporate, state and family owners will more often have direct representation on boards.[34] The role of the board may, however, vary with each of these different types of owners. For example, in corporate ownership (where we find cross-ownership, parent–subsidiary relations, strategic ownership, and friendly and hostile ownership situations), in some situations inter-organisational communication through interlocking directorates may be a main task of boards. In family firms a family council often exists, and the existence of family councils may affect the role of the other governance bodies. Executive ownership will influence boards and governance, but it is often considered to be a means to an end that is motivated by agency theory rather than a contextual variable.

Institutional owners

Institutional owners can be divided into various sub-groups, each with distinct characteristics and degrees of involvement in corporate governance.[35] One division is between pressure-sensitive institutions, pressure-resistant institutions and pressure-indeterminate institutions. The time perspectives of the ownership of these investors usually vary, and the type of ownership influences both the direction and kind of involvement in the boards.

Pressure-resistant investors have a long-term perspective of their ownership, whereas the perspectives of pressure-indeterminate investors are often short-term. Pressure-indeterminate institutional investors are often brokerage houses and investment counsellors. Pressure-sensitive institutional investors are investors who have business relationships with the firm. Their success and profitability will often depend on a good and strong relationship with the firm in which they invest. Therefore, in the event of conflict they will avoid challenging the management, preferring to sell their stock instead. Banks and insurance companies are often pressure-sensitive institutional investors. Board tasks in firms dominated by pressure-sensitive institutional investors will be service-oriented rather than control-oriented. Pressure-resistant institutional investors do not have any close business relationships with the firm, and thus they are also expected to remain independent of management. Such investors usually include public pension funds, mutual funds and foundations. These owners will, to a large extent, ask discerning questions and may vote differently from managers on strategic issues.

Venture capitalists

Venture capitalists contribute to the financing of young, unlisted dynamic ventures through equity or equity-like investments. The venture capital market is often divided into business angels and venture capital firms. Business angels are often wealthy individuals, while venture capital firms are professional investors who are often organised into firms or partnerships. Business angels and venture capital firms often have different approaches to market risks.[36] Business angels tend to rely upon the entrepreneur to protect them from losses. Consequently, they are more concerned with agency risks than market risks. Venture capital firms are more concerned with market risks, and they have learnt to protect themselves from agency risks through contractual arrangements. Venture capital firms often develop sophisticated tools to handle market risks.

There is both a hard side and a soft side to the contributions of VCs. The hard side is the capital they are providing to the firm. The soft side is the competence and mentoring they provide. A prioritised list of contributions from venture capitalists includes: helping with the acquisition of capital; serving as sounding boards; providing financial competence; giving a sense of economic safety; having involvement in the boards of directors; being a networking support; contributing to strategy development; contributing to the professionalism of the business; negotiating or litigating competence; being mentors; and helping with market competence, recruitment and technical/production competence.

Venture capitalists often demand seats on the boards where they provide capital, and the entry of a VC is often a key catalyst for the establishment of active boards.[37] Comparing boards in venture-capital-backed firms with boards in other small firms; they have a higher number of members, they have a higher number of outside board members, they have more frequent board meetings, and CEO duality is less common.

Venture capitalists are demanding investors. They retain the right to remove the entrepreneur from his or her position as CEO if he or she fails to meet agreed targets.

Types of business angels

VCs are not a coherent group. In addition to the differences between business angels and venture capitalist firms, within these two groups there are also major differences, which may be of crucial importance for entrepreneurs to know when approaching a venture capitalist. This is illustrated in table 5.4.

Table 5.4 illustrates four types of business angels. The *hobbyist* enjoys seeing business development and taking part in strategic decision-making. He or she uses capital as a tool to become a board member, and in that way to pursue his/her hobby. The hobbyist will

Table 5.4 *Different types of business angels*

Hobby angel	*Takeover angel*
Capital is used as a ticket to perform a hobby – mentoring and strategic management	Capital is used strategically to take over a firm – strategic decision-making and behavioural control
Consultant angel	*Capital provider angel*
Capital is used as a ticket to perform consulting services – advisory tasks	The only objective is to get return on investments – output control

Source: Politis and Gabrielsson 2005.

often be a mentor and be involved in strategic decision-making. The *consultant* gets involved in the board and the company through his or her own capital, but the main objective or business idea is to act as a consultant. The advisory tasks may be the most important. Boards may be gateways to consultancy; consultancy fees are invoiced. The only objective of the *capital provider* is to get return on his or her invested capital, and the main board task is output control. However, the capital provider will also be involved in other board tasks, including various service tasks, as this may impact the return on the investment. The *takeover*-oriented business angel wants to get voting control. Capital is used strategically to take over the firm, and the entrepreneur may be replaced if he or she does not serve the business angel.

Family firms

Family businesses are important because the majority of independent businesses are family-owned.[38] The objectives in family businesses are likely to differ from those in non-family businesses, and they are managed differently from non-family businesses. Developing governance systems in family businesses may have a significant impact on society.[39] Family businesses range from small shops to large empires, and core aspects of family business definitions include ownership, management, generation transfer, intentions to continue as a family business, family goals and interactions between the family and the business.[40] The most commonly used definition of a family business is one based on control with ownership rights. This definition includes major variations in family and business constellations. Sometimes a family has several businesses, and sometimes a business may have several family owners. Furthermore, there may be large families in small businesses, and small families in large businesses. There are also examples where the owners of a business are within a family, but the most influential individuals in the family are not direct owners of the business. Regardless of which family business definition is used, most businesses in most countries may be defined as family businesses.[41]

The family has traditionally been the model of governance for private businesses. For centuries families managed private estates, and in private businesses actual power is often in the hands of the family man acting as a sort of paterfamilias. Within the business he can act as he pleases as an owner, but also as a good father, respecting laws and business rules. Such figures are economically responsible for the business, and morally they are also responsible for their families, their employees and their environment. The ownership assumptions found in paternalistic logic are patently different from those derived from agency theory.[42] In paternalism, the owner has a face, and a heart as well; it is noteworthy that, even in the present day, most businesses have owners with faces and hearts.

A main concern in family businesses is balancing the interests of the family and the business. It is often found that business decisions are taken in the realm of the family and family values, rather than in the realm of the business. In studies about governance in SMEs we hear anecdotes about how important family is when making decisions in the business. It is reported that board meetings take place almost every day, but around the kitchen table. Other studies report how family concerns for the business are shared and discussed in family gatherings such as a Christmas party. Both the in-kitchen discussions and the Christmas parties can be important governance mechanisms in many small family businesses.

Some family businesses have family councils as a governance mechanism. Family councils are generally studied and discussed as a family governance mechanism in large families and very large family businesses.[43] Sometimes they may be formal, voluntarily included and described in family constitutions. But family councils may also be informal governance mechanisms, operating in the intersection of family concerns, ownership concerns, governance concerns and managerial concerns. However, very little, if any, attention is given to family councils or even family meetings in research into small businesses.

Altruism and stewardship theory, as well as paternalism, have been used to supplement or substitute agency theory in recent studies of family firms.

Subsidiaries and corporate ownership

A large number of firms are subsidiaries of other companies. The role of boards in subsidiaries varies. Some subsidiaries are just paper firms that are incorporated for practical reasons, such as tax avoidance purposes. The boards in these subsidiaries will quite often only be formal entities with no purpose other than to meet legal requirements. Other subsidiaries have their own identity that is related to, for example, customers, markets, employees and local societies. Various stakeholder issues may empower the boards in such subsidiaries.

The location of owners is a core concept when understanding subsidiary boards. Ingemar Bjørkman carried out a study of Norwegian and French subsidiaries of Swedish and Finnish parent companies, and he concluded that various board tasks depend on sociocultural factors in and the market size of the subsidiary's country, on internal control, on internal coordination and on external roles.[44] The boards in these subsidiaries were empowered by both internal and external actors, and arguments related to resource dependence tasks, advisory tasks and various kinds of control were found.

A distinction between local and central stakeholders should be made when trying to understand boards in subsidiaries.[45] Central stakeholders are those mostly related to the parent company. Local stakeholders are those mostly related to the subsidiary company. From the perspective of the subsidiary, the CEO and the board of the parent company may be considered as external actors, while customers, local employees and local societies may be considered as internal actors.

Boards of subsidiaries may be particularly important when a subsidiary is not fully owned, and the boardroom may then be an arena for competing ownership interest. This may also be the situation in joint ventures.

Other ownership types

There is a wide spectrum of ownership types, and the differences between the various ownership types may influence board tasks, the board working style and the background of the board members. Some

Table 5.5 *Ownership types arranged according to nature of ownership and nature of board involvement*

	No direct board involvement	*Direct board involvement*
Long-term ownership	**Institutional owners** – double independence – CEOs of other firms	**Industrialists** – management – owners – family
Short-term ownership	**Portfolio managers** – lawyers etc.	**Restructurers** – owners

firms have homogeneous ownership, while other firms have a mix of ownership types. Some ownership types typically have long-term involvement while other ownership types are more short-term. In some ownership types the owners are typically directly involved in the firm and in the board, while other ownership types will remain at arm's length from the operation and governance of the firm. This is illustrated in table 5.5.

Industrialists, restructurers, institutional owners and portfolio managers are examples of different ownership types. Their board involvement varies, and so too does the timescale of their ownership. It is indicated in table 5.5 that the different ownership types prefer board members to have either direct or indirect board involvement.

Among ownership types that may impact the board composition, board tasks and board working style we find mutual arrangements, partnerships, employee share ownership programmes (ESOPs), cooperatives and publicly owned corporations. Boards in universities, churches and religious organisations, not-for-profit organisations, political parties, etc. may also all be influenced in different ways by their ownership types.

The case of small firms: tasks and identities of 'outside' directors

In this in-depth summarising case the tasks and identities of outside directors in certain types of small and medium-sized enterprises are compared. We also compare the role of boards in family businesses, venture-capital-backed businesses and other SMEs.[46]

Family firms

Many SMEs are family businesses. There are, however, many definitions of family businesses; the broadest defines a family business as a firm in which a family has the voting control of the company.[47] This definition includes close to 95 per cent of all registered companies in Europe.[48] Here we use a common definition of a family business in order to highlight the special features of such firms; a firm that the CEO considers to be a family business. Boards in family businesses have been found to have relatively few directors, often consisting of one or two family members in addition to the owner-manager.[49] The board is also expected to have relatively little influence over the direction and performance of the enterprise, as the owner-manager may exercise power over the board through his or her central role in outside director selection and director remuneration, and by shaping the information provided to directors.[50]

Moreover, family businesses are often considered to have governance mechanisms other than the boards of directors. Examples of formal governance mechanisms include family councils and family meetings. The social interaction between family members may be considered another governance mechanism. The literature on family businesses, however, points out that, in family businesses where the second (or even a later) generation has assumed ownership control of the company, such family businesses often differ significantly in their governance structures compared with first-generation family businesses.[51] The complex ownership situation in many family businesses may consequently create demands from distant (non-involved) family members for organised systems that will exercise control and influence among the various branches of a family. Such an organised system could be a board of directors.[52]

Venture-capital-backed SMEs

Venture-capital-backed SMEs are firms in which professional investors have invested alongside management. For this reason they are often found in emerging industries where the entrepreneurial ventures have the potential to develop into significant economic contributors.[53] While family businesses by definition may be old and relatively mature firms in which everyday life is as important as maintaining traditions and building a future for the generations to come, venture-capital-backed firms will often be young and fast-growing companies in which the need for alertness and synchronicity in turn calls for short-term planning and frequent monitoring.[54]

Studies of boards in venture-capital-backed SMEs have indicated that venture capitalists are often a key stakeholder group exerting pressure to change and develop boards in SMEs. For example, studies of venture-capital-backed firms report that the boards are dominated by 'outside' board members, with VC-appointed directors being in control rather than the management.[55] The presence of VCs on the board of directors may, for example, help the firm's executives to focus their efforts on closely monitoring firm performance and in developing systems to reward innovation and creativity.[56] Moreover, VC-appointed directors may provide managerial competence and valuable resources through their experience and personal network (built up during their careers), all of which can be of great help for young entrepreneurial firms.[57] The adoption of 'outside' directors on the board is hence not only due to 'the power of the purse' – whereby the VC partnership wants to monitor the performance of both the CEO and the firm – but is also a way for these small entrepreneurial ventures to get access to the expertise and networking resources that the VCs possess.[58]

Subsidiaries, joint ventures, partnerships, etc.

Ownership structures other than the typical family firm or venture-capital-backed firm also feature in SMEs. Subsidiaries are one common example. The management in the parent company often constitutes the board in subsidiaries, and the parent company management is sometimes supplemented by employee directors, and even some outside directors. Joint ventures, partnerships and employee-owned firms are other ownership configurations in SMEs. Firms with such ownership structures may have particularly active boards, but the board members are most often the partners, and both of these examples (active boards and partners) have distinctive governance mechanisms and practices.[59]

'Outside' directors in SMEs

The discussion above indicates that a relevant question is: to what extent can our current understanding and conceptualisations of

Table 5.6 *Tasks and identities of 'outside' directors in SMEs*

	Agency theory – control	Resource-based view – advice and counsel	Resource dependence theory – managing resource dependencies
Family businesses			
Outsiders' contribution	Reducing information asymmetry among branches of the family, or for external stakeholders.	Bringing resources and competencies into the firm. Reducing the risk of 'inbreeding' and bringing a detached view to the family business.	Helping with contacts and networks during expansion (e.g. during internationalisation). Legitimisation during CEO successions.
Who is an 'outsider'?	Experienced non-family person in whom the family and external powerful stakeholder trust (often the family lawyer).	Experienced non-family person in whom the CEO/dominating family members trust (family friend, family lawyer, accountant or consultant).	Experienced non-family person in whom the CEO/dominating family members and other powerful stakeholders trust.
Venture-capital-backed firm			
Outsiders' contribution	Monitoring managerial and firm performance to maximise economic returns for equity holders (VCs and/or entrepreneurs).	Complementing entrepreneurs' lack of competence in key functional areas, such as finance, marketing, etc.	Using their network to recruit key personnel and to attract additional funding.
Who is an 'outsider'?	VC, VC-appointed director or other director in whom the VC trusts.	VC, VC-appointed director or other director in whom the VC trusts.	VC, VC-appointed director or other director in whom the VC trusts.
Other SMEs			
Outsiders' contribution	Reducing information asymmetry and protecting shareholders against managerial indiscretion.	Strengthening the resources and capabilities of the firm.	Offering legitimacy in the business community and influencing important stakeholder groups.
Who is an 'outsider'?	A non-executive shareholder, or businessperson not employed by the firm, in whom shareholders trust.	Experienced businessperson in whom the CEO trusts, often an executive in another firm.	High-profile person in whom external stakeholders trust.

'outside' directors be applied to SMEs without having to adjust the situation to compensate for differences in context? This question is based on the assumption that expectations with regard to boards may vary depending on the dynamics of board–stakeholder interactions and the relative power of various groups of internal and external stakeholders. Such dynamics and power balances may vary depending on the context in which the firm operates. In this respect, SMEs are often characterised either by ownership and control that is exercised by one or a few individuals, or by close relationships between owners and managers. The context of SMEs may consequently vary from the context of large Fortune 500 firms, and various ownership configurations may also raise questions about board compositional definitions similar to the insider versus outsider distinction.

Table 5.6 presents the tasks and identities of 'outside' directors in family firms, venture-capital-backed firms and other SMEs. The presentation is based on 100 empirical reports.

The 'outside' directors in *family businesses* make various contributions, depending on the theoretical approach considered. From an agency theory perspective the contribution of the 'outside' directors is mainly to reduce information asymmetry between various branches of the family, or between the family and important external stakeholders. From a resource-based perspective the tasks of 'outside' directors are those of bringing resources and competencies into the firm and bringing a detached view to the family business – a view that involves key stakeholder interests and public responsibilities. Also, particularly in more mature family businesses, the ability to avoid the risk of 'inbreeding' may be highly valued. The task of 'outside' directors from a resource dependence perspective is that of linking the firm to its external environment by networking activities. This is particularly the case in periods of expansion. Moreover, during CEO successions the 'outside' director may help the family business signal legitimacy and stability to external stakeholders.

Executives and CEOs in family businesses do not seem to avoid 'outside' directors, but they do not necessarily always welcome them either. Suspicion and family politics are common ingredients in the selection of board members, and the choice is not always in favour of the 'outsider'. Noteworthy mature family businesses (firms in the second or third generation) are more likely to employ 'outside' directors – either to monitor firm performance for various branches of the family or the firm's main stakeholders (i.e. banks) or as a sounding board for ageing CEOs.

Who are these 'outside' directors in family businesses? From the agency theory perspective the 'outside' director is a person in whom the family and powerful external stakeholders trust, often the family lawyer. From a resource-based perspective the 'outside' director is an experienced person in whom the CEO and the dominating family members trust. This may be a long-time family friend, the family lawyer or another individual the family has known for a long time. From resource dependence theory 'outside' directors are supposed to be boundary traversers, and in family firms they are experienced persons whom the CEOs, family members and other powerful stakeholders trust. All theoretical perspectives consequently highlight experience and trust as two main features for understanding the role and contribution of 'outside directors' in the family business context.

The contribution and definition of 'outside' directors in *venture-capital-backed firms* differ somewhat from those in family businesses. In an agency theory approach the contributions of the 'outside' directors in reducing managerial opportunism, and monitoring managerial and firm performance to maximise economic returns, are emphasised. When using the resource-based perspective, it is highlighted that 'outside' directors complement the lack of in-house competence in various functional areas. For example, the 'outside' directors often complement the management's lack of competence in finance, general management, marketing, etc. From a resource dependence perspective the 'outside' directors develop the contributions of the boards by using their networks. In this respect the 'outside' directors are mainly active in using their networks to find and recruit key personnel, and in receiving additional funding during the firm's various stages of development. From the CEO's point of view, the board was hence a much-valued resource despite the strong monitoring focus.

The 'outside' directors in the venture-capital-backed firms are the VCs, or an individual appointed by the VCs. It may happen that the entrepreneur appoints other 'outside' directors to counterbalance the influence of the VCs, but then it is a person who also is trusted by the VCs. A primary difference between venture-capital-backed firms and family businesses is that, while family businesses recruit directors in whom family members trust, venture-capital-backed firms recruit directors in whom the venture capitalists trust.

It is difficult to summarise the contribution of 'outside' directors in all the other SMEs, but here are some observations of differences from the above two categories (family firms and venture-capital-backed firms). From an agency theory perspective, in this residual group of firms 'outside' directors may primarily be recruited to check against managerial indiscretion and reduce the information gap between external owners and the management team. These are sometimes part-owners. This is the case both when there is a single owner, such as a parent company, and when the ownership is dispersed between several owners outside the firm. Using the resource-based perspective, the 'outside' directors' tasks in strengthening the resources and capabilities of the firm by contributing their expertise and experience are highlighted. Using resource dependence theory, 'outside' directors are described as helpful in offering legitimacy in the business community, influencing stakeholder groups and seeking to achieve competitive advantage through networking activities. Both the resource-based and the resource dependence perspectives indicate that 'outside' directors can be regarded as valuable resources that can be exploited at a low cost. This is because they bring in much expertise and give access to valued resources by making their business and personal networks available to the small firm.

The definitions of an 'outside' director in this group of SMEs also vary depending on the theoretical perspective adopted. Using agency theory, external owners will most often, through 'outside' directors, seek to influence company decisions. Using a resource-based perspective, an 'outside' director is defined as an experienced businessperson in whom the CEO trusts. These are often acquaintances who are CEOs in other firms. The resource dependence perspective describes an 'outside' director as a high-profile person in whom external stakeholders trust, chosen on the basis of his or her reputation.

These elaborations lead us to question previous universalistic approaches and general theorising when trying to understand the role and contribution of 'outside' directors across various types of SMEs. Contextual approaches are needed. From an agency theory perspective the most important qualification for 'outside' directors is their ability to be independent. However, should independence be defined in relation to the firm, the management or the owner family? In family businesses 'outside' directors are often defined as non-family directors. I have seen that 'outside' directors in family businesses tend to have strong ties to the CEO and/or the dominating family members. Their independence can therefore be questioned. It can even be the case that non-executive members of the family may be more independent than an 'outside' director who is recruited through the professional and private network of the CEO. In venture-capital-backed firms 'outside' directors are often defined as VC directors or VC-appointed directors – that is, directors who are independent of the entrepreneur, notwithstanding the fact that VCs also can deliberately withhold information, not perform as agreed and display short-term and self-interest-seeking behaviour at the expense of other stakeholders. In the remaining categories of firms 'outside' directors are often non-management shareholders. These observations clearly indicate that research on directorial independence in SMEs must include explicit discussions on what it is that directors are supposed to be independent of.

Moreover, the resource-based view stresses that 'outside' director qualifications other than independence are necessary. In this view 'outside' directors are supposed to have a good knowledge of the market and the industry in which the firm operates, so that their experience can improve firm performance. Resource dependence theory, on the other hand, stresses that 'outside' directors should have a well-developed personal and business network that can mediate trust and the establishment of links between internal and external stakeholders – in order to reduce internal resource dependencies. The various theoretically derived expectations of the role and contribution of the 'outside' director make it hard to find a person possessing all the necessary traits to act as an 'outside' director. Combinations of 'outside' directors' independence and expertise should be sought depending on the theory and context required.

Taken together, the results from the analysis indicate that 'outside' directors can be critical for effective boardroom governance in SMEs, but also that the traditional definition of an 'outside' director as a non-management director is an overly simplistic one. Our understanding of the role and contribution of 'outside' directors in SMEs seems, instead, to vary depending on the theoretical framework used, and the type of firm being studied. Hence, an open and context-based definition may be required to understand the various roles and contributions of 'outsider' directors in various SME settings. The concept of an 'outside' director is not generic and should not be used interchangeably between the different settings without considering thoroughly what the consequences will be.

Summary

Some of the contextual variables that are most commonly used in studies of boards and governance have been presented in this chapter, and among the most important are: resources; CEO tenure, ownership and top management team competence; national, geographical and cultural differences; variations in stakeholder set-ups and variations in legislation, including one-tier versus two-tier systems; differences in industries and competitive environments; firm size, including the comparison between large Fortune 500 corporations and small and medium-sized firms; firm life cycle phases, including start-ups, growth firms, mature firms, firms in crisis and firms at different thresholds – as, for example, IPOs; and ownership structures, including ownership dispersion and types, different kinds of family firms, institutional investors, venture capitalists, business angels and corporate ownership (including subsidiaries).

Not only do the contextual variables have a direct impact on the choice of board members, they clearly also influence the importance and relative power of various actors. The contextual variables have different characteristics. Attributes of the CEO, for example, may be considered as a contextual variable, but the CEO is also an important actor, resource and governance mechanism, and attributes of the CEO are influenced by board and corporate decisions and performance. Furthermore, the CEO may also moderate the various relationships in the model. In addition, other contextual variables, such as ownership, have similar attributes.

A contingency perspective of boards and governance implies that there has to be a fit between the context and governance designs. Recommendations in one contextual setting should not be applied in other settings without being given due consideration.

6 | Interactions: trust, power and strategising

The main concepts in this chapter are:
- a behavioural theory of boards and governance;
- actors and arenas;
- trust;
- emotions;
- power; and
- strategising.

An underlying theme in this book is that corporate governance is determined in the interactions between various actors. The interactions take place between human actors, and the interactions are thus at the heart of understanding the human side of corporate governance. These interactions play a seminal role in the understanding of boards of directors. The actor-based perspective is followed in this chapter; the objective is to present various aspects of these interactions between the internal actors, external actors and board members.

In the previous chapters I have described the various actors – their characteristics and goals. Interactions between them take place both inside and outside the boardroom. This chapter draws on various theories and bodies of literature to explain these interactions. Here, in what is the central chapter of the book, I aim to introduce the steps leading towards a behavioural theory of boards and governance. I also show how social and psychological processes taking place between the various actors may neutralise the effects described in prevailing theories about board task performance.

Research results concerning the various actors and how they interact are found in two main bodies of literature. These are, on the one hand, the work on social networks and social movement (which also includes the work on interlocking directorates), and, on the other hand, the work on TMTs (which explores the relations and interactions between

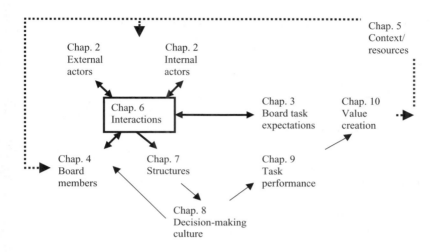

board members and important internal actors). The research stream on micro-strategising integrates some of these perspectives.

Studies of board interactions include responses to pressures – for example, through stock repurchasing plans,[1] the symbolic management of stockholders[2] and the circumvention of stakeholders' control.[3] Institutional theory has been used to explain responses to institutional pressure,[4] and political and psychological perspectives – including social network theory – have been used to explain independence and the selection processes of directors.[5]

Another body of interaction literature concerns the political dynamics surrounding the formation of alliances and partnerships,[6] including how firm behaviour responds to the interests and beliefs of the dominant coalition of stakeholders.[7] Recent works on micro-strategising have contributed to understanding these interactions outside as well as inside the boardroom.[8]

The layout of this chapter is as follows. In the first section I sketch a preliminary outline of a behavioural theory of boards and governance. The next section presents the interactions, including actors and arenas, trust and emotions. Then in the third section power and strategising are introduced.

The summarising in-depth case presented in this chapter is concerned with stakeholder management and the avoidance of corporate control.[9]

Towards a behavioural theory of boards and governance

In this section we present some elements that may be considered as building blocks in a behavioural theory of boards and governance.[10] A behavioural theory will

- focus on *strategising* more than on *objective alignments*;
- result in decisions taking place through *satisficing and problematic search* rather than through *rational decision-making*;
- allow boards to create value through the *deployment of knowledge* rather than through the *control of managerial behaviour*; and
- focus on *norms and learning processes* rather than on *outcome and structures*.

The main elements are presented first.

The behavioural theory of the firm perspective

Since the pioneering studies of Herbert Simon,[11] James March and Herbert Simon[12] and Richard Cyert and James March[13] the behavioural theory of the firm has been developed into a key perspective for understanding decision-making in organisations. The work of Simon and others can be considered as an attempt to link the abstract principles of the rational decision-making model in the economic discipline to concrete decision-making processes in real business settings. Nonetheless, little of this rich body of knowledge has spilled over into mainstream studies of boards and governance, where the rationality of agents is often still assumed. However, in line with calls for the need for a better capturing of processes and behavioural dynamics in and around the boardroom, studies have increasingly emphasised the need to apply theoretical concepts that can be related back to a behavioural framework. Four of the core concepts in the behavioural theory of the firm are examined below: bounded rationality,[14] satisficing behaviour,[15] organisational routines[16] and bargaining between coalitions of actors.[17] It is on these concepts that we start outlining a behavioural theory of boards and governance.

Bounded rationality

Recent research on boards and governance has addressed the issue of bounded rationality, which is a concept that refers to the actual complexity of decision-making in organisations.[18] This is not to say that agents do not strive to maximise utility, only that, in the real world, agents are not able to do so because of bounds on their intended rationality.[19] The business environment is complex and dynamic, and results in individuals being unable to understand all the linkages among the many variables around them. In this respect, the concept emphasises the fact that organisational actors do not fully comprehend the world they are living in.[20] This has two consequences in particular. In the first place, decisions cannot be regarded as optimal solutions to problems; all they can do is reflect solutions to satisfy particular aspiration levels.[21] These aspiration levels are determined by both history and the social environment. The historical aspiration level is set as a function of the organisation's past performance, whereas the social aspiration level is set by reference to meaningful reference groups. In the second place, and contrary to mainstream economic theorising, with its emphasis on individuals acting rationally in intent in the face of incomplete and asymmetric information,[22] a behavioural approach focuses more on subjective factors, such as cognitive biases and incompetence, as explanations for inefficient and ineffective decision-making.[23] The cognitive bias of organisational actors allows only imperfect mapping of the decision-making environment and rather limited, imprecise and selective information processing. Seen from this perspective, it may well be that the limited competence and incomplete knowledge among organisational members represent much more likely causes of organisational failures and inefficiencies than straightforward opportunism, which more or less assumes that individuals have full understanding of the opportunities available to them. This notion of bounded rationality has in the literature been called 'truly bounded rationality'.[24]

Satisficing and problemistic search

Another issue that has been addressed in recent research on boards and governance is 'satisficing'.[25] This concept refers to the fact that actors tend to accept choices or judgements that are 'good enough' based on their most important current needs, rather than searching for optimal solutions. The assumption of satisficing behaviour rests on the observation that decision-makers are concerned mainly with immediate problems and short-term solutions – something that has generally been called 'problemistic search'.[26] Problems are recognised, however, only to the extent that organisations fail to satisfy one or more of their self-imposed goals, or when such failure can be expected in the near future. Problem recognition itself is primarily driven by attention allocation and selection biases. When faced with a problem, decision-makers can be expected to search for solutions using simple heuristics or rules. The problem is regarded as solved as soon as an alternative is found that satisfies current goals, or if the goals are revised to a level that makes available solutions acceptable. When compared to optimising behaviour, it can be observed that satisficing behaviour potentially reduces the gains from behaving opportunistically. Decision-making in the behavioural theory is consequently seen as an experiential learning process, whereby firms adapt incrementally to their changing environment through learning and experimentation. Decision-makers learn by trial and error what can be done, and they adapt their goals, attention rules and search rules accordingly.

Routines and learning

A third concept that has come to prominence as a result of recent research is that boards of directors operate from the basis of 'routines' that are built up over time.[27] Routines can here be understood as the codified memory of the organisation, embodying the past experience, knowledge, beliefs, values and capabilities of the organisation and its decision-makers.[28] Routines consist mostly of experiential knowledge (learning by doing), which to a great extent is tacit and hard to codify. They are a source of control and stability, which both enable and constrain organisational action. On the one hand, they conserve the cognitive abilities of board members and channel and limit conflict among them. On the other hand, they direct attention to selected aspects of identified problem situations. In consequence, rules and routines are not purely passive elements in board behaviour but also serve as socially and historically constructed programmes of action that direct attention to specific aspects of a problematic situation. Boards are not victims of history, however, as routines can be changed by learning processes, such as imitation, or trial and error. Learning thus plays a central role in a behavioural framework.

Political bargaining and quasi-resolution of conflicts

The fourth concept is the issue of 'political bargaining' among coalitions of actors. Seen from this perspective, organisations can be depicted as complex political systems with agents organised in coalitions, some of them organised into sub-coalitions.[29] Coalition partners may have distinct preferences and objectives, which make negotiation and bargaining among coalition members common practice. Shifts in coalitions of organisational actors affect organisational decisions, goal-setting and problem-solving processes. Goal conflicts are solved through political bargaining rather than through objective alignment by economic incentives. Disagreement about organisational goals is dealt with in the context of ongoing bargaining processes among coalitions pursuing alternative objectives and priorities. Different coalitions may pursue conflicting goals, and organisations may encompass a variety of potentially conflicting and inconsistent goals by pursuing them sequentially. Goal formation is achieved by a series of procedures, including the application of local rationality and acceptable-level decision rules, as well as by devoting sequential attention to goals. The procedures for resolving conflicts do not necessarily lead to a consistent set of goals in the organisation. This means that organisations most of the time can be expected to have a considerable amount of latent conflicts and goals. Goal formation is hence seen as the outcome rather than the beginning of the bargain between coalitions. As such, goal formation and goal conflict may drive the search for additional information and new knowledge. In fact, from such a learning perspective, goal congruence and consensus may even be a hindrance rather than a stimulus to organisational development.

Elements in a behavioural theory of boards and governance

Building on the concepts outlined above, organisations can be depicted as coalitions of actors, within which organisational objectives and decisions are the outcomes of political bargaining between the actors. Organisational problems are dealt with by applying norms, problem-solving heuristics and memorised routines so as to reduce the complexity of decision-making by boundedly rational decision-makers. In order to analyse boards and governance in this setting, we may distinguish between the roles of the board in organisational decision-making and decision-making processes within the board. The behavioural perspective on boards and governance would, therefore, place emphasis on issues such as the analysis of strategising inside and outside the boardroom, problemistic search by board members, value creation through knowledge, and a focus on interactions and decision-making.

Value creation through knowledge

The existence of alternative goals in the behavioural approach provides inputs for additional information and knowledge. In fact, unlike agency theory predictions, the diversity of goals among internal and external actors can be considered beneficial, as it stimulates the discovery and active search for new knowledge as a by-product in the goal conflict resolution process. New knowledge enters the board decision-making process through the adjustment of aspiration levels and the formation of alternative dominant coalitions. Furthermore, diverse board members with different backgrounds and personalities will vary in the domains in which they have knowledge, the problems they have been exposed to and the problem-solving skills they have developed.[30] These conditions will, in turn, bring greater variety to the problems that the board identifies and the solutions it develops. Although empirical research on value creation boardroom culture is still scarce, a few recent studies have started to explore this issue – for example, how competence, creativity and cognitive conflicts among board members may influence board behaviour.[31] The value creation perspective, as here related to the goal and experience aspects, brings us to the value of process-oriented boardroom dynamics.[32]

Strategising inside and outside the boardroom

Consistent with the behavioural theory of the firm, a behavioural theory of boards and governance will consider organisations as multiple coalitions of actors. These actors may have conflicting interests and will achieve their goals through changing coalitions in the bargaining process within the corporation. In explaining decisions, a behavioural theory of boards and governance will focus on the political aspects of board behaviour,[33] and also on the allocation and use of power in the top echelons of the organisation and among alternative coalitions of actors.[34] A behavioural theory of boards and governance may in this connection analyse boards' involvement in political bargaining in order to achieve cooperation between coalitions of actors.[35] Following upon the analysis of power and trust relationships, the analysis can be extended to the more managerial aspects of political behaviour, such as how the symbolic rather than substantive aspects of stakeholder behaviour and expectations may be managed to benefit the interests of the dominant coalition within the organisation.[36]

The idea of distinguishing between the various coalitions of actors is not new in research on corporate governance.[37] A common way to identify the power and influence of coalitions is to make a distinction based on whether they operate within the strategic apex of the company – those who make decisions and take actions – or if they are placed outside this apex – those who seek to influence and control decisions and actions.[38] Shareholders are often considered to be the most important external actors, but, in management research, the list of external actors is deemed to be wider, including customers, suppliers, competitors, tax collectors and other state agents.[39] The CEO and the TMT are often considered the most important internal actors, but in many cases owners can also be considered internal actors. This is so especially in family firms and firms with concentrated ownership, which can be found in many medium-sized and small firms.[40] In the list of internal actors we may also find the families of the executives, and others with close psychological and financial ties to the CEO and the TMT.[41] Furthermore, it is argued that workers, most often regardless of their relationships with the management, should also be considered as internal actors.

In a behavioural theory of boards and governance the position of the board cannot be regarded as non-problematic. The formal role of the board is to consider 'the best interest of the firm' only.[42] Indeed, in a political context the question as to what the best interest of the firm is cannot be answered without reference to context and the particular dominant coalition of actors;[43] that is to say, the best interest of the firm is to be defined in the political bargaining between the actors. This, in turn, implies that the objectives of the firm, as seen from any particular coalition, cannot be regarded as the objective fundamentals for board decision-making. It also implies that the effectiveness of board decision-making cannot be analysed without taking the board decision-making context into account.

Problemistic search by the board: actors and arenas

In mediating between stakeholders, board members engage in a problemistic search for creating temporarily stable coalitions of actors that provide a solution to the problem at hand. Indeed, the bargaining process starts with defining corporate goals from the aspiration levels and expectations of stakeholders. A problemistic search by the board members will be triggered when organisational performance falls below stakeholder aspiration levels. Board members meet stake-holder expectations by using the information, expertise and other cognitive resources they possess to enhance consistency and coherence in the process of decision-making and control over firm resources.[44] The search for workable problem-solving heuristics will be aimed at finding solutions to the immediate problems of accountability. As such, the behavioural approach emphasises the political process involved in board decision-making[45] and the satisficing nature of board decision-making outcomes.[46] Satisficing is used as the guiding principle for decision-making, instead of trying to capture all opportunities to max-imize pay-offs – something that may reduce opportunism between organisational actors.[47] The alignment of outcome with sub-goals rather than with a profit objective may help in maintaining focus on tasks and duties in the organisation and in sustaining intrinsic moti-vation.[48] Thus, the analysis of how boards organise goal formation within the organisation (as well as the board's position and political role in the context of this process) may yield additional insights into the role of the board in organisational decision-making.

Norms and learning processes

A behavioural theory of boards and governance emphasises that board members rely on general rules and lessons based on past experience in making strategic decisions, rather than employing rational models of decision-making that require knowledge and information that they cannot have. The limits of bounded rationality prohibit the availability and understanding of a complete array of alternatives, which means that simple heuristics will be used to process the gathered information.[49] In particular, the decisions in the current period are informed and shaped by the environmental feedback that board members receive from their earlier decisions.[50] Learning among board members can hence be expected to be operationalised in the form of information-gathering and decision-making structures, procedures and rules.[51]

By applying simple decision-making heuristics, directors may enact decision-making scripts internalised from their participation on other boards in order to solve strategy and monitoring problems in their current organisation or board. This follows the idea that the partic-ular decision routines are encoded more deeply in the organisational memory, and are more likely to be recalled and enacted later in prob-lematic situations that are perceived as being similar. The reliance on rules in board decision-making facilitates action by presenting board members with readily available solutions to organisational problems. This reliance may also increase the board's ability to justify and defend its actions and decisions.[52] Board members cope with uncertainty and complexity reduction by routinely simplifying and structuring information through their perceptual filters and pre-existing knowledge structures.[53] Furthermore, the previous experiences of board members, their expectations and reference groups, and their routine procedures for information processing and learning are all highly relevant in coming to an understanding of board decision-making. In fact, the board of a specific corporation may have an organisational memory that is distinct and independent from the collective organisational memory of the individual directors as well as from a single director's individual memory. Through this perspective, board appointments and social network ties can moreover be seen as being embedded in the broader institutional environment – something that enables board members to learn about existing norms of appropriate beliefs and behaviour.[54] In this respect boards may be subject to processes of social construction in which the adoption of practices fulfils symbolic purposes rather than, or in addition to, efficiency requirements.[55] Director interlocks can consequently, from this perspective, be expected to encourage imitation not only through conscious choice but also by triggering the adoption of taken-for-granted board behaviour through less explicit socialisation processes.[56] The careful analysis of behavioural routines and mimetic processes in and around boards may thus provide insights into how boards and their members routinely use their past experiences in similar settings as scripts for solving problems in the current situation.[57] Similarly, the analysis of norms of board behaviour as another source of memorised socially constructed expectations may yield additional insights as far as the explanation of behaviour in and around boards is concerned.[58]

Building blocks in the subsequent presentation

So far we have presented four elements that may become building blocks in our attempts to construct a behavioural theory of boards and governance. These elements are also building blocks for the presentations in this book: problemistic search and interactions inside and outside the boardroom is presented in the coming section, followed by a section on strategising.

Norms and learning processes constitute a building block for understanding the evolution of rules and structures; they are presented in chapter 7. Value creation through knowledge is a topic that runs throughout this whole book; a value-creating boardroom culture is discussed in chapter 8

We have seen that behavioural theory is not just a theory about processes: a behavioural approach will also help us understand the importance of structures and norms.

Interactions inside and outside the boardroom

This section is about actors and arenas. I have already emphasised that boards do not work in a vacuum; in this book I use a definition of corporate governance in which the interactions between various actors, including board members, are at the heart.[59] Here I first identify the actors between whom the interactions take place. The interactions may, for example, take place between the various board members, between the board members and the TMT, or between the board members and actors who are outside the firm. However, there are many other interactions that may influence corporate governance – for example, interactions between members of the top management team, various kinds of interactions between external actors, and interactions between members of the TMT and various external actors.

Communication requires interaction between at least two actors, and it is the understanding of the communication more than the utterance or intention that determines the significance or the outcome of the communication.

In chapter 3 we have also seen that it is the interactions between the various actors that define board task expectations.[60] Internal actors are most likely to emphasise board tasks from internal perspectives, while external actors will emphasise board tasks from external perspectives. The contributions from social network theory and the TMT literature therefore help us to understand how board task expectations are influenced. Moreover, we expect that board task expectations help define not only what boards are supposed to do but also how it is to be done. Board task expectations provide directions for the selection of board members, and for board structures.

The interactions take place in various arenas and at various times. Not all arenas are equally accessible for all actors – even the board members. (Time and place are also discussed in this chapter.)

The actors have different kinds of power. The power relations are to a large extent influenced by the context, but also by the individual characteristics of the actors and their relational dynamics. Other important factors in understanding the interactions are, therefore, aspects related to trust, emotions and politics – including reactions to avoid external pressure, or techniques and strategies to exercise influence.

Actors and arenas

Corporate governance and corporate decision-making take place in the everyday strategic work of the various actors.[61] Decision-making takes place in various arenas. Some may be formal, but most arenas are informal, and there are both front-stage and back-stage arenas. Some arenas are open while others are closed. In addition, people may act in different ways in different arenas.

A formal arena is typically something that has been planned and scheduled, while an informal arena is about co-presence. The formal governance arenas will typically be board meetings and shareholders' meetings. There may also be many informal meetings where decision-making actors have a co-presence. Informal arenas are typically more relaxed and spontaneous, and in this way they may make a particular contribution in relation to creativity and openness in information sharing. 'Away days' can be considered as a hybrid arena:[62] these are the retreats or two-day meetings that some boards have in order for the members to get to know each other better and to discuss some issues in more detail.

Over the years I have frequently used the domestic lounge at Stockholm's Arlanda airport. On one occasion there was traffic chaos at the airport; the lounge quickly became packed, and I decided to sit down on a sofa at a table where a man in his early forties was sitting. He was from Finland. Fairly soon two more Finns entered the lounge, my sofa partner attracted their attention, and they sat down around our table. Not long after this my sofa partner summoned two Swedes, both in their sixties. It turned out that the five of them were all on their way to a board meeting in northern Sweden. The Finns were the owners, and the Swedes were two highly respected previous CEOs of large

Table 6.1 *Actors and arenas*

	Informal arenas	*Formal arenas*
Family context arenas	Home, ad hoc, family meetings, casual conversations, etc.	Family council, annual shareholders' meeting, formal family meetings, etc.
Firm context arenas	Ad hoc meetings, casual conversations, etc.	Board meetings, advisory board meetings, TMT meetings, other organized meetings, shareholder meetings, etc.

corporations. The conversation that took place around the table was, in reality, a board meeting. The discussion included many of the main issues that were on the agenda for the board meeting that afternoon. My perception was that they reached decisions on various sensitive issues without having the full board present. In other words, most of the decisions had been taken before the formal board meeting even started, and without the CEO and the local board members, including employee representatives, being present.

Much of the background discussion for board decisions takes place in locations other than formal board meetings. The formal board meeting thus often becomes no more than a 'rubber stamp' in relation to the decision-making.

In many firms the CEO and the board chair will have contacts between board meetings. It is not unusual for them to prepare the board meetings together, and for them to agree on what to propose to the board. Preparations such as this may be important and efficient with respect to the use of time, but they may also sideline the other board members. Their ability to attend to their various tasks may then be reduced.

Mattias Nordqvist studied actors and arenas in the context of governance in family businesses.[63] He distinguished, on the one hand, between the family context and the business context and, on the other hand, between formal and informal meetings. His framework is presented in table 6.1.

Within this framework the dynamics of actors and arenas in the strategic work of families was explored. The role of the 'Simmelian strangers' becomes apparent:[64] this term refers to an actor who is neither too close nor too far from the other actors with whom he or she interacts. Similar settings could be described outside family businesses – for example, the family versus business arenas could be exchanged with actors from political and business arenas in firms with governmental ownership. The stranger may have both a closeness and distance that provides possibilities and challenges. This is also one reason why strangers often get involved in strategic work quite quickly.

Unequal admittance to decision-making arenas

Not all actors – not even the board members – have equal access to the various decision-making arenas. The classic example is the woman who goes into the men's sauna and comments that she also wants to participate in the board decision-making. But there may also be many casual meeting places that establish the background for board decisions. However, it may not only be the physical arenas that are of importance. The choice of times at which board meetings are held may also be of importance in influencing which decisions are taken.

The following examples come from the 'board life story' project – a study of the role and contribution of women directors:[65]

Sometimes you must be on particular arenas to get to understand who makes decisions. In the leadership team of the company there were as many women as men. In a meeting we were discussing a difficult issue. Then we had a break, and all the girls went to the restroom to wash hands, and while we stood there doing so, we then decided what should happen.

In XX board you occasionally share a room with other women. You enter the bathroom with other women. Some common things like that build communion between women, making it easier to get in contact. You go to the swimming pool or to the sauna. It means a lot not to be alone as a woman on a board, in particular, during the breaks. During the actual meetings this doesn't matter so much. It is the time spent around the meetings that can be difficult. There are some arenas where you feel you are excluded.

These informal arenas, which are not planned to contribute to systematic decision-making and problem-solving, are genuinely important for the governance of organisations. One reason why informal arenas are important is that they include some people while others may be excluded. The boundaries are beyond the control of single individuals.

Table 6.2 *Frequency of interaction with chairperson involvement:*
examples

	Start-up	*Growth*	*Crisis*
Length of ordinary board meeting (hours)	7	3	4
Number of ordinary board meetings	7	10	16
'Away days' with overnight stay	0	1	1
Face-to-face chair/CEO meetings	9	16	22
Phone calls chair/CEO	24	22	53
Chairperson's meetings with bank	8	4	14
Chairperson's meetings with the press	5	1	2
Other informal firm-related meetings	21	75	53

In some ways, therefore, the informal arenas are typically controlled
by the firm's real power centres.[66]

Frequency of interactions
In chapter 5 I presented, from the 'one of the lads' study, the main
board tasks in three small firms to illustrate variations in different life
cycle phases. Above is a table displaying some of the interactions that
resulted from including the chairperson in the same firms[67] (the study
period was eighteen months).

Table 6.2 shows how the frequency of various kinds of interaction
may vary with contextual factors, in this case the life cycle phase of
the firm. The number as well as the length of board meetings may
vary. The number of meetings seemed to vary with the life cycle phase,
and the highest number of board meetings was in the case of crisis.
Unsurprisingly, boards are generally expected to act at times of crisis.[68] However, informal interactions between the board members will
probably be positively related to the length of the board meetings. If
board meetings are long then they will include meals, when it is also
possible to communicate and exchange information informally. This
is particularly the case when boards are arranging 'away days' with
overnight stays. CEO/chairperson interactions between meetings also
seem to be particularly frequent in situations of crisis. The table also
displays the other interaction partners of the chairperson.

Mark Macus in his doctoral dissertation studied the interactions
on boards in eight small or medium-sized US firms in the process of

making initial public offerings.[69] He explored various attributes of the interactions that stood out as registering distinctions between the firms, and he classified them as:

- interactions between the directors and top management;
- the frequency of board or committee meetings;
- the frequency of interactions between the directors besides boards or committee meetings;
- the frequency of face-to-face interactions between the directors (both at board or committee meetings as well as besides);
- the main interaction partner; and
- the fragmentation of the interaction network.

In some firms there are hardly any interactions between the directors and the top managers. Macus found that it was the extent of the interactions between the directors and the TMT that distinguished the fastest-growing firms in his sample from the other firms.[70] The highest incidence of interactions was in the fastest-growing firms. There was a rapid stream of interactions besides the regular board meetings. He concluded that, if top managers or directors can and do interact frequently and freely without restrictions or control by the CEO or chairman, information can flow more rapidly and unfiltered. The directors will then tend to have a better basis upon which to form their decisions and assess the company's situation. Top managers can also profit from the expertise and contact of the directors directly.

In some firms most of the interactions are face to face, while phone calls may be the most important means of interaction in other firms. A major difference between the firms was the variation in who the main interaction partner of the CEO was. In some of the firms the main interactions were with the directors representing the main owners. Legal aspects were then often emphasised. In other firms the main interactions were with the directors who had the most industry or entrepreneurial expertise or experience. It was also observed that the longer the directors had interacted the smoother the interaction became. The interactions were the smoothest when the board had remained unchanged over a long period; then many of the interactions became routine.

Actors and arenas: a garbage can model

There is interplay between different arenas in corporate governance and strategic decision-making. Different games may be played in different arenas, and the rules in each arena may vary. Actors may also play different roles in different arenas. However, discussions and experiences from one arena will be transferred across arenas. The overlap between the different arenas may be difficult for the actors to handle.[71]

The garbage can model takes the behavioural theory of the firm as its starting point.[72] Decisions are made based on streams of actors, arenas, questions and solutions. The actors have bounded rationality, and they make decisions based on satisficing and problemistic search. A solution to a question will be found in 'garbage cans', where actors and arenas are found together with questions and solutions. A garbage can model of boards and governance would imply that efforts should be made to sort streams so that related actors, arenas, questions and problems are kept together. Questions and solutions related to governance and strategic decision-making should be placed in the same garbage can as board members and the arenas where strategic and governance questions should be solved. One way of doing this is to make or require board routines or instructions stipulating the decision-making procedures for the board: which questions shall be put to the board during board meetings, and with what preparation? Corporate laws in Sweden and Norway have included clauses involving such routines or instructions to ensure that the employee-elected directors are at the arenas where the main questions are finding their solutions. These perspectives will be further elaborated in chapter 7.

Trust

Trust is a multifaceted concept and many distinctions could be made. This is illustrated in the following stories.[73]

'Driving to the board meeting we discussed our roles during the meeting. I had confidence in John's judgement. When working with John I find that checking is not necessary. John knows what it is all about.' The citation is from my field notes in the 'one of the lads' study where I was board chairperson in three small firms. John was one of the non-executive board members. He was a friend of mine, and as we were working in the same neighbourhood, he often picked me up in his car when we went to the board meetings. During the drive we usually discussed the agenda for the meeting, and how we should get our points across. I really trusted John. He always did what he promised to do, and he always had the expertise needed. Besides being able to trust his reliability, integrity and competence, our informal contacts between the board meetings were helpful in facilitating board decision-making.

Another person who had an impact on the board was Jerry. This is illustrated in the following extract: 'When I returned from my trip I found I had not been sent an invitation to the next board meeting. I therefore called Jerry (another outside director and a close friend of the owner-manager). I wanted to learn from him about the work of the board while I had been away. He told me that he was going to Germany and was unable to attend the meeting. I then called the owner-manager. He said he had not sent out the invitations for the meeting because Jerry could not attend. I then called Jerry again and we agreed upon a new date for the meeting.' As the new date for the meeting approached: 'I called the owner-manager about the meeting which was to be held the following Monday. Everything is prepared for the meeting, but Jerry could not come. He (the owner-manager) and Jerry were going to do some voluntary work at some place out of town during the weekend, and Jerry could not get back. I wanted to check whether Jerry would be available on the phone during our board meeting.' The board meeting took place without Jerry, but the date for the next meeting was set so that he could fit it into his diary. As the time for that next meeting approached, I wrote my field notes as follows: 'I had a message from the owner-manager on my voice mail so I called his private number. He said that Jerry had called him to say that he is taking his wife on a one-week vacation to the Canary Islands. He would therefore not be able to attend and he asked whether the meeting could be postponed. As there were no urgent matters on the agenda, we decided to postpone the meeting by fourteen days.' And then: 'Jerry suggested that we should have a two-day strategy meeting.' However, when the date for the strategy meeting came, Jerry was only able to attend it for two hours.

Jerry was one of the most successful businessmen in the local community. He had an excellent reputation and he was invited to join a number of boards. He was a board member of several companies and he was chairman and CEO of his own company. However, this man, who was competent, popular and trusted in the local business community, turned out to be unreliable as a board member in the company of his friend. Because of his other responsibilities, he did not have enough time for this board position and in practice he reduced the efforts to have an active board in his friend's company.

Recently in the management literature there has been an increased level of attention devoted to the role of trust.[74] Classical and neoclassical economics operate within an under-socialised, atomised conception of human action in a utilitarian tradition,[75] and usually focus on the specialised control mechanisms of price and authority, but there exists a class of more general control mechanisms that may be assigned the label 'trust'.[76] Pervasive evidence from numerous disciplines supports the inclusion of trust as a critical factor in investigations of transaction processes,[77] and indicates that trust is essential for understanding interpersonal and group behaviour and managerial effectiveness.[78] In establishing and sustaining cooperative exchange structures and networks, trust is considered to be important as a control mechanism.[79]

Trust between whom
Trust is generally a relational concept, and therefore it is necessary to clarify which individuals it is among whom trust is discussed. Secondly, the direction of trust must be considered. Thirdly, there are also different types of trust. In the basic framework of this book I have divided the actors into three main categories. These are the board members, internal actors and external actors. Within these main categories we can discuss the role of trust:

- between internal and external actors;
- between internal actors and the board members;
- between external actors and the board members; and
- between the board members.

This list is simplified, as I have also pointed out that it is not clearly defined who the internal and external actors are, and that there may be various subcategories of actors among whom trust relationships may vary.

Agency theory is premised on the belief that the principal does not trust the agent. This lack of trust is related to assumptions about information asymmetry and managerial opportunism. However, trust, or the lack of it, is also important between other actors – for example, between the board members and the management, between the shareholders and board members, and between the board members. We have also seen that agency relationships can function in different directions, and trust is therefore not just unidirectional: trust may go in both directions. However, before reaching any conclusions about the role of trust we also need to understand the different types of trust.

Types of trust
Despite the agreement on the importance of trust, there is no generally accepted definition of the concept. In a review of definitions of trust in the management literature, Larue Tone Hosmer proposes the following

definition: "Trust is the reliance by one person, group, or firm upon a voluntary accepted duty on the part of another person, group, or firm to recognise and protect the rights and interests of all others engaged in a joint endeavour or economic exchange."[80]

Some make distinctions between fragile and resilient types of trust.[81] Fragile types of trust are related to the capabilities of the trusted person, group or firm, while resilient trust is related to the integrity and ethics of the trusted party. Another and closely related distinction that seems to be of particular value in understanding boards and governance is the distinction between integrity-based types of trust and competence-based types of trust. Competence-based trust occurs when one person, group or a firm relies upon another person, group or firm to have sufficient competence to perform a task or assignment. Integrity-based trust occurs when one person, group or firm relies upon the moral integrity of another person, group or firm.

Most studies of boards and governance make implicit assumptions about trust, but few studies are precise in defining the term. In some studies I have employed Ian Macneil's relational norms[82] to define and make hypotheses about trust.[83] Others have, for example, used concepts and hypotheses connected with procedural justice.[84]

The point of reference from what Macneil calls 'contractual relations' is the whole relationship between exchange partners and how this relationship develops. He argues that long-term relations between exchange partners will best be taken care of by relational contracting. Trust and interdependence are central elements in relational contracting, and the relations should be characterised by relational norms emphasising role integration, preservation of the relationship, the harmonising of relational conflicts and supra-contract norms. In relational contracts trust will be the connection norm between the actors.

The trust aspects of relational norms can be compared with trust in stewardship theory, but they can also reflect paternalism, family relations and clans.[85] Some of my own research has indicated that trust is important in understanding directorates,[86] and that '[r]elational norms and trust seem to be of greater importance in understanding and monitoring small firms than large firms'.[87] The role of trust may vary depending on the stakeholder perspective being considered.

Procedural justice theory helps us understand how trust and positive relations develop. The extent to which board decisions are conducted in a procedurally fair manner influences the level of trust between board members. Trust in turn shapes the way board members respond to agency risks.

Contractual relations theory and procedural justice theory are both about the role of social capital in easing coordination between actors. Social capital is a dynamic concept and is based exclusively on trust.[88]

Direction of trust and the empowerment of boards

We have seen that there are various types of trust, and that because trust is a relational phenomenon we need to identify the actors between whom there are relations. However, the understanding of trust also requires an understanding of the direction of trust and the degree of trust. The empowerment for various tasks relates to the actors involved, the type of trust and the direction of trust.[89]

To recap, boards perform various tasks. The guiding framework in this book suggests three basic relations – between the external actors and the internal actors, between the internal actors and the board of directors and between the external actors and the board. The relations are characterised by different types of trust (competence-based types and integrity-based types), and the arguments put forward here are that different kinds of trust relations lead to the empowerment of boards for various tasks.

Boards of directors may be empowered by both the internal actors and the external actors. Although the board is a legal entity, and is formally empowered by law to monitor the management, boards are in reality empowered by the relationships between external and internal actors. Actors or stakeholders have various stakes (equity, economic and influence) and power (formal, economic and political). How and why the empowerment takes place seems to depend on the company's resource situation in relation to the environment, and will have consequences for board tasks (for example, legitimising, advising and controlling).

The lack of competence-based types of trust is positively related to the board's control tasks. The lack of integrity-based types of trust is positively related to the board's legitimisation tasks. The existence of both competence-based trust and integrity-based trust is positively related to the board's advisory tasks.

In theory, the board of directors, because of assumptions about managerial opportunism and lack of integrity-based types of trust, will be mandated to control management on behalf of the external stakeholders when there is a division between the residual claimants and the management of a firm.[90] In such cases, the board will monitor management on behalf of residual claimants. The external stakeholders may also require competent board members when a lack of managerial competency (competence-based trust) is assumed. The CEO will not need to empower a board of directors unless there is a lack of integrity-based trust (legitimacy tasks) and/or competence-based trust (advisory tasks). Both integrity-based types of trust and competence-based trust are important in the relations between external and internal actors/stakeholders, but trust in these relations will be negatively related to the external actors'/stakeholders' empowerment of the board.

The internal actors will empower the board with various tasks depending on the types of trust they have in the board members. Integrity-based types of trust in board–management relations may empower the board of directors with other roles.[91] If the internal actors trust the competence and the integrity of the board and its members, the board may be used by the internal actors for various support roles. With integrity-based types of trust the internal actors will also let the board ask discerning questions, and attempt to manipulate the board and avoid implementation of board decisions – thereby reducing the influence of the board.[92]

The external actors may empower the board both directly and indirectly. Direct empowerment involves some kind of direct pressure on the internal actors to have an outside board to monitor, and the actors will have their formal interactions with the company through the board of directors. The indirect empowerment will be more related to a signalling effect. If the board members withdraw, they send a signal to the stakeholders and the environment. The external actors will then be alerted to potential problems in board–management relations. The selection of board members is also a signal. Such indirect effects will have consequences for the actors' future evaluations of the company, and the external actors may react and make investigations if changes in board composition occur. The board of directors may legitimise the company in relation to external actors. The attention to this legitimising task will depend on whether the external actors trust the competence and integrity of the directors.

Emotions

What are emotions? Emotions may be both intra-individual and inter-individual. Emotions are socially constructed and situational, because they are dependent on relationships and interactions. Emotions evolve, transform and go in new directions as a result of institutional and organisational contexts. As such, they are experienced with different degrees of intensity, and can either be expressed or not expressed. Emotions and their representation are salient in interpersonal communication and interaction.[93]

Emotions are not necessarily a sign of irrationality. They may reflect social rationality, or even multi-rationality. Emotions may even be managed and nurtured to achieve desired objectives, such as loyalty, friendship, team spirit, sympathy, etc. Emotions may be driving as well as restraining forces, and to reject the importance of emotions in managerial life could also be to deny it the joy and worries associated with life in general.[94] Furthermore, emotions are not necessarily stable; they may be in a state of flux.[95]

Emotions in the boardroom

As I presented the issues that the management should deal with, Tony sighed and breathed heavily... Obviously he did not want to be involved in more board activities, and several times he tried to move the discussion on to other topics. When we discussed strategy, I talked about the concept of the 'driving forces'. But Tony tried to take over the discussion and to introduce other issues. He was obviously tired and reluctant to take on new responsibilities.[96]

This is a comment from the chairperson in a small firm. Tony was a senior executive director, and he felt that he was already working as much and as hard as he could. The top management team had already produced their own strategic plan, and Tony did not want to take on the extra work that the board required. He was exhausted and tried to protect himself.

There are emotions in the interactions between the various actors around the boardroom. They may be between the board members, between some board members and various internal and external actors, or between various individual and groups of internal and internal actors. The above example illustrates fatigue and exhaustion, but there are many types of emotions. Ethel Brundin lists the following types of emotions: happiness, anger, fear, frustration, hope, joy, surprise, disgust, hate, excitement, anxiety, sadness, depression, indignation, contempt, guilt, anguish, envy, jealousy, compassion, pity, embarrassment, shame, indignation, pride and intuition.[97] This list is not comprehensive, however. She found in a boardroom study that concern, frustration satisfaction, confidence, strain, bewilderment, resignation, abandonment and anger seem to be the most important. The different aspects are listed in order of importance.

How men and women directors interact

The literature looking into gender issues shows how boards may also be influenced by gender-related interactions. Men and women directors interact in various ways – for example, according to the following themes:

- ruling techniques;
- critical mass;
- women's networks;
- mentors; and
- flirtation.

The literature dealing with women in management has made the case that, whenever women and men interact, whether at 'work or at play, there is some level of sexuality involved. How they choose to deal with sexuality is determined by many factors.'[98] Such concerns have not been included in the literature regarding boards of directors. Flirtation and mentorship are, for example, found to be closely related. This is illustrated in the following stories from women directors.[99]

I think it is an advantage to be young, not necessarily very good-looking, but attractive and to be articulate, and also possess a glint in the eye.

I have had many advantages by being a woman. They have remembered me, and they have treated me as gentlemen. They have wanted to help me. Everybody has remembered me because I have been the only woman. [...] It may be an advantage to be a woman, but sex or gender does not mean much at the top.

I can allow myself some flirtatious behaviour that makes me acquire some knowledge of the other board members in a different way. I can see other sides of them than their male colleagues. You get knowledge about your male colleagues that they do not have about each other. Thus I may get support from them. I know a lot more about Thomas as a person. I have been dancing with him. It gives another kind of insight, understanding of behaviour, that I can use if I want.

The observations about attraction and flirtation are in line with observations about emotions and feelings in the boardroom.[100] People are emotional, feeling and affective human beings – not just cognitive machines – and no board members can disregard their feelings. People may have sympathies and antipathies towards each other. Even revenge may be related to boardroom behaviour. Some emotions may be long-lasting while others may be very short-lived, such as exhaustion.

There may be affective conflicts, not just cognitive ones, inside and outside the boardroom, and there are numerous stories and examples about how actors are very emotional when fighting or supporting each other.

Psychological ownership

Emotions are also related to ownership, and ownership has recently received attention as a psychological phenomenon; 'socio-symbolic ownership' is a term that may help us understand alternative perspectives of ownership.[101] Under certain conditions, organisational members can develop feelings of ownership towards the organisation and various organisational factors. Psychological ownership is the state of mind in which individuals feel as though a target of ownership is 'theirs'.[102] The core of psychological ownership is the feeling of possessiveness and of being psychologically tied to an object. When a property is grounded psychologically, it becomes 'mine'.

'Mine' is an extremely important concept in understanding organisations. Psychological ownership may have its roots in the individual possibly being in control of the target, intimately knowing the target or having invested the self in the target. A feeling of ownership will often be accompanied by a feeling of responsibility, but it may also result in resistance to change.

Emotions have been addressed most in relation to the governance of family firms, but the notion of psychological ownership can also be applied to governance in other organisations.

Power and strategising

The core of this section is to present the concept of strategising from behavioural theory. However, strategising is directly linked to the concept of power. Corporate governance policies may reflect direct as well as symbolic management by powerful actors in organisations. This may imply that firms with powerful top managers may adopt policies and practices to symbolise commitment to shareholder interests formally, but in practice they may fail in or avoid implementing them.[103] We have also seen that dominant actors in corporate governance and strategic decision-making may vary over time.[104]

Strategising – or, more precisely, micro-strategising – is an activity-based view of strategy.[105] It consists of the detailed processes and practices that constitute the day-to-day activities of organisational life and that relate to strategic outcomes. These are often invisible in traditional strategy research. Micro-strategising gets closer to the organisational activities that make up the system. Strategic activities involve people on the periphery, not only those at the centre. This is also evolving, and is more the case nowadays than earlier. The flexibility among actors about who they are and what they are doing may be a contribution from the strategising literature.

Power is a relational phenomenon. It is generated, maintained and lost in the context of relations with others. Power may be defined as a potential force that is situational and relational and comes into being in the actions between strategists. Emotions and power are important issues in board dynamics.[106] Board members need power to be able to contribute to strategising in the boardroom. The frequency of the reports in recent years concerning sudden resignations and changes of board members indicates that power struggles, embedded in emotions, are inherently related to emotions. Not only are these emotional power expressions indicators but sometimes they are clearly visible in various media discussions.

Influence and power

Power is an important concept when understanding behavioural perspectives on boards and governance, but what is power? Power may be difficult to observe directly. Therefore it is often studied through its sources or consequences. Robert A. Dahl's definition of power is often used as a starting point to understand power: 'A has power over B to the extent that A can get B to do something that B would not otherwise do.'[107] Power is a relation between actors, and this definition is related to influence. Power and influence are often seen as two sides of the same coin. It is also often argued that some resistance must be displayed if the power notion should be used, and some kind of submission or influence should be the result of the exercise of power. Power and influence may be exercised through politics and strategising inside and outside the boardroom.

Types of power

The literature on power is often divided into four main groups or dimensions. These are:

- direct power;
- indirect power;
- conscience-controlling power; and
- institutional/structural power.

Direct power is what is described in Dahl's power definition; you have power over me if you control something I need or appreciate. However, the direct power in the boardroom may have features other than power inside an organisation. Legally, the board members act like a collegium without a formal, hierarchical command structure. Direct power in the board is often related to voting rights, and the shareholders electing board members. It is a question of understanding the actors: Who has power over whom – and why? In addition to having this direct power over decision-making, boards may also have indirect power – for example, in relation to non-decision-making, and the power of influencing opinions.[108]

Indirect power in the boardroom setting is about not just the final decision-making but also who is setting the agenda.[109] This also includes alliances and who has been talking with whom outside the board meetings. This makes it important to understand the time and place of interactions.

Power may be exercised by controlling the consciousness of the actors.[110] Various techniques may be used to achieve this type of power – for example, techniques related to persuasion, education and manipulation.[111] Actors may be persuaded to act against their own interests. In the boardroom setting it has been usually been the case that certain actors have had sway over other actors about board tasks and accountability. Trust and emotions are also related to conscience-controlling power.

Institutional and structural power is about rationality and how to relate to power bases.[112] Strong institutional power is used inside the structure, while weak structural power is used and reproduced for identifiable actors. The institutional and structural power bases make it important to explore and understand the role of various kinds of internal and external influences – for example, TMTs, interlocking directorates, social networks, class elites, etc.

Some authors divide this latter group of types of power into structural power, ownership power, expert power and prestige power. Structural power is about the formal authority, ownership power is about the CEO ownership in the focal firm, expert power is often related to functional experience, while prestige power has been taken in various studies as elite education.[113]

Power and the boardroom

As power is the ability to influence others, board decision-making may be a power game.[114] In a recent study I collected the board life stories of eight women directors (the 'board life story' study).[115] They had experiences from more than 100 boards, and some of their stories illustrated the importance of understanding power in the boardroom. Most of the women had stories or statements about the board as an arena for an intense power game.

[O]thers used me in their power play. As I discovered what happened in the inner chambers, then I thought that I have been innocent too long. Yes, it is definitely a lot of power play.

It is a game and those not being experienced – and I feel that I have become experienced – they are getting completely manipulated. It is a lot of power in being like that. It is kind of nice to know that you master this game, but it is unnecessary that it shall be like that.

It takes some time before you see the power balance in a board. Who is deciding? It is not always the top person who decides. You need to find out who has the wheel in their hands.

One of the women told me that it was a shock for her to look at the power game taking place between the male board members inside and outside the boardroom. The observations of the women regarding the male directors and the power game were sorted into six sub-groups: the importance of nurturing contacts and networks; the 'network of *old boys*'; people of authority; people of prestige; people of power;

and alliance creation. Each of these sub-groups emphasises that women must understand and relate to their observations if they are to continue participating on corporate boards. It is not enough to have competence; there is also a need to relate to the power game.

Some of these sub-groups have been commented on in the literature – for example, in managerial[116] and class hegemony[117] literature, and interlocking directorates.[118] The women also perceived that the motives of their male colleagues for joining a board were a desire for prestige and to be around people of power or authority.[119]

The reality of power and influence inside and outside the boardroom requires the simultaneous, dynamic and complementary analysis of the context, content, will and skill in creating and using a constellation of power sources.[120]

Influences and alliances between board members

One aspect of power is that of creating alliances. Decision-making is influenced through the building of alliances. This was illustrated in the 'board life story' project, when the women clearly attributed power relationships to the boardroom. The women made observations as to how and why directors form ties or alliances. Creating alliances was the theme mostly referred to by the women with respect to power and processes. Alliances are a means of acquiring power and, therefore, tools for influencing board decisions. All but one of the women directors made similar comments.

You must not imagine that you can fight things through without having some allies.

It is important that you make alliances with the most influential and substantial board members, who are not necessarily the employee directors.[121] Board members are not all the same. You will easily get a feeling for whom the most influential board members are.

I haven't made phone calls in advance, and manipulated. However, this happens often on the board. I believe men do so more often than women. They talk before the meetings. They clarify ahead. I have attended many board meetings where I have been struggling to understand what's going on and suddenly something has been decided without having even been discussed.

The women observed that, when men wanted to be influential, they made alliances. Their stories showed that some of them just accepted these alliances as a part of the game, while others clearly disliked them. Although studies of boards of directors have recognised the role of alliances through interlocking directorates from inter-organisational and intra-class perspectives, the women directors emphasised alliances as part of the internal power mobilisation system practised by directors as a means of securing support in decision-making processes.

Internal influences

The dominating perspectives on corporate governance and control have tended to focus on how managers and internal actors have controlled organisations. Organisations operate in environments with exchange-based uncertainties, and managers use various tactics for preserving their autonomy and creating stability. There are two main theoretical perspectives that show the internal influences on the board members. These are upper echelon theory and managerial hegemony theory.

Upper echelon theory explains differences in firm-level success through differences in TMT and board composition.[122] The upper echelon is defined as the dominant coalition of powerful actors in an organisation; usually it is those who have formal positions in the top management team and the board of directors. Upper echelon theory has a focus on demography. It assumes the existence of considerable uncertainty with regard to decisions that are to be made, both in general and in interactions between managers and board members. The cognition and interactions of the upper echelon are shaped by their earlier experiences. Social integration and interactions between the board members and the members of the TMT are assumed to be two of the most important processes moderating the relationship between the demographics of the board members and corporate financial performance. The social embeddedness and social activities of board members are assumed to have positive effects on firms' strategic management.

Power circulation theory explains political dynamics among societal elites.[123] The top management level of an organisation is political, and it is characterised by shifting coalitions and continual power struggles.[124] Power circulation theory suggests that power disappears over time due to political obstacles arising from an increase in the number of competing and rival actors. Obsolescence and contestation are two interplaying mechanisms that form power circulation. Obsolescence implies that the CEO becomes stagnant and outdated due to ties with old decisions; contestation arises out of rivalry for the CEO position. Arguments from power circulation theory imply that powerful insiders may offer a counterweight against potential self-serving actions by CEOs.

A large number of studies and other observations show how managers manoeuvre to avoid control mechanisms from shareholders. Managerial dispositions involve efforts to subdue boards of directors' potential for control by recruiting board members, setting the boardroom agenda and investing in defence mechanisms for corporate control.

In the 'U'n'I' case, given at the end of this chapter, we see how corporate managers may circumvent corporate control by using various stakeholder management techniques, such as movement, 'multimatum' and manipulation processes.[125] The movement processes are characterised by the attitude that no hindrances are too big to be solved, and that the 'way is made while you walk'. It is about how to initiate processes and action without including the board or other constraining actors. 'Multimatum' is to do with monumental dynamism: when large organisations are on the move, they are hard to stop without considerable costs being incurred by those trying to stop them. 'Multimatum' is about how to influence the outcome of board decisions. Manipulation is described as playing one party off against the other. It is about how to neutralise certain board members.

Three groups of power base concepts were observed in the 'U'n'I' case. These were the concentration of institutional power, the CEO's charisma and relation-building abilities, and the friendship and power elites. These three groups are not quite distinct, as they appear to overlap and influence each other. The concentration of power has an institutional or organisational origin, CEO charisma has an individual origin in the main, and to a large extent the friendship and power elite power base seems to be a result of integrating the institutional and individual factors.

External influences

The main theoretical contributions to understanding the role of external actors' relations come from the work on interlocking directorates,[126] class elites,[127] social movements[128] and social network theory.[129] Agency theory contributes to the understanding of corporate control in emphasising input variables as the formal power of the external stakeholder, and in particular the shareholders. The formal power is related to voting rights. However, agency theory does not explain the external influences and processes going beyond voting rights. The literature on interlocking directorates, social movements and social networks helps us understand external influences on boards and governance.

Political and sociocultural elements can affect the diffusion process. Organisations are political arenas in which actors are engaged in contests over the rules and content of the governance of the organisation, indicating that there are coercive rather than mimetic processes at work.[130]

Social control and social distancing

The social norms in corporate elites may be in conflict with the legally mandated control tasks.[131] There will be a gap between these board task expectations and actual task performance, because of mutually reinforcing processes of social control methods in managerial elites, biases in director selection processes[132] and ignorance in board decision-making. Social control in corporate elites filters the board members' efforts in their control tasks on behalf of shareholders.[133] This social elite control may take place as informal social sanctioning. An example of such sanctioning is referred to as social distancing from directors on other boards.[134] Board members avoiding the filters from managerial elites are likely to be informally ostracised from board affairs. This will mean that they will not be invited to informal meetings, and others are therefore less likely to build on their comments at formal meetings.[135]

Institutional investors and corporate managers can be considered as contenders for corporate control. Agency theory has had considerable influence on the rhetoric used to describe governance policies, but less influence on practice.[136] While the rhetoric of governance has changed considerably in recent years, the actual practice has changed little. Boards and governance should thus be understood from an institutional perspective.[137] Corporate managers may formally be adopting governance policies according to agency theory or the prevailing logic in the business and investor communities, but they may also decouple these policies from actual organisational practices. Actual governance practices tend to reflect the interests and beliefs of corporate elites.[138]

A collective consciousness may be made possible by a high level of social homogeneity and overlapping directorships. These mechanisms help create a group identity. However, group-level identity may not be enough to secure social control. Individuals may have personal interests that violate the collective interest of the group. Social control involves processes in the social system that serve to counteract non-compliant tendencies that, in turn, may violate the large social group. The literature on social psychology suggests that people have a fundamental motivation in seeking inclusion and avoiding exclusion from social groups that are important for their self-identity.

It has been argued that corporate governance reforms have stagnated because of social processes in the corporate elite. Sociological perspectives on boards of directors have long suggested that boards are the locus of control processes. The board members become socialised into the expectations of the corporate elite.[139] The corporate elite is typically defined as the leaders and board members of large corporations. Boards may provide a locus for the social sanctioning of directors who have acted against the priorities of corporate leaders. Members of the corporate elite may lobby against issues of public interest to advocate alternative interests from which they themselves will gain.

Social control may vary from legal sanctioning to relatively subtle informal sanctions. Social distancing is a relatively informal kind of control.[140] A mechanism observed in boards and governance, social distancing involves a range of specific behaviours, or the withdrawal of behaviours, towards non-compliant group members[141]. Social distancing may include neglecting to ask opinions of out-of-favour board members, not inviting them to informal meetings or social activities, and in other ways preventing them from participating in the group. Social distancing may also involve paying less attention to remarks from the non-compliant individuals and not recognising their contribution to the group. Gossip among group members can also be used. Group members may also initiate discussions on a topic with which the nonconformist is not familiar, and thus keep the person out of the group.

Social distancing is a near-universal phenomenon, but it is strongest in groups that are socially cohesive because of demographic homogeneity and network ties between the members. This is typically the case among board members and the corporate elite. Normative expectations tend to be strong in such groups, and that also makes it easier to identify deviant behaviour. Cohesion is enhanced not only by overlapping board memberships but also by the 'small world character of the interlock networks, in which the average number of links between any two directors in the network is very small, but also by club memberships, school ties, and a persistently high level of demographic homogeneity'.[142] Social distancing is likely to occur when group members can interact or avoid interaction with the noncompliant individual while simultaneously carrying out their collective activity.

James Westphal and Poonam Khanna have found in their study of social distancing in the boardroom that board members with very high reputations will be less likely to experience social distancing than board members with lower reputations.[143] Board members may be less reluctant to compromise their social capital by distancing themselves from these high-status directors. Furthermore, Westphal and Khanna find that social distancing is a temporary sanction. People who experience social distancing will be less likely to participate in other elite-threatening activities, and social distancing will disappear after a period of 'good' behaviour. Board decisions are typically made unanimously, and any indications of initial reservations will most often be worked out informally ahead of board meetings. Board members who do not want to participate in elite-threatening changes may in this way be able to withdraw their support for such changes.

To overcome the problems with social control from corporate elites it is suggested that boards should be required to have members drawn from substantially different socioeconomic and professional backgrounds. These should be people who have not been socialised in the norms of the corporate elite.

The U'n'I case: power and strategising

In this in-depth summarising case I present the power and strategising techniques displayed by a CEO in circumventing board and stakeholder control.[144]

In August 1992 UNI Storebrand, Norway's largest insurance company, went into public administration because of bankruptcy threats. The corporate management of the company had failed in its hostile takeover bid for Skandia, the largest Swedish – and

Scandinavian – insurance company. In its takeover bid, UNI Storebrand had violated the interests of the stockholders, the Norwegian
public and their representatives in Parliament and bureaucracy, corporate democracy, and the interest of the creditors. The takeover bid
resulted in a loss of billions of dollars for stakeholders, creditors and
customers.

UNI Storebrand was the result of a merger between the two largest
insurance companies in Norway – UNI and Storebrand, approved by
the Norwegian authorities in January 1991. In 1989 UNI had tried
to merge with another large Norwegian insurance company (Vesta),
but the plans were thwarted by the government. Before the merger
between UNI and Storebrand, UNI had been the largest life insurance
company in Norway while Storebrand had been the largest non-life
insurance company. In both the life and the non-life sectors, the new
company (UNI Storebrand) had domestic market shares of between
30 per cent and 50 per cent. In 1991 UNI Storebrand had an average of 4,661 employees, Skandia in Sweden an average of 11,321.
The merged company was a public joint-stock company, but the
UNI Foundation owned 30 per cent of the stock (the UNI Foundation was established because UNI was a mutual insurance company
before the merger with Storebrand). The equity of the UNI Foundation was the accumulated result of the non-life activities of UNI
Insurance. In the merger, the Storebrand CEO became the new CEO
of UNI Storebrand, while the CEO of UNI and the UNI Foundation became the chairman of the board. I now present some of the
power bases and techniques that the CEO used to circumvent corporate
control.

Power bases

The power bases observed included institutional, individual and integrated sources. The institutional power bases were related to the power
derived from organisational size and power (such as economic power),
the individual power bases were related to the characteristics of the
manager as an individual, and the integrated power bases were the
additional power arising because of simultaneous institutional and
individual power. The power bases are shown in table 6.3 and are
illustrated in relation to various types of stakeholders.

Table 6.3 *Power bases*

	Equity/ shareholders	*Economic/competitors, suppliers, etc.*	*Environmental/employees, society in general*
Institutional: *Concentration of institutional power*	Ownership structure made it possible to set conditions for the election of board members	Financial power made it possible to use directors and executives in interlocking directorates	Employees, politicians and bureaucrats were afraid to oppose due to potential repercussions
Individual: *CEO charisma and relation-building abilities*	He made everybody enthusiastic about his plans	He was considered to be a managerial genius and was awarded the 'Best Manager Prize'	He was considered to be a man of discretion, acting morally within every domain of social responsibility
Integrated: *Friendship and power elites*	The board chairman defined his role as supporting and inspiring the CEO	He was in the core of power elites, sharing common leadership ideologies	He shared ideologies and was on friendly terms with influential politicians and bureaucrats

Institutional: concentration of power

UNI Storebrand was the largest investor in the Norwegian financial market. Even though the stockholders and governmental bodies alike were aware of the possible danger related to this concentration of power, they were more victims than monitors of this power. The press reported that politicians, bureaucrats and corporate managers were all afraid to oppose the sphere of the UNI CEO because of potential personal or financial repercussions.

According to agency theory, the board of directors is considered to be one of the principal means for stockholders to control management in the case of a separation of ownership and control. Another mechanism is the market for corporate control. UNI Storebrand's board composition was decided by a charter, which stated that there should be ten board members, four of whom were to be elected as employee representatives, two from the UNI Foundation (including the chairperson) and four representing other stockholders. The CEO and the top management group also attended the board meetings, but they had no voting rights.

Even though the four outside directors were among the most influential executives of major Norwegian corporations, the board composition and the board's behaviour indicated that managerial hegemony existed, and that in reality the stockholders had little influence. The board chairperson commented to the press, just after he had been appointed to his position, that his main job was to support and inspire the CEO. The Skandia takeover bid had been on the board agenda nineteen times, and the CEO and his administration received unanimous support every time. A public investigation report indicated, however, that the CEO used the chief officer of the Ministry of Finance in Norway as a hostage in relation to the board's considerations. The members of the board were subsequently sued by the stockholders for not having looked after their stakes when supporting the Skandia takeover bid. One of the main accusations concerned the board's lack of concern for the takeover defences adopted by Skandia. The importance of Skandia's unequal voting stock defences had been commented on in a major Swedish journal a few days before UNI Storebrand started its takeover bid. These defences included the provision that no stockholder could vote for more than thirty shares at the annual shareholders' meeting, and the CEO of Skandia formally requested that all stockholders be given proxies to distribute their voting rights.

UNI Storebrand also had direct and indirect interlocks with other corporations. The ownership structure of UNI Storebrand made it possible for the corporate management to set the conditions for the election of outside board members. They were (with one exception) top executives of some of the most influential Norwegian corporations, but none of them was in the core of the personal network of the CEO. As a large financial institution, supposed to be the financial locomotive in Norwegian industry, UNI Storebrand actively used its board members and top executives in interlocking directorates to influence other corporations. UNI Storebrand was clearly the Norwegian corporation with the most interlocks in the country's industry: it had direct or indirect interlocks with about 50 per cent of the largest Norwegian firms. These interlocks indicated a concentration of institutional power and mutual independence, and may have had a potential impact on the development of networks and power elites. Some of the corporations in this network represented large financial sources, and the top management and the board of directors in some of them have been sued for insufficient evaluation/consideration of the economic and financial consequences of supporting UNI Storebrand's takeover bid.

Individual: CEO charisma and relation-building abilities

The individual characteristics of the CEO are heavily emphasised in the UNI Storebrand case. His relationship-building abilities, personal charisma and friendly behaviour seem to have legitimised his actions. He was compared to an evangelist, preaching his gospel in such a way that everybody said: 'Hallelujah and amen.' He was considered to be a person of high moral integrity with regard to every aspect of social responsibility. Most of the employees adored him; they were probably more loyal to him than to the corporation. He was considered to be the 'wonder boy' of Norwegian management. Because of his personal integrity, his love of communicating, his reciprocity and his respect, the CEO was awarded Norway's 'Best Manager Prize' in 1991. He generated enthusiasm for his plans and visions.

Integrated: friendship and power elites

Integrated power is defined here as the power that stems from combining institutional and individual power. The U'n'I case clearly shows how friendship ties between individuals in power elites across organisations are crucial in understanding strategic management and stakeholder control. In the U'n'I case, these elites seemed to evolve from a common ideology, the most apparent of these being related to politics, university background and a shared leadership ideology. The groupings resulted in 'a network of old boys', wherein politicians, bureaucrats and corporate leaders supported and encouraged each other.

In light of the UNI Storebrand crisis, three elite networks were revealed. The first network ('the old boys' club') consisted of twenty to thirty of the Norwegian corporate managers. Rather than being one defined group with a distinct inner core, this network had several levels. The core of the group was characterised by giving terms of trade to both business and government. One of the members of the network explained: 'To be a member of the "old boys' club" involves it being possible to arrange anything if you know the group and the rules of the game. The members are members of each other's board of directors; they own each other's companies and decide each other's compensation.' The UNI Storebrand crisis almost destroyed this network.

The second network was 'the presidents' club'. This club was a more exclusive variant. The group developed around a US management consultant who had become a guru in Norway. His leadership philosophy was based on the belief that leadership is a profession and that leadership skills are independent of the business or corporation to be led. Between seven and ten of the presidents of large Norwegian corporations were members of this group. They met twice a year to cultivate a common leadership ideology and to discuss marketing trends and corporate strategies.

The third network was an example of how industry leaders and politicians come together. The group was the close network of the Secretary of Finance in Norway. Together with his political advisers he met regularly with eight of the country's industrial and financial leaders.

The CEO was in the core of each of these networks. He was on particularly good terms with the members of the Norwegian Cabinet. He was, half officially, declared to be a social democrat, and he shared the vision of the Norwegian Prime Minister that Norwegians had to be active in forming the inner financial market being brought into being in Europe. The process of involving the politicians in the Skandia takeover bid started in the office of the Prime Minister. At this meeting the CEO was alone with the Prime Minister, and the CEO informed him of his plans. From then on the CEO cultivated good relations with the Secretary of Finance and his closest advisers.

Strategising techniques

Observations about the processes of stakeholder management are sorted into three concepts: movement, 'multimatum' and manipulation. The concepts are illustrated in table 6.4.

Movement: 'The road is made while you walk'

The UNI Storebrand case showed a proactive response of movement to avoid stakeholder control. "The road is made while you walk", a quotation from Ferdinand Finne, a Norwegian novelist, was adopted as a slogan. The concept refers to one of the ways the corporate management of UNI Storebrand dealt with laws, regulations and other forms of stakeholder control. The quote refers to setting off towards a destination without knowing what obstacles will appear and how you will overcome them, yet still having faith that solutions will be found. It was reported that, at corporate management meetings, the CEO would usually smile when confronted with comments that his plans were not in accordance with laws and regulations. His response to such comments was: 'The road will be made while we walk.' He saw that laws and decisions by governmental bodies and other stakeholder groups were changed 'as he was walking'. As a corporate manager he had thus far succeeded in whatever he tried: why should he not succeed this time? These observations are also reinforced by a citation from his personal diary: 'Think positively about what you can do with the situation. Push worries ahead of you.'

The board of directors, business leaders, financial institutions, politicians, employees and society in general all seemed to be blinded by his earlier successes, and they tended to believe that he would continue achieving his vision in the future.

Multimatum: requesting approval after the point of no return

UNI Storebrand used the risky, but obviously effective, escalator technique of putting oneself and another party in a position of mutual destruction unless the other party acts to save them both.

Table 6.4 *Strategising techniques: processes of stakeholder management*

	Equity/ shareholders	*Economic/competitors, suppliers, etc.*	*Environmental/employees, society in general*
Movement: *"The road is made while you walk"*	Corporate management was far ahead of the board in strategy formation	Business leaders and financial institutions tended to believe he would be successful	Laws and regulations were changed if they did not agree with the corporation's behaviour
Multimatum: *Requesting approval after the point of no return*	The raid was on the board's agenda after dispositions had been made	Creditors and partners would suffer losses if they did not provide support	The governmental regulatory bodies were faced with a moral dilemma
Manipulation: *Playing one party off against another*	The board was kept informed about positive signs from government	Industry leaders and financial institutions thought he was supported by government	Politicians and bureaucrats thought he was supported by a united Norwegian industry

One of the frequently used descriptions of the corporate strategic response to corporate control was that 'approval was requested after the point of no return'. The Norwegian Parliament and other governmental control bodies had presented requirements to UNI and Storebrand in order to avoid any undesirable consequences from the corporation's behaviour in relation to customers, competitors, financial institutions and society in general. In 1989 UNI, the second largest insurance company in Norway, had wanted to merge with Vesta, the fourth largest. This proposed merger was prevented after a thorough discussion in Parliament, which resulted in a bill that prohibited any of the largest Norwegian insurance companies from merging. In 1990 the two largest Norwegian insurance companies, UNI and Storebrand, merged, in direct defiance of the bill. The firms had relocated together and had integrated their IT systems and all their organisational and marketing structures and systems before requesting approval. The stock market and the Norwegian equivalent of the Security and Exchange Commission, most Members of Parliament, the Norwegian price authorities and even the members of the social democratic Labour Party opposed this merger.

The main formal reason for letting UNI and Storebrand merge was that the amalgamated company would become the driving force for Norwegian industry by investing in Norwegian firms. During the autumn of 1991 the firm 'asked' the Norwegian Secretary of Finance whether the Norwegian state would join UNI Storebrand in buying the Swedish insurance company Skandia, or whether the Cabinet would allow UNI Storebrand to invest all its Swedish resources in the Skandia takeover bid. In a secret letter of 12 November 1991 from the corporate director (chief of staff) of UNI Storebrand, Credit Supervision (the main Norwegian governmental body for controlling financial institutions) was told that unless it made concessions UNI Storebrand would suffer destructive losses. By that time UNI Storebrand had already bought 20 per cent of the shares in Skandia without concessions.

The board of directors also faced the managerial ultimatum tactics of requesting approval after the event in the Skandia takeover bid, and financial institutions and partners were unable to withdraw from obligations without suffering severe losses.

Manipulation: playing one party off against another
One aspect of the manipulation that occurred in UNI Storebrand involved a kind of co-optation of the decision-making process without

letting the co-opted parties have any influence. It seemed to be the CEO's style to make frequent briefings to the official governmental authorities and the control bodies, but never to ask permission. The CEO did not get any promises from the Prime Minister at their meeting, but neither did he get the opposite – any rebuffs. The atmosphere at this meeting was such that UNI Storebrand on several occasions explicitly declared that the Norwegian Prime Minister supported the takeover bid; moreover, these declarations were never denied. The CEO played one party off against another. The Cabinet thought the CEO was supported by a united front of Norwegian industries, and the industry leaders thought he was supported by the Cabinet. Due to the crisis, stockholders and financial institutions considered legal proceedings against the Norwegian authorities for not having stopped the scheme. It was at this stage that the political parties debated whether the authorities' relations with UNI Storebrand's unsuccessful Skandia takeover bid should lead to a motion for a vote of no confidence in Parliament against the Secretary of Finance and the Prime Minister.

Another example of the use of manipulation emerged when, in interviews, both employees and stockholder activists described how the CEO and the board chairman actively tried to suppress comments from the shareholders at the general assembly meeting in May 1992. This was done by directly and personally contacting and threatening shareholder activists, and by attempting to manipulate the assembly. At the assembly meeting 800 employees were allowed admittance, and they were instructed to applaud whatever the corporate management said and to react negatively to whatever was said by potential opposition figures.

Summary

Various concepts related to interactions inside and outside the boardroom have been introduced in this chapter. The main concepts from the behavioural theory of the firm have been truly bounded rationality, satisficing and problemistic search, routines and learning, and political bargaining and the quasi-resolution of conflicts. With direct application to boards and governance, we have strategising, value creation through knowledge, norms and learning processes, informal, formal and hybrid arenas, unequal admittance, frequencies of interaction, relational norms, integrity- and competence-based types of trust, the direction of trust, emotions, and psychological and socio-symbolical ownership. Concepts related to power and influencing techniques have also been introduced, including social control, social distancing, institutional, individual and integrated types of power, and movement, multimatum and manipulation techniques to circumvent stakeholder control.

In this chapter I have presented interactions that take place both inside and outside the boardroom. I started by proposing a first step towards a behavioural theory of boards and governance, suggesting that

- value creation through knowledge;
- strategising;
- problemistic search; and
- norms and learning processes

are all elements that may become building blocks in creating a behavioural theory of boards and governance. The illustrative and summarising case at the end of this chapter highlighted techniques for circumventing corporate control.

In this chapter I have explored the attributes of the interactions, including the attributes of the actors and arenas. Board decision-making is influenced by activities in various arenas, and not all the actors have the same access to the various arenas. Trust and emotions are also among the attributes highlighting the human sides of corporate governance. The importance of emotions is clear from the reports and observations as to what really happens in corporate governance, but it is underestimated from a research and discussion perspective.

Distinctions were made between different types of trust. I presented:

- competence-based kinds of trust; and
- integrity-based kinds of trust.

Trust is a relational phenomenon. It is also important, therefore, to understand the relationships between those whom we found to have trusting relationships, and the direction of trust. Trust is a cornerstone for effective board interactions, and trust between the various actors empowers boards for their tasks.

Boards are embedded in social institutions. Boards' tasks, board composition and boards' working structures are results of requirements and pressure from the environment. In this chapter I have also presented strategising and the political dynamics surrounding the boardroom. Power and strategising are closely related. Power does not refer to the attributes of individual people but to the relations between the actors. Strategising is an activity-based view of strategy, and it concerns the detailed processes and practices which constitute the day-to-day activities of organisational life and which relate to strategic outcomes. Strategic activities involve individuals both outside and inside the boardroom.

In chapter 7 I present the structures and norms to be found around the boardroom. They often reflect the rule-of-thumb guidelines resulting from problemistic search and satisficing. The evolution of codes of best corporate governance practice is rooted in the need for such guidelines.

7 | *Structures and leadership*

The main concepts under consideration in this chapter are:
- rules;
- codes;
- norms;
- structures;
- leadership;
- committees;
- the CEO's work description;
- board instructions;
- board evaluations; and
- 'away days'.

How can good corporate governance be developed? In this chapter I present various ways – and attempts – to improve corporate governance. The chapter is structured around the concepts of norms, rules, structures and leadership, and starts by outlining some theories that seek to explain how boards behave. It is not always formal laws or regulations that are the most important factors here but, rather, we often find that it is symbols, norms, perceptions of justice, and board leadership and informal regulations that are calling the tune.

Extensive efforts have been made in recent years to develop codes of best practice for corporate governance. These practices are attempts to regulate the 'rules of the game' in order to achieve some kind of accountability and reliability. In this chapter I outline the development of some of these codes before presenting arguments about board structures and board leadership.

Formal structures and leadership can be viewed as being on a continuum. Formal structures and active leadership may serve as substitutes for each other. However, I argue that both leadership and structures are important for enhancing board effectiveness.

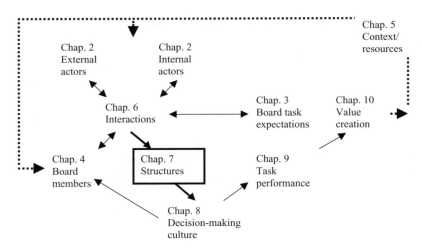

In the guiding framework of the book I have placed this chapter between that on interactions (chapter 6) and that on decision-making (chapter 8). However, I also argue that structures and leadership influence the direct relationship between the board members and board decision-making.

Rules, norms, structures and leadership

Theories of rational decision-making often highlight how rules serve to constrain action and behaviour. They also show how rules empower and facilitate action. In this way, the likelihood is increased that organisational actions will be taken rather than postponed. I now present some theories explaining the role of rules and norms.

Formal and informal structures and norms

The Higgs review in the United Kingdom[1] and most of the recent literature on reforming corporate governance have contributed to developing and formalising structures and norms. Formal and informal board structures and norms, including board leadership, mediate the impact of the interactions and the board's decision-making culture, and they may moderate the dynamics among the various board members. The development of rules for the boardroom is often explained in terms of imitative processes and institutional theory.[2] However, even though boards adapt rules and structures as a response to demands from external actors, actual practices seem to be tailored to the needs and demands of internal actors.[3]

Most rules are informal. Various descriptions exist concerning informal rules and norms in the boardroom.[4] These descriptions have generally reflected the perspectives of managerial hegemony and class hegemony. However, the recent development of codes of best practice has led to a formalisation of rules and structures. Most of these codes represent investor perspectives, but we also see codes reflecting the perspectives of other external and internal actors. The codes often include requirements in connection with board evaluations, the CEO working description, board instructions, board leadership and board committees.

Symbolic management

Reliance on rules can be understood from strategic choice perspectives[5] and from institutional theory.[6] While various attempts have been made to contrast these theories in research into boards of directors,[7] informal rules are generally found to be more important than formal rules.[8] How rules form both decisions and actual board behaviour has to some extent been ignored in studies of boards and governance. A behavioural theory on boards and governance will, however, emphasise the consequences of rules for board decision-making.

Institutional action theory

The institutional theory of action has been formulated by James March and Johan P. Olsen.[9] The theory focuses on the consequences of rules in structuring organisational action and decision-making, and it touches upon inertia in organisations. Rule-based actions characterise organisational decisions, and when individuals and organisations fulfil their identities they follow rules or procedures that they see as being appropriate to the situation in which they find themselves. A reliance on rules also characterises major decisions made by boards of directors.[10] Corporate boards of directors are guided in their decisions both by historical precedents and by formal rules that are not easily modified as board actions become institutionalised and norms of appropriate beliefs and behaviour become established.

Three aspects of the institutional theory of action are particularly important in explaining boards and governance.[11]

- Organisational decisions are enacted through the application of appropriate rules.
- History is important in shaping the rules and routines that structure behaviour.
- There is an interplay between cognitive and political factors in the generation and maintenance of organisational rules.

Compared with other versions of institutionalism, this perspective emphasises organisation-level rules rather than the effects of the broader institutional environment.

The identities of the decision-makers are important in understanding institutional action theory. Their identities will contain values, experiences and roles – including their social identification and points of reference. Board members share a common identification resulting from shared values, commitments and demographic characteristics. The theory assumes that decisions are made by matching situations to rules according to the identities of the actors. The adjustments to the rules will be influenced by their identities.

Procedural justice

Procedural justice theory examines the impact of the decision-making process. The theory defines a fair or just process as one that is perceived as being conducted according to norms of impartiality and respect.[12] Aspects of formal procedural justice along with the conduct of decision-making actors contribute to individual actors' perceptions of procedural justice. These include the opportunity the individual actors have to provide input to the decision, the attention their input receives, the timeliness of the feedback they are given on decision outcomes, and the sufficiency of justification. The style of interaction, including the extent to which decision-makers treat the individual actors with dignity and respect, also affects perceptions of fairness.

Perceptions of procedural justice impact on attitudes and behaviour. They will, for example, increase decision acceptance and commitment to decisions. They will also reduce antisocial and counterproductive behaviour.

The assessment of procedural justice builds trust in the decision-making process. It indicates the trustworthiness of decision-makers, and assures individuals that their self-interest is protected in the long run. Furthermore, procedural justice is important to individuals because it affirms their status and value to the group or organisation. Being treated with fairness, dignity and respect are important signals about the status of the individual actors in a group. Such signals are especially important in boards as their infrequent meetings cause the impact of the interaction to appear greater, and because board membership is often in itself a motivation to serve on boards.[13]

Structures or leadership

Corporate governance designs balance the needs for structures and leadership. Agency theory focuses on how structures direct the outcomes of decisions, and formalisation serves to objectify rules, making the rules appear more legitimate and objective. Most research on board structures has been into CEO duality: who should be the leader of the board? However, very little research has been carried out into the role and tasks of board leadership.

John Roberts, Terry McNulty and John Stiles[14] emphasise the pivotal importance of board leadership, and they claim that the role of the chairperson is 'vital to the board members' engagement in various ways', and 'their own conduct does much to set the culture of the board'. Leadership and structure may influence the board decision-making culture. However, little research attention has been given to systematically exploring the behavioural perspectives of board leadership. At the end of this chapter I present various aspects of board structures and board leadership.

'Rules of the game'

We now come to the rules of the game. Some rules are formal and some are informal. Some are based on rational choice, while other rules have emerged from practice and after influence from various internal and external sources. Tony Whisler has grasped the importance of the informal rules of the game, and he presents them in a schedule of seven articles.[15] His list of rules is descriptive, and it takes in the conflicting practices and norms that have evolved into boardroom rules and norms.

In the remainder of this chapter we see how Whisler's rules of the game contrast with some of the efforts to develop codes of good corporate governance; we also see, however, that the list of informal rules of the game in practice may still describe the situation as it really is in boardrooms.

Table 7.1 *'Rules of the game'*

Article I Inside the boardroom
- No fighting
- Support your CEO
- Serve your apprenticeship
- No crusades
- Do your homework
- Participate

Article II Understand why you are here
- We are here to give counsel, make judgements and oversee the commitment of corporate resources
- We are responsible for assessing and, if necessary, replacing top management
- We don't manage the company
- We don't set the strategy
- We are responsible for assuring the long-term survival of the firm
- We cannot abdicate our responsibilities
- Officially, we are here to act in the shareholders' interests

Article III Outside the boardroom
- Keep your distance from subordinate company executives
- Be prepared to discuss matters individually with the CEO
- Don't talk about company business with others
- Watch for straws in the wind
- Watch for talent

Article IV Assessing board invitations
- Join a winner: you are what your board (and its company) is
- Try to stay close to home
- Decline or resign officially only for reasons of overload
- Trade up slowly and unobtrusively
- Officially, deprecate the personal significance of your director's fee

Article V Getting new blood
- Prime beef = CEOs of other companies (big and rich is best)
- Try to add lustre to the board
- We should try to add a woman or a minority-group member to the board, but only if they are 'truly qualified'
- Look hard at lawyers, investment bankers and consultants before inviting them onto the board
- No crusaders

Article VI Assessing the CEO
- He should have a plan for making the company bigger and richer
- He should heed our counsel
- He should have outstanding subordinates
- He should not surprise us
- He should tell us everything

Article VII Disposing of the CEO
- Don't rush
- Make sure you have overwhelming director support
- Don't wait too long

Source: Whisler 1984.

Rules reduce ambiguity and provide a set of acceptable solutions, and rules contain both cognitive and political factors. A primary source of rules is the organisation's historical experience. Rules may be seen as history-dependent, socially constructed techniques applied in the enactment and reproduction of social structure.[16] They include both the formally codified standards and norms that structure conduct in organisations. Rules are given a concrete form in the policies, programmes, procedures, routines and conventions that form an organisation.[17] Rules contain the knowledge, capabilities, beliefs, values and memories of an organisation and its members.

Rules may channel political conflicts in organisations, and may serve as a form of political truce that temporarily suspends hostilities and conflicts. Rules are also tools that empower and control organisational practices. In the absence of rules political action may be organised, and the likelihood of decisions and actions being postponed or avoided will increase. Rules are, therefore, a source of organisational inertia and a guide for organisational practice and change.

The evolution of codes

A reliance on rules facilitates action by presenting board members with readily available solutions for organisational problems. Reliance on rules provides for accountability and reliability in organisational activities[18] and enhances the ability of board members to meet their fiduciary responsibilities. Corporate boards of directors are accountable for their actions and decisions. Reliance on the prevailing rules increases the board's ability to justify and defend its actions and decisions.

There has been rapid development of various codes of good corporate governance. These codes are sets of best-practice recommendations regarding the structure and behaviour of boards. They often contain sets of norms on the role of boards of directors, on relationships with shareholders and top management, on auditing and information disclosure, and on the selection, remuneration and dismissal of directors and top managers. Specific code recommendations vary across countries, but generally they rest on the principles of adequate disclosure and appropriate checks and balances in the governance structure. Codes are important when other mechanisms attempting to improve governance fail.

Main types of codes

Which problems do codes solve? Should there be the same codes for all kinds of firms – small as well as large – and all kinds of ownership? Should family firms and firms listed on stock exchanges have the same codes? Finally, codes adapted from international or US situations may be wrong when applied in other countries.

Authors and corporate governance definitions

Codes are devised for many purposes and by various actors – for example, stock exchanges, governments, directors' associations, managers' associations, professional associations and investors. Norms are not objective, often being the result of an ideological struggle. The objectives of the various actors may vary, but the development of codes across countries and actors still tends to converge. The convergence of codes seems to be driven by mimetic processes rather than by research or rational choices.[19]

The first recognised code of good corporate governance was presented in the late 1970s, and it was developed by the Business Roundtable in the United States. This code was a response in the early takeover movement to the trend of corporate criminal behaviour. The Business Roundtable is a management organisation in the United States, but in most countries it has been the stock exchange or investor groups that have formulated the first codes. Moreover, these codes have mostly been directed towards firms that are listed on the stock exchanges. Codes have been developed in countries under various legal systems, and many of the codes have been adopted elsewhere with only limited local or national adjustments. Very little scientific evidence exists regarding the appropriateness of codes adopted in various countries. Codes often contain quantifications without flexible solutions; often a clear focus is also missing, including the definition of value creation; there is also ambiguity about implementation.

Enforcement: comply or explain

Codes of best practice can be formal or informal, and some codes are general while others are specific. Some principles or standards are in many codes formulated as 'shoulds' while other standards are formulated as 'musts'. Codes are also enforced in different ways. *Comply or explain* is the enforcement standard mostly used in codes influenced by stock exchanges. Codes from stock exchanges most often require a section in the annual financial reports to be devoted to boards and corporate governance practices; divergences from the requirements in the codes have to be explained here.

Despite the voluntary nature of the early codes, they influenced firms in several ways – for example, through legitimacy or effectivity arguments. Compliance was important for the reputation of the firm, and the guidelines were expected to improve firm performance. However, various studies have shown that compliance tended to be with the letter of the 'law', not necessarily with its spirit.

Content of codes

The content of the codes has been evolving as societies have experienced practical challenges in relation to corporate governance. However, independence has remained a key concept in most codes over the years. The board and a majority of its board members are generally presumed to be independent. A variety of attributes or definitions of 'independence' have been used, however – for example, financial and psychological independence, independence from the management and independence from individual owners or stakeholders. To meet these independence criteria most codes include requirements about the insider/outsider ratio, the separation of the CEO and chairperson positions, the existence of independent board committees, and regular meetings without the presence of the CEO or inside directors.

Most codes also include paragraphs on transparency and accountability, and on regular board evaluations. Corporate governance sections in corporate annual financial reports are often mandatory, and in these sections the boards report how they meet the requirements in the codes. In some codes there exist very specific requirements about what has to be reported. These often also include a stakeholder policy and information about the competency and demographics of individual board members. Disclosure requirements for the remuneration of board members and corporate management may also be included in the codes.

Some codes also have sections dealing with the boards' working style. These most often cover areas such as CEO working descriptions, board instructions, the introduction of new board members, etc.

Some influential codes or laws

The Sarbanes–Oxley Act

The Sarbanes–Oxley Act was introduced in the United States in 2002. It was, esentially, a result of political expedience and uneasy compromise following the scandals in corporations such as Enron, Tyco, etc., and contained few of the ingredients of considered public policy.[20] Nonetheless, its introduction was the largest incursion ever of state control into corporate governance. Previously, public policy on corporate governance in the United States had mainly been referred to in state laws, with the consequence that most large firms were incorporated in Delaware. However, the Sarbanes–Oxley Act does not penetrate to the heart of corporate governance but just 'nibbles at it around the edges'. Its main practical content concerns auditors, disclosure and the protection of whistle-blowers.[21]

The NYSE Code

Stock exchanges have had a major impact on corporate governance regulations and codes. This has particularly been the case in countries such as the United States, which has limited state-level regulations. The New York Stock Exchange (NYSE) has been one of the main actors. A major development took place in 1978, when it was required that all listed companies should have an audit committee made up of a majority of outside directors. The immediate consequence was that listed companies needed to have at least two outside directors. The outsider/insider ratio of the listed firms increased gradually from 1978, and after the corporate scandals in 2002 a new listing standard was introduced, with the requirement that listed companies should have a majority of independent outside directors. Listed firms had two years to comply with this standard.[22]

The Higgs Report and the Combined Code

In the United Kingdom the Higgs Report on the role and effectiveness of non-executive directors was presented in 2003, with the intention of preventing the emergence of major corporate governance failures in the country. The Higgs Report was a follow-up to earlier British codes, such as the Cadbury Report (1992),[23] the Greenbury Report (1995),[24] the Hempel Report (1998)[25] and the Turnbull Report (1999).[26] The Higgs Report was predicated on behavioural perspectives and the dynamics of actual board behaviour to a greater extent than most other codes. The Combined Code, as presented in the final Higgs Report, included such requirements as about 50 per cent of non-executive directors having to be independent, the absolute separation of the chief executive and the board chairperson positions, an enhanced role for the senior independent director (both within the board and in relation to shareholders) and the specification of a normal term of six years for non-executive directors. These were all traditional structural requirements, intended to promote the boards' control tasks. However, the Higgs Report also had an innovative focus on board relationships and behaviours, as it contained provision for evaluating the balance of skills, knowledge and experience of the board.[27]

The Higgs review also summarised the responsibilities of the board chairperson. These include:

- leading the board, ensuring its effectiveness on all aspects of this role and setting its agenda;
- ensuring the provision of accurate, timely and clear information to directors;
- ensuring effective communication with shareholders;
- arranging the regular evaluation of the performance of the board, its committees and individual directors; and
- facilitating the effective contribution of non-executive directors and ensuring constructive relations between executive and non-executive directors.[28]

Codes in continental Europe

Among influential codes in continental Europe we have the Tabaksblat Code in the Netherlands, the Cromme Code in Germany and the Viénot codes in France.

The Tabaksblat Code, dating from 2003, clearly states that the starting point for a company is a long-term form of collaboration between the various parties involved.[29] A two-tier board system exists in the Netherlands, and both the management board and the supervisory board have overall responsibility for weighing up the interests of a broad set of stakeholders, generally with a view to ensuring the continuity of the company.

The German Corporate Governance Code (the Cromme Code) was amended in May 2003, originally having been introduced by a governmental commission.[30] A two-tier board system exists in Germany. This code aims to make the German corporate governance system transparent and understandable; its purpose is to promote trust. In the code it is stressed that good corporate governance requires open discussion between the management board and the supervisory board. The code contains principles about the following: one share, one vote; no more than two former members of the management board are to be members of the supervisory board; supervisory board members are not to exercise directorships (or similar positions) or advisory tasks for major competitors of the enterprise; members of the management board of a listed company are not to accept more than a total of five supervisory board mandates in non-group companies; the election or re-election of members of the supervisory board at different dates and for different periods of office is required so as to enable changing requirements to be taken into account; and supervisory board members are to receive fixed as well as performance-related compensation. Performance-related compensation should contain a long-term component. If a member of the supervisory board takes part in less than half the meetings of the supervisory board in a financial year, this is to be noted in the report of the supervisory board.

Corporate governance in France has been influenced by the Viénot Reports and the Bouton Report.[31] In France there is the freedom to choose between a one-tier or a two-tier board system, but most principles in the codes refer to the one-tier system. The French codes are more specific on regular board evaluations than many other codes.

The OECD principles

The OECD principles of corporate governance were first endorsed in 1999 by the OECD ministers.[32] It has since become a benchmark for policy-makers, investors, corporations and other stakeholders worldwide. The OECD guidelines emphasise the need to adapt corporate governance principles to the legislation and culture in each country.

Board structures

'There should be a clear division of responsibilities at the head of the company between the running of the board and the executive responsibility for running the company's business. No one individual should have unfettered powers of decision.'[33] Most corporate governance codes have sections relating to board structures. These sections include suggestions or requirements not just about the relationships between the CEO and the board but also about the relationships between the board members, and the boards' relations to the external actors.

Among important issues in the discussion on board structures we find the questions of CEO duality, board committees, the CEO work description, board instructions and various board maintenance activities.

CEO *duality and independent chairs*

CEO duality is a question that is raised in relation to board composition, board structures and board leadership structures.[34] CEO duality is one of the four 'usual suspects' in research into boards of directors.[35] There is a strong sentiment among board reform advocates for the need to separate the positions of the CEO and the chairperson. This separation, largely grounded in agency theory, is to do with concerns over the managerial dominance of the board.[36] However, supporters of stewardship theory argue that corporations benefit from CEO duality and a unified leadership.[37] Unified leadership removes internal and external ambiguity about who is responsible for firm processes and outcomes.

In the United States and United Kingdom the separation of the roles of CEO and chairperson has probably been the most debated issue about corporate governance reforms – as we have seen above. But this separation of roles is already compulsory in the European two-tier governance systems. The US corporate governance activists Paul MacAvoy and Ira Millstein hold that this separation has to be an imperative in corporate governance reforms. They argue that boards will not be knowledgeable, aware or active when there is CEO duality. 'It is contrary to human nature to expect total objectivity from the CEO regarding his or her performance relative to strategies he or she has helped formulate.'[38] The chairperson should be independent in order to ensure the impartial provision of information that is necessary to gain an informed insight. Part of the board leadership role is that of setting the board agenda, and the chairperson has to be the agent for the board in setting the agenda and obtaining the necessary information about CEO performance and the implementation of decisions regarding corporate strategies.

Empirically, based on a large-scale meta-analysis of the relationship between CEO duality and corporate financial performance, Dalton,

Daily, Ellstrand and Johnson did not make any findings that support CEO duality or the separation of the roles.[39]

Committees

In most codes it is suggested or required that various committees should be established, responsible for carrying out in-depth analyses of specific business-related activities for the full board. Generally, three committees are specified. These are the audit committee, the nomination committee and the remuneration committee, but recommendations for additional committees may also be found. However, the call for the establishment of committees is mostly targeted at large corporations.

The committees suggested in an Anglo-American framework are board committees, and the committee members are often elected from amongst the board members. However, in some other countries, such as the Scandinavian countries,[40] the committees suggested may be committees reporting to the annual shareholders' meeting rather than to the board. The composition and mandate of these committees will thus vary from the board committees even though their titles will be similar.

Audit or control committees

The codes recommend that audit committees should have a clear relationship with the board.[41] The audit committee should be in regular communication with the external auditors, and at least once a year it should have a formal meeting with the external auditors without the CEO or executives being present.

The audit committee should have explicit authority to investigate matters within its term of reference, and have all the resources that it needs to do so, with full access to all necessary information. The committee should be able to obtain external professional advice and to invite outsiders with relevant experience to attend if necessary.

The primary tasks of the audit committee will be to:

- understand the corporation's risk profile and oversee the corporation's risk assessment and management practices;
- understand and have familiarity with the corporation's internal control systems; and
- review the corporation's procedures for addressing compliance with the law and important corporate policies, including the corporation's code of conduct and board decisions.[42]

Nomination committees

Nomination committees are also recommended in most codes of best practice, which should lead the process for board appointments and make recommendations to the board. A nomination committee should have a majority of non-executive directors,[43] but the board chairperson should normally lead the nomination committee.[44]

There should be a formal, rigorous and transparent procedure for the appointment of new board members.[45] Appointments should be made on merit and against objective criteria. The board should satisfy itself that plans are in place for the orderly succession of appointments to the board.

The nomination committee should evaluate the balance of skills, knowledge and experience on the board and, in light of this evaluation, prepare a description of the role and capabilities required for a particular appointment. For the nomination of a chairperson, the nomination committee should prepare a job specification. It is also recommended in the Combined Code that no individual should be appointed to the chairmanship of a second FTSE 100 company.[46] A separate section in the annual report should describe the work of the nomination committee.

Remuneration committees

A remuneration or compensation committee should look at the overall compensation structure of the corporation to determine if it establishes appropriate incentives for management and employees at all levels.[47] The Higgs Report suggests that the remuneration committee should consist exclusively of independent non-executive directors.[48] The committee should determine and agree with the board a framework (or board policy) for the remuneration of the CEO, the board chairperson and other members of the executive management that it is authorised to consider. It is suggested that the remuneration of the non-executive directors should be a matter for the chairperson and the executive members of the board.

In recent years many corporations have moved towards remunerating directors and management with stock options and other equity compensation geared to the corporation's share price. This trend may align the interests of the board members and the management with the interests of the shareholder. However, equity compensation should be carefully designed to avoid unintended incentives, such as an emphasis on short-term market value changes.[49]

CEO *work description*

The recommendation of a CEO work description has its roots in agency theory. A CEO work description generally states that the CEO and senior management run the corporation's day-to-day business activities. It is generally the responsibility of the CEO and the senior management to operate the corporation in an effective and ethical manner. In a two-tier board system, the responsibilities of the CEO will often be that of the executive board.

A CEO work description will clarify the charges of the CEO, and it will also clarify *when* and in relation to *which questions* the CEO shall put decisions before the board. Issues that are of major importance or that are outside the main business of a firm are usually dealt with by the board, and a CEO working description will often specify what is within the mandate of the CEO.

A CEO work description will also include sections on cooperation with the board and which items should be prepared and presented before the board – including how and when they should be prepared. Such items may include strategic planning, annual operating plans and budgets, the selection of qualified management and the establishment of an effective organisational structure, the identification of managerial risks, and good financial reporting.

A formal CEO board work description is compulsory in some countries, and it is recommended in several of the codes. The CEO work description is a main element in what is called *reserved power*. If the board has reserved power this means it makes formal statements about *delegated power* to the CEO. Reserved power defines the thresholds of decision that are delegated to the CEO on a number of key issues. Reserved power statements impose constraints on managerial actions.

Board *instructions*

A key argument in favour of board instructions is that they empower the board in relation to the management. Board instructions provide predictability, and the informal rules of the game provided by board instructions become either visible or challenged. A main objective for some board instructions is to incorporate minorities and newcomers into the actual work of the board. This is illustrated in Sweden and Norway, where firm-specific board instructions are compulsory in firms that have employee-elected board members. Various codes of best practice also require that the firm-specific board instructions are to be communicated in the corporate annual reports, with the intention that shareholders and other stakeholders thereby gain an internal benchmark of how the board in the particular firm is supposed to work.

Board instructions not only include lists that detail the tasks of the board but also describe thoroughly how the board is to meet its tasks. Such instructions are made at national level in corporate laws, but codes of best practice made by various stakeholder groups may, as we have seen, present firm-specific board instructions. Here I emphasise the board instructions developed in each firm to formalise and disseminate the firm's internal rules of the game.

In Sweden the board's statutory instructions include its formal work plan, instructions to the CEO and various reporting instructions. They serve as guiding documents for the board's work, and at least once a year the board must review the relevance and currency of these instructions.[50]

The board instructions may be very firm-specific, and can also be a working document that serves to help the board in improving its own performance. The document ensures that all board members are aware of the proceedings of the board, the agenda setting, meeting arenas and meeting forms.

In some codes a corporate governance committee is recommended,[51] and the mandate of such a committee includes developing and maintaining board and corporate governance instructions. Also included is the responsibility of board evaluations and external corporate governance reporting. Some codes also recommend a work description for the tasks of the board chairperson. There is a degree of overlap between the responsibilities of the corporate governance committee and the work description of the chairperson. The appointment of a deputy chairperson is also often recommended.

Board meeting structures

Board meeting structures describe the required number of meetings, the length of meetings, structures within the meetings, participation in meetings, etc. 'Away days' and meetings without the participation of executives are among the suggestions in various codes.

The number of board meetings varies across countries and in line with such contextual variables as firm size. The number of board meetings tends to be higher in times of crises than in normal situations. The length of the meetings is considered to be one of the main constraints for board power. Jay Lorsch and Elisabeth MacIver have found that lack of time at meetings is the major constraint for board contributions.[52] Longer meetings may permit the board members to discuss and explore key issues in depth, while more frequent meetings may help directors stay up to date on emerging corporate trends. Board meetings must, in general, permit sufficient time for discussion and a healthy 'give and take' between the board members and the management.[53] There should be enough meeting time for key strategy and governance issues to be discussed properly.[54]

Boards should have a formal schedule of matters specifically reserved for the board members to decide on collectively. A schedule of these matters should be given to the board members on appointment and should be kept up to date. The non-executive directors should also have the opportunity to meet without the CEO or other corporate executives being present.[55] Boards are recommended to have a thorough evaluation of the CEO and his or her performance at least once a year. This evaluation should take place without the CEO being present.

Various facilitating structures designed to involve board members are suggested by various authors.[56] These may include:
- 'away days' or 'two-day' meetings;
- informal dialogue between board members between board meetings;
- informal dialogue between board members and executives between board meetings;
- more time spent at board meetings;
- strategy on the agenda rather than routine items;
- structures to revisit issues so that they can be resolved via an iterative process over time;
- processes of information sharing, challenge and open debate;
- presentations of executives; and
- shades of opinions among executives to be revealed.

The idea of 'away days' is one mechanism that includes many of these facilitating structures. They may help the board members to get to know one another and thus also develop cohesion, they may provide the ability to explore and use knowledge and competencies from other boards and they may be a way for board members to gain more firm-specific knowledge. 'Away days' may provide for informal dialogue between the board members, and also between board members and the executives.

Notice, information, minutes and voting

Various recommendations are made to ensure that board members receive sufficient information for their decision-making. This is emphasised in, for example, the Cadbury Code – as well as in various other influential codes. Boards should meet regularly and receive due notice of the issues to be discussed, supported by the necessary paperwork.[57] When arranging a meeting schedule for the board, each corporation should consider its nature and the complexity of its operation.

The board should be supplied in a timely manner with information in a form and of a quality sufficient to enable it to discharge its duties.[58] Boards should not take decisions on important matters that have not been placed on the agenda. In some codes it is recommended that the people responsible for a particular business should be present at the meetings, and anyone who is indispensable for answering questions in greater depth should also be on hand.[59]

The Swedish codes include specifications regarding the board minutes.[60] They have to make a clear presentation of the matters discussed, and should include the supporting material available for each item and the details of the decisions taken. The minutes are to be sent to the directors as soon as possible after the board meeting.

The board instruction may also contain directions about voting at board meetings. The main questions include which and how many members need to be present as well as the voting order, including trial voting and whether the chairperson has a double vote.

Ethics and whistle-blowing

It is suggested that ethics codes and rules about whistle-blowing should be included in board structures. The OECD principles state that boards should apply high ethical standards, and they should take into account the interests of stakeholders.[61] A code for the handling of confidential information should be included in the board instructions.[62]

Conflicts of interest may be a major issue for some boards, and directions for how to deal with them are also included in some board charters or instructions. The board should be informed if any of the board members see a conflict of interest arising, and it is recommended that the board – without the board member(s) in question being present – should decide how this person(s) should be involved in the decision-making in the actual case.[63] Insider trading and abusive self-dealing should be prohibited.

Stakeholders, including individual employees and their representative bodies, should be able to communicate their concerns about illegal or unethical practices freely to the board, and their rights should not be compromised for doing this.[64] A corporation should have a code of conduct outlining effective reporting and enforcement mechanisms.[65] Employees should have a means of alerting the board to potential misconduct without fear of negative repercussions.

The Enron case emphasised the need for there to be formalised ways for employees to have direct communication with board members without passing over the CEO (if only to reassure the CEO that he is not being passed over!). Generally, it is recommended that the CEO should be advised of significant contacts between board members and senior management.

Board maintenance mechanisms

Procedures to educate and integrate new directors rapidly are considered to be important for developing effective boards. Board maintenance mechanisms include board and board member education, the introduction of new board members, board evaluation, etc.

Board education

It may take time for board members to define a value-added role for the board itself, but, as the highest authority in the corporate structure, the board is responsible for its own job specification, including the boardroom culture. The Cadbury Code emphasises the role of board members' training in this regard and articulates their role as follows: 'The weight of responsibility borne by all directors and the increasing commitment which their duties require emphasise the importance of the manner in which they prepare themselves for their posts. Given the varying backgrounds, qualifications and experience of directors, it is highly desirable that they should all undertake some form of internal or external training; this is particularly important for directors . . . with no earlier board experience.'[66]

The chairperson should ensure that the directors continually update their skills and knowledge, as well as their familiarity, with the company in order to fulfil successfully the board members' tasks – both on the board and on board committees. The company should provide the necessary resources for developing and updating its directors' knowledge and skills.[67]

Introduction of new members

Orientation to a new job is important for optimal performance. However, the orientation of new members has been missing on most boards. Traditionally, it has been assumed that whoever becomes a board member will know what the role is about and what he or she has to do. Increasingly, however, boards are realising the value of introducing new board members to the firm and the board, including the boardroom culture.

Newly appointed board members should be entitled to expect a proper process of induction into the company's affairs. 'It is then up to the individual directors to keep abreast of their legislative and broader responsibilities.'[68] The chairperson should ensure that new board members receive a full, formal and tailored induction on joining the board.[69]

The Higgs Report includes an induction checklist.[70] It suggests as a general rule that a combination of selected written information, together with presentations and activities such as meetings and site visits, will help to give a new appointee a balanced and realistic overview of the company. The induction process should build an understanding of the nature of the company, its lines of business and the markets in which it operates. It should also build a link with the company's employees, including meetings with senior management, visits to company sites other than the headquarters to learn about products and services, and meeting people in an informal way. The induction programme should also build an understanding of the company's main relationships, including meetings with auditors and developing a knowledge of, in particular, who the major customers, supplier, shareholders, etc. are.

Board evaluations

Board evaluations are among the mechanisms now receiving increasing attention in the corporate community. MacAvoy and Millstein make some additional proposals for improving corporate governance.[71] These proposals include the requirements that board members must be familiar with the information systems that the CEO relies on, formal and regular evaluations of management performance must be made by the board, boards should assure themselves about the integrity of the management, and boards should establish procedures to familiarise themselves with alternative strategies and innovative products, and structure their meetings so that issues central to the performance of the company are given sufficient time for the board to consider options, and not just listen to reports.

Various suggestions have been made with respect to the objectives and various forms of board evaluations. Externally related objectives are related to transparency. Internally related objectives are related to developing the internal effectiveness of the board by assessing the way in which the board operates, by checking that the important issues are suitably prepared and discussed, and by measuring the actual contribution of each director to the board's work through his or her competence and involvement in discussions.

The board should undertake a formal and rigorous annual evaluation of its own performance and that of its committees and individual directors.[72] The French corporate governance codes contain a separate paragraph on board evaluations.[73] 'For good corporate governance, the board of directors should evaluate the board's ability to meet the expectations of the shareholders having entrusted authority to it to direct the corporation by reviewing from time to time its membership, organisation and operation (which implies a corresponding review of board committees).' Accordingly, each board should think about what the desirable balance is for its membership. The board of directors should also from time to time consider the adequacy of its organisation and operation for the optimum performance of its tasks.

The form of board evaluation may vary, but in most codes it is recommended that the evaluation should be formal and regular, taking place at least once a year. There also exist suggestions about how evaluations should be performed and which agents should conduct them. Board evaluations may, for example, be implemented under the leadership of an independent director, with help from an external consultant. The shareholders should be informed each year in the annual report of the evaluations carried out, and of any steps taken as a result. The internal rules of operation of the board of directors could provide for a meeting once a year, at which time the evaluation of the chairman's and chief executive officer's respective performance would be carried out and the participants could reflect on the future of the company's executive management.

In the Combined Code it is suggested that it should be recorded in the corporate annual report how performance evaluation of the board, its committees and its members has been conducted.[74]

'Two-day' meetings and annual retreats or 'away days'

'Two-day' meetings or 'away days' enable the board members to build relationships away from the formal setting of the boardroom. 'Away days' should take place at least once a year, but various successful companies follow the practice of having several 'away days' per year. Some firms even try to have the setting of 'away days' for all board meetings.

'Away days' may provide good opportunities for board development and education, board evaluation, visiting sites away from the headquarters, strategy discussions or various other topics needing more in-depth discussions. 'Away days' may also be a good way for new board members to get to know the firm and the other board members.

In addition to in-depth formal discussion on topics given priority, such 'away days' or retreats will often be important for the boardroom culture and how board members work together. The board members will meet each other, relate to each other and get to know each other. 'Away days' promote long and comprehensive discussions, positive social interactions and relationship-building activities outside the boardroom, and ensure that the board members stay together at least for a certain period of time.

Board leadership

Various codes have recently included warnings that board leadership should be more than a 'box-ticking' activity, stating that it should go beyond checking compliance with various codes and requirements. In my interview with women directors in the 'board life story' study some of the women came forward with the following and similar comments:

I have never experienced good chairpersons. A good chairperson helps all board members into the discussion and utilises all the resources that exist in the board. All board chairpersons I have experienced have been men.

That of letting people be able to say what's on their mind, without letting the discussion slide. He stopped the debate when it was about to get away from the topic or repeat itself, and then drew conclusions based on his own directions. He used the phrases or formulations being used by others in the debate. If I for example used the phrase 'relevant problem' he would use the same phrase, but put in his own context. But still I felt that I had been heard – very astute. But he was also very raw. He was making conclusions – so that all felt that they had been heard; but later they appreciated that he had been following his own opinions. He had a lot of opinions himself.[75]

One of the women indicated that many chairpersons are not good at utilising the boards themselves as a resource, while another was fascinated by how the chairman manipulated the board when he formulated decisions.

In academic research the roles and tasks of the board chairperson have, so far, received very limited attention. Discussions regarding chairpersons have mainly been about CEO duality and chair independence, ownership and compensation, chair age and tenure, full- or part-time positions and whether the chairperson used to be the CEO.

Board leadership structure and CEO duality

CEO duality, as has already been mentioned, is a measure of board leadership structure; it is the term used when the CEO is also the chairperson. According to agency theory predictions, CEO duality promotes entrenchment by reducing board monitoring effectiveness. CEO duality is not allowed in most systems, where a separation between executive tasks and board tasks is compulsory. This is the case in the continental European two-tier board systems, and in the Scandinavian systems. A separation of the CEO and chairperson positions is also one of the requirements to be found in most corporate governance codes. The existence of CEO duality is consequently disappearing rapidly in the United Kingdom, but in the United States there are still many who argue in favour of it, the importance of unity of command being the main factor they single out. In research, this argument is supported by promoters of stewardship theory.

CEO duality has also been among the most used concepts or variables in research into boards and governance, and it is among the concepts often labelled the 'usual suspects'. Despite the large number of studies that have been conducted using CEO duality as a concept, no clear correlations have been found between the existence of CEO duality and firm financial performance.[76]

A question related to CEO duality is that of whether the chairperson position should be full-time or part-time. A full-time non-executive board chairperson is increasingly to be found in large UK corporations. The ongoing discussion in the United Kingdom is thus also about whether the full-time board chairperson is independent from the CEO. Corporate governance guidelines in the United Kingdom, including the Higgs Report of 2003,[77] include recommendations about having outside directors, separate from the CEO and the chair, who can lead the outside board members in meetings when independence is of particular importance. Another recommendation found in other countries is that the full-time board chairperson should have his or her office located away from the offices of the corporate executive leadership.

A main reason for the board to have a leader separate from and independent of the CEO is that it needs a leader whose primary task is to help the entire board in formulating and carrying out its tasks. The ideal board will consist of individuals with different specific attributes, experience and expertise. The directors are, typically, outsiders with constraints on their time and resources that make it harder for them to obtain the inside knowledge needed to perform their tasks. 'One member of the board, independent of the CEO, should therefore have the primary responsibility of and devote the time necessary to getting the other directors informed by helping them focus on the issues that are important to the shareholders, and on the risks facing the corporation.'[78] The leadership tasks in a board will therefore include coordination, integration, communication and moulding a group of individuals into a good working team.

Leadership roles and style

Few boards have clear expectations about the roles of a board chair, and few evaluate the effectiveness of their chairperson.[79] Board chairpersons range from effective to neglectful, from domineering to self-serving. Chairs consciously or unconsciously perform various tasks, and they have a variety of leadership styles. The chair's leadership behaviour affects the board's effectiveness, because the board is a social system that contains a mix of personalities and relationships.[80] These relationships extend beyond the boardroom and the board members.

It is the task of the chair to provide effective board leadership, and thus also to be a team leader and to ensure that the characteristics of an effective team are present. This includes the board culture; the board culture provides the context in which the board functions.

The board chair sets the tone for much more than board meetings. The chair orchestrates board self-development and evaluations. An engaged chair leads to an engaged board.

Chair or leader

Richard and Lana Furr use the following taxonomy of personality types among board chairpersons:[81]

- the pliant chairperson;[82]
- the 'my way' chairperson;
- the 'in the weeds' detail chairperson;
- the 'no leadership ability or interest' chairperson;
- the self-serving chairperson; and
- the procrastinating chairperson.

There are many combinations of the various personality types. The pliant chairperson is a supporter or a pleaser who does not have any mind of his or her own. This person is constantly trying to find the position of the people on the board whom he or she feels the most drawn towards or whom he or she is committed to pleasing or supporting. The pliant chairperson can be tactful, gracious, humble, likeable and caring, but may let other board members dominate, visibly or indirectly, through backroom conversations. The 'my way' chairperson may ask for others' views, but only one answer is acceptable. This is often communicated in a pleasant and tactful manner, rather than a bullying, argumentative or emotional way. If it had been done in a less tactful way the board members would not have been willing to remain with the board. The 'in the weeds' detail chairperson may be great at details. This may be important at a functional level, but not for a board chairperson at the strategic level. The details may be very time-consuming, and overlap with the tasks of the executives, and meetings may be very boring to visionary, strategic thinkers.

The chairperson with no leadership ability or interest may be good technically – creative, an engineer, a computer guru, a financial wizard – whose love and gift is in dealing with the product. He or she may even be one of the founders of the company. Boards with such chairpersons will essentially be leaderless and not well managed in terms of good governance. The self-serving chairperson is the person who primarily seeks to meet his or her own needs. The procrastinating chairperson is indecisive and unwilling to commit to a path forward until the last minute. Items for discussion may often be postponed.

In the board literature, various leadership roles are defined. Among the various roles we find chair, coach, mentor, integrator, mediator, negotiator, figurehead, entrepreneur, strategist, supporter, etc. However, in the leadership literature a leader is often defined as someone who creates conditions that enlist and focus the talent and energy of others towards a common purpose, vision and set of goals. This differs from the perceptions of a board chairperson who mainly ratifies the agenda of board meetings, chairs the discussions in the boardroom and makes sure that decisions are formulated and ratified. This chairperson definition does not adequately take into account the human side of boards and governance. A more in-depth discussion and investigation of the various roles and tasks of the board chairperson is needed.

A good board chairperson is a coach.[83] A good coach works to derive satisfaction through the achievement of others. The role of a chairperson will be to support both the CEO and the other board members.[84] The chairperson should support the CEO in setting the board's agenda and managing the information flow to the board. Board chairpersons should also support the effectiveness of the board as a whole, and bring out the potential that is in the board as a team.

Mentoring new board members is another critical aspect of the responsibilities of the chairperson. He or she should provide them with the counsel needed to become active, productive contributors as speedily as possible. It is a task of the chairperson to meld the board into a cohesive group, and to make each individual director feel that he or she is equal. As a team leader the board chairperson should be able to build consensus. The board chairperson or a lead director cannot command, issue instructions or deliver mandates.[85] The chairperson must never forget that the people on the board are his or her peers, each with valuable insights and talents to contribute. The board chairperson assumes additional responsibilities, not greater authority.

As a figurehead and role model, the chairperson must possess a level of personal integrity that instils trust in others. Peers expect exchanges with the chairperson to be confidential and that the information will be used constructively.

The chair's role is to act as a mediator, creating continuous, honest communication between the CEO and the board members. The communication part of this role also includes the ability to read the silent communication and the body language of the board members. The chair should maintain communication with both internal and external actors.

Leader attributes and style

Some surveys have been conducted to explore the attributes of the board chairperson. Good board chairpersons share a number of core qualities and experiences.[86]

- An impressive track record and a wide network of contacts.
- Experience as an executive and a non-executive director.
- Personal presence and high standards of personal integrity.
- Intelligence and the ability to think strategically.

The effective chairperson upholds the highest standards of integrity and probity.[87] A good board chairperson will be a role model who lives by the core values of the company. Chairpersons are expected to give clear directions for adherence to the company's ethics. This means encouraging the right behaviour both inside and outside the boardroom.

There are, however, several factors that make good chairpersons stand out from the rest. A good chairperson works well with the CEO, achieves openness and transparency at board meetings, continuously improves board performance and has an open leadership style. A good chairperson counsels and challenges the CEO in a collaborative rather than confrontational way. A good chairperson has interpersonal and leadership skills and the ability to communicate effectively. Empathy and self-awareness are more and more critical; arrogance is a debilitating barrier. Great chairpersons demonstrate leadership that inspires and excites enthusiasm.

Leadership during meetings

In an article in *The Corporate Board*, Susan Bloch describes what makes a great board chairperson.[88] A great chairperson creates a climate where everyone contributes. An outcome of good board leadership can be openness and interactions between board members – a climate of transparency and trust.[89] Humour and generosity are key qualities. The best chairpersons are listeners who are sensitive to the dynamics of the meeting. They help present the choices to the board and ask the board to make decisions, reserving their own opinions until they summarise and help draw conclusions from the discussion. A bad chairperson interferes and seeks to dominate the proceedings: a good chairperson enquires and involves, seeking to build a strong board that can deliver optimum performance, and making sure that everyone contributes for the benefit of the whole.

The board chairperson is responsible for the agenda, and a great chairperson will run a flexible process.[90] This means that the board addresses the right work, in the right way and at the right time. The chairperson is responsible for managing the board to ensure that sufficient time is allowed for discussions of complex and ongoing issues. Board processes must allow for robust levels of discussion with contribution from all directors. The effective chairperson encourages active engagement by all the members of the board. Setting the agenda is not only a matter of getting papers distributed on time; the chairperson must also ensure that there is a good debate, that options are presented and that the fundamental assumptions are tested. Setting the agenda also includes setting the style and tone of board discussions so as to promote effective decision-making and constructive debate.

A good chairperson will know the skills, abilities and the personalities of the other board members. He or she needs to be sensitive to all people attending the meeting. A good chairperson will also know the history of the board; he or she will remind the board of its past decisions and commitments, to avoid backtracking and 'reinventing the wheel'.[91]

Leadership between meetings

The chairperson will also be involved between the meetings. A chairman once told me that, before every meeting, he set aside time to think through how each and every board member could be encouraged to participate during the meeting, how they would react and how he should respond to them.[92] Good chairpersons will prepare for the role, and they will do their best with the boards they inherit. They will also seek to improve the quality of the board by getting the mix of experience, skills and personalities to meet the needs of the company. The chairperson will be very sensitive to encouraging board members to retire at the appropriate time and in the search for new members. The best teams will need the best players, and a chairperson should therefore ensure that the best players are on board. A good chairperson should also evaluate his or her own position. At different times in a company's life it needs different things from its board and the chairperson; a chairperson should therefore also recognise when it is time to withdraw.

A good board chairperson ensures effective communication with shareholders and ensures that the members of the board develop an understanding of the view of major investors.[93] Good chairpersons will have communication with internal and external actors such as employees, shareholders, politicians, journalists, etc. They must also work well with the CEOs to create a no-surprise environment.[94]

Good chairpersons will prepare for the role. They will do this by familiarising themselves with their duties and obligations, doing the organisational homework, performing independent investigations and enquiries and communicating with the CEO and key stakeholders. Chairpersons may also benefit from thinking through each meeting thoroughly beforehand, and anticipating alternative input and reactions from the various board members.

The case of board evaluations

In this in-depth summarising case we present a system for board evaluation.[95] It is often argued that it is necessary with an evaluation of the accountability and knowledge of board members to maximise the boards' value-creating potential.[96] However, empirical studies have shown that board evaluations are far from common practice, and the process of evaluating the whole board is even rarer than that of evaluating individual board members. A board evaluation process can in this respect be helpful for defining how various board tasks contribute to value creation, and to balance and meet the interest of the firm's various stakeholders.

Before starting a board evaluation process four questions should be asked: who, what, for whom and how? A board evaluation system will consist of these four elements:

Table 7.2 *Board evaluation systems*

EVALUATOR

	Board-to-board evaluation	Board-to-market evaluation

Self-evaluation
 	
Board
  committees
 	
Consultants
	Objectives:
	  effectiveness
	  improving behaviour
		Objectives:
		  self-legitimising
		  meeting legal requirements

Researchers
 	
External
  agents
	Market-to-board evaluation
	
	Objectives:
	  legitimating evaluation
	  practice effectiveness
		Market-to-market evaluation
		
		Objectives:
		  accountability control
		  reputation-building

ADDRESSEE   Self-development   Academic, research   Owners, investors, etc.
                Internal board committees   External board committees

- the agents performing the evaluation (self-evaluation, consultants, etc.);
- the issues being evaluated (accountability, knowledge, etc.);
- the addressees or the stakeholders behind the evaluation (internal stakeholders, external stakeholders, the board itself, etc.); and
- the way the evaluation is performed (schemes, interviews, observations, etc.).

Together, these four elements will help meet the purpose of an evaluation. In table 7.2 we illustrate the main elements of this board evaluation system.

The addressees or the stakeholders are presented on the horizontal axis, and the agents of the evaluation are presented on the vertical axis. The board-to-market evaluation has now become compulsory through various codes of best practice under the heading 'comply or explain'. To a large extent it is a self-legitimising approach. A key function of the market-to-market evaluation is transparency to meet accountability requirements. The main objectives for market-to-board and board-to-board evaluations are creating accountability and effectiveness. This is done through the securing and development of the knowledge and skills of the board members. It is the responsibility of the individual directors to use their knowledge and skills to create accountability.

This may be promoted through a board-to-board evaluation; however, a market-to-board evaluation will be of more help in evaluating the knowledge and skills of the board members than a board-to-board evaluation.

Board task expectations are – as shown above – developed from various theories, including agency theory, stakeholder theory, resource dependence theory and resource-based theory. Different expectations may exist among various stakeholders, including various groups of shareholders. The board will need to balance these expectations. Board task performance is, in reality, the tasks the board is already performing. Creating board accountability will be consist of aligning actual board task performance with board task expectations. Various interactions, the knowledge and attributes of the board members, the board structures and norms, and the board decision-making culture may all hinder or secure this alignment. The creation of accountability will include the tasks of selecting, motivating and developing board members and the decision-making culture through board leadership and structures.

A major contribution of board evaluations is to structure the inner working of boards in order to align the knowledge and competency of the outside board members with the various parts of the value chain.

Summary

The main concepts addressed in this chapter have been symbolic management, institutional action theory, formal and informal rules, codes (developed by various types of actors and in different countries), norms, structures and leadership (roles, styles and attributes). Included in board structures are concepts such as committees (audit, nomination and remuneration), CEO duality, the CEO work description, board instructions, board evaluations and 'away days'.

In this chapter I have presented a variety of ways and means to try to improve corporate governance. The chapter has been structured around the concepts of norms, rules, structures and leadership. Extensive efforts have been made in recent years to develop codes of best practice for corporate governance, to regulate the rules of the game in order to achieve some kind of accountability and reliability.

Codes of best corporate governance practices have been developed in many countries and by various national legislatures. Some of the codes have also achieved the status of national codes, but the under-lying ideologies are hardly discussed. Most of the codes have used a shareholder value perspective and applied agency theory, though the content of the codes varies.

In this chapter I have presented proposals about board structures and leadership, including:

- CEO duality and board composition;
- the existence, use and composition of committees;
- CEO work descriptions;
- board instructions, including board meeting structures, board infor-mation, ethics, etc.;
- board maintenance mechanisms, such as board education, new mem-ber introductions, board evaluations and 'away days'; and
- board leadership tasks.

The board structures are the rules of the game. They may be general or firm-specific, they may be formal or informal, and they may be rooted in different types of norms. Boards, board members and the management will have various kinds of incentives to follow the rules of the game. The board chairperson may also have an important role in defining and implementing these rules.

There may be some substitution effects between formal board struc-tures and board leadership, but it is also a task for the board chairper-son to make sure that proper structures exist. Furthermore, we have challenged the traditional role of the chairperson. The board chairper-son can be considered as a coach, whose role it is to bring out the potential of each board member and to meld the board into a cohesive group.

8 | *The decision-making culture*

The main concepts covered in this chapter are:
- criticality and independence;
- creativity;
- cohesiveness;
- openness and generosity;
- preparation and involvement;
- use of knowledge and skills;
- cognitive conflicts;
- groupthink and diversity;
- vicious and virtual dynamics; and
- process-oriented boardroom culture.

In this chapter I present the board decision-making culture. The decision-making culture is what characterises the board as a team or a work group. In the framework of this book the decision-making culture is presented as a mediator between the board members and board task performance.[1] The interactions and structures are mediating the relationship between the board members and the decision-making culture. In the framework figure at the start of this chapter I have included two additional arrows – one arrow from the board members and one arrow from structures to the other new arrow. These arrows illustrate not only that the individual board members may have a direct impact on the decision-making culture but also that both interactions and structures influence or moderate this relationship.

A shortcoming in many of the codes is that they do not see the human side of corporate governance, and thus a board is rarely seen as a team. The boardroom culture is rarely discussed. Boards are closed institutions, and few other than the board members themselves have witnessed boards in action. Richard Leblanc and James Gillies argue that, if the study of governance is to continue, there should be more focus and research on boards in action. 'Decision-making failure in

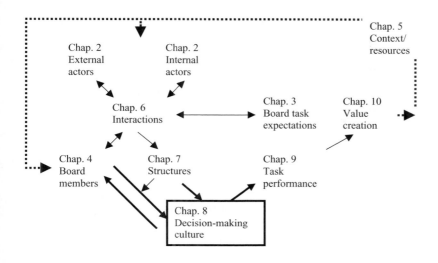

boardrooms has less to do with the lack of supposedly independent directors and more to do with the independence of mind, and the competencies and behaviours of the directors sitting around the board table. This includes how they are chosen, how they are led, how they work together, and how they retire from the board.'[2] The missing ingredient in understanding and researching boards of directors is the human side of governance.

In chapter 6 we explored some of the processes taking place between actors inside and outside the boardroom. In this chapter the focus is on how the board members are working like a team or a strategic decision-making group. In this chapter I present the board as a social system, and demonstrate that the outcomes of board efforts are a result of the board functioning as a high-output work group.

I start this chapter by presenting the board as a team. Aspects of team dynamics, including cognitive perspectives, are presented, followed by dimensions of the boardroom culture. Core concepts are:

• cognitive conflicts and diversity;
• criticality and independence;
• creativity;
• cohesiveness; and
• commitment.

The importance of preparations, involvement, openness and generosity are emphasised in particular.

Various aspects of the boardroom culture may appear as paradoxes.[3] Boards are simultaneously supposed to have distance and closeness, independence and interdependence, trust and distrust, etc. Some of these paradoxes are discussed. There are often needs to balance various perspectives and relationships, and various cycles of virtuous or vicious dynamics may result from improper balances. This chapter ends with an illustration of the process-oriented boardroom dynamics in the TINE Group case from the 'fly on the wall' study.

The board as a team

What distinguishes boards from work groups or teams? The board is presented here as a work group, and we ask if the interactions between board members are very different from the interactions between top management team members.[4] A board is a group of people who are characterised by having only a few face-to-face meetings, with more members than the typical working group, who are highly complex and perform multifarious tasks, and who have severe time constraints in working on them. As a consequence, boards are especially vulnerable to interaction difficulties.[5] Board effectiveness is likely to depend on socio-psychological processes, in particular those processes leading to group participation, the exchange of information, and critical discussions.[6] In this section cognition is the starting point, continuing with lists of team characteristics of board members, and ending with concepts of board culture.

It is uncommon to consider the board as a team. One reason for this is that the board meets only infrequently.[7] However, a corporate board is a group of people who have a psychological dependence on one another. Directors may be sued as a group, and thus they also depend on each other. Whether they like it or not, all board members are part of a group, with its own dynamics and patterns that affect how it acts. Board members will have to relate to group norms rather than to individual norms.[8]

Cognition

In a seminal article by Daniel Forbes and Frances Milliken, boards are presented as a strategic decision-making group.[9] The authors draw on literature on small-group decision-making, and they discuss criteria that may distinguish effective boards from ineffective ones. Their analysis focuses on the fact that, for the boards' service and control tasks to be performed effectively, it is necessary that board members cooperate to exchange information, evaluate the merits of competing alternatives and reach well-reasoned decisions.

Boards can be seen as 'large, elite, and episodic decision-making groups that face complex tasks pertaining to strategic processes'.[10] Forbes and Milliken argue that, because boards are not involved in implementation, the output that they produce is entirely cognitive in nature. They also argue that boards are particularly vulnerable to process losses. Process losses are the interaction difficulties that prevent groups from achieving their full potential. Therefore, board effectiveness is heavily dependent on socio-psychological processes, and in particular those pertaining to group participation and interaction, the exchange of information, and critical discussions.

Board effectiveness is defined as the board's ability to meet its task expectations and to continue working together.[11] These are the classic task and maintenance criteria in group effectiveness models. Both are board-level outcomes, but, although they are different from firm performance, both of them contribute to it.

Characters

When exploring the board as a work group it is important to identify each of the team members, and how they interact. Each board member may have his or her individual contribution.

Contributions and strategic positioning of team members
One of the main outcomes from our 'fly on the wall' study of the TINE Group was the exploration of the dynamics among the various board members. The board members of the TINE Group had different contributions to make with respect to decision-making.[12] Not only were the contributions a matter of individuals having exact knowledge, but the decision-making was a result of processes among the board members. The different board members took various roles in these processes.

- Crusaders: some were crusaders, or mostly issue-oriented. For them, the most important thing was not to get a unanimous decision but to raise issues – often as a response to their relationships with external stakeholders.

- Strategists: some were chiefly interested in influencing decision outcomes. The chairperson was clearly also in this group, and this group would be highly aware of the processes needed to secure the intended outcome. The strategists were aware of techniques that could be used to get their interests accepted. They were able to render the crusaders passive or isolate them, and to convince the supporters.
- Supporters: some were mainly process-oriented. They had various reasons for taking these roles, but a major reason was that they wanted to support the chairperson or the CEO, and some had other outlets or arenas for influencing decisions.

The combination of the different orientations seems to contribute to a decision-making culture characterised by creativity and critical attitudes, as well as openness and generosity.

The contributions of the board members varied depending on the issue in question. It was clear that some board members had more contributions to make in internally oriented issues than in externally oriented ones, and vice versa. Some board members had more contributions to make in financially oriented questions, while others had more contributions to make in operational or more quality-oriented aspects. Some board members had particular contributions when relating to the past, while others were good in relating to the future. The various orientations made it possible for the board members to complement each other in various advisory tasks as well as in control tasks.

Director types: functional and dysfunctional

Similar observations were made in the boardroom in Canadian firms.[13] Based on 'fly on the wall' studies Leblanc and Gillies used a categorisation of director types, and found that change agents, consensus builders, counsellors, challengers and conductors were positively related to board efficacy and corporate performance, while controllers, conformists, cheerleaders, critics and caretakers were negatively related. Table 8.1 shows the list of Leblanc and Gillies's functional director types and table 8.2 shows the list of their dysfunctional director types. All the descriptions of the director types are dynamic and relational.

Table 8.1 *Functional director types*

- 'Conductor chairs' are superior chairs who relate very well to directors and management, have a keen interest in effective governance, possess remarkable leadership skills and serve at the hub of all important board activity.
- 'Change agents' act as catalysts for bringing about fundamental change (for example, by replacing the CEO, fighting a takeover, developing a new strategy). Retired CEOs of successful enterprises make excellent change agents.
- 'Consensus builders' act as conciliators, disarming and resolving conflict through their interpersonal and communication skills. Former senior politicians make exceptional consensus builders.
- 'Counsellors' have strong persuasive skills, high credibility and the ability to work on a one-to-one basis with a variety of people. They are coaches, connectors, mentors and negotiators.
- 'Challengers' ask the tough questions: they know when to speak, what to say and how to say it, and their questions cause managers to rethink key decisions. Lawyers, accountants, consultants and academics often make effective challengers.

Source: Leblanc and Gillies 2005.

Culture concepts

A team is more than the sum of its members, and understanding effective boardroom dynamics involves looking into the decision-making culture among the different board members. Lessons from psychology may be used to understand the board as a team, but a board may be different from other teams or small decision-making groups. Investigating how boards may be different from other small decision-making groups is a major challenge in corporate governance research. The gauntlet is taken up by Forbes and Milliken,[14] and they summarise various aspects of board decision-making cultures. They use concepts such as cognitive conflicts, cohesiveness, effort norms and the use of knowledge and skills. Creativity, commitment, criticality, care, consensus, etc. are other concepts used to describe the boards' decision-making culture.

Some of the concepts most widely used are criticality, creativity, cognitive conflicts, cohesion and commitment.

- Cognitive conflict is concerned with the presence of issues related to conflict between board members. Forbes and Milliken suggest that it

Table 8.2 *Dysfunctional director types*

- '**Caretaker chairs**' are unable to run board meetings effectively, do not manage interpersonal conflict and dissent and do not have effective working relationships with other directors, the CEO or the management team. They should be replaced if they cannot improve.
- '**Controllers**' dominate the board process through skill, tact, humour or anger. They are very dangerous, particularly when the board contains dysfunctional director types who cannot neutralise them.
- '**Conformists**' are non-performing, cooperating directors who support the status quo and seldom prepare for, or take part in, any serious discussion. They are well liked due to past success or relationships, and may be former CEOs, regulators or politicians who now have limited credibility.
- '**Cheerleaders**' are enthusiastic amateurs who constantly praise directors, the CEO and the management team but are unprepared for meetings, unaware of strategic issues facing the company and often ask inane questions. At worst they are regarded with contempt, and at best they are referred to as 'sleepers', 'non-performers' or 'ineffective'.
- '**Critics**' constantly criticise and complain, with an abrasive tone and ill-chosen words. They are referred to as 'manipulative' and 'sneaky' by fellow directors and they lack the ability for 'constructive dissent' possessed by challengers or change agents.

Source: Leblanc and Gillies 2005.

should be operationalised through the frequency of conflicts about ideas and the extent of differences of opinion on the board.
- Criticality is about independence, and much of the literature is influenced by agency theory. However, it concerns not only demographic or formal independence but real independence as well, which leads to independence in behaviour or decision-making.
- Creativity in the boardroom is about the contribution from individual board members and also from the board as a team. There may be processes in the boardroom resulting in creative proposals as well as creative solutions to various problems.
- Cohesiveness is defined as the degree to which board members are attracted to each other and are motivated to stay on board.
- Commitment and effort norms are defined as group expectations about the intensity of individual behaviour. It could be operationalised by the board carefully scrutinising the information provided by the firm prior to the meetings, the board members taking

notes during the meetings, or the board members actively participating during the meetings.

Various authors argue that it is a positive boardroom climate or decision-making culture that matters most for creating accountability.[15]

The board decision-making culture

Forbes and Milliken present a model of board processes and their impact on board effectiveness.[16] Important elements in their model are cognitive conflicts, cohesiveness, effort norms and the use of knowledge and skills. They all refer to board processes that represent various aspects of the board decision-making culture, and they mediate the relationships between board demography and structures and board-level outcomes.

In the 'value-creating board' surveys carried out in Norway we used various operationalisations suggested in the existing board literature to measure the boardroom culture and investigated various underlying concepts and the relationships between them. The various measures could be sorted under headings such as critical attitudes and independence, creativity, preparations/involvement, openness/generosity and cognitive conflicts. The cohesiveness measures are related mostly to preparation/involvement, but also to openness/generosity. Creativity is related to critical attitudes. In some settings we also found that independence is related to preparations/involvement and creativity is related to openness/generosity.

Criticality and independence

Criticality (or critical attitudes) is highly related to the independence concept. Criticality involves the board as a team having, in general, an independent, questioning attitude. Information and suggestions from the CEO will generally be questioned by the board members in the boardroom, and the board members will critically find their own information and carefully scrutinise the information being provided by the CEO, after which the board will reach its decisions independent of the CEO.

Theories about social movements and class elites take the independence discussion outside the executive versus non-executive arena.

There may be ties – either weak or strong – between executives and groups outside the firm, and these groups may support each other's behaviour and direct decisions to create benefits for individuals belonging to this group or class – even though such decisions may be negative for the firm or the shareholders as a whole. Pluralistic ignorance is a bias in group decision-making. A large proportion of the group members may privately reject group norms or practices, but believe that most other group members accept them. This bias in such perceptions of board members reduces the propensity for individual directors to speak out and express their concerns. Board members tend to overestimate the extent to which they are on their own with some critical questions.

Criticality goes beyond demographic or structural independence, but at the same time it does not fully cover the independence concept. It is possible to be not just critical without being independent but also independent without being critical. Criticality covers the critical, questioning part of independence.

Criticality is concerned with asking critical questions about the information and the decision proposals presented by the management. Criticality will thus include the board members finding their own information beyond what is presented by the management; it will involve the fostering of a culture of open dissent. It is argued that the best-performing companies are those which have boards with a membership that remains unchanged for an extended period, and which regard dissent as an obligation and treat no subject as being *undiscussable*.[17]

Creativity

Creativity in the boardroom has two main aspects. First, that the creativity and curiosity of the individual board members are stimulated and used; and, second, that creative processes exist in the boardroom. Creative processes go beyond the creativity of each individual director. Creativity in the boardroom is about how creativity is stimulated and takes place in the interactions between the board members, and between the board members and the management. Directors present issues or solutions that by themselves may not be creative, but they can be an input to the understanding, thinking and imagination of the others and thus trigger creativity.

There may be processes in the boardroom that result in creative proposals as well as creative solutions to various problems. A creative boardroom culture will generally require aspects of openness/generosity, cognitive conflicts/diversity and questioning. Creativity and curiosity will be stimulated when people with diverse backgrounds and perceptions are together in a setting in which they willingly give to and support each other without fear of harming their own reputation or the consequences of what they are saying or doing. Creativity is even further supported when this culture also encourages critical and independent questioning.

Creativity may be a result of impulsive decision-making, but impulsiveness and speed may be the opposite of creative processes and process orientation.

Cohesiveness

Board cohesiveness refers to the degree to which board members are attracted to each other and are motivated to remain on the board. Cohesiveness is related to affection, and it captures how board members like to meet and be on a board together. It reflects the ability of the board to continue working together.[18]

Board members who are attracted to each other will appreciate coming together for board meetings, and assign a very high priority to being a part of the board. Cohesiveness will also include having a good atmosphere at board meetings. The board members may then often experience a higher level of satisfaction than in situations where there is little or no cohesiveness.

Cohesiveness is expected to impact on future board processes. Organisational commitment research indicates that organisational commitment, including effort norms, preparation and involvement, openness and generosity, will be influenced by cohesiveness and a good boardroom atmosphere.

Good atmosphere

The development of a good boardroom atmosphere was considered to be one of the main contributions of women directors in the 'board life story' project. The women interviewed illustrated how women were able to create a good atmosphere in the boardroom.[19] The women directors were very sensitive to having a good atmosphere in the boardroom: these are some examples of the comments they made. 'The company secretary told that after I came, the atmosphere changed. It was not so tough any more. Things loosened up. It became more relaxed. Some more laughter.' 'Many have pointed out that the tone is different with me as a woman there. And I have wondered many times whether it is because I am a woman – or whether it is because it is me. I think it is possible to have some humour. I allow myself to present comments that can make the others smile.' The women directors gave further examples of how the board members liked to see each other and looked forward to the board meetings. The good atmosphere also facilitated openness and generosity among the board members.

Supportive decision style
Studies have found that active and powerful boards have an encouraging and supportive decision-making style that is friendlier than passive and less powerful boards.[20]

Openness and generosity (use of knowledge and skills)

Openness and generosity are concerned with the use of knowledge and skills: how board members can accept and recognise that they may be wrong in their considerations, and how they willingly give advice based on private knowledge, ideas and points of view. Furthermore, openness and generosity relate to how board members openly and freely communicate personal preferences and considerations.

Openness and generosity are also about the use of knowledge and skills. It is of little value to have skilled and knowledgeable persons on a board if they do not use these skills and knowledge.

Openness
Probably the most significant recommendation that real-world governance experts agree on with respect to boardroom dynamics is that boards need to have an open and challenging interchange between directors and the CEO and between the directors themselves.[21] Boards that work well have constructive, critical dialogue between the board members and senior management. Such open dialogue is the single best indication of board effectiveness. It is even claimed by Sir Adrian Cadbury that openness between board members, as well as being fundamental to the working of an effective board, also sets the tone

for relationships throughout the company. Trust and confidence are built on openness and on the willingness of all board members to say what they think, even if it may be critical of colleagues and of their proposals.

Openness can be achieved in various ways, but cohesiveness and a good atmosphere in the boardroom are clearly important. 'Away days', visits to company sites, participation in committees, etc. can all contribute to openness. The importance of creating a climate of trust and candour has been argued by various authors.[22] The CEO and the board chairperson may influence such an atmosphere. Important information should be shared with the board members in time for them to read and digest it.

Revealing ignorance

Openness is closely related to the appreciation of diversity. Diverse viewpoints have contributed to lively discussions, particularly on the strategic directions of the company. 'Independent, intrepid, informed, diverse (in background and expertise) directors willing to speak up when concerned or in doubt and to challenge management and each other are crucial to healthy and constructive boardroom dynamics and to effective corporate governance.'[23]

These last comments concern the asking of questions and being willing to reveal ignorance. The following comments reflect how some women directors value their contributions by asking questions.[24]

I am often good at asking questions that give the others something to reflect on. I believe that they experience it as interesting, and I am not critical. I am not asking questions to criticise. I ask questions to see whether there is something we need to illuminate. I am trying to include other perspectives – to get a broader discussion.

Women often ask questions that nobody else dares to ask. Girls dare to ask some very relevant simple questions – is it millions or billions?

Such questions may be important for developing a process-oriented boardroom culture.[25]

Openness is related to preparations. The questions the board members ask during a board meeting, and even the very words chosen, demonstrate the director's understanding of an issue.[26] To ask a question proper preparations have to be made. The board documents have to be read, and time has to be invested in order to understand the complexities of an issue. At many ineffective board meetings directors sit in silence, assuming that the other board members have not noticed that they are unprepared, and also assuming that the collective incompetence is not noticed.

Generous use of knowledge and skills

A distinction must be made between the presence and the use of knowledge and skills. An assumption in most of the board and governance literature is that existing competence will be used. However, this may not be the case. Openness and generosity are crucial for utilising the knowledge and skills of the board members. On the one hand, openness and generosity are reflected in the fact that the board members know and use each other's competence. The use of knowledge and skills is related to the behavioural dimensions of social integration, and refers to a group's ability to cooperate.[27] On the other hand, the openness and generosity criterion also obliges the board members to use their own competency generously.

Forbes and Milliken suggest that the use of knowledge and skills can be measured, as 'people on [boards] are aware of each other's areas of expertise; [...] when an issue is discussed, the most knowledgeable people generally have the most influence, [and] task delegation on [boards] represents a good match between knowledge and responsibilities'. The use of knowledge and skills is different from cognitive conflicts; it refers to the process by which the board members' contribution is coordinated. Cognitive conflicts relate to the content of the board members' contribution.[28]

Preparation and involvement (effort norms)

Norms were introduced in the previous chapter as a concept that could be used to direct group behaviour. Effort norms are a group-level construct that refers to the group's shared belief regarding the level of effort each individual is expected to put into fulfilling a task. It is about preparation and involvement, or the expected commitment of the board members as a group.

Forbes and Milliken suggest that preparation and involvement, or effort norms, can be measured and realised with questions that 'carefully scrutinise the information provided by the firm prior to meetings', by 'researching issues relevant to the firm prior to meetings', by 'taking notes during meetings' or by 'participating actively during meetings'. Effort norms are also about the time and availability of the board members.

Preparations: women and men

The women in the 'board life story' project provided many examples of how their male counterparts did not prepare properly.[29] Women were, in general, better prepared than men. The men's lack of preparation was considered by some women to be very arrogant, and valuable time at board meetings was lost as a result. The board members who turned up poorly prepared – or even completely unprepared – were often business executives with a high reputation, and they often had many board assignments. The lack of preparation often reduced the board members' independence, and it supported managerial dominance. However, the unsatisfactory preparation of male directors also presented opportunities to the women. By doing their homework well, the women gained the ability to influence decision-making and to improve their status as directors – even though they had often been elected as tokens. Although the women had less board experience, and in the corporate hierarchies they ranked several levels lower than their male counterparts, the women directors soon proved to have a great positive impact on board performance. Sometimes this even started a positive virtuous circle for improving board behaviour and board effectiveness: as the 'old boys' did not want to be caught asleep, the female representation obliged the male directors to improve their preparations as well.

Here are some of the illustrations from the women directors:

Many of these men did not have time to prepare properly. They had many board assignments and often many operative duties. They can attend a board meeting and read the board documents, keeping one page ahead.

One issue that I found to be a fundamental difference between women and men was that I found the women to be much better prepared than the men ... It is the regulars, and they can boast that they have such a photographic reading capacity that it enables them to go through a document in three seconds and get an impression. That is nonsense. The consequence is that they have to talk hot air – to keep the meeting running – while they read their documents, and take a lot more time. The advantage for these women is that they can take the men by surprise by being prepared, and the men just have to try to follow.

I have seen that male members of this board open the envelope in the lift. We often used to joke by saying that the boardroom should be as far as possible away from the garage. The quality of the board meetings was a function of the distance between the boardroom and the garage.

Involvement and time

How active are the board members during the meeting, and how highly do they value their role as a board member? Involvement is more than just attending a meeting; it is also about the attention given and activities undertaken during the meetings, as well as between the meetings.

How much time should board members invest in performing their duties, and how available are they when urgently needed? 'Away days' or retreats have been mentioned as important tools for developing boards, but not all board members are equally available for such activities. Cohesion and a good atmosphere seem to be important motivators for the involvement and the use of time of the board members.

Speed of decision-making

Board processes and decision-making style can also be characterised by the speed of decision-making. Slow versus quick decision-making, uninformed versus informed decision-making and impulsive versus deliberate decision-making have all been used as measures in studies.[30] An effective board decision-making speed is related not only to the length of board meetings. Participating boards may not be faster in their decision-making than many passive boards, but they will be more deliberate and informed.

Cognitive conflicts

The concept of cognitive conflict refers to the task-oriented differences in judgement between group members.[31] It can be defined as disagreements in judgement over the content of the tasks being performed, including differences in viewpoints, ideas and opinions. Cognitive conflict implies that the board members may have different opinions on important board issues, that they bring with them different perspectives on what is the best for the company and that they have very different ways of arguing and reasoning. The existence of cognitive conflict is expected to impact on both criticality and creativity. Empirically, we found only limited overlap between the cognitive conflict measure and the other measures of boardroom culture.

Groupthink and diversity

The groupthink concept has been used in the literature about cognitive conflicts in the boardroom. Groupthink is common in many board-rooms.[32] Conformity is a typical attribute among board members, and the boardroom culture often discourages dissent. However, one of the most important links in a virtuous circle is the board members' capacity to challenge each other's beliefs and assumptions.Groupthink and conformity are clearly related to creativity, critical attitudes, openness and generosity.

One of the most important aspects with regard to cognitive conflict is that variations in perceptions are used. It is not enough to have different backgrounds and various perceptions; the boardroom culture must ensure that this variation is used. Cognitive conflicts and diversity may therefore not in themselves be characteristics of the boardroom culture; what is needed is to have a culture that uses the knowledge and skills of board members with various backgrounds and perceptions.

Disagreements and affective conflicts

Cognitive conflicts have been defined as task-oriented conflicts, but such conflicts may relate to more than just which tasks should be done and the objectives of performing these tasks. There may, for example, be disagreements about what is best for the firm: this can be termed *goal conflict*. There may also be disagreements about how to achieve what is best for the firm: this can be termed *policy conflict*. Policy conflict may be related to how tasks should be performed and when. There may also exist various ways of arguing or reasoning among the board members.

Conflict is in general a strong and negatively loaded concept, but there may be different degrees of strength in the disagreements or con-flicts. Clearly, the conflicts may go beyond perceiving issues in dif-ferent ways or from different perspectives. The ways the conflicts or disagreements are handled will vary. On some boards disagreements are not encouraged and all decisions have to be made unanimously. The culture on other boards accepts differences in opinion, and boardroom voting need not always be unanimous.

Cognitive conflicts are often time-consuming, but usually they are considered to be beneficial; some conflicts may be harmful, however. Affective conflicts are generally considered to be harmful. Affective conflict is the dysfunctional and emotional conflict that arises from incompatibilities or disputes between decision partners.[33] A conflict may start out as a cognitive conflict, but a long-term cognitive conflict may end up as an affective conflict. In this way conflict dynamism may take place.

Paradoxes and dynamics

We have seen that the boardroom culture may be described by various paradoxes,[34] and that the culture is dynamic. Paradoxical pairings, such as creativity and criticality, and cohesion and cognitive conflicts, were introduced. Such paradoxes and dynamics of the boardroom culture have been discussed by various authors. Among such pairings we find:

- distance and closeness;[35]
- independence and interdependence;[36]
- trust and distrust;[37]
- engaged but non-executive;[38]
- challenging but supportive;[39]
- independent but involved;[40] and
- open dissent but respect, trust and candour.[41]

Some theoretical and empirical contributions have been made on solving these paradoxes, but their academic content and their relationships have not been fully developed.[42] Managing paradoxes involves an approach that accepts tension.

Paradoxes

Listed above are some of the paradoxes presented for describing effective boardroom culture.[43] In the following summary and description of some of these paradoxes, terms such as 'challenging', 'questioning', 'probing', 'discussing', 'testing', 'informing', 'debating' and 'encouraging' appear frequently.

Engaged but non-executive

Among the pairings we find that there should be simultaneously distance and closeness, that of engagement and non-executivity, and independence and involvement.

Non-executive directors will not be as knowledgeable about the firm and its business as executive directors, but the non-executive directors can increase their knowledge. Without knowledge, critique and critical questioning may be difficult. Building this knowledge may go beyond attending board meetings and reading the papers for the board. Ways of increasing the knowledge of non-executives include meeting and socialising with executives, visiting plants and attending company events, etc. John Roberts, Terry McNulty and Philip Stiles argue that non-executive directors will in this way be engaged, but at the same time they should not take on executive roles.[44] Over-involvement in executive tasks may create a destructive friction between executives and non-executives.

Directors should be independent but involved. Roberts, McNulty and Stiles also argue that non-executive directors should display independence of mind, and have the confidence to act it out in boardroom discussions. Creativity and criticality, and debate and dialogue, should be encouraged in place of formal appraisals of executive proposals.

Critical attitudes and trust

Trust and distrust as well as cohesion and conflicts should be balanced. The board members should be challenging and supportive. Distrust and trust are not to be postulated *ex ante*, but at any point in time elements of trust and distrust should both exist. Criticality is not the same as disloyalty, and asking questions is a link to creativity and diversity.

A key skill of non-executives is to draw upon the objectivity that their distance from the day-to-day management gives them, as a basis for questioning and challenging. One of the most important skills for board members in questioning is the ability to do so in a way that is felt to be both helpful and supportive for the CEO and the executives.[45] Non-skilful questioning may result in frustrated executives who, in response, hide or hold back information and minimise the role of the board and the non-executives.

A key challenge is balancing critical attitudes and trust. Well-placed trust grows out of active enquiry rather than blind acceptance.[46] A culture of open dissent should be encouraged, but also with respect, trust and candour.[47] This is a link to openness and generosity. The development of good boardroom structures may facilitate the simultaneous achievement of independence and trust. Formal board structures, including 'alone-meetings' and the formalisation of information flows outside the boardroom, are examples of such structures.

Independence and interdependence
Is it possible to attain simultaneously independence and interdependence, yin and yang, distance and closeness, or masculinity and femininity? Independence and interdependence have been described as yin and yang.[48] Boards integrating both independence and interdependence are purported to make the greatest contribution to company performance. The independence criterion is based on neoclassical assumptions, which, in the main, consider the group and organisational processes inside the board as a black box, while the interdependence criterion opens the black box and focuses on such processes.

The recent literature on corporate governance reforms has had a strong and almost excessive focus on independence. Independence may be a legitimate goal in structuring a board. However, interdependence may *also* be key to making boards strong and active. If the control tasks require independence then the task of strategic partnership requires interdependence. The interdependent board of directors is a group of people who are able to come together in an environment of great trust and respect and combine their diverse knowledge, talents and perspectives for the strategic benefit of the company.[49]

Vicious or virtuous dynamics

The existence of the various paradoxes indicates the importance of balancing contrasting perspectives. There is a need to balance distance and closeness, distrust and trust, independence and interdependence. It is, however, very easy to lean more towards one side than the other in such paradoxes; then a reinforcing vicious dynamic easily develops. Such reinforcing cycles of control and collaboration are described by Chamu Sundaramurthy and Marianne Lewis in an article about the paradoxes of governance.[50]

Reinforcing cycles of control and collaboration

The dynamics related to of each of these balances could easily lead
to either a positive or a negative decision-making culture. Macro-
level social processes and micro-level social processes reinforce each
other. Passive board norms may enable top managers to engage in symbolic management practices that may give the impression that boards
are controlling management. Furthermore, symbolic management of
shareholders may allow passive board norms to exist.

Groupthink and distrust are core concepts used by Sundaramurthy
and Lewis. They examine reinforcing cycles that foster strategic persistence and organisational decline.[51] The reinforcement of dysfunctional dynamics arises when only one perspective is taken into account.
With an emphasis on closeness, trust and interdependence rooted in,
for example, stewardship theory,[52] groupthink may easily be a consequence of a collaborative emphasis and cohesiveness in the governance
team. Groupthink – even with increasing collaboration and commitment – may lead to strategic persistence, but also to rigid mental maps
and failure.

On the other side, a control emphasis with vigilant, outsider-
dominated boards and a focus on distance, distrust and independence
will suppress stewardship, and board management polarisation will
increase. The dominance of distanced and independent board members
will probably result in financial and outcome-based controls rather
than behavioural, internal and strategic controls. This may lead to
shortened time horizons and risk avoidance from managers. Greater
control and distrust may also spur declining intrinsic motivation and,
again, management's learning capacity.[53] Curiosity and creativity may
be repressed, and learning become tied to the specific situations in
which extrinsic awards apply. This may have consequences for mould-
breaking innovations and change.[54] This may also lead to strategic
persistence and failure.

Virtuous dynamics

Virtuous and self-correcting dynamics or cycles may develop when
fostering the paradoxes and balancing the various perspectives. Self-
correcting cycles may result in strategic flexibility and organisational
renewal, instead of the strategic persistence and failure stemming from
the reinforcing cycles. However, the balancing is not only a question
of finding a middle ground but also one of including both elements

simultaneously in a proper balance. Trust and distrust must not be perceived as bipolar concepts but as different concepts. The opposite of trust is not distrust; the opposite of distance is not closeness; the opposite of independence is not interdependence. Thus it is possible to increase the attention simultaneously to collaboration and control, to closeness and distance or to trust and distrust.

Sundaramurthy and Lewis make the following propositions on how to foster self-correcting cycles:

- encouraging trust (in others' capabilities), distrust (of human limitations), and cognitive (task-related) conflict among governance actors;
- promoting diversity (for example, insider–outsider mix, heterogeneous backgrounds) and shared understanding (for example, board/management strategic decision-making, informal and formal interactions); and
- external interventions.[55]

An important point is creating an atmosphere of openness and trust in which the board members and executives are encouraged to speak up. The board members must learn not only to trust each other and the management but also, through familiarity with human limitations, to know when not to trust. Rational controls should complement trusting board–management relations.

Including and involving board members with diverse backgrounds in strategic decision-making and interactions will create a greater familiarity with the firm's goals, and a shared understanding may be achieved. Informal communication between external board members and a wide range of executives is one way to proceed. The board should consist of members who trust and challenge one another and engage directly with senior managers on critical issues facing the board.[56]

External constituents, including consultants, institutional investors and shareholder activists, will, unlike the decision-makers on the board and in the TMT, be less likely to view strategic change as ego-threatening.

The case of process-oriented boardroom dynamics

In one of our research projects we were 'flies on the wall' in the corporate boardroom of the TINE Group in Norway.[57] The TINE Group is a cooperative with about 5000 employees. The corporate board consisted of fourteen directors – ten elected by the owners and four elected by the employees. The CEO and other people from the TMT were not formal members of the board with voting rights, but five of them participated during most board meetings.

Observing the boardroom culture

Our first and immediate observation as we entered the boardroom was the positive atmosphere among the board members. We identified a definite and supportive decision-making culture. This was confirmed during our further observations, even though we later got a more detailed and distinctive picture. The atmosphere in the boardroom was characterised by friendliness and openness, but with a strictly structured meeting agenda.

Here are some of our observations.

- First, the board members clearly enjoyed being together. They looked forward to the board meetings and to seeing each other. That was the case for all the board members, including the union representatives, the CEO and the TMT.
- Second, we got the general impression that the board was a well-functioning social system in which trust and confidence were built on openness and the willingness of all board members to contribute and to say what they thought. The board members were not sitting on the fence defending themselves. They were open to sharing information and knowledge and to entering into arguments. However, they were generally also open to and willing to accept alternative outcomes from the board decision-making processes.
- Third, the board members devoted considerable time to their work on the board. Huge piles of documents were read before each meeting, and all the board members were involved as board members of subsidiary companies. They had regular meetings with the owners through the regional membership organisations. Many of the board members were willing to spend close to 50 per cent of their working hours on activities related to the TINE board.
- Fourth, we found that creativity was stimulated through the variety in the personalities of the board members and various task-related conflicts. We observed the variation in contributions among the board members. Most of the owner-elected representatives had similar backgrounds, but there were so many representatives that the differences in personalities became very evident. This was

illuminated by the nicknames we gave them – for example, the crusader, the politician, the analyst, the strategist, the sound farmer's wisdom, the summariser, the women alibi, the unionist, etc. We also observed how managerial interests were challenged by various regional interests, employee interests, societal interests, gender-related interests, etc.

The above observations gave a picture of a process-oriented decision-making culture. Great emphasis was given to hearing all voices, to involving the whole board and to attaining unanimous decisions. This was a very time-consuming process, and the board meetings did last a long time. However, this decision-making culture – the cohesiveness, the openness and generosity, the involvement and use of time, and the creativity – set the scene for board-level dialogue on a strategy that enabled part-time board members to shape the thinking of executives and vice versa. The board members' involvement inside and outside the boardroom made it possible to bridge the gap between the knowledge of the board members and the executives. Our conclusion was that the culture in the corporate board of TINE embedded board decisions – both in relation to the corporate management and in relation to the owners. The boardroom was a communication arena that, with its focus on processes, shaped the context for strategic debate.

How to create a process-oriented decision-making culture

Our observations made us reflect upon the elements necessary to create a process-oriented decision-making culture.

The chairperson

Board leadership may have important effects on group performance. The TINE board chairperson was a full-time, non-executive chairperson. One aspect of being non-executive is that he did not have a permanent office at the TINE headquarters, and one of his main tasks was related to working with the owners and other external stakeholders. He was, without doubt, the leader of the board. He was the one running the process leading to the establishment of the present TINE Group, and he had chaired the board that selected the present CEO. The chairperson acted like an industrialist building an empire. It was important for him personally that both TINE and the board were working well. He was the one, as the builder of an empire, who was setting the standards. Thus he also displayed enormous involvement.

The chairperson was highly respected. He was praised for creating enthusiasm among the board members, and he was good at running processes. He has a role model with high integrity. Sometimes the board members even made decisions based on loyalty to him more than on the contents of the particular case. One of his mottos was 'When you search for the best in others, then you will find the best in yourself'. He was clever and enthusiastic about including and using the potential of the individual board members. We observed, however, that he was also skilled in using a large number of techniques in influencing board decision-making outcomes. Such techniques included preparatory discussions with the CEO and other board members, detailed personal mental preparation before each meeting, summarising discussions, and arranging the voting order.

Codes and norms

Codes of best practice exist, first and foremost, to create norms and structures that ensure that board decision-making takes place in efficient and just ways. They are there to create board effectiveness and to bridge the gap between board task expectations and actual board task performance. Norms may be formal as well as informal, and informal 'rules of the game' may be more important than formal regulations and structures. Norms may include expectations about attendance, advance preparations for meetings, values and corporate cultures, and ethical standards. Our observations were that the board norms at TINE reflected norms from cooperatives and not-for-profit organisations rather than those from investor groups and stock markets, from managerial hegemony and business elites, or from family businesses. Process-oriented board involvement is one such norm. There is a tradition that boards are both the formal and the real decision-makers, and the board members are very conscious that decisions need to be embedded among the members. The use of time, commitment and independence were among the norms we observed.

Meetings and structures

The board structures at TINE include the length and frequency of the meetings, board-management relations and the attendance of the

TMT at the meetings, preparations and presentations of the items on the agenda etc.

One main feature is that board meetings in practice usually lasted two days, and quite often a third day was added – for example, when there was a strategy seminar, a board development seminar, council meetings or the annual owners' meeting. In most cases some social activities (or at least a dinner) were arranged in the evenings. The board members therefore had considerable time to socialise and to discuss matters in a setting other than the formal meetings.

One reason for having such long meetings was so that all the board members should be able to voice their opinions, and on most major items on the agenda the chairperson was inviting a 'round'. This meant that each board member was asked to give his/her opinion. A consequence of this practice was that a comment or an idea from one person often triggered ideas from the others. This initiated some very creative sessions: several times we observed how a comment from one person led to discussions that resulted in important and relevant decisions.

The long meetings were needed to cater for the presence of people from the top management team. The various items on the agenda were prepared by various persons in the TMT and their respective staff. They also made decision proposals and presented the case for the board. Most often the decision proposals were changed after the discussions in the boardroom. The CEO and the board chairperson were clearly open to these changes, and they did not seek any kudos from having their own proposals accepted. It was possible, as several of the directors in the TMT were present at the board meetings, to express subtly nuanced opinions on various issues. This made it easier for the board members to get involved in creative discussion.

At every meeting there was an item on the agenda called 'open post'. On this item the board members were invited to introduce issues they wanted to have discussed, and the CEO and the chairperson also introduced issues they were planning to put on the agenda at a later meeting.

Informal communication

Formal communication between the TMT and the board should go through the CEO, and the CEO's communication should be with the chairperson. However, TINE had a structure wherein the members of the corporate board and the members of the top management team were on the same subsidiary company boards. A system of internal interlocking directorates existed, and this system created professional and friendship ties between members of the corporate board and the TMT. These interlocks facilitated communication and coordination.

These examples have demonstrated that the board structures at the TINE Group made it possible for the board members to develop the context for the strategic debate. They shaped the content, context and conduct of strategy and important decisions, and their influence was continuous and not confined to discrete decision episodes.

Decision- versus process-oriented culture

We got a picture of a process-oriented boardroom culture at TINE. Many of the features we saw are almost the opposite of present practice and recommendations in corporate governance development. In table 8.3 we contrast aspects of a traditional, decision-oriented boardroom culture with the process-oriented culture we found in the case of TINE.

Board task expectations are criteria for board effectiveness. The main board task expectations at TINE were embedding and participation in strategic decision-making. The boardroom culture was characterised by cohesiveness, openness and generosity, preparedness and involvement, and creativity. Codes of best practice and agency theory emphasise the control of managerial opportunism and the ratification of decisions as board effectiveness criteria. The boardroom culture should display codes of best practice that can be described by criticality and independence.

Various aspects of board dynamics are listed. The decision-making speed at TINE was slow and the board meetings were lengthy. The board consisted of members of long standing. The opposite characteristics are often recommended in codes or in practice.

In TINE there were a large number of board members, diversity among board members was encouraged and appreciated, and the strategists were the dominating board members. In practice elsewhere we often find that having a small number of directors is encouraged, and that board members are homogeneous. The type of board member advocated in the ongoing corporate governance debate can be categorised as barbarian, and the recommendation is that they should replace many of the present board members, who are classified as supporters.

Table 8.3 *Process-oriented versus decision-oriented boardroom culture*

	Decision-oriented (practice and codes)	Process-oriented (observed at TINE)
Board effectiveness		
Criteria for board effectiveness – main board tasks	Controlling managerial opportunism and ratification of decisions	Embedding and participation in strategic decision-making
Effective boardroom culture	Independence	Criticality Creativity Cohesiveness Openness and generosity Preparedness and involvement
Board dynamics		
Decision-making speed	Fast	Slow
Length of meetings	Short	Long
Time spent by board members	Little	Much
Director number	Small	Large
Director background	Homogeneous	Heterogeneous
Director personality types	Crusaders/barbarians	Strategists
Board–management relations	Distance	Closeness
Board–management relations	Distrust	Trust
Boardroom norms influence	From finance	From leadership
Board leadership	Decision-maker and chairperson	Coach and leader
Decision-making	Information and voting	Communication and negotiations
Dynamics	Vicious circles	Virtuous circles
Results and value creation		
Decision outcome	Pre-determined	Open
Decision consequences and ownership interests	Short-term	Long-term
Value creation definition	Narrow	Comprehensive

In the TINE case presented above closeness in board–management relations is discussed, and trust was described as a basic characteristic of the boardroom relations. The board was like a work group, and boardroom norms were influenced from the leadership literature rather than the finance literature. The chairperson in TINE was a role model, a coach and a leader, while chairpersons in other companies/firms act as trouble-shooters, decision-makers and chairs.

At TINE, decision-making took place through negotiation and communication, the decision outcome was open, and the decision consequences and ownership interests were long-term. The opposite is often the case in practice. In TINE we observed dynamism with virtuous development circles. The assumptions behind the prevailing theory of corporate governance, managerial opportunism, have been severely criticised because they may lead to vicious development circles. Furthermore, we found at TINE a comprehensive value creation definition that was clearly beyond pure shareholder value logic.

Summary

The main concepts in this chapter have been criticality and independence, creativity, cohesiveness, openness and generosity, preparation and involvement, the use of knowledge and skills, cognitive conflicts, groupthink and diversity, vicious and virtual dynamics and process-oriented boardroom culture.

So far throughout this book I have argued that the key to good corporate governance can be found in human or social factors rather than structural factors, and what distinguishes the best boards is that they are robust and effective social systems.[58] The chief elements of such boards include a virtuous cycle of respect, trust and candour; a culture of open dissent; a fluid portfolio of roles; and individual accountability and performance evaluation. Board members should be chosen not only on the basis of their individual track records but also on the basis of how they fit into the team environment or boardroom culture, and their compatibility with the other members of the board.[59] Research in social psychology and group dynamics has served as a theoretical basis for many contributions to board theories.[60] It has been shown that communication processes and information sharing are the main predictors of group performance.

In this chapter I have presented the board as a social system, and explained that the outcomes of board efforts are the results of the board performing as a well-functioning work group. Having presented the board as a team I then presented the dimensions of the boardroom culture. The dimensions were sorted under the following headings:

- criticality and independence;
- creativity;
- cohesiveness;
- openness and generosity;
- preparation and involvement; and
- cognitive conflicts.

Openness and generosity have been considered to constitute one of the most important recommendations for developing good boardroom dynamics. They relate to using the knowledge and skills of the board members. Boards need to have an open and challenging interchange between the directors themselves. Preparations and involvement are related to effort norms and commitment.

Various aspects of the boardroom culture appear as paradoxes. Boards are, at one and the same time, supposed to have distance and closeness, independence and interdependence, trust and distrust, etc. Proper balances with respect to these pairings of characteristics may contribute to virtuous cycles of boardroom dynamics.

9 | *Actual task performance*

The main concepts in this chapter are:
- board task performance;
- board strategy involvement;
- strategic decision-making;
- output control;
- internal control;
- behavioural control;
- quantitative control;
- qualitative control;
- reputation building and networking;
- advice and counsel; and
- mentoring and collaboration.

In 1971 Professor Mace wrote his seminal book about boards of directors, entitled *Directors: Myth and Reality*.[1] The central observation was that there is a gap between board task expectations and board task performance. He described board task expectations as myths, as boards were in reality doing something else. The board tasks he described as myths were those of (a) establishing objectives for the corporation, (b) asking discerning questions and (c) hiring, remunerating and firing the CEO. He found that boards were not involved in these tasks. In reality, the tasks boards were involved in were (a) providing advice and counsel to the CEO, (b) offering some sort of disciplining value and (c) acting in crisis situations. In chapter 3 I presented theoretically derived expectations regarding board task involvement; the objective of this chapter is to present the realities of board task involvement.

Board members rarely make clear distinctions between the various board tasks.[2] The distinction in this book between the various board tasks has a theoretic background; all the same, board members still use various frameworks to describe what they are doing or what boards are supposed to do. These frameworks usually stem from the ongoing

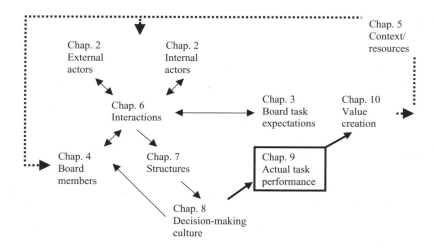

public corporate governance debate or the existing management literature. Sometimes their frameworks may be very practical and micro-issue-oriented. Furthermore, board members approach boards from various perspectives, and they have various backgrounds. Their perceptions of how boards are involved in various tasks thus also vary. Perceptions will be influenced by the role of the actor: various studies have, for example, found that the board chair will generally rate board task involvement higher than the CEO does.[3] The perception of other board members will vary, but they will rarely rate board task involvement higher than the chairperson does.

In chapter 3 I presented six groups of theoretically elaborated board tasks. These were output control, internal control, strategic control, network tasks, advisory tasks and strategy participation or mentoring tasks. In the literature and research about board tasks they are often grouped. I sorted the tasks based on whether the board tasks served external or internal actors. Control tasks are often related to tasks serving external actors, while 'service' is the label often used for tasks serving internal actors – such as the CEO, for example. Board tasks can also be sorted depending on the focus of the board members' attention; the example in chapter 3 used internal focus, external focus or strategy focus. An alternative description of the focus could be to have the categories of focus on the past, focus on the present or focus on the future. The outline in this chapter uses the concepts of strategy, control and service.[4]

The few studies that have empirically studied board task performance have often made a distinction between board task involvement and various measures about the results of board tasks, such as strategic orientation, restructuring, CEO compensation and selection, etc. Here I also make this distinction, and in this chapter I present board task involvement; in chapter 10 I present the outcome of board task involvement.

This chapter is laid out in three main sections:
- board strategy involvement;
- board control involvement; and
- board service involvement.

Within strategy, control and service involvement I explore various empirically elaborated board tasks, all of which relate to the board task expectations in chapter 3. This chapter is illustrated with examples from the 'value-creating board' surveys.[5] Also, at the end of this chapter I present an in-depth case study that summarises this and previous chapters. The case study will also present results from the 'value-creating board' surveys. In the case study I present examples of how to operationalise and measure concepts from this and preceding chapters.

Strategy involvement

Strategy may be defined as the development, maintenance and monitoring of the firms' core competencies with the purpose of achieving long-term results and survival. Strategic decision-making involves resolving uncertainty, complexity and conflict.

Strategies can be defined at various levels. Corporate strategy is about defining the type of business the firm should be involved in. Corporate strategy may be considered as the development of decisions that set and clarify the corporate ideas and values, long-term objectives and mission. Business strategy, on the other hand, sets the standards for how a firm should compete and position itself in relation to competitors and resource providers. Corporate strategy can be defined as 'the pattern of company purposes and goals – and the major policies for achieving these goals – that defines the business or businesses the company is to be involved with and the kind of company it is to be'.[6] The corporate strategy differentiates a corporation from its competitors, and it reconciles what a company may do in terms of opportunity. This concept of corporate strategy involves not only financial objectives but also economic, social and personal purposes.

Board strategic involvement covers corporate mission development, strategy conception and formulation, and strategy implementation. The board can be involved to various degrees in each of these areas. Strategy formulation includes reviewing executive analyses or corporate strengths and weaknesses, discussing various forecasts, examining the CEO assumptions about the firm's environment, assisting in developing new strategic options and aiding the selection of corporate strategy.[7]

The processes of strategic decision-making are usually described in terms of either a top-down or a bottom-up approach. Strategic activities may take place at multiple levels in a firm, and there may be many iterations ensuring that the boards are involved at various levels. In a top-down approach the board will frame the strategic context, while the implementation and detailed formulations will take place at lower levels of the organisation. In a bottom-up approach the context and content will be formulated in the organisation, while the board's task will, to a large degree, be to ratify. Studies have shown that the board may have the largest contribution when it formulates the strategic context.[8]

Strategic management and strategic control

The board's strategy involvement has rationales from external and internal perspectives. The external control perspective is concerned with ensuring the ability of various actors to influence and control company performance. Business development and value creation provide the rationale for the other perspective: board involvement may improve creativity in the strategy development process. It is argued in the strategy literature that the board must make sure that management has a process for developing, evaluating and choosing between strategic alternatives.[9] Participation in the strategy development process is also a tool board members may use to become more acquainted with the firm and the industry.

In the agency theory literature the strategy process is divided into strategic management and strategic control.[10] The execution of these tasks, according to agency theory, should be divided between the management and the board. The task of the management is strategic management, which consists of decision formulation and implementation. The board should be involved in strategic control: this includes decision ratification and evaluation.

The discussion of the board's goal-setting and strategy involvement has centred on whether the board should only ratify decisions presented to it by the management or whether it should also be involved in shaping the content, context and conduct of strategy.[11]

Collaboration[12] and mentorship[13] are two concepts used in connection with board involvement in strategic management. Collaboration is the conceptual opposite of control. Proponents of stewardship theory argue that the board's task is collaboration: this means, in practice, that the board and the management collaborate in developing the firm through strategy formulations and implementation. In a similar way, mentorship is the opposite of monitoring or control. The theoretical underpinning for the role of mentorship is, again, stewardship theory, and it is argued that the board's task is to mentor or coach the management rather than to control it. A mentorship approach means that, in practice, boards should be involved in strategy formulation and implementation.

Table 9.1 below is from the 'value-creating board' survey, conducted in Norway, and it illustrates how various actors in the boardroom may perceive the board's involvement in the strategy process. The four stages in the process are formulation, ratification, implementation and evaluation. There is no CEO duality in the sample. CEOs attend board meetings, but most often without voting rights. In Norway one-third of the board members may be elected by the employees from among the employees.

Table 9.1 demonstrates that the chair and the other outside board members give higher responses on the various strategy involvement questions than the CEO and employee-elected board members. The biggest differences occur in three of the four questions between the outside board members and the employee-elected directors. Among the board members who were not chairs or CEOs, 160 were women. There were no differences between the men and the women in their responses about the board's strategy participation.

Strategy ratification gets the highest ratings, followed by strategy formulation. Control with strategy implementation gets the lowest ratings. The differences in ratings between implementation and control with implementation are only minor.

Table 9.1 *Board strategy involvement perceptions*

	CEO	Chair	Outside	Employee
Develop long-term strategies and overall objectives	5.22	5.80	5.94	5.10
Ratify long-term strategies and overall objectives	5.37	5.85	6.10	5.28
Implement decisions about long-term strategies and overall objectives	4.92	5.45	5.76	4.95
Control implementation of long-term strategies and overall objectives	4.96	5.35	5.69	4.84
N	c.500	c.300	c.300	c.200

Responses from Norwegian firms with between fifty and 5000 employees, based on a seven-point Likert-type scale where a value of 7 means 'highly agree'.
N = number of responses.

Embedding the board's strategic decision-making

The agency theory argument about the board's strategic involvement is disputed in theory as well as in practice. If the board is to have an impact on the strategic direction of a company it needs to be involved in more than just ratification and evaluation. The board's strategic involvement needs to be properly embedded, and the board should also be involved in shaping the content, context and conduct of strategy. This argument is displayed in table 9.2 below.[14]

The three levels of board strategy involvement described in table 9.2 indicate that the board and its members may have a higher involvement in the strategy process than just the taking of strategic decisions. The middle column indicates that board members may also act as consultants and collaborators or mentors for the management in their strategy development. In that way, they help shape the strategic decisions. However, strategies should be embedded within the board, and if the board is to be genuinely powerful in influencing the future of a company then it must also be involved in shaping the context and conduct of strategies. The board will then develop the context for the strategic debate, establish the process and methodology for strategy development,

Table 9.2 *Choice, change and control as parts of strategic conduct*

	Ratifying strategic decisions	*Shaping strategic decisions*	*Shaping the content, context and conduct of strategy*
Definition	Influence is exerted inside the boardroom at the end of capital investment decisions	Influence occurs early in the decision process as part-time board members shape the preparation of capital investment proposals by executives	Influence is continuous and not confined to decision episodes
Board behaviour	Inside the boardroom, boards take decisions to accept, reject or refer capital investment proposals	Consultation with part-time board members by executives, either formally or informally, whilst a capital investment proposal is being prepared enables board members to test ideas, raise issues, question assumptions, advise caution and offer encouragement Executives 'sieve' capital investment proposals in anticipation of the need for board approval	The board develops the context for strategic debate, establishes a methodology for strategy development, monitors strategy content and alters the conduct of the executives in relation to strategy
Board involvement	All boards take strategic decisions	Some boards shape strategic decisions	A minority of boards shape the context, content and conduct of strategy

Source: McNulty and Pettigrew 1999.

monitor the strategy content and alter management's conduct in relation to strategy. Most boards are involved in taking strategic decisions,
some boards shape strategic decisions, but few are involved in a continuous shaping of the content, context and conduct of strategies.

Several hurdles have to be surmounted if part-time board members
are to be fully involved in the third step of strategy making. There
must be an increase in the attention given to strategy, and the contribution of board members may be facilitated by, for example,[15] 'away
days', informal dialogue between board members in between board
meetings, informal dialogue between board members and executives
in between meetings, the time spent at board meetings, focusing on the
agenda more than on routine items, several iterations of issues over
time, processes of information sharing, challenge and open debate, the
presentations of executives, and the uncovering of subtle nuances of
opinion between different executives.

Diversity and cognitive perspectives on boards and strategy

Most research into how boards contribute to strategy has been related
to how boards deal with the conflict resulting from divergent preferences of principals and agents. How cognitive perspectives influence
the board strategy contribution has, so far, received limited attention.[16]

In chapter 8 I demonstrated how diversity and cognition are related.
Diversity in the boardroom is a main question related to board composition, but diversity goes beyond the issues of women or minority
representation and having members from different professional backgrounds. It is possible to differentiate between observable and non-
observable types of diversity.[17] The observable types are more likely
to evoke actions than the non-observable types. These two types are
not mutually exclusive. Among the non-observable types of diversity
it is possible to list individual capabilities, personalities and values.
Differences in personalities and values can create major differences in
orientation towards various issues, and they may also influence interaction styles. Diversity in the composition of boards may affect board
behaviour through affective, cognitive, communication and symbolic
processes.

Violina Rindova has made a contribution to the investigation of
what boards have to do with strategy from diversity and cognitive

perspectives.[18] She shows how the board's involvement in strategy involves resolving conflict, complexity and uncertainty. Conflict comes from diverging interests among the various actors; complexity is related to interactions among multiple actors and events; uncertainty comes from information asymmetry between the various actors, and from incomplete information about the future impact of social, technological and economic factors. The complexity and uncertainty of strategic decision-making requires various types of knowledge among the decision-makers, and various ways of processing knowledge. Various types and degrees of complexity and uncertainty will thus necessitate various types of knowledge and diversity from the board members as well as putting demands on the board's working style. From a cognitive perspective, Rindova predicts that both board involvement and diversity in knowledge among board members will increase as complexity and uncertainty increase.

Table 9.3 illustrates how the board's strategic involvement is seen from a cognitive perspective rather than from a traditional governance perspective rooted in legalistic theory and agency theory.[19]

The columns represent limitations and possibilities, and the possibilities are emphasised in the cognitive perspectives: what appears as a limitation may with a cognitive approach be turned into a possibility. Directors may contribute with general problem-solving expertise even though they do not have firm-specific knowledge. They may find efficient ways of communication and information processing even though their time spent on board work is limited. They may lack familiarity with the everyday problems in the company, but they may provide stimuli based on external variation. Not only will directors control managerial decision-making and intervene if performance declines, they will continually contribute to decision quality through scanning, interpretation and choice. Directors related to organisational stakeholders may – even though they are dependent 'yes-sayers' – be a source of representative variation, and board members with multiple directorships may benefit from increased exposure and expertise even though they may have more time constraints. Strategic decision-making is about seeing possibilities under cognitive constraints and complexity and uncertainty. This is also the case for the board's strategy involvement. The diversity and cognitive perspectives fit nicely into a behavioural theory of boards and governance.

Table 9.3 *Differences in the evaluation of board effectiveness in strategy contribution*

Frequently suggested directors' limitations	Likely grounds for directors' ineffectiveness from a traditional governance perspective	Likely grounds for directors' effectiveness from a cognitive perspective
Directors have limited firm-specific knowledge	Limited knowledge prevents directors from making substantive contribution to strategic decisions	Directors rely on general problem-solving expertise and transfer skills from other organisational contexts
Directors spend too little time on board work	Directors cannot process the complex information necessary to make strategic decisions	Directors process and structure information as experts, leading to efficiency and speed gains
Directors are too removed from the everyday problems of the firm	Lack of familiarity limits directors' potential contributions	Directors focus on and notice different stimuli and provide external variety
Directors' role is to control managerial decision-making	Directors intervene only if performance declines	Directors contribute to decision quality through scanning, interpretation and choice
Directors from a customer or a supplier firm are less independent	Less independence leads to 'yes-saying'	Directors related to organisational stakeholders may be a source of representative variety
Multiple directorships reduce time for and familiarity with each of the firms	The potential ineffectiveness of limited time and firm-specific knowledge is magnified	A curvilinear relationship: additional board memberships increase exposure and expertise up to a point

Source: Rindova 1999.

Control involvement

We often find that there is a distinction between internal and external control mechanisms.[20] The board of directors is the main internal control mechanism, while the market for corporate control is often, at least in the US setting, considered to be the main external control mechanism. Here we are addressing the board's control tasks, and these tasks may also be internally and externally oriented.

Control can be seen as the question: who has the basic control over key decisions? The control tasks may follow a stepwise logic or process,[21] including mandate clarification (stakeholder analysis), the setting of goals and strategies (strategy process), the ratification of plans and budget-based goals and strategies (budgeting process) and the control and evaluation of budgets and strategy implementation.

The first tasks were presented and discussed in the previous section on strategy involvement. The implementation of this process may take place in various ways. The variations mainly relate to what the board's responsibilities are compared to what the managerial responsibilities are.

Stakeholder analysis and strategic process

Mandate clarification can be carried out either at an aggregate level, for the whole board, or for the individual directors. Many observations have indicated that board members have only vague or general ideas about their mandates. Few have an awareness of how various stakeholders or actors have an interest in directing the boards' task involvement, and how they relate to that. There is often a general idea that they should do what is best for the firm, and nobody should represent any particular stakeholder. However, what is best for the shareholders is often equated to what is best for the firm. A regular stakeholder analysis will help the board balance the stakes and power of various stakeholders.

Board control tasks are sometimes divided into strategic control and operational control.[22] Operational control will often follow ordinary twelve-month planning cycles, and performance will be measured against goals and budgets. Management performance will often be tracked against cost and revenue objectives. Strategic control will more often be long-term and based on non-financial information.

Strategic control is sometimes also contrasted with financial control. Under a system of strategic control, managers are evaluated on the basis of how strategically desirable the decisions were before the implementation (*ex ante*) and on the basis of financial performance after the decisions had been implemented (*ex post*). Under a system of financial control, managers are rewarded primarily on the basis of their success in meeting performance criteria; the *ex ante* counterparts of financial controls are budgets.

Control, entrenchment and tools for evaluations

We have already seen in chapter 6 that CEOs may have various ways to circumvent the board. Among the entrenchment mechanisms available to CEOs is the alteration of individual assessments, situation assessments and performance assessments.[23] They may also neutralise internal control mechanisms. Boards may be well aware of the inefficiencies of internal control mechanisms; some of the inefficiencies will be intractable while others can be addressed.

To perform the control tasks, various kinds of information and tools are needed. Various checklists may be compiled with regard to directors' information, as follows.[24]

- Comparing sales, costs and balance sheet and cash flow information with earlier periods.
- Information on the firm's share of the market.
- The minutes of management committee meetings.
- Key media articles on the company and major competitors.
- Consumer preference surveys etc.
- Employee attitude surveys.

The management's comments should also be provided. They should include the reasons for their views, and the likely consequences from acting on them, such as for the rest of the year.

This list shows the tasks that the board should be involved in and the kind of information it should demand.

Boards will also exert power over management by management control systems, by assessing top management and by determining top management incentives and sanctions. Furthermore, boards may possess reserved power. Having reserved power means that the board makes formal statements about delegated power to the CEO. The board defines the thresholds of decision that are delegated to the CEO on a number of key issues. Reserved power statements make constraints on managerial actions.

Inside directors may have an important role in strategic control. In complex organisations it is often difficult to implement effective methods of internal control because information about the relationships between managerial behaviour and financial performance can be hidden. Those who are participants in the decision process have access to information that is relevant to assessing managerial competence and the strategic desirability of initiatives – regardless of their short-term or long-term performance outcomes. Part-time board members may lack the amount and quality of information needed to control managerial behaviour.

Inside directors usually have greater access to subjective information about top managers' performance – for example, the decision process and the decision-making quality. Outside directors will generally have limited contact with the day-to-day decision processes of the firm, and will thus often lack the kind of subjective information needed. Outside directors may – because of their experiences – be able to make detached judgements about the strategic decisions of top managers, but the very nature of strategic decisions make them unique and unstructured. Outside directors will therefore need additional information about firm processes. This may require time and relationship types that challenge the state of being independent.

Perceptions about board control involvement

In the 'value-creating board' surveys we collected perceptions about board control involvement in a similar way to those for board strategy involvement. The results, displayed in table 9.4, are sorted based on results from factor analyses.

There were only a few differences between the responses from men and women. Contributions to charity, CEO remuneration, top management team incentive systems and human resource policy were rated higher by women than men. The natural environment and customer satisfaction were rated higher by men than women. The differences may show real differences, as not all boards have women directors, but it may also reflect differences between the sexes in how the questions are perceived or in how directors of different gender want to report their perceptions. The implications of table 9.4 are discussed in following sections.

Table 9.4 *Board control involvement perceptions*

		CEO	Chair	Outsider	Employee
Output	Financial return to owners	4.47	4.88	5.03	4.18
	Natural environment and CSR	3.69	4.43	4.40	3.80
	Contribution to charity	2.26	2.74	2.87	2.45
Quantitative	Cost budgets	4.90	5.39	5.63	5.29
	Investments and use of capital	5.17	5.62	5.89	5.33
	Liquidity and payments	4.46	5.14	5.35	4.95
	Risk management	5.16	5.62	5.92	5.38
	Sales and marketing budgets	4.56	5.03	5.34	4.93
Behaviour	CEO performance	4.55	4.90	4.92	3.66
	CEO remuneration	4.26	4.71	5.18	3.91
	TMT incentive system	3.27	4.08	4.32	2.84
Qualitative	Human resources policy	3.42	4.17	4.02	3.21
	Organisation and human resources	4.12	4.78	4.61	3.54
	Product quality and customer satisfaction	4.19	4.97	4.91	4.30
	N	c.500	c.300	c.300	c.200

Responses from Norwegian firms with between fifty and 5000 employees, based on a seven-point Likert-type scale where a value of 7 means 'highly agree'.
N = number of responses.

Output and quantitative types of control

Output control, financial and quantitative-oriented types of control are often considered to be external types of control. Control and evaluation may be conducted based on *ex ante*, externally given standards. External control will often require less time and effort than behavioural and quantitative types of control. External and part-time board members will therefore also often find it easier to relate to these types of control. Both output control and quantitative types of control will generally be financially or accounting-oriented, and the focus is largely based on past performance.

Compliance with the formal tasks related to laws or regulations may also be a form of external control. There are laws that emphasise the board's and the board members' liability in meeting employment and labour issues, environmental issues, tax and fiscal issues, competition and customer issues, etc. The formal tasks may be related to financial reporting and the annual report, the annual shareholders' meeting, the signing of forms, and various issues in relation to shareholder registers etc.

Output control

Environmental assessment and conversations with stakeholders are important for output control, as is transparency. In the 'value-creating board' surveys output control was assessed with three measures: the evaluation of the financial return to shareholders; the evaluation of issues related to the natural environment and corporate social responsibility; and the evaluation of contributions to charity. It was very evident that the boards were not involved in evaluating contributions to charity. Their involvement in the natural environment and CSR was also limited. Finally, their involvement in the financial return to shareholders was lower than their involvement in any of the measures categorised as quantitative control. The chairperson and the other outside, non-executive board members give higher ratings on the output control questions than the CEO and the employee-elected board members.

The low board involvement in output control may be due to the fact that the board is only one of several governance mechanisms for output control. Output control may be conducted by people or institutions outside the board, and those institutions focusing on output control may prefer to place board members to safeguard the boundaries of the firm or to protect the rights of stakeholders than to develop the organisation.

Quantitative control

In the 'value-creating board' surveys quantitative control was assessed using five measures: the board's involvement in the evaluation of cost budgets; the evaluation of investments and capital expenditures; the evaluation of liquidity and payments; the evaluation of risk management and the firm being subject to proper control; and the evaluation of sales and marketing budgets. The evaluation of risk management and the evaluation of investments were the two items that got the highest ratings among all fifteen control involvement items surveyed. All five quantitative control items also got higher ratings than the items measuring the other types of control involvement. The involvement in quantitative control was rated significantly higher by the non-executive outside board members than by the chairperson. The employee-elected board members rated their involvement in this type of control higher than did the CEOs.

Behavioural and qualitative kinds of control

I have described how strategic types of control are mainly related to the future, and that financial and other externally oriented types of control are mainly related to the past. A characteristic of behavioural and qualitative types of control is that, first and foremost, they relate to the present. Furthermore, they generally also have an internal focus.

Strategic and financial control, which we looked at earlier in other contexts, may both also be related to internal control. One aspect of internal control is operational control: this tracks management performance against cost and revenue objectives. Operational control is mostly financial, and often it does not explicitly take into account long-term and non-financial aims. This kind of control was presented in the quantitative control section. Strategic control, on the other hand, is more qualitative and long-term, so aspects of strategic control will be presented under the qualitative control heading.

Many of the codes of best practice make suggestions as to internal control. The internal control concept has traditionally been used by auditors and accountants. The main tools in the board's involvement in internal control are the use of an audit committee and the board's active relations with auditors. A key responsibility for an audit committee may be to monitor if the management is acting in accordance with decisions made by the board. In general, however, good relations and frequent contact with internal as well as external auditors may be important in the internal control tasks.

Nevertheless, the board's internal control involvement goes beyond the use of auditors and an audit committee. Boards are responsible for overseeing and ensuring that proper internal control systems exist, and that the board members themselves assess management. This includes the hiring, firing and remunerating of the CEO. The board has two main classes of internal control options available for this task. It can either alter the incentives of the managerial team, or it can dismiss it.[25] One of the main tasks of the board is to select and 'deselect' the CEO. Even though it is the formal task of the board to select the CEO, in reality it is often the incumbent CEO who exercises most influence on selecting his or her successor. Recently we have seen an increasing number of situations in which the CEO has been fired; this is to a large extent a result of external pressures, including shareholder activism.

Another aspect of internal control is the board's disciplining role. Boards will often serve a disciplining task just by existing or having meetings.[26] The fact that the CEO and executives are aware that outsiders will be examining what they have done forces them to do a little better. Decision-making and information gathering will thus also be somewhat more informal with a board requiring reports more regularly when they have more frequent meetings than when they meet infrequently. The CEO can also use the board as a disciplinary tool in relation to the rest of the organisation. The CEO can make the people lower down in the organisation think that the board is asking disciplining or controlling questions.[27]

Behavioural control

Three questions were used in the 'value-creating board' surveys to indicate behavioural control. These were the level of involvement in assessing the work of the CEO, in the evaluation of remuneration to the CEO and in the evaluation of incentive systems to the top management team. The differences between the responses from the outside non-executive board members and the responses from the employee-elected board members were very big for these questions. The responses from the chairpersons and the CEOs were in between the extremes, with the responses from the chairpersons closest to the outside directors. The outside directors and the employee-elected directors gave their highest rating for the board's involvement in the evaluation of CEO remuneration, while the chairpersons and the CEOs gave their highest ratings for its involvement in the evaluation of the CEO's behaviour.

In the survey there were also questions about who had the most influence last time there was a change in the TMT, and the last time there was a change in the compensation package to the CEO. The CEO and individuals in the TMT clearly had the strongest influence when people in the TMT were being changed. The chairperson also had some influence, but others such as the outside board members, the employee-elected directors and other external actors had little influence. In the question about the CEO compensation package it was very clear that the chairperson had the greatest influence. Other outside board members also had some influence, but the employee-elected board members had very limited influence. The employee-elected board members indicated that the CEO had as much influence as the outside board members.

Many codes of best practice argue that separate remuneration committees should be established to ensure that independent CEO assessment and remuneration takes place. 'Alone meetings', where the outside directors meet without the CEO's presence, are also clearly advised.

Qualitative control

Three measures were used to indicate qualitative control. These were the boards' involvement in evaluating the company's human resources management (HRM) and recruitment policy, the boards' involvement in evaluating the company's organisation and human resources, and the boards' involvement in evaluating product quality and customer satisfaction. Sometimes boards use quality indices to evaluate human resources, employee satisfaction and attitude surveys, customer satisfaction, etc.[28] These may form useful benchmarks on progress towards various stated goals

The ratings of the boards' involvement in qualitative control were generally lower than the ratings of the behavioural control questions. The chairperson generally gave the highest ratings, but the ratings from the other outside board members were very similar. The highest ratings were given to the boards' involvement in the evaluation of product quality and customer satisfaction, and the lowest ratings were given to the evaluation of human resources policy. The employee directors had higher ratings than the CEOs on product quality and customer satisfaction. The low ratings from employee directors on the issues concerning human resources and the behavioural control questions may reflect the gap between their ambitions to influence these issues and what they experience in reality.

Service involvement

The service tasks are sometimes called the institutional tasks of the board as they function at the institutional level of the firm.[29] The service tasks have strong theoretical foundations from resource dependence theory, as the board is helping to acquire critical resources; they serve to legitimise the firm in the environment.[30] Service tasks also include how the board members are involved in providing advice and guidance through their experience and expertise. The advisory tasks of boards have received significant attention in managerial hegemony theory.[31] More recent arguments are, however, derived from the resource-based view of the firm,[32] and also from stewardship theory.[33] According to these theories the boards are evaluated based on their contribution to value creation, and not only to control.

Table 9.5 shows results from the 'value-creating board' surveys about how various categories of board members rate the boards' involvement in nine issues related to service tasks. Four different factors were extracted through factor analyses: these were involvement in resource dependence tasks, two factors related to involvement in advisory tasks, and one factor indicating mentorship.

Male board members generally rated these questions higher than female board members. There were no differences between the sexes on the questions about legal and financial issues and about mentorship. As in the case for the control questions, the different answers may show genuine differences, as not all boards have women directors. Boards with women may be less involved in the various service issues; various other analyses indicate so. However, it may also reflect differences between the sexes in how the questions are perceived or how directors of different gender want to report their perceptions. Comments about the various service tasks are presented in the following section.

Resource dependence tasks

Three questions were used in the 'value-creating board' surveys to indicate the boards' involvement in the various resource dependence

Table 9.5 *Board service involvement perceptions*

		CEO	Chair	Outsider	Employee
RD[a]	Building networks	4.33	4.81	4.79	4.64
	Lobby and legitimise	3.65	3.97	3.92	3.67
	Advise through networks	3.80	4.38	4.10	3.93
Top-down advice	General management (HRM, strategy, organisation) issues	4.72	5.26	5.31	4.42
	Legal and accounting technical issues	4.17	4.39	4.72	3.85
	Financial issues	4.29	4.77	4.98	4.15
Dialogue advice	Technical issues	3.50	3.81	4.01	4.00
	Marketing issues	4.42	4.81	4.98	4.43
Mentoring		3.78	4.33	4.12	3.53
	N[b]	*c.*500	*c.*300	*c.*300	*c.*200

Responses from Norwegian firms with between fifty and 5000 employees, based on a seven-point Likert-type scale where a value of 7 means 'highly agree'.
a RD = resource dependence tasks.
b N = number of responses.

tasks. The questions were about the boards' contribution to building networks, their contribution to lobbying and legitimacy, and how the firm uses the network of the board members to get advice. Building networks received the highest ratings while lobbying and legitimacy had the lowest ratings; the low rating may be caused by a somewhat negative connotation to the lobbying concept.

There were no big differences in the answers from the various categories of respondents. The highest ratings were given in the responses from the chairpersons and the other outside board members. The lowest ratings were given by the CEOs. The resource dependence tasks may be considered to be the service tasks with external focus or orientation.

Reputation building and networking

The legitimacy and reputation tasks of the board have long been identified. The board is often the primary signalling source for the organisation's intentions and purpose.[34] For instance, CEOs may want to add individuals to the board to improve the firm's reputation in environmental matters. Sometimes the involvement and activities of such board members may be unimportant, as they function as 'window displays' or 'ornaments on the corporate Christmas tree'. Board members with high integrity, power or reputation may make the environment positive for the firm, but legitimacy and reputation building may be more related to who the board members are than what they do. Making the board members visible may therefore be important for developing board effectiveness.

Networking and lobbying usually require more activity and involvement than legitimacy and reputation building. Networking may take place in various ways – for example, through co-optation and interlocking directorates.[35] Interlocking directorates may contribute to inter-organisational coordination through communication and information sharing, and may also contribute to influencing the decision-making in other firms. The networking and lobbying tasks of the board may often be activated by including board members with high social capital and access to the elements in the environment that the firm may need to influence.

Bridging competency and biased advice
There is a strong tradition that boards may help, by acquiring critical resources, to reduce uncertainty and to serve as a legitimising function for the organisation.

In a similar fashion, board members may also give the firm access to the knowledge resources in the network of the board members. The problem with this kind of advice is the bias in advice seeking. This can also lead to biased advice: the advice is given based on the board members' network ties, and such ties are often social and related to existing business and friendship ties.[36] Bias emanating from business ties may be based on functional background similarity and interdependent relationships. Furthermore, friends are expected to provide social support, and friends tend to affirm each other's self-serving attributions.

Advice and counsel

The board members may serve as sources of information – like tentacles in the environment. However, the advisory tasks of boards are mainly related to the competency of the various board members. Diversity is considered an important board composition characteristic for providing proper advice. From an advisory perspective, diversity will be reflected in the board members having competencies that supplement the competencies of the management.

A board focusing on advisory tasks may not be a decision-making body, but it can indicate that the management should look into areas it feels the management has not yet carefully explored. The board can post words of warning to the management, and these will have an effect on management thinking.

The advice and service tasks may be performed as parts of the regular board meetings, but they may also be performed outside the meetings as individual counselling from board members to the management. In some boards there are arrangements whereby the board members receive additional remuneration for the counselling they are performing outside the meetings. Often this is a motive for consultants to become board members.

In the 'value-creating board' surveys, questions were asked about five different advisory tasks: general management questions; human resource management, strategy and organisation, legal and accounting technical questions; financial questions (corporate finance and investments); technical questions (including also production and information technology); and marketing questions. Two groups resulted from the factor analysis. One group was related to overall questions about general management, law and finance; this group can be labelled 'top-down' advice. The other group seems to be more related to production and markets, and it can be labelled 'dialogue' advice.

Overall questions and top-down advice

The differences in responses between the four groups of respondents were higher on the overall questions than on the production/market-oriented questions, and also on the questions about the resource dependence tasks. The main difference lay in the low responses from the employee directors on the three overall advice questions.

The highest ratings were on general management advice. Advice may be classified as either generalist or specialist advice. Generalist advice is often related to strategic decision-making, leadership, HRM and the development of organisational resources. Generalist advice is often at an overall and general level and is different from control. However, the practical conduct of control of these issues may take the form of advice.

The high ratings may confirm that the board is a group of generalists, not specialists, who can advise the CEO on all kinds of problems – suggesting new ideas, new services and new improvements for what is being done, and also providing criticism on what is not being done.

The two other overall questions were about legal advice and financial advice. The financial expertise in companies varies; some CEOs therefore find it valuable to have financially oriented people as board members. The same is the case with legal advice. Advice on financial issues was rated higher than advice on legal issues.

Production and markets: dialogue advice

The other group of advisory questions is directed at technical issues, production, products, markets and marketing. These are questions normally at the core of any organisation, and the board members' knowledge and competency in these areas will thus supplement existing knowledge and create a possibility for dialogue and interaction.

The impact of technology on almost all companies is sufficiently great for it to provide opportunities for board members with technological knowledge to provide advice on technological questions. Board members offering technological advice may often have backgrounds different from those of other board members. They may also be younger, in particular if the competency needed is related to investments in new technology. In the surveys, advice on market issues was rated higher than advice on technical issues.

Mentoring and collaboration in strategic management

The last question on board tasks in the 'value-creating board' surveys was on mentoring. Mentoring and collaboration was introduced in this chapter in the section about the board's strategic involvement. Mentorship and collaboration tasks are mentioned in the literature as two similar tasks, with stewardship theory as the theoretical rationale for both of them. These tasks are distinctly different from the advisory task, as the boards or the board members take a more direct responsibility for value creation than when service tasks are involved.

However, mentoring and collaboration are clearly different. In mentoring the board takes the responsibility for helping and supporting the CEO and the management. In collaboration the board takes an independent responsibility to collaborate with the CEO and the management to achieve value creation. Collaboration in strategic decision-making is not a separation of decision control and decision management tasks. Collaboration is based on trust, and the management and the board will, from their different perspectives, contribute not only to ratifying strategic decisions but also to shaping the context, content and conduct of strategies.[37]

Although mentoring has been used in particular in relation to honeymoon effects,[38] it has also been used in relation to boards in small entrepreneurial firms.[39] The honeymoon effect postulates that a board will try to support, help and mentor a newly chosen CEO. However, after some time, as the new CEO becomes more independent, the board will cease to function as a mentor and become more active as a monitor.[40]

The literature about business angels has described the mentorship role of rich and experienced people wanting to support and mentor young entrepreneurs and new initiatives. However, such mentorship involvements do not need to be altruistic. If the tasks of boards go beyond minimising agency costs and instead are about value creation, mentoring and supporting entrepreneurs or managers may certainly be a way to effective board involvement.

Moreover, the board of directors may serve as a kind of sounding board – a wall to bounce the ball against. Many CEOs experience isolation to some degree, and therefore feel a need to have a partner to discuss things with. Sometimes they encounter situations in which they need to have somebody to talk to. Issues and questions may be raised or presented, even though the real need is more to have somebody who can listen than somebody who can respond and answer.

The case of board task involvement

The in-depth summarising case in this chapter relates concepts presented in this chapter to concepts presented in previous chapters. A basic idea underlying the arguments in this book is that the internal dynamics of boards affect how they undertake their tasks. The framework in this book builds on the model of Shaker Zahra and John Pearce.[41] Zahra and Pearce argue that the relationship between board composition and corporate financial performance must be split into various intermediate steps. Among these steps they argue for board member characteristics, board structures and board processes, and board task performance. Furthermore, they present three clearly different board tasks – strategy, control and service – and argue how context, board member characteristics, board structures and board processes, in different ways and to various degrees, impact the various board tasks. The variations in effects on the different board tasks are illustrated here. I also show empirically that there is a need to open the 'black box' of actual board behaviour in order to understand and develop board effectiveness, and to go beyond studies of traditional measures of board composition.

Board accountability is discussed in chapter 3, and various expectations of board task performance, which are theoretically elaborated, are presented. Various contextual factors are presented in chapter 5, and board composition and board member characteristics feature in chapter 4. There are four board members attributes that are often included in studies of boards of directors: the number of board members, the ratio of outside directors, CEO duality and shareholding by board members. These four attributes are often called the 'usual suspects'.[42] However, various other board member attributes – such as the board members' general and firm-specific knowledge, as well as incentives – are presumed to be important, but they are more difficult to measure. In chapter 7 board structures are presented; these may be measured by the number and length of board meetings, the use of 'away days', etc. Board structures may also be measured by their compliance with various codes of best corporate governance practice. In chapter 8 I look at the board decision-making processes, and I argue that board effectiveness also depends on how well the board works as a team.

Variables and measures

My empirical analysis is from the 'value-creating board' surveys data. The dependent variables are various board task involvement variables, and the independent variables are some of the variables presented in the earlier chapters. In the analysis we used responses from approximately 300 board chairpersons in firms with between fifty and 5000 employees.[43]

The six board task involvement measures used in the analysis are as follows.

- Quantitative control: this was measured as the mean of the five items listed in table 9.4. Quantitative control was used as an indicator of external types of control.
- Behavioural control: this was measured as the mean of the three items listed in table 9.4. Behavioural control was used as an indicator of internal types of control
- Qualitative control: this was measured as the mean of the three qualitative control items listed in table 9.4. Qualitative control is an internal type of control, but it is long-term and can also be used as an indicator of strategic control.
- Network: this was measured as the mean of the three items related to resource dependence tasks listed in table 9.5.
- Advice: this was measured as the mean of the five items about advisory tasks listed in table 9.5.
- Board strategy involvement; this was measured as the mean of the four items listed in table 9.1.

The six variables correspond generally to the six theoretically elaborated board tasks presented in chapter 3.

Among the contextual variables presented in chapter 5 I selected indicators of ownership, firm size and the experience of crisis.[44] Two ownership variables were used: more than 10 per cent state ownership, and a family business perception. Firm size was measured on the basis of the number of employees.

Two main sets of variables were used to measure the attributes of the board members. The first set was the 'usual suspects', including the number of board members, the outsider ratio, CEO duality[45] and the level of shareholding by the board members. The second set of variables consisted of the board members' intrinsic motivation, their firm-specific knowledge and their diversity.[46] Intrinsic motivation was measured as the mean of three variables related to awareness of liability, personal and professional standards, and reputation.[47] Firm-specific knowledge was measured as the mean of six particular items dealing with the board members' firm-specific knowledge.[48] Diversity was measured as the mean of five items.[49]

Board structures (chapter 7) were also measured by two sets of variables. The first set was about board meetings, while the second set was related to recommended maintenance mechanisms in codes of best corporate governance practice. Three meeting variables were used: the number of regular board meetings, the length of regular board meetings and the use of two-day meetings or 'away days'. We measured six different board maintenance or code compliance variables.[50] The variables concerned the existence of 'alone' meetings, board development activities, CEO work descriptions, new member introductions, regular board evaluations and board instructions.

Four decision-making culture variables from the discussion in chapter 8 were used:[51] cohesiveness,[52] openness and generosity,[53] preparation and involvement[54] and critical attitudes.[55]

Analyses

Six main models were analysed. The differences in the models were the dependent variables. In each model the variables were introduced in eight steps: first, the ownership variables; second, the firm size; third, the crisis variable; fourth, the 'usual suspects'; fifth, the other board member variables; sixth, the various board meeting variables; seventh, the six code compliance variables; and, eighth, the four board culture variables.

Table 9.6 shows how much of the variation in the board task performance variable is explained after a new step is introduced. The significance signs indicate the significance of the change from the previous step.

Variations in explanation vary across the various types of board task performance.[56] Table 9.6 shows that the variation in board strategy involvement is explained the most, followed by the variation in behavioural control. The variation in quantitative control is explained the least. The introduction of firm size and the 'usual suspects' increases the explanation of the variation in strategy involvement and behavioural control considerably. Firm size does not explain anything of the variation in the other board tasks. It is a similar situation with the 'usual suspects' – they do not explain much of the variations in the other tasks.

The overall picture indicates that step 5 and step 8 add the most to the explanation of the variations in board task performance.

The context

The three first steps in the analysis included only contextual variables. Ownership explained variations in behavioural control, firm size

Table 9.6 *Predictors of board task involvement*

	Control			Service		
	Quantitative	Behavioural	Qualitative	Network	Advice	Strategy
1. Ownership	0.005	0.045**	0.024'	0.009	0.013	0.028'
2. Firm size	0.006	0.105***	0.026	0.012	0.013	0.121***
3. Crisis	0.022'	0.108	0.026	0.038*	0.014	0.122
4. 'Usual suspects'	0.025	0.258***	0.040	0.069	0.069*	0.224***
5. Knowledge, diversity, incentives	0.154***	0.295*	0.185***	0.177***	0.220***	0.357***
6. Meetings	0.187'	0.346**	0.223*	0.207	0.241	0.416***
7. Code compliance	0.194	0.360	0.256	0.260'	0.245	0.465'
8. Decision-making culture	0.238*	0.403**	0.303*	0.339***	0.327***	0.493*
N	206	206	206	206	206	206

*Linear hierarchical regression analysis.

R^2 and F-change significance: ' = 10%, * = 5%, ** = 1%, *** = 0.1%.

N = number of responses.

explained variations in behavioural and strategy involvement, and crisis explained variables in networking.

There is a negative relationship between being a family firm and behavioural control. However, being a family firm is also correlated with size, and various other independent variables, including the number of board members, the outsider ratio, etc. Being a family firm is also negatively related to board strategy involvement and qualitative control. We did not find any relationship in step 1 between state ownership and involvement in any of the board tasks. However, in the full model we found a negative relation between state ownership and strategic involvement.

Firm size, as mentioned above, significantly contributes to explaining behavioural control and strategy involvement. In step 2 we found positive relationships between firm size and these variables. However, these relationships did not appear in the full models. There were significant correlations between firm size and the 'usual suspects'. In the full model firm size was negatively related to the network variable.[57] However, any relationship with involvement in the other board tasks is absent. The crisis variable was positively related to quantitative control and networking,[58] thereby indicating that both quantitative control and networking are particularly important in situations of crisis.

The board members

Attributes relating to the board members were included in two steps. The 'usual suspects' were included in step 4, while knowledge, diversity and incentives were included in step 5. Table 9.6 shows that the inclusion of the 'usual suspects' increased the explanations of the variations in behavioural control, advice and strategy involvement. The coefficients reported in step 4 showed that the number of board members and the outsider ratio were positively related to board strategy involvement. The positive relationship between the number of board members and strategy involvement also existed in the full model.[59] The positive relationship between outsider ratio and strategy involvement disappeared in step 5 as the more detailed attributes of the board members were introduced.

The coefficients reported in step 4 also showed that there was a positive relationship between behavioural control and the outsider ratio. The relationship was negative between behavioural control and board members' ownership. These relationships also remained in the full model.[60] The relationship between advice and board member ownership was similar, but not as strong.[61]

The addition of knowledge, diversity and intrinsic incentives increased the explanatory power of all models significantly. With quantitative control they were all positive,[62] but the significance decreased as the boardroom culture variables were introduced in step 8. The relationship between firm-specific knowledge and behavioural control was positive in step 5, but it gradually decreased as more variables were introduced. Qualitative control was significantly positively related to firm-specific knowledge and intrinsic motivation, but the significance of intrinsic motivation decreased in step 8.[63] Firm-specific knowledge was positively related to the network variable in all steps, but the significance was somewhat reduced in step 8.[64] With advice and strategy the positive relationship between firm-specific knowledge and diversity was the most important, but the significance of diversity disappeared as the boardroom culture variables were introduced.[65]

Firm-specific knowledge and diversity were generally the board member variables contributing the most to board task performance. Firm-specific knowledge had both direct and moderated effects, while the effects of diversity were to a large degree moderated by the boardroom decision-making culture.

Board structures and leadership

Board structures were included in two steps. In step 6 we included the format of meetings, and in step 7 we included various maintenance structures recommended in codes of best practice. In our analyses we did not include variables concerning the chairperson's leadership style. Steps 6 and 7 both increased the explanatory power of the models, but the significance of each step was not particularly high.

Quantitative control was related only to 'two-day' meetings and the length of the board meeting, but the significance of the relationships was not particularly strong. Behavioural control was positively related to 'two-day' meetings.[66] A positive relation with the number of meetings was found in step 6. Qualitative control was positively related to 'two-day' meetings and negatively related to the existence of a CEO working description.[67]

'Two-day' meetings were positively related to the network variable in step 6, but the significance decreased and disappeared in the following steps. Board evaluations and new member introductions were also positively related to the network variable. The significance was not particularly strong, however, and it decreased when introducing the boardroom culture variables in step 8. None of the board structure variables was significantly related to the advisory tasks. Strategy involvement was highly positively related to the existence of 'two-day' meetings.[68] None of the other variables was significantly related to board strategy involvement.

Board decision-making culture

The explanatory power of each of the models increased significantly when the decision-making culture variables were introduced in step 8. The point has already been made that the boardroom culture mediated the effects of the board member attribute variables on board task performance.

The variables used were openness and generosity, preparation and involvement, critical attitudes and cohesiveness. None of the variables was individually significantly related to quantitative control. The preparation and involvement variable was positively related to behavioural control,[69] while the openness and generosity variable was significantly positively related to qualitative control.[70] Openness and generosity were also significant positively related to advice.[71] Cohesiveness was positively related to networking.[72] Preparation and involvement were positively related to strategic involvement.[73]

The discussion in chapter 8 showed how the boardroom culture variables intercorrelate in various ways. The interpretation of the impact of the individual boardroom culture variables therefore needs to be carried out with care.

Predictors of board task performance

The analysis presented here is generally based on a model with intermediate steps. This means that board members influence board structures, board structures influence the decision-making culture, and the decision-making culture influences board task performance. However, as I have indicated several times, there may be both direct and moderating effects. It is a direct effect when, for example, the number of board members influences board task performance without any intermediate links. It is a moderating effect when, for example, the size and direction of the relationship between the number of board members and the decision-making culture are changed by variations in board structure. Diversity, for example, may be important for various board tasks but it does not help unless there is a decision-making culture or board structures that value diversity.

We have, however, seen here that there are variations and similarities in predictors of board task performance. The explained variation among the board task variables itself actually varied: the variations in strategy involvement and behavioural control were explained the most. We also found that some predictor variables that were positively related to some task performance variables were negatively related to other task performance variables.

Variables that in general explained the most in actual board task involvement were:

- the firm-specific knowledge of the board members;
- the use of 'away days';
- openness and generosity; and
- preparation and involvement.

Firm size, family ownership, the experience of crisis, the number of board members, and diversity also gave significant contributions to the explanations of the variations, but the scale of the contributions varied depending on the task performance variable, and the contributions were generally also mediated by other variables.

Summary

Among the concepts presented in this chapter are board strategy involvement (content, context and conduct of strategy), financial control, output control, internal control, behavioural control, quantitative control, qualitative control, resource dependence tasks, reputation building, lobbying and networking, bridging competence, advice (dialogue and top-down), and mentoring and collaboration in strategic decision-making.

In this chapter I have presented and discussed concepts and findings in relation to boards' strategy involvement, boards' control involvement and boards' service involvement. This chapter is the empirical side of chapter 3. In chapter 3 I examined board task expectations as they are presented in various theories; here, in chapter 9, I have presented what boards are doing in reality, and the presentations are based on empirical observations. Observations from the 'value-creating boards' surveys were used to develop, illustrate and measure concepts.

Table 9.7 contains a presentation of the concepts used to describe board task involvement. There are many ways of categorising board task involvement or performance. Board task involvement is dichotomised by many authors, and generally the dichotomy reflects the existence of both external and internal perspectives. The external perspectives are usually called control tasks or monitoring tasks whereas the internal perspectives are usually called service tasks – but collaboration, resource provision and even mentoring are used by some authors.

We often find that board tasks are divided into three main groups – control, strategy and service. Board strategy involvement may, however, be related to both internal and external perspectives. In chapter 3 I presented theoretical expectations in relation to six board tasks. These were output control, internal control, decision control, networking and resource dependence tasks, advisory tasks and collaboration and mentoring tasks. The left-hand columns of table 9.6 show how these tasks are related to the general use of the control, service and strategy concepts.

Column IV in table 9.7 lists most of the actual board tasks or concepts presented in this chapter. This column also indicates how these actual and empirically elaborated tasks are related to the expectations. Column V in the table also gives a guide as to how we measured board task involvement in the in-depth summarising study. The variables used in the study are as follows.

- Quantitative control: this also reflects financial and operational control. We also measured other aspects of output control, such as board involvement in following up or controlling returns to shareholders, corporate social performance and employee health, environment, and safety. However, board involvement in these output measures was different from what it was in the quantitative control measures.
- Behavioural control: this reflects internal control and is about board involvement in assessing CEO performance and remunerating the CEO and the top management team. We did not measure if and how the board designs internal control systems.
- Qualitative control: this may reflect decision and strategic control. It measures board involvement in following up on organisational resources, human resources, products and markets. Board

Table 9.7 *Summary of board task concepts*

I	II	III	IV	V
		Zahra and Pearce 1989	Task expectations from chapter 3	Task performance concepts in text	Task performance measures in case analysis
Controlling	Control	Output control	Output control	
				Financial control	Quantitative control
				Quantitative control	
		Internal control		
			Operational control	
			Internal control	
			Behavioural control	Behavioural control
			Qualitative control	Qualitative control
		Decision control		
			Strategic control	
	Strategy			Strategy involvement
		Collaboration and mentoring	Strategy involvement	
			Collaborating	
			Mentoring	
Collaborating	Service	Advisory	Dialogue advice	Advice
			Top-down advice	
		Networking	Bridge competence	Network and lobbying
			Networking	
			Lobbying	
			Reputation and legitimacy	

involvement in decision ratification and resource allocation is not directly included in this measure.

- Strategy involvement: this includes not only the ratification of important decisions but also board involvement in the formulation, implementation and control of strategies. This variable will also reflect any collaboration between the management and the board in strategic management. Our measure of mentorship had an additional characteristic other than the strategic involvement measure.

- Advisory tasks: these include both the top-down type of advice and the dialogue kind of advice.
- Networking and lobbying tasks: these reflect bridging, network building and lobbying. We did not measure board involvement in legitimacy and reputation building.

The in-depth summarising case clearly showed variations and similarities in the predictors of board task performance. The study showed that the explained variation among the board task variables itself actually varied. The variations in strategy involvement and behavioural control were explained the most. We also found that some predictor variables that were positively related to *some* task performance variables were negatively related to *other* task performance variables. The number of board members, the outsider ratio and board members' ownership are among the examples. The variables that generally explained the greatest variation in actual board task involvement were:

- the firm-specific knowledge of the board members (chapter 4);
- the use of 'away days' (chapter 7);
- openness and generosity (chapter 8); and
- preparation and involvement (chapter 8).

Diversity was also one of the variables with considerable explanatory power.

10 | *The value-creating board*

Important concepts in this chapter include:
- corporate financial performance;
- corporate social responsibility;
- mergers;
- divestments;
- process innovation;
- product innovation;
- organisational innovation;
- domestic market venturing;
- international market venturing; and
- the value chain.

This chapter links with chapter 2. In that chapter I presented various definitions of corporate governance, and explained that the different definitions would also emphasise various aspects of value creation. In this chapter I present relationships between boards and value creation, but I also link value creation back to the various actors or stakeholders.

In this book I highlight behavioural perspectives and the human side of governance. Certain assumptions are therefore embodied in the value creation discussion.

- First, the fiduciary duty of the board is not only to minimise agency costs but also to create value. The duty of boards is not only to protect wealth but also to create wealth.[1]
- Second, a time perspective must be included when evaluating value creation. A distinction between long-term and short-term value creation can be made. My emphasis is more long-term than short-term.
- Third, the corporate governance definitions presented in chapter 2 indicated that value creation can be seen in relation to how it

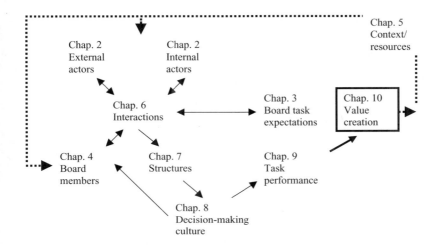

optimises value for certain individual actors or groups of actors, but value creation can also be seen in relation to the firm itself. A distinction between various external and internal value creation considerations and measures therefore needs to be made. Furthermore, value or wealth creation can consist of doing what is best for the firm; therefore, I will also consider value creation throughout the whole corporate value chain.

- Fourth, the duty of boards includes balancing the distribution of value to the various stakeholders. The different actors may have differing value creation preferences, however, as evidenced by the struggles between ideologies, and the strategising among various actors or groups of actors. Ethics and corporate social responsibility are important aspects of value creation that need to be taken into account – even under a shareholder supremacy definition of corporate governance.

- Fifth, contingency perspectives must be used to understand value creation. Various contextual factors will influence the perception of value creation. What is considered to be value creation for firms in some contexts may not be considered to be value creation for firms in other contexts.

This chapter has two main parts. The first part contains a discussion about the relationships between board tasks and internal and external value creation, and touches on both economic and social value creation.

Table 10.1 *Types of value creation*

	Internal value creation	*External value creation*
Economic value creation	Internationalisation, merger, restructuring, entrepreneurial posture, innovation, venturing	Financial performance: stock market returns, accounting returns, sales growth, etc.
Social value creation	Employee well-being, workplace safety, workplace ethics, programmes for employee training, etc.	Corporate social performance and ethical behaviour, family welfare, product quality and customer satisfaction, environmental sustainability, job creation, etc.

The second part consists of reflections on the contribution of boards to the whole corporate value chain.

External and internal value creation

My value creation definition has to be seen in the light of the corporate governance definitions presented in chapter 2. A key distinction is that between firm-external and firm-internal value creation. Another distinction can be made between economic value creation and social value creation. This is illustrated in table 10.1.[2]

This section has three parts: the first about external economic value creation, the second about social value creation, and the third about internal economic value creation.

Boards and corporate financial performance

Most discussions and studies of boards of directors link aspects of board demographics with corporate financial performance.[3] Corporate financial performance can be measured in several ways, and different actors may be more interested in some measures or aspects than in others. The different measures may well reflect the different kinds of value creation.[4]

A main distinction in financial performance indicators is whether they are accounting-based or market-based indicators. There is some disagreement as to the extent to which any board or executive decision might influence these measures. It is argued that accounting-based indicators – such as the return on assets, the return on equity and the return on sales – are subject to manipulation, may systematically undervalue assets, may create distortions due to various depreciation and valuation policies, may differ in methods for consolidating accounts and may lack standardisation in handling international accounting conventions,[5] all of which are disadvantages. Financial accounting returns are also difficult to interpret across industries. On the other hand, market-based indicators have several advantages. They reflect risk-adjusted performance and are less affected in comparisons between industries or countries. However, they are subject to forces beyond the management's control, and boards often find that accounting measures provide the most convenient targets for CEOs to reach. Accounting measures thus often provide a benchmark for boards in their evaluation of CEOs and firm performance.[6]

The majority of studies of boards and corporate financial performance have looked at how the four 'usual suspects' influence various performance measures. The 'usual suspects' are, as presented earlier,[7] the number of board members, the outsider ratio, CEO duality and the shareholding of board members.[8] Dan Dalton, Catherine Daily, Alan Ellstrand and Jonathan Johnson have conducted several meta-analyses on these studies, and generally they have found that the results are not clear-cut but ambiguous.[9]

Most published studies use arguments from agency theory regarding board independence, incentives and the control tasks to explain corporate financial performance. One of the problems arising from these studies is that few of them have been able to distinguish between the effects based on agency theory arguments and those from other board task theories. The independence measures have often been the same as resource and knowledge measures, and measures of control tasks are rarely differentiated from service tasks. As has been remarked before, boards are most often treated as a 'black box', with the human side not included.

Another feature in many of the studies is the contextual background. Ownership, industry, CEO power, etc. are typically either used as contextual or supplementing predictor variables, but most samples are from large US corporations – most often Fortune 500 firms.[10] Boards in small and medium-sized US firms and firms in other countries are hardly addressed at all.

Boards and corporate social performance

Corporate financial performance may, for many actors, be seen as an end in itself. However, financial or economic performance may also be seen as a means to achieve something else. This is particularly emphasised when corporate responsibility goes beyond shareholder value. John Elkington's 'triple bottom line' (see table 10.2[11]) is a term often used to reflect and evaluate corporate responsibility.[12] For the business, the triple bottom line encapsulates what traditionally are seen as three distinct spheres of sustainability: environmental factors, social factors and economic factors.

The 'triple bottom line' argument is that firms should have economic, social and environmental objectives: in other words, corporations should act as good citizens. Corporate citizenship is about taking account of the total impact a firm has on society and the natural environment. It implies a structuring that moves from short-term transactions towards relationships that seek to capture stakeholders' loyalty through ever more surgical interventions that align profitable opportunity with their social identities and underlying values. Elkington argues that the three different spheres are not independent but interdependent.

Various measures of corporate social and environmental responsibility have been used in studies of boards and governance, including lawsuits and illegal activities, CSR scales, reputation, social concerns, environmental reporting, etc.[13] Studies have also used downsizing, growth and contributions to charity – and even the number of women or employee board members – as indicators of corporate social responsibility. Some of these studies use instrumental stakeholder theory as the theoretical rationale. This stakeholder approach holds that CSR, ethics and taking stakeholder concerns into account will benefit the firm.[14]

What if morality comes with prohibitively high costs? Business cases for women directors and minorities demonstrate that it benefits the firm to have them there, but would we have women directors even if it did not benefit the firm? Is it likely that sustainability and the natural

Table 10.2 *Elkington's triple bottom line*

Environment
Organisations create environmental impacts at various scales, including local, national, regional and international. These occur in relation to air, water, land and biodiversity resources. Some are well understood, while others present sustainable measurement challenges owing to their complexity, uncertainty and synergies.

Social
The social dimension of sustainability captures the impact of an organisation's activity on society, including on employees, customers, the community, the supply chain and business partners. Social performance is a key ingredient in ensuring an organisation's ability to deliver high-quality environmental and economic performance. Many stakeholders believe that reporting and improving social performance enhances reputation, increases stakeholder trust, creates opportunities and lowers costs.

Economic
Organisations affect in many ways the economies in which they operate, including through their use of resources and the creation of wealth. These impacts, however, are not fully captured and disclosd by conventional financial accounting and reporting. Therefore, additional measures are required to capture the full range of an organisation's economic impacts. Sustainability reporting has rarely embraced economic measures of data, although there is a lengthy history of measuring certain economic effects – for example, of company relocation, closure and investment.

Source: GRI Guidelines July 2000.

environment will continue to receive emphasis whatever the associated expenses? These are some of the core questions in corporate social responsibility. Some aspects of CSR are regulated by law while other aspects are left to the integrity of the board and the board members to decide.

Some studies have shown that public ownership and family ownership contribute to corporate social value creation. It has also been argued that women board members, employee-elected board members, politically elected board members, etc. contribute to corporate social 'value creation'. The empirical support for these hypotheses is, to the best of my knowledge, decidedly thin, however. Again, a limitation in these studies is the 'black box' approach. These studies do not consider what is taking place inside the boardroom, and the political dynamics and strategising therein is clearly able to influence the outcome. A major problem here is the cause and effect problem. We already know that boards and firms that give high attention to women and minority directors are firms that give high attention to corporate social performance; the uncertainty is whether it is the women and minorities that influence this performance or vice versa.

Boards and internal economic value creation

The presentation of boards and internal value creation is divided into three main sections. First I look at external innovation. External innovation has been applied as a concept that refers to extrinsic – as opposed to intrinsic – sources of innovation.[15] This includes issues related to strategic content, internationalisation, mergers and divestments. Thereafter I discuss corporate entrepreneurship, before addressing the relationships between board task involvement and corporate innovation.

Board task performance and external innovation

Expenditure on innovation and expenditure on research and development (R&D) are often seen as two sides of the same coin. Innovation is much more than R&D, however. Some authors make distinctions between internal and external innovation. External innovation is related to buying and selling businesses. Firms focusing on external innovation will often rely on internal control systems. Mergers and acquisitions will have a negative indirect effect on internal innovation through the control systems used to implement this strategy.[16] As firms acquire new firms or units the attention of boards will move from strategic control and management to financial control. Acquisition is thus considered to be something of a poison pill for internal innovation.[17] Active involvement in financial control tasks may be negative, especially in industries relying on innovation.[18]

Restructuring, including downsizing and divestments, has often been seen as a form of external innovation. The concept of external innovation often refers to possibilities for the firm and its investors in the environment rather than within the firm itself. However, research has shown that downsizing and divestments often follow inadequate corporate governance,[19] but that a takeover threat may trigger board activity.

Some illustrations of these concepts and relationships are displayed in table 10.3. The results of correlation analysis between the board task performance variables and some variables about external innovation/strategic content are displayed in the table. The results are from the 'value-creating board' survey.[20]

The first row in table 10.3 shows the relationships between the experience of a takeover threat in recent years and the present level of board task involvement. The figures indicate that previous takeover threats have influenced the board's involvement in each of the board tasks. This trend in the relationship sounds more plausible than a relationship tending in the other direction. The most significant relationships were associated with quantitative control and strategy involvement.

The table also shows positive relationships between networking and R&D costs. This may have alternative explanations. It may indicate that R&D costs can be an easy-to-communicate measure, but that R&D is not something that boards are usually involved in. It may also indicate that board members may be used to lobby for or bridge links to sources of research funding. Looking for potential external cooperation partners for sharing R&D costs may be another explanation. Merger activity is positively related to behavioural control, networking and strategy involvement. International activities are positively related to behavioural control and strategy involvement. Boards may be involved when framing decisions about international activities, but it does not seem as though the advice and network tasks of the board members are very important for international activities.

The only indicated relationship with restructuring is strategy involvement, but there are significant differences between, on the one hand, networking and advice and, on the other hand, the contribution of strategy to restructuring. The table clearly displays that the various board task performances differ in their relationships with merger activity, restructuring and international activities. The same difference is not found with respect to a takeover threat.

Corporate entrepreneurship and entrepreneurial posture

As we have just seen, the contribution of external innovation to value creation can be disputed. Corporate innovation and corporate entrepreneurship are not always the same. Corporate entrepreneurship can – in contrast to various aspects of external innovation – contribute to value creation by developing a work environment that supports

Table 10.3 *Board task performance and strategic content*

	Quantitative control	Behavioural control	Qualitative control	Networking	Advice	Strategy
Takeover threat	0.30**	0.13*	0.13*	0.15*	0.24**	0.30**
R&D costs	0.06	0.02	-0.03	0.14*	0.08	-0.03
Merger activity	0.06	0.19**	0.07	0.18**	-0.06	0.23**
Restructuring	0.09	0.05	-0.03	-0.05	-0.07	0.12'
International	0.10	0.16*	-0.06	-0.05	0.04	0.14'

* Firms with between fifty and 5000 employees.

N = c.250, Pearson's product moment correlation coefficients.

Two-tailed significance: ' = 10%, * = 5%, ** = 1%.

corporate and individual growth, creating opportunities for employees to use their creative skills and fostering a culture of cross-functional collaboration.[21] Entrepreneurial activities often have a long-term perspective, and risk aversion, careerism and short-term-based reward systems may discourage the entrepreneurial efforts of managers. Boards should therefore have a role in ensuring that executives focus on long-term value creation and corporate entrepreneurship.[22]

However, owners and board members are not always proponents of long-termism and entrepreneurial processes. Many owners are short-term-oriented, and adopting an entrepreneurial orientation at the board level can be very time-consuming.

The entrepreneurial posture is oriented towards internal innovation. As such, it may be seen as a stance that encourages the processes leading to such innovation. In understanding the impact of board task performance on corporate innovation, it may therefore be important to understand the relationship between board task performance and entrepreneurial posture.

An entrepreneurial posture is defined as one of innovativeness, risk-taking and proactivity.[23] It may also include strategic renewal: this means building or acquiring new capabilities and then creatively leveraging them to create value.[24] Organisational innovation may be a starting point for strategic renewal. Strategic renewal is the evolutionary process that promotes, accommodates and utilises new knowledge and innovation in order to bring about change in the core competencies of the organisation or its product or markets.[25]

When will boards influence strategic change? Boards are usually recognised as having the potential to affect strategic change in an organisation. However, this potential is not always used. Studies have shown that there are various demographic and process-related features of boards that indicate a tendency towards change, while other features imply a preference for the status quo.[26] It is also argued that outside board members will tend to implement strategic change that is similar to what they are used to in their home company.[27] Board members will tend to develop attitudes that justify their earlier behaviour.

Implanting corporate entrepreneurship projects often requires fundamental changes in the organisation's culture, structure and management styles. Such changes will involve uncertainty, and cannot take place without support from management.[28] Studies of the relationship between corporate governance and corporate entrepreneurship have found that long-term perspectives and CEO involvement seem to be important. Outsiders, including shareholders, may lead companies away from an entrepreneurial orientation.[29]

Corporate innovation

We now turn to internal innovation, in contrast to the external innovation looked at earlier in this section. Corporate internal innovation can be defined as a company's commitment to creating and introducing new products, production processes and organisational systems.[30] Corporate innovation may also include venturing. Venturing means that firms expand their operations either by entering new markets or by expanding their operations in existing markets.

Innovation is an important outcome of firm processes, and is one aspect of internal value creation in a firm. It is critical for firm performance. Various studies have explored how innovation relates to corporate financial performance. Researchers have also tried to look into how boards may impact on innovation. However, innovation often requires investors and owners to adopt a long-term and patient approach.

Studies have found that board strategy involvement has a positive impact on internal innovation, while financial control has a negative impact. Financial control necessarily involves financial targets; as a result, the board and the management become increasingly focused on the short term, and reduce investments in products and processes, etc. that will not generate a pay-off in the short term. The implementation of innovation may be very complex, and innovation will therefore, as discussed earlier, be highly dependent on managerial involvement. The greatest degree of board contribution to internal innovation is thus expected to be through its strategy involvement.

In a study of medium-sized US companies I, along with Shaker Zahra and Donald Neubaum,[31] looked at the impact of corporate governance on five types of corporate innovation. These were:
- product innovation;
- process innovation;
- organisational innovation;
- domestic market venturing; and
- foreign market venturing.

We found some correlations between the types of innovation and the 'usual suspects'. We found an inverse U-formed relationship between the number of board members and each of the types of innovation. Neither large nor small boards were positively related to innovation. The outsider ratio was negatively related to all types of innovation. CEO duality was negatively related to the first four types of innovation. Outside directors' stock ownership was positively related to product innovation, domestic venturing and foreign venturing. In this study we also explored the effect of different kinds of institutional owners. We distinguished between pressure-resistant institutions, pressure-sensitive institutions and pressure-indeterminate institutions.[32] Pressure is considered in relation to managerial influence. Pressure-resistant institutions typically have a long-term perspective on their investments. We found that there was a positive relationship between all types of corporate innovation and pressure-resistant institutions. We also found negative correlations between corporate innovation and pressure-sensitive institutions.

The measures in this US study were used in the 'value-creating board' survey.[33] Table 10.4 displays the relationships between board task involvement and the different types of innovation. Board task performance was measured though a questionnaire to the chairpersons, and corporate innovation was measured through a questionnaire to CEOs. The study covered medium-sized Norwegian companies. The table also displays correlation coefficients.

Four features immediately become apparent when studying table 10.4. First, the correlation between board task performance and corporate innovation is generally low. Second, there are significant relationships between board strategy involvement and corporate innovation. Board–management collaboration seems to influence corporate innovation. Third, some types of board tasks are related to foreign market venturing; this is an activity that seems to be supported by board control activities. Fourth, organisational innovation is positively related to internal control. Organisational innovation seems to be linked to integrated control systems.

Value creation throughout the corporate value chain

The recent literature has taken a fresh look at boards' tasks in the whole corporate value chain and not just in the final value distribution part of the chain. A main proponent of this perspective is Bernard Taylor, who wants a move from 'corporate governance to corporate

Table 10.4 Board task performance and corporate innovation

	Quantitative control	Behavioural control	Qualitative control	Networking	Advice	Strategy
Product	0.10	0.07	0.04	0.04	0.09	0.14*
Process	0.04	0.08	-0.06	0.02	0.05	0.12'
Organisational	0.01	0.15*	0.10	0.02	-0.05	0.12'
Domestic	0.02	0.00	0.00	0.01	-0.03	0.08
Foreign	0.15*	0.11'	-0.03	-0.02	0.00	0.17**

N = c.250, Pearson's product moment correlation coefficients.
Two-tailed significance: ' = 10%, * = 5%, ** = 1%.
Firms with between fifty and 5000 employees.

Table 10.5 *Board tasks and the corporate value chain*

Inbound logistics	Operations	Innovation	Resource allocation	Imple-mentation	Value distribution
Board networking and resource provision	Board advisory tasks	Board involvement in strategy through mentoring and collaboration	Board qualitative and decision control tasks	Board behavioural and operational control tasks	Board output and financial control tasks

entrepreneurship'.[34] According to Taylor, the drive for short-term profits puts too much focus on value distribution rather than enhancing the prosperity of the business throughout the whole value chain. In addition, we saw in the first section of this chapter that there were strong positive correlations between innovation and the board's strategy involvement. However, value creation is more than just innovation and corporate entrepreneurship. This is illustrated in table 10.5, which shows how the different board tasks presented above may relate to and influence the various elements in the value chain.[35]

The term 'value chain' was used by Michael Porter in his book *Competitive Advantage*.[36] A value chain analysis describes activities within and around an organisation, and relates them to a competitive analysis of the strengths and weaknesses of an organisation. Primary activities are inbound logistics, operations, outbound logistics, marketing and sales, and service. Support activities are infrastructure, human resource management, technology development and procurement. Here I do not follow Porter's value chain in detail but I use it to show that boards can contribute to value creation by their involvement in different elements of a company's value chain. Board involvement can be seen as support activities, and various tasks may relate to the various phases. Phases in which boards can be involved are, for example, inbound logistics, operations, innovations, resource allocation, implementation and distribution. The order of sequence among the phases will be discussed, and it clearly varies between firms. The order presented here embodies a resource-based approach more than an opportunity-based approach. Here I use the value chain approach for board evaluation purposes.

Table 10.5 demonstrates that board members simultaneously need to balance accountability and knowledge. The accountability dimension is emphasised through the need to balance and meet the interests of various stakeholders. The knowledge dimension is emphasised through the need to use their knowledge and skills to support continuously and effectively the creation of value. However, neither concept is fully developed, and the relationships between the value chain phases and board tasks are more complex than those that are illustrated.

- The first phase is inbound logistics, which is about securing and providing resources. A firm depends on various kinds of resources. The resources are to various degrees controlled by the external environment. Board networking tasks, including the whole range of managing resource dependencies, may be of particular importance in this phase.
- The second phase is operations, which can include production, sales and marketing, finance, law and general management. Board advisory or consultancy tasks may be of particular importance in this phase.
- The third phase is innovation, which can be considered as the development of products, processes, the organisation and markets. The board strategy involvement through mentoring and collaboration may be particularly important in this phase.
- The fourth phase is resource allocation. Resource allocation and decision-making involve making decisions that are important for the long-term development of the firm. In this phase the boards have an important decision ratification and control task.
- The fifth phase is implementation. With respect to implementation the boards have a behavioural control task, including that of hiring, compensating and firing the CEO.
- The sixth and final phase is value distribution. This phase includes decisions on how corporate results or assets should be allocated to various stakeholders. CSR considerations should also be allocated to the various stakeholders. Board output control tasks and negotiations are important in this phase.

Understanding board tasks from a value chain perspective helps us understand that the board may have several tasks going on simultaneously, and that all tasks may contribute to value creation. This goes beyond the arguments that board tasks depend primarily on firm contexts such as the firm's life cycle, including experience of crisis;

company size; the ownership structure, including ownership type and dispersion; the industry and the industrial environment; national, geographical and cultural differences; and the CEO tenure and characteristics. However, the context may have an impact on how the contribution in various phases should be balanced. The value chain approach is still novel, and there is a need for conceptual development and empirical investigations.

The next section looks at how the attributes of the board members and the board working style may contribute to value creation.

Board member competence and the value chain

After having identified board tasks that are related to various value-creating activities, the challenge is to identify the most appropriate board members. Here I make an attempt to identify the requirements in terms of board members' attributes for each of the phases in the value chain. I do so by identifying the obstacles to effective board task performance.

Obstacles for board members

What are the obstacles that prevent outside directors from contributing to effective board task performance? The lack of independence is the main argument in agency theory, while a lack of time has been discussed by many authors. Board members often serve on multiple boards in addition to doing their regular job, which leaves them with limited time for their various assignments – which in turn leads to a risk of an insufficiently engaged board working style.

Lack of knowledge is an additional issue. Outsiders are often regarded as bringing in different kinds of knowledge, networks and perspectives from those that already exist in the firm. Outside directors do not always have sufficient expertise and firm-specific knowledge, however, to understand and evaluate complex firm decisions. Lack of understanding can reduce the board's potential contribution to a minimum.

I argue here that there are various obstacles in the way of the board members' contributions in the various parts of the value chain. It is therefore a challenge to recruit and develop board members who, as a collegial body, can use their knowledge and skills to align board task expectations and actual board task performance, and thus create accountability. The general argument from a shareholder value point of view is that there is a need for independent and detached outside board members. But a value chain analysis would suggest that too many independent and detached outside board members risk damaging accountability. The trade-off costs – in terms of a lack of firm-specific knowledge, the lack of involvement and the deficiency in understanding that comes from the lack of such knowledge – may hinder the embodiment of actual board behaviour in relation to board task expectations.

Board member types

I argue that different competencies and types of knowledge are needed to make contributions in the various steps in the value chain and the corresponding board tasks. Based on the value chain analysis, we recognise the need for board members to play various roles:

- liaison facilitators and resource providers;
- consultants, supporters and advisers;
- mentors and collaborators;
- decision-makers and analysts;
- evaluators and controllers; and
- negotiators and advocates.

The roles can be played by different board members, and some board members may perform more than one role. However, boards can realise their full value-creating potential only by collectively ensuring that all these roles are enacted simultaneously.

The liaison facilitators and resource providers have various networking tasks, including ensuring legitimacy, contacting and lobbying. The characteristics of the resource providers are discussed in the literature in terms of resource dependence theory.[37] These board members should have large networks among the groups that are the most important for the firm, and they need to enjoy credibility in these groups. Sometimes, and for some firms, it may be important for resource providers to relate to financiers, including the banks, sometimes to politicians and public authorities, and sometimes to customers, suppliers or competitors. The knowledge needed is more related to who they are than to what they do. The resource provision tasks can in some cases be obtained by external consultants, but often it gives more credibility and commitment when this competency is to be found among the board members.

The advisers, supporters and consultants may contribute to firm operations by giving advice on issues such as finance, marketing, general management and leadership, and legal and technical issues. The board members may – from a knowledge-based or resource-based perspective, through their personal and intangible skills and competencies – be valuable resources for the firm. There may be alternative ways for a firm to obtain these resources – for example, through consultants in the market place or through employment in the hierarchy – but sometimes board membership may be the only way of providing certain resources that are valuable, rare, non-substitutable and inimitable in a manner that provides long-term competitive advantage.

With regard to collaborators and mentors, board members may take on mentoring roles for the firm and the CEO, including those of being a sounding board and a discussion partner. This will involve outside board members who, through their openness and generosity, share their experiences, knowledge and time with the CEO. Board members with diverse backgrounds and characteristics should involve themselves in creative processes leading to innovative activities in relation to, for example, products, processes, the organisation and markets. The board members may in this way contribute to the formulation and formation of the content and context of strategic decisions.

Board members are also decision-makers and analysts, and they must understand the implications of the decisions they are to ratify. The task of boards will normally be to make decisions on issues that are important with respect to the size of and consequences for the firm. Therefore, there is a need for board members who combine integrity, maturity, responsibility and risk-taking behaviour on behalf of stakeholders with both long-term and short-term perspectives.

The behavioural control tasks involve board members taking evaluator and controller roles and having sufficient time, knowledge and independence to evaluate managerial performance. It may be difficult for outside board members, who tend to have less than full-time involvement with the board and the firm, to be sufficiently informed. However, routines should be developed that allow board decisions and other external obligations to be followed up, including ethical standards, accounting, etc. Board members should make time available in order to acquaint themselves with the main products and activities of the firm, the major risks, the market situation of the firm, the organisational culture, etc. Board members should also have the time and opportunity to meet regularly with the top management team.

Table 10.6 *Boards and value creation*

Value creation	Resource acquisition	Operation	Innovation	Resource allocation	Implementation	Distribution
Chaps. 3 and 9 Board task	Networking, lobbying, legitimacy	Advisory and supporting	Strategic management, collaboration and mentoring	Strategic control and decision-making	Internal and behavioural control	Output control and negotiation
Chap. 8 Board culture	Commitment	Commitment Cognitive conflicts	Commitment Cognitive conflicts Cohesiveness Creativity	Critical attitudes Cognitive conflicts	Critical attitudes Commitment Cognitive conflicts	Critical attitudes
Chap. 7 Board leadership	Counsellor Figurehead	Counsellor Supporter	Coach	Change agent Strategist	Conductor	Challenger Chair
Chap. 7 Board structures	Evaluations	Evaluations	Evaluations 'Away days' Long meetings Introductions	Instructions Descriptions Long meetings Introductions	Evaluations Description Instructions Committees Alone meetings Long meetings Many meetings	Consensus builder Evaluations Instructions Committees Many meetings
Chap. 4 Board members	Liaison facilitators and resource providers Relational capital	Consultants, supporters and advisers Outsiders General and function-oriented knowledge	Mentors and collaborators Large boards Outsiders Board process knowledge	Decision-makers and analysts Personal ownership	Evaluators and controllers Outsiders Firm-level knowledge	Negotiators and advocates Integrity

In terms of the roles of advocates and negotiators, board output control tasks are important for value distribution. The board members need to balance the stakes and interests of various internal and external actors. Often board members have particular responsibilities for safe-guarding the interests of certain stakeholders or owners – for example, various family branches in family firms, short-term versus long-term investors, managerial versus ownership perspectives, corporate social responsibility and employee issues, etc. These tasks have implications for board members' role as negotiators.

These are the various requirements that are needed for outside board members to make contributions in the different phases in the value chain. The point to emphasise is that a lack of knowledge may be a major hindrance for outside board members' ability to maximise boards' full value-creating potential.

The board working style and value creation

In table 10.6 I have combined the results from table 9.6 with the value chain reflections presented above. Table 10.6 indicates how boards may contribute to value creation throughout the whole value chain. Six parts of the value chain are included, and I have indicated board tasks, the attributes of board members, the board culture, board leadership and board structures that may be of particular importance in each of the parts. One of the main differences between a value chain approach and a contextual approach (for example, a life cycle approach) is that the value chain approach makes it clear that all value-creating activities normally take place at the same time. This implies that the various board tasks also need to take place at the same time, and that there will be many simultaneous requirements placed on the board members, the board culture, the board leadership and the board structure in general.

The inputs in the table are indicators; they use the concepts from the preceding chapters as illustrations. Some of the inputs are based on the empirical analysis that was presented in chapter 9, where it was shown how various decision-making culture attributes were impor-tant for different board tasks. In table 10.6 I have mostly used the concepts discussed in earlier studies, but openness and generosity, and preparedness and involvement, can easily be applied as well. I also found that board tasks were influenced by variations in board member demography (chapter 4) and board structure (chapter 7). Evaluation is a powerful tool; it is valuable for most of the tasks. 'Away days' are also listed as a very powerful tool – especially in relation to board strategy involvement. The board leadership attributes were not included in table 9.6, but are concepts presented in chapter 7. The concepts from chapter 7 are supplemented with Leblanc's functional director types, presented in chapter 8.

From a value chain perspective the optimal solution would be that all the concepts illustrated in table 10.6 should be present at the same time.

Summary

The key concepts presented in this chapter include corporate financial performance, corporate social responsibility, mergers, divestments, process innovation, product innovation and organisational innovation, and domestic and international market venturing.

Of the two main parts to the chapter, the first part is about internal and external value creation, with emphasis on the relationships between boards and corporate innovation, while the second part is about value creation through the whole value chain, linking concepts from earlier chapters of the book to value creation.

In addition to making a distinction between internal and external value creation I also introduced a distinction between financial and social value creation, and I presented stakeholder approaches, CSR perspectives and Elkington's 'triple bottom line' as supplements and alternatives to financial value creation. Such perspectives are often seen as instrumental in relation to financial performance, but firms do not necessarily benefit from having high moral standards – at least, not in the short run.

The numerous studies on board and financial performance have all been carried out in relation to the 'usual suspects' and various measures of financial performance in large US corporations. Although these studies have so far met the requirements in the dominating scholarly paradigms related to data, methods and theory,[38] recently they have been criticised for not opening the 'black box' of actual board behaviour, and for producing results that are weak or ambiguous.

The focus of the first part of the chapter was on the relationships between board task performance and corporate entrepreneurship. In the presentation of internal value creation I distinguished between internal and external innovation, and between corporate entrepreneurship and corporate innovation. External innovation is related to buying and selling businesses. Outside board members may find it easier to relate to external innovation than to internal innovation. In my internal innovation definition I included an entrepreneurial behaviour or posture perspective. The entrepreneurial posture is defined as one of innovativeness, risk-taking and proactivity, and I defined internal innovation in relation to product innovation, process innovation, organisational innovation and market venturing.

We found that innovation was strongly related to the board's strategy involvement, and using a value chain approach I illustrated how various board tasks may contribute to value creation throughout the corporate value chain. A value chain approach is an analytical tool that may be used to identify how boards can contribute to value creation; this chapter has demonstrated how and where the various concepts presented in this book can be used in such an approach. The value chain approach illustrates how many of the board task theories presented in chapter 3 can be combined. This approach also shows how a large number of tasks, cultures, leadership styles, structures and board member attributes can be simultaneously present and balanced. It differs from some contingency approaches, which indicate that the paradoxes[39] of distance and closeness, independence and involvement, trust and distrust, engagement and non-executivity, criticality and support, open dissent and respect, trust and candour can all be solved by separation based on context and time.

11 | *The human side of corporate governance*

Just as the title of this book is *Boards, Governance and Value Creation*, underlining the fact that it is premised on how boards of directors can contribute to creating value, so the subtitle is *The Human Side of Corporate Governance*, as the focus and overarching theme of the book has been on the human aspects of the subject. In this final chapter I first reprise the preceding chapters before presenting a list of contributions, then, finally, I make some summarising observations about ethics, balancing boards and the human side of corporate governance.

Main points in the various chapters

This book has followed a logic described in the framework in chapter 1. A separate chapter has been devoted to each box in the framework.

Framework and definitions

In chapter 1 the guiding board and governance framework was introduced. The framework presents the human side of corporate governance by opening up the 'black box' of actual board behaviour; in most discussions and studies of corporate governance this box is closed. The contingency and evolutionary perspectives are also fundamental elements in the framework. Actual board behaviour and corporate governance are rooted in various learning and influencing loops. These processes and loops are to be found at societal, institutional, organisational, group and individual levels.

Chapter 2 was about the actors, and in it I presented definitions of corporate governance. Four different types of corporate governance definitions were discussed:
- the managerial definition;
- the shareholder supremacy definition;

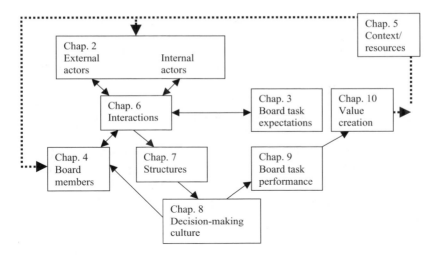

- the stakeholder definition; and
- the firm definition.

The values and ideologies of various internal and external actors were presented. Corporate governance is about who and what really count; this includes a struggle between various ideologies. However, a simple shareholder supremacy understanding of corporate governance was brought into question. This was illuminated through the application of the various corporate governance definitions, which were seen to be biased and to reflect the values of those promoting them. In chapter 2 we also saw how corporate governance definitions emerge over time, and that practice often precedes theory.

Board task expectations and theories

In chapter 3 I presented board task theories. This chapter was about accountability and board task expectations, and started with a typology of board task expectations. The following board tasks were presented:
- board output control tasks;
- board networking tasks;
- board internal control tasks;
- board advisory tasks;
- board decision control tasks; and
- board collaboration and mentoring tasks.

Each group of tasks had theoretical rationales. Various theories have contributed to the understanding of board tasks and accountability issues, and most theories are clearly rooted in a defined value-creating perspective. Various actors thus also tend to favour or avoid identifying with them or their value-creating consequences.

The first group of theories consists of those in which boards are, in practice, passive 'aunt' boards. This group consists of property rights theory, legalistic theory and managerial hegemony theory – theories that have their roots in economics, law and sociology respectively. 'Box-ticking' may be a main board task, based on these theories, as a consequence of the evolution of corporate governance codes. The second group of theories comprises those defining a firm as an instrument for external 'barbarian' actors. Agency theory is the benchmark for these theories, as they are all positioned in relation to it – albeit in different ways. The theories presented in this group are agency theory, stakeholder theory, stewardship theory, game theory and paternalism. In general, various types of control are the board tasks implied in these theories. The third group of theories consists of institutional 'clan' theories. Networking tasks and the social capital of board members are important in social capital and social network theory. The fourth group of theories comprises resource theories, in which the purpose is to create value for the firm. Networking, lobbying and legitimacy are important board tasks in resource dependence theory. Resource-based theories focus on the advisory tasks and the human capital of the board members.

'More than the usual suspects'

The board members are, obviously, important actors in the boardroom. Their characteristics, composition and compensation are presented in chapter 4. It is important to identify these three concepts and to distinguish between them. However, they relate to each other, and characteristics, compensation and composition should not be viewed in isolation when exploring boards and value creation.

Included in board member characteristics is competence. Seven types of board member qualification criteria were presented, based on arguments from theory and board task expectations. These were firm-specific knowledge, general and function-oriented competence, process-oriented competence, relational competence, personality, negotiation skills and ownership. The term 'compensation' was used to describe the board members' incentives and motivation. Internal as well as external incentives are included; and the incentives go beyond independence and shareholding. Motivation from liability, reputation and personal and professional standards were also introduced. The question of board composition relates to the size and configuration of the board with respect to its members' competence, characteristics and compensation.

Context and resources were presented in chapter 5. Not only do the contextual variables have a direct impact on the choice of board members, they clearly also influence the importance and relative power of various actors. The contextual variables have different characteristics: some, for example, may also be governance mechanisms and results. A contingency perspective of boards and governance implies that there must be a fit between context and governance designs. Recommendations in one contextual setting should not be applied in other settings without full consideration.

Interactions: the chapter in the centre

Interactions were the topic of chapter 6. The emphasis on the human side of corporate governance was more evident here than elsewhere. I started this chapter by presenting a step towards a behavioural theory of boards and governance. The suggested building blocks in this theory were:
- value creation through knowledge;
- strategising;
- problemistic search; and
- norms and learning processes.

In this chapter the attributes of interactions were investigated, including the attributes of actors and arenas, trust and emotions, and strategising, including power and influence.

Board working style

Structures, rules, norms and leadership were presented in chapter 7. Extensive efforts have been made in recent years to develop codes of best practice for corporate governance. These represent efforts to regulate the rules of the game in order to achieve some kind of

accountability and reliability. Various attempts at ways to improve corporate governance were discussed. There may be substitution effects
between formal board structures and board leadership, but it is also
a task for the board chairperson to make sure that proper structures
exist. Furthermore, we have challenged the traditional role of the chairperson. The board chairperson can be considered as a coach, whose
role it is to bring out the potential of each board member and to meld
the board into a cohesive group.

Chapter 8 contains a discussion on boardroom culture. Throughout
this book I have argued that the key to good corporate governance is
human or social factors and not structural factors, and what distinguishes the best boards is that they are robust, effective social systems.
In chapter 8 I presented the board as a social system, in which the
outcomes of board efforts are the result of the board performing as
a high-powered, functioning work group. In addition, the following
dimensions of the boardroom culture were presented:
- criticality and independence;
- creativity;
- cohesiveness;
- openness and generosity;
- preparation and involvement; and
- cognitive conflicts.

Openness and generosity have come to be considered one of the
most important recommendations for developing good boardroom
dynamics.

Board task performance and value creation

In chapter 9, which is about actual board task performance, I presented
and discussed concepts and findings in relation to boards' strategy
involvement, control involvement and service involvement. This chapter is the empirical side of chapter 3: in it I discussed what boards do
in reality, with the arguments based on empirical observations. Observations from the 'value-creating boards' surveys were used to develop,
illustrate and measure concepts.

The in-depth summarising study at the end of chapter 9 clearly
showed variations and similarities in predictors of board task performance. The study showed that the explained variation among the
board task variables itself varied. We also found that some predictor

variables that were positively related to some task performance variables were negatively related to others. Variables that generally gave the best explanations for board task involvement were:

- the firm-specific knowledge of the board members;
- the use of 'away days';
- openness and generosity; and
- preparation and involvement.

Chapter 10 deals with boards and value creation. This chapter has two main parts: in the first, about internal and external value creation, the relationships between boards and corporate innovation are emphasised, and the second is about value creation through the whole value chain.

The focus of the first part of chapter 10 is on the relationships between board task performance and corporate entrepreneurship. We found that innovation was strongly related to the board's strategy involvement, and based on a value chain approach we demonstrated how various board tasks may contribute to value creation throughout the corporate value chain. A value chain approach differs from some contingency approaches. It shows how a number of tasks, cultures, leadership styles, structures and board member attributes should be simultaneously present and balanced, and not separated by time or context.

Contributions

Thoughtful readers are the target group for this book, which has been written in a management tradition with an emphasis on strategy. The objective of the book has been to stimulate thinking. This objective has two sides. First, it is not supposed to be a handbook that presents final answers to various questions. It is a research-based book that, it is hoped, will help the reader reflect on and gain greater understanding of boards and governance. Second, it is also an objective of the book to communicate actionable knowledge.

The first major contribution of the book is a framework that attempts to integrate much of the present practices, discussions and research about boards and value creation. This has been an ambitious task, and there are clearly many integrative challenges to be solved. Many novel concepts and typologies are suggested in order to integrate various streams of logic. Another main proposition is that it redirects attention from impersonal models of boards and governance to the human side of corporate governance. The interaction of human actors in value-creating processes is the core of corporate governance, and it is argued that an understanding of human behaviour must be a building block when developing board and governance practices. The book also introduces a research agenda and suggests possibilities for cumulative research. Research questions and relationships, concepts and measures are presented. These main propositions will be summarised below, but first some more specific conclusions are listed.

Conclusions

This is a summary of some conclusions illustrating the human side of corporate governance.

- The 'black box' of the boardroom needs to be investigated. Intermediate steps, contingency and evolutionary approaches should be used in understanding boards and governance.
- Corporate governance should be viewed in terms of actors in interactions. The actors and their relationships are characterised by trust, emotion and power.
- The values, goals and objectives of corporate governance are not set a priori but are the results of strategising and biased arguments derived from competing ideologies.
- Board accountability does not have a single focus but involves a number of tasks. An understanding of the various tasks is important for developing board effectiveness and value creation.
- Boards must not perform just a single task at a time but they continually need to balance various tasks.
- The impact of board leadership and processes is underestimated. Team and team leadership attributes should be exploited in corporate governance.
- The competency of board members is not utilised sufficiently. Board members need to spend time together conducting in-depth discussions in order to get the most out of their joint resources.
- Various board maintenance mechanisms may have considerable implications for board effectiveness. Boards should give priority to board evaluations and other board self-development activities.

We have seen that the human side of corporate governance goes far beyond understanding the relationships between the 'usual suspects' and corporate financial performance. This should have implications both for research and for practice.

Novel concepts and typologies

This book represents an attempt to integrate literature and discussions from different perspectives. The current state of understanding of boards of directors can be compared to the descriptions given by blind people encountering an elephant for the first time. I have here tried to amalgamate perspectives from various disciplines, from various theories and from research and practice. Such attempts are important to facilitate communication and accumulate knowledge. My starting point has been from management and strategy research, a background that has shaped my focus and directed the development of many of the concepts.

The classification logic and guiding framework

The various propositions, concepts and typologies are presented in the framework that has also guided the presentation of this book. This is a framework for understanding behavioural perspectives of boards and governance. The framework may at first seem very complex – indeed, it is complex – but it is at the same time a very simplified picture of the human side of corporate governance. The framework is also a classification logic that can help us sort our observations, and thus also help us make more informed evaluations and recommendations.

Summaries of definitions, tasks and theories

Various definitions of corporate governance were compared in chapter 2. Corporate governance was presented there as a struggle between ideologies, with the different definitions to a large extent reflecting the various ideologies. Four main definitions were summarised in table 2.1: the managerial, shareholder, stakeholder and firm definitions. The understanding of value creation and board tasks varies in line with which definition is the most influential. In chapter 2 I also argued why it may be better conceptually to conceive of actors as opposed to stakeholders.

Throughout this book I have drawn a distinction between board roles and board tasks. The board role concept has been widely used in earlier literature, but it has several limitations. It does not properly distinguish between board working structures and the tasks that boards are performing. The role concept is also loaded with many connotations that are not properly dealt with in the board literature. A typology of six board tasks was presented in table 3.1.

In tables 3.2 and 3.3 I sorted and described various theories regarding board tasks. Agency theory has been the dominant theory explaining boards and corporate governance, but comparisons with other theories are needed. The presentation in chapter 3 contains a comprehensive introduction to and discussion of various theories that are used in different disciplines to explain and investigate boards.

Various novel frameworks and approaches
Various concepts and typologies were also presented in chapters 4 to 6 – for example, different types of owners (chapter 5) and the distinctions between actors and arenas, different types of trust and various strategising techniques (chapter 6). In table 7.2 a system for board evaluation was presented, a process-oriented boardroom culture was summarised in table 8.3, and a value chain approach to analysing board effectiveness was summarised in table 10.6.

Redirecting attention

It has been an objective of this book to direct attention to the human side of governance, but I have also tried to integrate this in a value creation perspective. The human side has been integrated in four main ways.
- Defining who and what really count.
- The existence of power and emotions.
- The use of human and social capital.
- Learning and evolutionary processes.

The 'who and what really count?' question was addressed in chapters 2 and 3. The presence of power and emotions outside and inside the boardroom was the focus of chapter 6. Power, trust, emotions and strategising characterise the relationships between the various corporate governance actors.

The importance of human and social capital was put forward in some of the theories in chapter 3, in chapter 4 human and social capital were presented at both individual (characteristics) and aggregate board level (composition) and in chapters 6 to 9 the use of it was explored. We have seen that various board tasks set requirements for different types of human and social board capital (chapter 9). Furthermore, the use of board capital (human and social knowledge and skills) is influenced by the interactions inside and outside the boardroom (chapter 6), how board members are motivated and compensated (chapter 4) and the existence and use of board structures and norms, including the development and employment of codes of best practice (chapter 7). However, the most important elements in the value-creating use of board capital are the boardroom culture (chapter 8) and board leadership (chapter 7).

Chapter 5 dealt with contextual factors, but learning and evolution were also introduced. Board members learn both at individual and group levels, and the outcome of past board decisions and behaviour may impact the future context, including the power of the various actors. A dynamic capabilities approach to board capital should therefore be taken.

A research agenda

A research agenda has been introduced. This agenda includes various research questions, concepts, variables, measures and methods. The overall research questions are indicated in the guiding framework, and the arrows in the framework may indicate propositions or hypotheses. Throughout the book it is also clear, however, that other relationships may exist, and some are also indicated. The framework is influenced by an intermediate step approach, in which there are various mediating factors between the 'usual suspects' and corporate financial performance. In some places I have indicated that there may be moderating effects and not only mediating effects. One such example is found in the introductory figures to chapter 7 and chapter 8. Board leadership and structures not only mediate the relationships but also moderate or influence them. Furthermore, there may be direct relationships. The attributes of the board members may, for example, have a direct impact on the decision-making culture, board task performance or value creation. This is indicated in the above-mentioned figures and in the data analysis in the end of chapter 8.

In this book I introduce many theories that are useful in studies of boards and governance. In chapter 3 there was a thorough presentation of a number of theories explaining or predicting various board tasks. Theories explaining board member selection were presented in chapter 4, theories about social control, trust and power were presented in chapter 6, procedural justice theory and institutional action theory were presented in chapter 7, and theories related to group processes were presented in chapter 8.

Each chapter contains groups of concepts that relate to each other. In each group there may be other concepts, and how they relate to each other remains to be explored. This should be carried out both theoretically and empirically.

Various variables and measures have been presented. The overall framework was used in the 'value-creating board' surveys, and many of the variables and measures used in these surveys are presented in this book. Most of the operationalisations are found in chapter 9 and chapter 10. Most of the measures stem from other studies, and the measures have also been used in other research projects.

Various research methods are needed to explore boards of directors, and results from several types of methods are presented in this book. Some research projects have applied traditional quantitative approaches relying mostly on archival data, while others have been very qualitative. The 'value-creating board' surveys collected responses through questionnaires from various respondents on each board. This is illustrated in tables 9.1, 9.4, 9.5, 10.3 and 10.4. Responses were also collected at various points in time. The surveys were originally conducted in Norway, but they were replicated in various other countries.

We have also seen some examples from the 'one of the lads' study (chapters 5 and 6), the 'fly on the wall' study (chapter 8), the 'board life story' study (chapters 7 and 8) and the 'U'n'I' study (chapter 6). Each study had a distinct focus. In efforts to research boards of directors we should not simply replicate each other but, rather, find ways to supplement each other and integrate various perspectives and methods.

Reflections

In this final section I present some summarising reflections on three topics that have permeated the whole book. These are:
• board ethics (arenas for board ethics);
• balancing boards (aunts, barbarians or clans); and
• behavioural perspectives (the human side of corporate governance).

Arenas for board ethics

Ethics has been a topic of discussion throughout this whole book and has been related to what a corporation is, to corporate social responsibility and to the struggle between ideologies. Ethics relates to the use of theories and the assumptions in various theories. Ethics is also important when considering how actors relate to one another, and influences board decision-making. Finally, ethics is important in relation to the board members' accountability, responsibility and liability.

Board ethics discussions will be found in various arenas. In this book I have broached the subjects of corporate ethics, the board's ethics, managerial ethics and the board members' ethics. I have also raised the question of corporate governance ethics: this is the system-level ethics related to theory development, laws and regulations. Recently, agency theory and the shareholder supremacy approach have been on the receiving end of considerable criticism for being unethical.[1] This viewpoint will not be discussed in this summary, however. Instead, I will outline some of the differences between utilitarian and deontological ethics, before presenting arenas for board ethics.

Utilitarian versus deontological ethics[2]
Utilitarian ethics is, first of all, about goals and objectives, but it is also related to consequences.[3] It is concerned with why things are done. Deontological ethics is about instrumental values, and it is concerned with how things are done. When discussing board ethics both types should be included. Traditional economic theory, including agency theory, builds the neoclassical paradigm.[4] This paradigm is based on utilitarian ethics. Organisation theory and sociology also include, to a greater extent, deontological ethics.

Utilitarian ethics is strongly related to stakeholder analyses. What objectives does the firm have? What objectives do the various actors have? What are the consequences of firm actions for various stakeholders? In deontological ethics, values are attached to how things are done. Decisions may be ethically wrong even though ethical objectives are met. They may be wrong because they are done in a wrong way. A classical example is the experiments carried out on human beings during World War II.

Corporate ethics

Corporate ethics is presented in various earlier sections. All of chapter 2 was related to corporate ethics. In chapter 3 some of the theories – such as stakeholder theory – were about corporate ethics, and corporate ethics arguments were used in the discussion about agency theory. Corporate ethics codes were mentioned in chapter 7. Corporate ethics was also included in chapter 9 in the discussions on output control, and in chapter 10 in the discussions on social value creation.

The news media regularly report stories about unethical corporate behaviour. Corporate ethics is a responsibility of the board, and in the literature the board has been considered as the superego of the corporation.[5] Various corporate governance codes also suggest or require that corporate ethics codes should be developed, and that the boards are responsible for doing so.

The setting of the ethical tone of the firm may be considered a strategic task of the board, as the board is crucial in setting the ethical framework for the firm. A common manifestation of this task is the production of a corporate code of ethics.[6] Ethics codes may contain paragraphs dealing with CSR, various ethics standards – for example, with respect to bribery – and rules about whistle-blowing. Corporate ethics codes may act as benchmarks for boards. Corporations are also recommended to make separate social reports, or at least have separate paragraphs on that aspect in the annual report.

Reputation building and corporate volunteering are themes within corporate ethics, but corporate ethics may also be philanthropic and related to altruism.

The board's ethics

The second arena for board ethics is the board's own ethics. The board's own ethics has two main parts: external and internal. The external part is about accountability. Are the boards doing what they are accountable to do? Are expectations (chapter 3) and task performance (chapter 9) aligned? The internal part is about the working style of the board, including working structures and leadership (chapter 7) and the decision-making culture (chapter 8). Are boards creating accountability by developing and following good working styles?

The board's own ethics is about how the board is ensuring that it does what it is supposed to do. Is the board developing and using good working structures? For example, is sufficient time being set aside for board meetings, is the board actively improving its own performance through various maintenance mechanisms, and how well does the board decision-making culture match the board's tasks to ensure that they are given priority?

The board's ethics is also about the interaction and processes between the board members (chapter 6). Are all the board members included in the decision-making processes? How does the power game in the boardroom take place – through power techniques and strategising? What are the roles of trust and emotions in the boardroom?

Managerial ethics

The managerial ethics discussion is, first and foremost, the issue of managerial opportunism and the criticism of managerial hegemony. There are many examples of how managers circumvent the boards and corporate control so as to pursue their own objectives. We do not need to go far to find examples of how managers give themselves benefits beyond what is best for the firm and its stakeholders. These objectives do not always need to be criminal, but can be a misuse of the trust bestowed upon managers. There are also examples where board chairpersons and boards accept and approve of such unethical behaviour.

Managerial opportunism is the central question in agency theory (chapter 3), and also to a large extent in the ongoing corporate governance discussion, in most research on corporate governance and in the development of codes of best corporate governance practice (chapter 7). The main recommendation to avoid managerial opportunism is for the board to be independent (chapter 4). The ethical counterpart of independence is that the board members have integrity. Integrity is how you behave when nobody else is watching you.

Boards are expected to perform various control tasks to prevent managerial opportunism. These include output control, behavioural control and strategic control. In chapters 7, 8 and 9 I presented various board structures and tools that may be important for avoiding managerial opportunism.

The board members' ethics

The questions about board ethics can also be applied to the motives for being a board member and to how the board members use their board memberships. Board member motivation is presented in chapter 4. Issues concerning insider trading, liability and golden parachutes have been raised. Negligence of board duties and liability should also be addressed. Board members' ethics is intimately connected with the integrity of the individual board members.

The question of board members' ethics is addressed as soon as a person is asked to become a board member. Self-assessments should be done by the candidate in order for him or her to establish if he/she will be able to meet expectations and contribute to value creation. An estimation of involvement and competence should be carried out. Ethics and adverse selection are also related.[7] If a candidate knows that sufficient time and commitment cannot be given adequate priority to take the board responsibilities properly, then this will be a matter of ethics.

It is a question of board member ethics when the board members themselves decide on their own benefits and remunerations. A classic situation is related to social movement and managerial hegemony theories.[8] These may indicate that board members can let the CEO receive high compensation while at the same time expecting that this will have positive consequences for themselves. Board members may also make decisions on behalf of the firm that may give benefits to them personally or to actors with whom they are involved. Individuals may also, as board members, contribute to decision-making that is motivated by their emotions – including anger, revenge and feelings of antipathy.

Board members' ethics is also related to how the board members treat each other, and about how each board member contributes to a value-creating decision-making culture.

Ethical dilemmas

Ethics is not just a question of right or wrong. Ethical reasoning and decision-making is, first of all, a question of choosing between various alternatives that may be good or bad. It is the latter that may cause the biggest problems. Some of these issues were addressed in the strategising techniques of 'multimatum' presented in chapter 6.

Boards will need to make decisions from among competing interests. Long-term and short-term interests may be in conflict. The interests of the employees may also be at variance with the interests of the shareholders or other stakeholders. Questions of downsizing, divesting, etc. are never easy to take when social concerns are included. And what about firing a CEO?

Boards and board members will encounter situations in which they need to make decisions from among options that may all be wrong. In the 'one of the lads' study we had to choose which creditors we should pay and which should suffer. Sometimes boards and board members may consider doing something that is illegal if the alternative is worse than such an indiscretion. Situations related to bankruptcies often pose such dilemmas.

ABC and the 'value-creating' board

Is there an ideal board or an ideal board composition? In chapter 7 various codes of best practice were introduced, and some of the codes give clear recommendations about ideal boards. Boards and board practices are benchmarked in relation to these codes, and boards often need to comply with them. This is a box-ticking approach to the problem of the ideal board.

In chapter 9 we presented board involvement, and there are arguments that the ideal board is also active. Terry McNulty and Andrew Pettigrew argue for the maximalistic board rather than the minimalistic board.[9] I argue, however, that there is a need to go further. Here I present an ABC for professional boards. The professional board needs to be in balance. ABC is an acronym for the concepts I presented in chapter 3: aunt, barbarian and clan. I use these concepts in a typology of boards, as displayed in table 11.1.

This board typology is directly related to the classification of board theories presented in chapter 3, and the table corresponds to table 3.2.

Boards have typically been 'aunt' boards and, in larger firms, also 'clan' boards. Waves of shareholder activism have resulted in pressure to have 'barbarian' boards. However, it is not likely that there will be equilibrium with a pure 'barbarian' board. From the 'barbarian' situation boards may return to being 'aunt' or 'clan'. The challenge is, however, to develop them into becoming 'value-creating'. That will imply achieving a balance of the various rationales, tasks and relationships. Direct efforts must be taken to get boards to the value-creating situation, and efforts must be made to keep them there. However, this is still a more sustainable situation than that for the 'barbarian' board.

Table 11.1 *Board typology: aunt, barbarian and clan*

Barbarian board	Value-creating board
Rationale from finance	Integrated rationale – strategy
Monitoring board	Participative board
Control tasks	Balances control and service
Distance and hostility	Balances distance and closeness
Independent – external	Balances independence and
Do not trust the management	interdependence
Is not trusted by the management	Both integrity- and competence-based trust
Aunt board	Clan board
Rationale from law	Rationale from sociology
Passive board	Collegial board
Formal tasks	Service tasks
Dependent – dominated by management	Closeness
	Interdependence
No competence-based trust – no expectations	Trusted by the management

Aunts

'Aunt' boards have been so-named because their board composition and selection are a result of convenience. Such boards often consist of people who are willing to see their names appear as board members. Often they are individuals who have been appointed just to meet formal requirements: nobody ever intended them to have to make contributions. Usually they are family members or friends of the management or owners. Many of them will, necessarily, be women; the female–male ratio will be higher here than on other boards.

'Aunt' boards are reactive and passive. They are mostly involved in value protection and formal tasks, including 'box-ticking', output control, value distribution, some sort of discipline and action in crises. They have their primary rationale from law, but it is also described in property rights and managerial hegemony theory.

Members of 'aunt' boards will often be dependent on the management, but they are not trusted to do anything other than rubber-stamping. Members of such boards often refrain from challenging

CEOs, not only because they support him or her but also because they have little to contribute.

Barbarians

This category has received its name from the finance literature. The 'barbarians' are elected or selected by external actors. 'Barbarians' are outsiders and independent of the management; they have their own agenda. This is the kind of board that is promoted by most codes of best practice (chapter 7). This category has its rationale in agency theory, but this kind of board is also discussed in other theories, such as stakeholder theory. The objective then is to create value for external stakeholders.

'Barbarian' boards are monitoring boards, and they perform various control tasks. They ask discerning and critical questions, and independently hire, fire and compensate the CEOs. 'Barbarians' have a distant, and sometimes hostile, relationship with CEOs. They do not trust the management, and the management do not trust them. This is not a stable situation. When CEOs realise that they are not trusted they start to treat the board members in a similar way. CEOs have many ways to avoid being controlled by 'barbarians'. Some of them were touched on in chapter 6.

However, CEOs have the ability to adjust to the expectations of the 'barbarians'. When there are independent directors, CEOs will spend more time in political processes integrating with the directors. CEOs will try to sell their merits and the success of strategic decisions. This communication may occur at the expense of constructive dialogue, however.[10] CEOs act in this way because of their human nature; they will try to gain control over their dependencies, and, if independent directors assess CEO performance and decide the remuneration and future of the CEO, CEOs will try to exercise their authority to influence the outcome.

Abundant evidence exists that CEOs seek advice from the board only if they have a high level of personal trust in the board and the board members. Barbarians on the board will, therefore, also reduce the amount of advice that CEOs seek from the board.

Clans

The rationale of 'clan' boards is based on sociology. It is described in such institutional theories as social networks, social movement and class hegemony theory. The 'clan' members are individuals in an inner circle who constitute a distinct network. A successful director must help perpetuate and protect the values of this network. The main objective for 'clan' boards is to create value for internal actors and business elites. However, these 'clan' board members may also provide important service resources to the firm, particularly through their social networks, but also through their own advice.

The 'clan' members tend to support each other during board meetings. There are mechanisms of social control that make board members interdependent; theories of social control were presented in chapter 6. In practice, there will be mutual trust between the CEO and the board members. The board members will not ask critical questions.

'Clan' boards may be important knowledge providers, and the 'clan' members may act as mentors. 'Clan' boards may be important 'window displays' helping to legitimate the CEO and the firm.

The balanced and value-creating board

Boards should not be classified just as 'aunts', 'barbarians' or 'clans'. An ABC for boards would imply that boards should contribute to value creation. From a strategic management perspective boards should have an integrated rationale reflecting both internal and external value creation, and boards should contribute throughout the whole corporate value chain.

The 'value-creating' board is a collaborating and participative board, but also a board that can balance control and service tasks. It can balance distance and closeness, independence and interdependence. It can also balance integrity- and competence-based trust.

Various theories help us study value-creating boards. In table 3.2 we classified resource dependence theory and the resource-based view of the firm as 'value creation' theories. This classification is only partly correct. These theories have a focus on value creation in the firm, and they have a long-term perspective, but they do not explicitly balance control and service, or independence and interdependence. Furthermore, stewardship theory was classified as a 'barbarian' theory. The focus is on value creation for external stakeholders, but it makes assumptions about trust, closeness and collaboration rather than about distrust, distance and control. Both stewardship and resource theories may help us develop a theory of value-creating boards. Game theory and property rights theory may also make important contributions.

Game theory contributes to an understanding of balances, the importance of social contracts and long-term perspectives. Property rights theory is about team production; its contribution to a theory of the 'value-creating board' is the argument that it is those who add value, assume unique risk and possess strategic information who should be board members.

The human side of corporate governance

Here I finally turn again to the human side of corporate governance. Three sections will be presented here before the book concludes with a few final comments on the implications. The sections look at myths and realities, the steps towards a behavioural theory, and new paradigms of governance.

Myths and realities: creating accountability

This book started by introducing the landmark contribution of Miles Mace – *Directors: Myth and Reality*. The difference between myths and realities is the human side of corporate governance. Understanding and reducing this gap between board task expectations and board task performance contributes to creating accountability. The main contributions of this book in developing effective boards and reducing the gap between myths and realities are the guiding framework for exploring behavioural perspectives of corporate governance, and the steps taken towards a behavioural theory of boards and governance.

Towards a behavioural theory

The steps towards a behavioural theory of boards and governance were presented in chapter 6 – the central chapter of the book. The building blocks in the behavioural theory of the firm include assumptions about bounded rationality, satisficing and problemistic search, routines and learning, and political bargaining and the quasi-resolution of conflict. These components were used as background for the main elements in a behavioural theory of boards and governance. The following main elements were suggested:

- focus on strategising more than objective alignments;
- decisions to be made through satisficing and problemistic search rather than by rational decision-making;

- boards to create knowledge through the deployment of knowledge rather than through control of managerial behaviour; and
- there will be a focus on interactions and processes rather than on outcome and structures.

More work needs to be carried out to develop a behavioural theory of boards and governance further.

New paradigms of governance

In this book we have encountered issues of concern to corporate governance and boards of directors in the past and in the present, and we have been challenged about the future. The past was different from the present. The understanding and conduct of corporate governance are fast-changing. The problems, concepts, explanations[11] and theories[12] have changed, and many of the governance institutions and mechanisms today did not play the same role even as recently as a generation ago. Corporate governance institutions, including boards of directors, are challenged now, and in the future they will be even more challenged.

The pace of change being experienced today as we move towards an information and knowledge economy is continually accelerating, and the market place is becoming increasingly global. As we move towards a knowledge-based economy, it may transpire that the underlying assumptions in agency theory are too simplistic, or even wrong.[13] The corporation as a legal entity developed out of its ability to protect not just shareholders but other stakeholders as well. In the new economy human capital investors will be critical, and employees will often be in the same position as financial capital providers. This means that multiple principal–agent relationships, rather than a single one, will need to be regulated. There is also a need to break out of the short-termism that has evolved following the shareholder value movement. The attention of managers should be focused on managing the company and not just the share price.

New organisational forms are arising, and human capital seems to be replacing much of the importance of financial capital. New approaches and new solutions to the corporate governance problem will be forthcoming.[14] This brings us back to the questions raised in chapter 2. Will this bring new paradigms of governance? Will this bring changes to the 'who and what really count' question? And who should define corporate governance?

Implications

Three objectives for this book were set out at the beginning of the first chapter. By understanding the human side of corporate governance, we should be able to:

- investigate how boards can contribute to value creation;
- highlight the behavioural and ethical dimensions of corporate governance; and
- present a coherent and unifying framework.

We have taken some steps in the direction of investigating how boards contribute to value creation, and in integrating behavioural dimensions and ethics into corporate governance. Some steps were also taken towards developing a behavioural theory of boards, and a cohesive, coherent and unifying guiding framework was presented. Together, these moves have given a picture of the human side of corporate governance.

Notes

Preface

1 The most complete presentation is in Huse 2005.
2 The dissertation was published in Norwegian, but it resulted in several publications, including Huse 1993a, Huse 1994b, and Borch and Huse 1993.
3 The most comprehensive presentation is published in a Norwegian report. The results in English are found in Huse 1993c, which is based on a presentation at the Academy of Management in Atlanta in 1993. Elisabeth Ljunggren was the assistant in this project.
4 The results are published as a Norwegian-language book: Huse and Halvorsen 1995. Various parts of the study are published elsewhere, including a conceptual article in *Long-Range Planning* (Huse 1998).
5 The main contribution from this study is Huse and Eide 1996.
6 The results from this project are published in various places, including Bilimoria and Huse 1997 and Huse and Solberg 2006.
7 The results from this study are presented and published in several places, including Huse, Minichilli and Schøning 2005.
8 This programme is ongoing and several publications are in the pipeline.
9 See, for example, Huse and Rindova 2001.
10 See, for example, Halme and Huse 1997.
11 See, for example, Gabrielsson and Huse 2002.
12 See, for example, Huse and Gabrielsson 2004, Huse, Neubaum and Gabrielsson 2005 and Zahra, Neubaum and Huse 2000.

Chapter 1

1 Mace 1971.
2 Zahra and Pearce 1989.
3 Johnson, Daily and Ellstrand 1996.
4 Pettigrew 1992: 169.
5 Forbes and Milliken 1999.
6 Pettigrew 1992.
7 Huse 2000, 2005.

8 See, for example, March and Simon 1958 or Cyert and March 1963 for the behavioural theory of the firm, and Van Ees, Gabrielsson and Huse 2005 or Huse 1993b for its application to boards of directors.

9 Lawrence and Lorsch 1976.

10 Blair 1995, Huse and Rindova 2001, Wright, Filatotchev, Buck and Bishop 2003.

11 Sundaramurthy and Lewis 2003.

12 Gomez 2004, Pye 2004, Useem 1993.

13 Galaskiewicz and Wasserman 1989, Westphal, Seidel and Steward 2001.

14 Johnson, Hoskisson and Hitt 1993, Judge and Zeithaml 1992.

15 Cyert and March 1963.

16 Eisenhardt and Martin 2000.

17 Shen 2003, Sundaramurthy and Lewis 2003, Westphal and Zajac 2001.

Chapter 2

1 Monks and Minow 2004, for example, identify the shareholders, the managers and the board members as the most important actors, but various other actors are also identified.

2 Parts of this section are adapted from Huse and Rindova 2001.

3 Demb and Neubauer 1992, Lorsch and McIver 1989.

4 Environmental Protection Agency.

5 Agency theory, managerial hegemony theory and stakeholder theory are among the theories presented in chapter 3.

6 Mintzberg 1983, Pfeffer and Salancik 1978, Selznik 1949, Zahra and Pearce 1989.

7 These are usually the main elements presented in the theory of the firm.

8 Blair 1995. Margaret Blair uses a team production approach rooted in property rights theory. See the presentation of property rights theory in chapter 3.

9 See also Monks and Minow 2004.

10 Charkham 1994: 1.

11 See Aguilera and Jackson 2003.

12 See, for example, Huse and Eide 1996.

13 See, for example, Mintzberg 1983.

14 See, for example, the Higgs Review 2003.

15 Aguilera and Jackson 2003: 460–1.

16 See, for example, Jensen and Ruback 1983.

17 See Pfeffer and Salancik 1978 for an overview of resource dependence theory. Resource dependence theory is among the theories presented in chapter 3.

18 See, for example, Jones 1995.
19 The increase in managerial remuneration in the last decade was, in fact, much higher, but this has to be offset against the fact that shareholder activism started in the 1980s.
20 See, for example, Monks and Minow 2004: 235–9.
21 Berle and Means 1932.
22 See, for example, Fama and Jensen 1983b and Jensen and Meckling 1976.
23 When the benefits from control are lower than the costs of control there will be no incentives to control.
24 The concepts of principals and agents are presented in chapter 3 in the section on agency theory.
25 Aguilera and Jackson 2003.
26 Aoki 1984, 2001, 2004.
27 See Aguilera and Jackson 2003.
28 Discrete contracts are, for example, defined in transaction cost theory (see chapter 3). Discrete contracts stand in contrast to relational contracts. A discrete contract is one in which no relation exists between the actors – or, more specifically, the contracting parties – apart from the simple exchange of goods. Its paradigm is the transaction in neoclassical microeconomics. However, every contract involves relations apart from the exchange of goods itself. Relational contracts, including a comparison between discrete and relational contracts, are the focus of Macneil's relational contracts theory (Macneil 1980).
29 Correctly known as the Committee on the Financial Aspects of Corporate Governance; see Cadbury 1992.
30 Kochan 2003.
31 Parts of this section have been adapted from Huse 2003b.
32 *Business Week*, 7 October 2002: 58.
33 Child and Rodriguez 2003, Kochan 2003.
34 See, for example, Ghoshal 2005.
35 Kochan 2003.
36 Huse and Rindova 2001.
37 Child and Rodriguez 2003, Kochan 2003.
38 Fiss and Zajac 2004.
39 This is evidenced by, for example, Blair 1995 and Lazonick and O'Sullivan 2000.
40 This is also evidenced in business school teaching; see, for example, Fiss and Zajac 2004 and Gioia 2003.
41 Blair 1995.
42 Agency theory assumptions are presented in the following paragraphs and in chapter 3.

43 See also Grandori and Soda 2003.
44 A more detailed presentation and critique of agency theory is found in chapter 3.
45 Kochan 2003.
46 Margit Osterloh and Bruno Frey (2004) argue that these efforts make 'governance structures for crooks'.
47 Ibid.
48 See the presentation of game theory in chapter 3. See also Aoki 2004.
49 Child and Rodriguez 2003.
50 See, for example, Taylor 2001.
51 Ibid.

Chapter 3

1 See, for example, Forbes and Milliken 1999 for the use of these concepts.
2 When referring to the resource-based view of the firm more often than not I also include therein the development of the knowledge-based view of the firm and the competence-based view of the firm. Sometimes, however, it is more appropriate to make a direct reference to the knowledge-based view or the competence-based view.
3 Giddens 1984: 30.
4 Monks and Minow 2004.
5 See Aguilera and Jackson 2003.
6 Hung 1988.
7 Pearce 1983.
8 Fama and Jensen 1983a, 1983b.
9 Pfeffer and Salancik 1978.
10 See, for example, Barney 1991.
11 Davis, Schoorman and Donaldson 1997.
12 The theoretical rationales and examples of empirical studies relating to each of the tasks are presented in Huse 2005.
13 Pfeffer and Salancik 1978.
14 Baysinger and Hoskisson 1990.
15 Gabrielsson and Huse 2005.
16 Fama and Jensen 1983a.
17 Baysinger and Hoskisson 1990, Stiles and Taylor 2001.
18 McNulty and Pettigrew 1999.
19 The origin of the aunt, barbarian and clan framework is presented in detail in Huse 2003. The quadrants in table 3.2 relate also to those in table 11.1 (p. 310). The two dimensions reflect various dualities or paradoxes – e.g. control and service, independence and interdependence, distance and closeness. I have avoided presenting these concepts in the

table as most of the theories are somewhat more complex than what can be integrated directly in such a framework.

20 See, for example, Lynall, Golden and Hillman 2003.
21 That contracts are incomplete is a basic assumption in property rights theory; see, for example, Grossman and Hart 1986.
22 See Alchian and Demsetz 1972.
23 See, for example, Blair 1995, Blair and Stout 2001, Grandori 2004 and Kaufman and Englander 2005.
24 See, for example, Grossman and Hart 1986.
25 See Zahra and Pearce 1989: 292.
26 The corporate laws that were introduced in the late 1990s in Sweden and Norway made legal requirements of board instructions and CEO work descriptions to enhance the employee-elected directors' contributions.
27 Reprinted as a Harvard Classic in 1986; a short version is found in Mace 1972.
28 Lorsch and MacIver 1989; see also Herman 1981 and Patton and Baker 1987.
29 This argument is developed further in chapter 7.
30 Jensen and Meckling 1976: 308.
31 Agency theory is, according to Williamson 1996: 173, defined by Jensen and Meckling (1976, 1979), Fama (1980), Fama and Jensen (1983b, 1985) and Jensen (1983, 1986).
32 See Eisenhardt 1989 and Fama and Jensen 1983a.
33 See Berle and Means 1932 and Jensen and Meckling 1976.
34 These assumptions also underlie other theories – e.g. property rights theory and transaction cost theory. They are presented here because agency theory has received such a prominent place in the corporate governance literature.
35 Jensen and Meckling 1976: 312.
36 Ibid.: 308.
37 Ibid.: 325. Michael Jensen and William Meckling define bounding costs in this way: 'Suppose that the owner-manager could expend resources to guarantee to the outside equity holders that he would limit his activities which cost the firm [F]. We call these expenditures "bonding costs", and they would take such forms as contractual guarantees to have the financial accounts audited by a public accountant, explicit bonding against malfeasance on the part of the manager, and contractual limitations on the manager's decision making power (which impose costs on the firm because they limit his ability to take full advantage of some profitable opportunities as well as limiting his ability to harm the stockholders while making himself better off).'

38 Fama and Jensen 1983a: 303–4.
39 See, for example, Hillman and Dalziel 2003.
40 See, for example, Fama and Jensen 1983a.
41 See ibid. for more descriptions and examples.
42 Child and Rodriguez 2004.
43 Hill and Jones 1992.
44 Child and Rodriguez 2004: 95ff.
45 See, for example, Aoki 2004.
46 See, for example, Pettit and Singer 1985.
47 Examples are Perrow 1984, Etzioni 1988 and Ghoshal 2005.
48 In a posthumously published manuscript (Ghoshal 2005).
49 Through various contributions from, for example, Andrew Pettigrew.
50 See the following section about transaction cost theory. Agency theory focuses on incentives rather than on governance mechanisms.
51 See, for example, Aoki 1984.
52 Donaldson 1990, Davis, Schoorman and Donaldson 1997. Stewardship theory is presented in a separate section.
53 See, for example, Schulze, Lubatkin, Dino and Bucholtz 2001.
54 Freeman 1984; see also Mitchell, Agle and Wood 1997. Stakeholder theory is presented in a separate section.
55 Alchian and Demsetz 1972; see also, for example, Aguilera and Jackson 2003 and Grandori 2004. Property rights theory is presented in a separate section.
56 Gnan, Huse and Montemerlo 2005; see also Johannisson and Huse 2000. Paternalism is presented in a separate section.
57 See Macneil 1980. Relational norms are presented in chapter 6 in the section on types of trust.
58 Williamson 1996: 173 defines transaction cost theory through the following contributions: Williamson 1975, 1979, 1985, 1988, Klein, Crawford and Alchian 1978, Klein 1980, 1988, Klein and Leffler 1981, Teece 1980, Alchian 1984 and Joskow 1985, 1988.
59 See, for example, Fama 1980.
60 See Näsi 1995.
61 Freeman 1984.
62 See, for example, Mitchell, Agle and Wood 1997.
63 Ibid.: 857.
64 Freeman 1984: 46.
65 Clarkson 1995, Preston 1990.
66 See the section on common agency theory.
67 Donaldson and Preston 1995, Mitchell, Agle and Wood 1997.
68 Fombrun 1996, Fombrun and Rindova 1994.
69 Jones 1995.

322 *Notes to pages 54–9*

70 See Donaldson 1990. Lex Donaldson uses the classical arguments from organisation theory about theory X and theory Y in his criticism of agency theory. Agency theory assumptions about motivation can be compared with theory X assumptions about lazy and opportunistic human beings. Donaldson argues that these assumptions should be replaced by theory Y assumptions about self-motivated and trustworthy actors.
71 Davis, Schoorman and Donaldson 1997.
72 See also Gabrielsson 2003.
73 See, for example, Sundaramurty and Lewis 2003.
74 Goel and Erakovic 2005, Hillman and Dalziel 2003, Shen 2003.
75 See, for example, Cable and Shane 1997.
76 Aoki 2004.
77 See ibid. for a presentation of comparative institutional analysis and game theory.
78 Some of this paragraph is extracted from Gnan, Huse and Montemerlo 2005; see also Johannisson and Huse 2000.
79 See Huse 1993b.
80 Johannisson and Huse 2000: 359.
81 See, for example, Brundin 2002 and Johnson, Melin and Whittington 2003.
82 Additional institutional theories are presented in chapter 7.
83 Hung 1998.
84 Scott 1995.
85 DiMaggio and Powell 1983.
86 See, for example, Hillman and Dalziel 2003.
87 Burt 1992.
88 See, for example, Coleman 1990 and Burt 1992.
89 Burt 1997.
90 Useem 1984, Mizruchi 1996, Zajac and Westphal 1996.
91 See, for example, Gulati and Westphal 1999.
92 See Granovetter 1985. The formulations used are from Lynall, Golden and Hillman 2003.
93 Gulati and Gargiulo 1999.
94 Burt 1992.
95 Granovetter 1973.
96 See Burt 1997. The structural hole argument draws on several lines of network theorising that emerged in sociology during the 1970s, most notably, Granovetter (1973) on the strength of weak ties, Freeman (1977) on betweenness centrality, Cook and Emerson (1978) on the power of having exclusive exchange partners, and Burt (1980) on the structural autonomy created by network complexity.
97 Davis and Thompson 1994.

 98 Ibid.: 156.
 99 Useem 1982, 1984, Zahra and Pearce 1989.
100 See, for example, Richardson 1987 for an extended description of direct/indirect and directional/non-directional interlocks.
101 Richardson 1987 has a detailed presentation of these four theories.
102 Ibid.
103 Useem 1984.
104 Daft 1989, Palmer 1983, Pennings 1981, Richardson 1987.
105 Palmer 1983, Useem 1982, 1984.
106 Pfeffer and Salancik 1978.
107 See Pfeffer and Salancik 1978.
108 See, for example, Pfeffer 1972.
109 Selznik 1949.
110 See, for example, Pfeffer 1972.
111 See, for example, Carpenter and Westphal 2001 and Westphal 1999.
112 Hillman, Cannella and Paetzold 2000.
113 The contributions that generally are considered to be the most ground-breaking for development of the resource-based view of the firm are Penrose 1959, Wernerfelt 1984 and Barney 1991.
114 Also including the knowledge-based view of the firm and the competence-based view of the firm.
115 Zahra and Filatotchev 2004.
116 Barney 1991.
117 Barney, Wright and Ketchen 2001.
118 See, for example, Barney 1991.
119 See, for example, Macus 2002: 41–2.
120 Macus 2002: 60.
121 See, for example, Collin 2004: 25.
122 'DM culture' refers to the decision-making culture presented in chapter 8.

Chapter 4

  1 Vance 1983: 31.
  2 Finkelstein and Mooney 2003.
  3 The word 'compensation' is used here for alliteration purposes. The meaning contained in the word 'motivation' may perhaps convey more precisely the nuance that is intended.
  4 See chapter 7.
  5 Hillman and Dalziel 2003.
  6 Finkelstein and Mooney 2003. Catherine Daily, Dan Dalton and colleagues have, in a large number of publications, presented

meta-analyses of the relations between 'usual suspects' and firm financial performance.

7 CEO duality occurs when the CEO also chairs the board. CEO duality is often referred to in the context of board structure. Accordingly, I also present CEO duality in chapter 7, which is about board structures.

8 Hillman and Dalziel 2003.

9 See, for example, Johannisson and Huse 2000. In this study we follow two firms as they recruit their first outside board members.

10 The 'hierarchy and market' notions and discussion refer to transaction cost theory. See chapter 3.

11 See the presentations in chapter 3 of transaction cost analysis and the resource-based view of the firm.

12 This is what Hillman and Dalziel call relational capital.

13 From Nahapiet and Goshal 1998. See also Hillman and Dalziel 2003.

14 Hillman and Dalziel 2003: 388.

15 See also Huse and Solberg 2006 about how women may make contributions to corporate boards.

16 See, for example, Certo 2003 and Mizruchi 1996.

17 See, for example, Kosnik 1987.

18 See, for example, Kosnik 1990.

19 See chapters 2 and 3.

20 See, for example, Osterloh and Frey 2004.

21 See, for example, Lorsch and MacIver 1989 and Mace 1971.

22 See, for example, Hermalin and Weisbach 1988, 1991.

23 See, for example, Fama and Jensen 1983a and Hermalin and Weisbach 1988.

24 Jensen 1993.

25 Pfeffer and Salancik 1978: 172.

26 See, for example, Burt 1980.

27 Firstenberg and Malkiel 1994: 34; see also Dalton, Daily, Johnson and Ellstrand 1999.

28 Yermack 1996.

29 Various arguments for small and large boards are presented by Dalton, Daily, Johnson and Ellstrand 1999.

30 Dalton, Daily, Ellstrand and Johnson 1998.

31 Kosnik 1987.

32 See Baysinger and Butler 1985.

33 See, for example, Hagen and Huse 2006.

34 This situation is presented in more detail in chapter 7 in relation to the Higgs Report.

35 See, for example, Milliken and Martins 1996.

36 See, for example, Forbes and Milliken 1999.
37 Daily and Dalton 2003.
38 See, for example, Huse and Solberg 2006 and Bilimoria and Huse 1997.
39 These issues are discussed further in chapter 8, especially in the research illustration there. More about women directors is also found in the case prsented at the end of this chapter.
40 See, for example, Lorsch and MacIver 1989. This list is a result of a research project published in Huse 2003a.
41 See, for example, Lorsch and MacIver 1989. The arguments in this paragraph are also supported empirically in a research project on board members in small Norwegian firms published in Huse 2003a: 111–14.
42 Co-determination and socio-technical systems, as expounded by the Tavistock School (Einar Thorsrud), characterised the Norwegian working climate in the 1960s.
43 AS companies are privately held joint-stock companies while ASA companies are publicly traded joint-stock companies, but not necessarily listed companies.

Chapter 5

1 Zahra and Pearce 1989.
2 See, for example, Greene, Brush and Brown 1997 and Borch, Huse and Senneseth 1999.
3 Borch, Huse and Senneseth 1999.
4 Zahra 1991.
5 Shen 2003.
6 Berle and Means 1932 and Fama and Jensen 1983a.
7 Berle and Means 1932.
8 See, for example, La Porta, Lopez-de-Silanes and Shleifer 1999 and Thomsen 2004.
9 Aguilera and Jackson 2003.
10 Aguilera and Jackson claim that this classification only partially fits the variations within Europe including eastern Europe, east Asian countries and multinational corporations.
11 Van Ees and Postma 2004. The cultures in both countries are changing rapidly as a result of efforts to standardise corporate governance practices between countries.
12 Filatotchev and Toms 2003.
13 Grandori 2004 and Huse 2003b.
14 See, for example, Fama and Jensen 1983a or Alchian and Demsetz 1972.
15 See, for example, Halme and Huse 1997.

16 See, for example, Huse, Neubaum and Gabrielsson 2005 or Zahra, Neubaum and Huse 1997.
17 Huse 2000.
18 See, for example, Johannisson and Huse 2000.
19 See, for example, Huse 1998.
20 For details of the 'one of the lads' study, see, for example, Huse 1998.
21 See, for example, Lorsch and MacIver 1989 and Mace 1971.
22 See, for example, Huse 1998 and Lynall, Golden and Hillman 2003.
23 Weber 1956.
24 Quinn and Cameron 1983.
25 Lynall, Golden and Hillman 2003.
26 Daily and Dalton 1992a and 1992b, Johannisson and Huse 2000, Gedajlovic, Lubatkin and Schulze 2004.
27 Zahra and Filatotchev 2004.
28 Certo, Daily and Dalton 2001.
29 Gedajlovic, Lubatkin and Schulze 2004.
30 See, for example, the section on new paradigms of governance in chapter 2 and the presentation of property rights in chapter 3.
31 Nordqvist 2005: 36–9.
32 See, for example, Pedersen and Thomsen 2003.
33 See chapters 2 and 3.
34 Gedajlovic and Shapiro 1998.
35 Zahra, Neubaum and Huse 2000.
36 Fiet 1995.
37 Gabrielsson and Huse 2002.
38 This section is developed from Gnan, Huse and Montemerlo 2005.
39 Astrachan and Shanker 2003, Corbetta and Montemerlo 1999.
40 Astrachan, Klein and Smyrnios 2001.
41 La Porta, Lopez-de-Silanes and Schleifer 1999, Westhead and Cowling 1998.
42 Johannisson and Huse 2000.
43 Lansberg 1999, Ward 1991.
44 Bjørkman 1994.
45 Huse and Rindova 2001.
46 The case presented here comes from Gabrielsson and Huse 2005.
47 See, for example, Neubauer and Lank 1998 or La Porta, Lopez-de-Silanes and Schleifer 1999.
48 See, for example, Mustakallio 2002.
49 Ward and Handy 1988, Huse 1990, Cromie, Stephenson and Monteith 1995, Corbetta and Tomaselli 1996, Haalien and Huse 2005.
50 Ward and Handy 1988, Johannisson and Huse 2000.
51 Gersick, Davis, McCollon Hampton and Lansberg 1997.

52 Neubauer and Lank 1998.
53 Timmons and Bygrave 1986, Fried and Hisrich 1995.
54 Manigart and Sapienza 2000.
55 Rosenstein 1988, Rosenstein, Bruno, Bygrave and Taylor 1993, Fried, Bruton and Hisrich 1998, Gabrielsson and Huse 2002.
56 Fried, Bruton and Hisrich 1998, Markman, Balkin and Schjoedt 2001.
57 Deakins, O'Neill and Mileham 2000, Politis and Landström 2002.
58 Rosenstein 1988, Gabrielsson and Huse 2002.
59 Gulati and Westphal 1999, Goodall and Warner 2002.

Chapter 6

1 Kosnik 1987.
2 Westphal and Zajac 1998.
3 Huse and Eide 1996.
4 DiMaggio and Powell 1983, Meyer and Rowan 1977, Oliver 1991.
5 Westphal and Zajac 1995, Zajac and Westphal 1996.
6 Ocasio 1994, Selznick 1957.
7 March 1962.
8 Johnson, Melin and Whittington 2003.
9 Huse and Eide 1996.
10 This section is co-authored with Hans Van Ees and Jonas Gabrielsson. It is extracted from Van Ees, Gabrielsson and Huse 2005.
11 Simon 1945, 1955.
12 March and Simon 1958.
13 Cyert and March 1963.
14 Ocasio 1999, Osterloh, Frey and Frost 2001, Hendry 2005.
15 Hendry 2005.
16 Ocasio 1999, Zahra and Filatotchev 2004.
17 Huse and Rindova 2001.
18 Simon 1955, March and Simon 1958, Cyert and March 1963.
19 Hendry 2005.
20 Ibid.
21 Cyert and March 1963; see also Levinthal and March 1993.
22 Eisenhardt 1989.
23 Hendry 2002, Foss 2001.
24 Osterloh, Frey and Frost 2001; see also Radner 1996.
25 Hendry 2005.
26 Cyert and March 1963.
27 Ocasio 1999, Zahra and Filatotchev 2004.
28 March and Simon 1958, Cyert and March 1963, Nelson and Winter 2002.

29 March 1962, Cyert and March 1963.
30 Rindova 1999.
31 Pettigrew and McNulty 1995, Huse 1998, Pettigrew and McNulty 1998, McNulty and Pettigrew and 1999, Gabrielsson and Winlund 2000, Huse, Minichilli and Schøning 2005.
32 Huse, Minichilli and Schøning 2005.
33 Zald 1969.
34 Aguilera and Jackson 2003.
35 Ocasio 1999, Hendry 2002, Johnson, Melin and Whittington 2003.
36 Huse and Eide 1996.
37 Jensen and Meckling 1976.
38 Mintzberg 1983, Huse 2000.
39 Freeman and Reed 1983, Huse and Rindova 2001.
40 Gabrielsson and Huse 2005.
41 Kosnik 1987.
42 Blair and Stout 2001.
43 Huse and Rindova 2001.
44 Rindova 1999.
45 Ocasio 1994, Huse and Eide 1996, Ng and DeCock 2002.
46 Hendry 2005.
47 Baumol 2004.
48 Grandori 2004, Osterloh and Frey 2004, Windolf 2004.
49 Hendry 2005.
50 Cyert and March 1963.
51 Ocasio 1999.
52 Westphal and Zajac 1998.
53 Rindova 1999.
54 See, for example, Judge and Zeithaml 1992, Westphal, Seidel and Stewart 2001, Aguilera and Cuervo-Cazurra 2004 and Jonnergård, Kärreman and Svensson 2004.
55 Westphal, Seidel and Stewart 2001, Aguilera and Cuervo-Cazurra 2004.
56 Westphal, Seidel and Stewart 2001.
57 Ocasio 1999, Westphal, Seidel and Stewart 2001.
58 Huse, Minichilli and Schøning 2005.
59 See chapter 1, the section on value creation and board effectiveness.
60 See chapter 2.
61 See the doctoral dissertation of Mattias Nordqvist for an interesting presentation of the arenas and actors of corporate decision-making: Nordqvist 2005.
62 Ibid.
63 Ibid.: 247.
64 Ibid.: 257, with reference to Simmel 1950.

65 See, for example, Huse and Solberg 2006.
66 See Sjöstrand and Tyrstrup 2001, Melin 1998, Cyert and March 1963 or Nordqvist 2005.
67 This is from the 'one of the lads' study that I conducted in the beginning of the 1990s, for which I was the chairperson. The results are reported in various books and article, such as Huse 1998.
68 Mace 1971, Lorsch and MacIver 1989.
69 Macus 2002.
70 Ibid.: 134.
71 See, for example, Nordqvist 2005.
72 March and Olsen 1976.
73 This is from the 'one of the lads' study. See, for example, Huse 1998 and earlier instances in this chapter and chapter 5. This paragraph is extracted from Huse 1998: 223.
74 Bromiley and Cummings 1995, Hosmer 1995, Korsgaard, Schweiger and Sapienza 1995, McAllister 1995, Macneil 1980, Ring and Van den Ven 1992, 1994.
75 Etzioni 1988, Frank 1988, Granovetter 1985.
76 Bradach and Eccles 1989, Macneil 1980.
77 Browning, Beyer and Shetler 1995, Ring 1993.
78 Hosmer 1995, McAllister 1995.
79 Dwyer, Schurr and Oh 1987, Jarillo 1988, Larson 1992.
80 Hosmer 1995: 393.
81 See, for example, Ring 1996.
82 Macneil 1980.
83 See, for example, Huse 1993a, Borch and Huse 1993 or Huse 1994a.
84 Procedural justice is presented in a separate subsection in chapter 7. See, for example, Sapienza, Korsgard, Goulet and Hoogendam 2000.
85 See Huse 1994c. See also Donaldson 1990 on stewardship theory, and Collin 1990, Sjöstrand 1985 and Ouchi 1980 on clans.
86 Borch and Huse 1993, Huse 1993a.
87 Huse 1993a: 235.
88 See the presentation in chapter 3. See also Fukayama 1995.
89 This subsection is a summary of an empirical analysis presented in Huse 1996 and 2000.
90 Fama and Jensen 1983a, Jensen and Meckling 1976.
91 Donaldson 1990, Donaldson and Davis 1991.
92 Demb and Neubauer 1992, Huse 1993a.
93 Brundin 2002: 82.
94 Sjöstrand 1997.
95 Brundin 2002.

96 This story is from the 'one of the lads' study; see, for example, Huse 1998: 223.
97 Brundin 2002.
98 Harriman 1985: 13.
99 The examples are taken from the 'board life story' study; see, for example, Huse and Solberg 2006 or Bilimoria and Huse 1997.
100 Huse 1998, Brundin and Nordqvist 2004.
101 Nordqvist 2005. Socio-symbolic ownership combines symbolic interactionism and psychological ownership.
102 See, for example, Pierce, Kostova and Dirks 2001: 299.
103 Westphal and Zajac 1994, Zajac and Westphal 1995.
104 See also Cyert and March 1963 (dominant coalition) and Melin 1998 (power centre).
105 Johnson, Melin and Whittington 2003. See also Ravasi and Zattoni 2006.
106 Pettigrew and McNulty 1995, Brundin and Nordqvist 2004.
107 Dahl 1957: 202.
108 These are the core concepts of the doctoral thesis of Pinying Zhang Wenstøp. In her thesis she uses data from the 'value-creating board' surveys; see Wenstøp 2005.
109 Bachrach and Baratz 1975.
110 Lukes 1974.
111 Huse and Eide 1996.
112 Foucalt 1982, Luhman 1988, Giddens 1984.
113 Finkelstein 1992.
114 Yukl 1998.
115 The 'board life story' project; see also Huse and Solberg 2006.
116 Such as Mace 1971.
117 Useem 1984.
118 Pennings 1980, Richardson 1987.
119 Mace 1971, Whisler 1984.
120 Pettigrew and McNulty 1998.
121 In several European countries some of the board members are elected by and among the employees.
122 Hambrick and Mason 1984.
123 Michels 1962.
124 Ocasio 1994.
125 Huse and Eide 1996.
126 Pennings 1980, Richardson 1987.
127 Useem 1984.
128 Stearns and Mizruchi 1993, Mizruchi and Stearns 1988, Davis and Thompson 1994, Davis 1991.

129 Larson 1992.
130 Fiss and Zajac 2004.
131 This section is strongly influenced by the work of James Westphal, in particular in Westphal and Khanna 2003. Some paragraphs are taken almost directly from this article.
132 Westphal and Zajac 1995.
133 Westphal and Khanna 2003.
134 Ibid.
135 Ibid.
136 Westphal and Zajac 1998.
137 Powell and DiMaggio 1991, Oliver 1991.
138 Westphal and Zajac 1998, Zajac and Westphal 1995.
139 Useem 1982, Palmer and Barber 2001.
140 Westphal and Khanna 2003: 364.
141 Ibid.: 365.
142 Ibid.: 366.
143 Ibid.
144 This case presentation is taken from Huse and Eide 1996.

Chapter 7

 1 Higgs 2003.
 2 Aguilera and Cuervo-Cazurra 2004.
 3 Westphal and Zajac 1998.
 4 Lorsch and MacIver 1989, Patton and Baker 1987, Whisler 1984.
 5 Child 1972.
 6 March and Olsen 1976.
 7 Judge and Zeithaml 1992, Ocasio 1999.
 8 Ocasio 1999.
 9 March and Olsen 1989.
10 Ocasio 1999.
11 Ibid.: 385.
12 Sapienza, Korsgaard, Goulet and Hoogendam 2000: 337; see also Tyler 1989 and Tyler and Lind 1992.
13 Forbes and Milliken 1999.
14 Roberts, McNulty and Stiles 2005.
15 Whisler 1984.
16 Giddens 1984: 21.
17 Ocasio 1999: 386.
18 Hannan and Freeman 1977 and 1984.
19 Cuervo-Cazurra and Aguilera 2004, Thomsen 2004.
20 Monks and Minow 2004: 248–9.

21 The Sarbanes–Oxley Act contains, for example, regulations about the prohibition of audit and non-audit services from the same audit firm, detailing how auditing should be controlled by an independent audit committee composed of members of the board of directors, with a maximum of five years of individual responsibility for senior auditors. Furthermore, it includes regulations concerning increased financial and non-financial disclosure, the disclosure of all material from balance sheet transactions within the past six months, the prohibition of personal loans, a code of ethics for senior financial officers, a requirement that a company audit committee should include one member who is a financial expert, the protection of whistle-blowers and a requirement for the management certification of accounts, and penalties including fines of up to $1 million and ten years' imprisonment can be imposed for transgressions

22 The NYSE code also includes regulations about how non-management directors must meet without management in regular executive sessions, about mandatory committees comprised solely of independent directors, about how the chair of the audit committee must have accounting or financial management experience and about how the audit committee must have sole responsibility for hiring and firing the company's auditors and firing the independent auditor. 'Independent' is defined as having no material relationship with the company (either directly, or as a partner, shareholder or officer of an organisation that has a relationship with the company) and a requirement for a five-year 'cooling-off' period for former employees of the company and for their family members. Directors' fees must be the sole compensation an audit committee member receives from the company. The company has to adopt a code of business conduct and ethics.

23 The Committee on the Financial Aspects of Corporate Governance; Cadbury 1992.

24 The Greenbury Report, by the Study Group on Directors' Remuneration; Greenbury 1995.

25 Committee on Corporate Governance 2003.

26 Institute of Chartered Accountants in England and Wales 1999.

27 Roberts, McNulty and Stiles 2005.

28 Higgs 2003.

29 The Dutch Corporate Governance Code, *Principles of Good Corporate Governance and Best Practice Provisions*, the Corporate Governance Committee chaired by M. Tabaksblat, 9 December 2003.

30 Government Commission, German Corporate Governance Codes, 21 May 2003.

31 The Viénot Reports date from 1995 and 1999, the Bouton Report from 2002. For more details, see AFEP/MEDEF 2003: *The Corporate Governance of Listed Corporations*, produced by AFEP (Association Française des Entreprises Privées) and MEDEF (Mouvement des Entreprises de France), October 2003.
32 The OECD principles date to 2004.
33 See *The Combined Code (Revised)*, Committee on Corporate Governance 2003, section A.2: 5.
34 See, for example, chapter 4 and the section on board leadership below.
35 See, for example, the introduction to chapter 4.
36 See Dalton, Daily, Ellstrand and Johnson 1998.
37 Davis, Schoorman and Donaldson 1997.
38 MacAvoy and Millstein 2003: 100.
39 Dalton, Daily, Ellstrand and Johnson 1998.
40 See, for example, the Swedish *Code of Corporate Governance*, Swedish Government 2004.
41 See for example, Cadbury 1992, paragraph 4.35.
42 See, for example, Business Roundtable 2002.
43 Cadbury 1992, paragraph 4.30.
44 Committee on Corporate Governance 2003, section A.4: 8.
45 Ibid.
46 Ibid., section A.4.3: 8.
47 Business Roundtable *Principles of Corporate Governance*, 2002.
48 Higgs 2003, Summary of the principal duties of the remuneration committee.
49 See, for example, Osterloh and Frey 2004 and Business Roundtable 2002.
50 See, for example, Swedish Government 2004, codes section: 29.
51 See, for example, Business Roundtable 2002.
52 Lorsch and MacIver, 1989: 83.
53 See, for example, Business Roundtable 2002.
54 See Letendre 2004: 101–2.
55 See, for example, Business Roundtable 2002.
56 McNulty and Pettigrew 1999.
57 Cadbury 1992, paragraph 4.23.
58 Committee on Corporate Governance 2003, section A.5: 9.
59 See, for example, the Swiss *Codes of Best Practice for Corporate Governance*, issued by the Swiss Business Federation in 2002.
60 See, for example, Swedish Government 2004, codes section: 30.
61 OECD *Principles of Corporate Governance*, 2004.
62 See, for example, the *Handbook of Corporate Governance Reports* (the Italian codes), Assoziacione fra le società italiane per azonini 2004.

63 See, for example, Swiss Business Federation 2002.
64 See, for example, OECD 2004.
65 See, for example, Business Roundtable 2002.
66 Cadbury 1992, paragraph 4.12.
67 Committee on Corporate Governance 2003, section A.5.
68 Cadbury 1992.
69 Committee on Corporate Governance 2003, section A.5: 10.
70 Higgs 2003.
71 MacAvoy and Millstein 2003.
72 Committee on Corporate Governance 2003, section A.6: 10.
73 AFEP/MEDEF 2003, paragraph 9.
74 Committee on Corporate Governance 2003: 23.
75 Huse and Solberg 2006.
76 Dalton, Daily, Johnson and Ellstrand 1999.
77 Higgs 2003.
78 MacAvoy and Millstein 2003: 116.
79 Furr and Furr 2005.
80 Ibid.
81 Ibid.: 14–15.
82 Richard and Lana Furr use the term 'chairman'; I have made the change to 'chairperson'.
83 Cadbury 2002: 177.
84 MacAvoy and Millstein 2003: 117.
85 Mattson 2002.
86 Bloch 2005.
87 Higgs 2003.
88 Bloch 2005.
89 Ibid.: 7.
90 Ibid.: 10.
91 Ibid.: 10.
92 Jostein Frøyland of the TINE Group.
93 Higgs 2003.
94 Bloch, 2005: 10.
95 The system is based on that outlined in the PhD dissertation of Alessandro Minichilli.
96 Conger, Finegold and Lawler 1998.

Chapter 8

1 Forbes and Milliken 1999: 490.
2 Leblanc and Gillies 2005: 23.

3 'Duality' may technically be a more correct conceptual term than 'paradox' (Janssens and Steyart 1999), but I prefer to use the term 'paradox' as it is generally more relevant than 'duality' in the discussion here.
4 Smith, Smith, Olian, Sims, O'Bannen and Scully 1994.
5 Forbes and Milliken 1999.
6 Ibid.: 492.
7 Stiles and Taylor 2001: 113.
8 Alderfer 1986.
9 Forbes and Milliken 1999.
10 Ibid.: 492.
11 Ibid.
12 Huse, Minichilli and Schøning 2005.
13 See Letendre 2004 or Leblanc and Gillies 2005.
14 Forbes and Milliken 1999.
15 See, for example, Forbes and Milliken 1999, Roberts, McNulty and Stiles 2005, Sonnenfeld 2002.
16 Forbes and Milliken 1999.
17 Sonnenfeld 2002: 111.
18 Forbes and Milliken 1999: 493.
19 Huse and Solberg 2006.
20 Pearce and Zahra 1991.
21 Cadbury 2002: 88.
22 See, for example, Sonnenfeld 2002.
23 Letendre 2004: 104.
24 From the 'board life story' project; see, for example, Huse and Solberg 2006.
25 Daily and Dalton 2003.
26 Leblanc and Gillies 2005: 24.
27 Forbes and Milliken 1999: 495.
28 Ibid.: 496.
29 Huse and Solberg 2006.
30 Pearce and Zahra 1991.
31 Forbes and Milliken 1999: 494.
32 Sonnenfeld 2002.
33 Higashide and Birley 2002.
34 'Duality' may be a more correct conceptual tem than 'paradox' (Janssens and Steyart 1999). My use of the term 'paradox' is commented on in footnote 3 above.
35 Huse 1994c.
36 See, for example, Huse 1994a, 1994c or Lewis 2003.
37 See, for example, Huse 1994a, 1994c or Stiles and Taylor 2001: 2.

38 Roberts, McNulty and Stiles 2005.
39 Ibid.
40 Ibid.
41 Sonnenfeld 2002.
42 See, for example, Demb and Neubauer 1992, Huse 1993a, 1994a, Roberts and Stiles 1999 or Sundaramurthy and Lewis 2003.
43 Some of the balancing perspectives may be more urgent in corporate governance systems with a one-tier structure (as they work in the United Kingdom and the United States) than in systems where some of this balance is already made by having governance bodies with distinctly different roles.
44 Roberts, McNulty and Stiles 2005: 13.
45 Ibid.: 14.
46 John O'Neil, cited in ibid.
47 Sonnenfeld 2002.
48 Huse 1994a.
49 Lewis 2003.
50 Sundaramurthy and Lewis 2003.
51 Ibid.
52 Davis, Schoorman and Donaldson 1997.
53 Frey 1997.
54 Sundaramurthy and Lewis 2003: 405.
55 Ibid.: 407–11.
56 See also Sonnenfeld 2002.
57 The presentation here is based on Huse, Minichilli and Schøning 2005.
58 Sonnenfeld 2002.
59 Stiles and Taylor 2001: 116.
60 See, for example, Macus 2002.

Chapter 9

1 Mace 1971; see also Mace 1972.
2 McNulty, Roberts and Stiles 2005.
3 Such comparisons have been carried out in, for example, Huse 1994c and in the 'value-creating board' surveys. The evaluation of the board working style does not follow the same patterns across different categories of respondents.
4 Zahra and Pearce 1989.
5 See the presentation in the preface.
6 Andrews 1981: 104.
7 Zahra and Pearce 1990: 165.

8 Stiles and Taylor 2001: 47.
9 See, for example, Andrews 1981.
10 Fama and Jensen 1983a.
11 McNulty and Pettigrew 1999.
12 See, for example, Sundaramurthy and Lewis 2003.
13 See, for example, Shen 2003.
14 The table and arguments are as developed by McNulty and Pettigrew 1999.
15 See, for example, McNulty and Pettigrew 1999: 69–70.
16 Rindova 1999.
17 Milliken and Martins 1996.
18 Rindova 1999.
19 Ibid.: 969.
20 See, for example, Walsh and Seward 1990.
21 See, for example, Huse and Halvorsen 1995.
22 Stiles and Taylor 2001: 63–6.
23 Walsh and Seward 1990: 430–2.
24 See Monks and Minow 2004: 207; the list is adapted from one by Walter J. Salmon.
25 Walsh and Seward 1990: 427.
26 Mace 1971: 22–7.
27 Ibid.: 25.
28 See more, for example, in Stiles and Taylor 2001: 68.
29 Judge and Zeithaml 1992.
30 Pfeffer and Salancik 1978.
31 Mace 1971.
32 Barney 1991.
33 Davis, Schoorman and Donaldson 1997, Sundaramurthy and Lewis 2003.
34 Stiles and Taylor 2001.
35 For more on co-optation, see the paragraphs about resource dependence theory (Pfeffer and Salancik 1978) and the sections about interlocking directorates (Richardson 1987) in chapter 3.
36 See McDonald and Westphal 2003 for an analysis of this topic.
37 McNulty and Pettigrew 1999; see also the previous section on strategy involvement.
38 See, for example, Shen 2003.
39 Johannisson and Huse 2000.
40 Shen 2003.
41 Zahra and Pearce 1989.
42 The 'usual suspects' are presented by, for example, Finkelstein and Mooney 2003.

43 Our variables were based on more than fifty items, and all items were fully completed by 205 board chairpersons. The data was collected in 2005.

44 The experience of crisis was measured as the squared mean of four items taken as the experienced degree of crisis for the three most recent years. The questions were about financial crisis, sudden crisis based on external events, internal actor-related crisis, and the experience of external pressures to replace the CEO or the board.

45 No CEO duality existed in our sample.

46 These variables were measured through seven-point Likert-type scales.

47 Selected on the basis of Hermalin and Weisbach 1988.

48 Selected on the basis of Hillman and Dalziel 2003.

49 Selected on the basis of Milliken and Martins 1996.

50 They were all single item measures on a five-point Likert-type scale.

51 Each of them was measured as the mean of three items on a seven-point Likert-type scale.

52 The following items were used: the board members' appreciation of being together during meetings; having a pleasant atmosphere during the meetings; and giving high priority to being a member of this board.

53 The following items were used: the board members' acceptance and acknowledgement of the risk of making mistakes in opinions; willingness to give advice based on private knowledge, ideas and points of view; and openly communicating personal preferences and evaluations.

54 The following items were used: board members giving much and sufficient time for their board involvement; always being available if the board position should require it; and always being very well prepared for board meetings.

55 The following items were used: board members being very active in finding their own reports in addition to what is provided by the CEO; asking critical questions about proposals initiated by the management; and asking critical questions about information supplied by the management.

56 My analysis has been complex and comprehensive. A large number of dependent and independent variables were included, but many variables have been omitted in order to simplify the analyses and presentations. For example, among the contextual variables only a few ownership indicators, only one life cycle indicator, no industry indicators and no CEO attributes were included. More variables about board members could also have been included, such as gender, employee directors, etc. I did not include any variables from chapter 6 about power and strategising, trust, emotions, etc., and additional variables about board structures could have been included. I did not include any indicators about

the board leadership and the board chairperson. Some indicators of the board decision-making culture, such as creativity and cognitive conflicts, were also left out in my analysis. Furthermore, my analyses used linear multiple regression techniques, and the analyses included only some direct and mediating effects. I did not include here moderating and spurious effects. More complex and sophisticated analyses could have been used. Additional analyses have shown the importance of various interaction effects – for example, between board member competency, and board structures and culture.

57 The standardised coefficient was –0.24 and the significance was 0.02.

58 The relationships were significant in all steps in the analysis. In the full model the standardised coefficient between crisis and qualitative control was 0.18 and the significance was 0.01. For networks the standardised coefficient was 0.22 and the significance was 0.002.

59 The standardised coefficient was 0.17 and the significance was 0.04.

60 The standardised coefficients were 0.17 and –0.20, and the significances were 0.02 and 0.005, for outsider ratio and board member ownership respectively.

61 Both outsider ratio and board member ownership were significant in step 4, but in the full model only the negative relation with board member ownership was significant. The standardised coefficient was –0.17 and the significance was 0.03. The negative relationship with board member ownership increased as the other board member attributes were introduced.

62 In particular, firm-specific knowledge.

63 The standardised coefficient between firm-specific knowledge and qualitative control was 0.25 with a significance of 0.001.

64 The standardised coefficient in the full model was 0.21 and the significance was 0.008.

65 The standardised coefficient in the full model between firm-specific knowledge and advice was 0.28 and the significance was 0.000; between firm-specific knowledge and strategy it was 0.22 with a significance of 0.002.

66 The standardised coefficient in the full model was 0.18 and the significance was 0.02.

67 The standardised coefficients in the full model were 0.21 with a significance of 0.01 for 'two-day' meetings, and –0.21 with a significance of 0.02 for the CEO work description.

68 The standardised coefficient in the full model was 0.21 and the significance was 0.008.

69 The standardised coefficient in the full model was 0.17 and the significance was 0.02.

70 The standardised coefficient in the full model was 0.22 and the significance was 0.007.
71 The standardised coefficient in the full model was 0.27 and the significance was 0.001.
72 The standardised coefficient in the full model was 0.17 and the significance was 0.03.
73 The standardised coefficient in the full model was 0.16 and the significance was 0.02.

Chapter 10

1 See, for example, Tricker 1984.
2 The layout of this table is as suggested by Jonas Gabrielsson.
3 See, for example, Gabrielsson and Huse 2004.
4 See, for example, Huse 1993a, 1994b and 1994c.
5 See Dalton, Daily, Ellstrand and Johnson 1998: 274.
6 Ibid.
7 For example, in chapter 4, chapter 7 and chapter 9.
8 Finkelstein and Mooney 2003.
9 See, for example, Johnson, Daily and Ellstrand 1996, Dalton, Daily, Ellstrand and Johnson 1998 and Dalton, Daily, Johnson and Ellstrand 1999.
10 Evidence and more detailed arguments are presented in, for example, Gabrielsson and Huse 2004 and Huse 2000. See also Daily, Dalton and Cannella 2003.
11 From Zadek 2001: 110.
12 Ibid.: 105; see www.sustainability.co.uk.
13 See, for example, Graves and Waddock 1994, Halme and Huse 1997.
14 See, for example, Jones 1995.
15 See, for example, Hitt, Hoskisson, Johnson and Moesel 1996.
16 Hitt, Hoskisson, Johnson and Moesel 1996.
17 Hitt, Hoskisson, Ireland and Harrison 1991.
18 Hitt, Hoskisson, Johnson and Moesel 1996.
19 Hoskisson and Turk 1990.
20 In this analysis I used a sample of Norwegian firms with between fifty and 5000 employees. Data was collected from various sources, including separate questionnaires to CEOs and board chairpersons. The sample consisted of some 300 firms where responses from both CEOs and chairpersons were received. Some 250 responses were so complete that they could be used in the present analyses. The same board task performance variables that were presented in chapter 9 were used once again.

Responses to the board task performance variables were given by the board chairpersons. The R&D cost is the ratio of firm R&D expenditure to sales. Merger, restructuring and takeover threats were measured as the sum of CEO and chairperson responses. Merger and restructuring were both measured as the sum of two items. One question was used in the takeover threat variable. International activities were measured only by the responses from the CEOs.

21 Zahra 1996: 1715.
22 Ibid.
23 Covin and Slevin 1991.
24 Zahra 1996: 1715.
25 Floyd and Lane 2000: 155.
26 See, for example, Golden and Zajac 2001, Westphal and Fredrickson 2001, Goodstein, Gautam and Boeker 1994.
27 Westphal and Fredrickson 2001.
28 Zahra 1996.
29 Ibid.
30 Zahra, Neubaum and Huse 2000.
31 Ibid.
32 Pressure-resistant institutions included public pension funds, mutual funds, endowments and foundations. Pressure-sensitive institutions included insurance companies, banks and non-bank trusts. Pressure-indeterminate institutions included corporate pension funds, brokerage houses, investment advisory firms and private companies.
33 All the items were measured on a 7-point Likert-type scale. Product innovation included being the first company in the industry to introduce new products to the market place, creating radically new products for sale in new markets, creating radically new products for sale in the company's existing markets and commercialising new products. Process innovation included investing heavily in cutting-edge process-oriented R&D, being the first company in the industry to develop and introduce radically new technologies, pioneering the creation of new process technologies and copying other companies' process technologies (reverse engineering). Organisational innovation was measured as being the first in the industry to develop innovative management systems, being the first in the industry to introduce new business concepts and practices, changing the organisational structure in a significant way to promote innovation and introducing innovative human resource programmes to spur creativity and innovation. Domestic market venturing was measured through entering new markets, promoting new domestic business creation, diversifying into new industries in Norway, supporting domestic new venture activities and financing domestic start-up business

activities. Foreign market venturing was measured by entering new foreign markets, expanding international operations, supporting start-up
business activities dedicated to international operations and financing
start-up business activities dedicated to international operations. All
measures with one exception were identical with Zahra, Neubaum and
Huse 2000 (where there was one additional question on product innovation). We did not include it because the discriminant validity to process
innovation was too low.

34 Taylor 2001.
35 The section about value creation through the whole value chain contains
extracts from Huse, Minichilli and Gabrielsson (forthcoming).
36 Porter 1985.
37 Hillman, Cannella and Paetzold 2000.
38 Management and, in particular, corporate governance research is
inspired by the US 'publish and perish' syndrome. The implications of
this are the use of easily available data, the use of already accepted
methods and the dominance of agency theory. See, for example,
the discussions about the 'lamp' and 'hammer' syndromes in Huse
2000.
39 See chapter 8.

Chapter 11

1 See chapters 2 and 3.
2 A discussion of the various types of ethics in relation to corporate governance is found in Etzioni 1988.
3 Consequence ethics is another type of ethics, but it is related to utilitarian
ethics.
4 Etzioni 1988 is a critique of the neoclassical paradigm. The discussion
about utilitarian and deontological ethics is the core of the book. The
neoclassical paradigm is characterised by assumptions about individual
and intentionally rational opportunistic actors. See the theory presentations in chapter 3.
5 Stone 1975.
6 Stiles and Taylor 2001: 39.
7 See the presentation of agency theory in chapter 3.
8 See the theory presentations in chapter 3. See also the presentations of
influencing and social control in chapter 6.
9 See, for example, McNulty and Pettigrew 1999.
10 Westphal 2002.
11 See, for example, Pye 2004.

12 See, for example, Gomez 2004 or Gomez and Korine 2005.
13 The arguments in this paragraph are also put forward in Huse 2003b: 217–18.
14 See, for example, Grandori 2004 for thought-provoking new approaches and new solutions to the corporate governance problem.

References

AFEP/MEDEF 2003. *The Corporate Governance of Listed Corporations.* Paris: Association Française des Entreprises Privées/Mouvement des Entreprises de France, available at www.ecgi.org/codes/documents/cg_oct03_en.pdf.

Aguilera, R. V., and A. Cuervo-Cazurra 2004. Codes of good governance worldwide: what is the trigger? *Organisation Studies*, 25: 415–43.

Aguilera, R. V., and G. Jackson 2003. The cross-national diversity of corporate governance: dimensions and determinants. *Academy of Management Review*, 28: 447–65.

Alchian, A. A. 1984. Specificity, specialization, and coalitions. *Journal of Economic Theory and Institutions*, 140: 34–9.

Alchian, A. A., and H. Demsetz 1972. Production, information costs, and economic organization. *American Economic Review*, 62: 777–95.

Alderfer, C. 1986. The invisible director on corporate boards. *Harvard Business Review*, 64 (6): 38–52.

Andrews, K. R. 1981. Corporate strategy as a vital function of the board. *Harvard Business Review*, 59 (11): 174–84.

Aoki, M. 1984. *The Co-operative Game Theory of the Firm.* Oxford and New York: Clarendon Press.

2001. *Towards a Comparative Institutional Analysis.* Boston: MIT Press.

2004. A comparative institutional analytic approach to corporate governance. In A. Grandori (ed.), *Corporate Governance and Firm Organization: Microfoundations and Structural Forms.* Oxford: Oxford University Press.

Assoziacione fra le società italiane per azioni 2004. *Handbook of Corporate Governance Reports.* Rome: Assoziacione fra le società italiane per azioni, available at www.ecgi.org/codes/code.php?code_id=65.

Astrachan, J. H., S. Klein and K. Smyrnios 2001. The F-PEC scale of family influence: a proposal for solving the family business definition problem. *Family Business Review*, 15: 45–58.

Astrachan, J. H., and M. C. Shanker 2003. Family businesses' contribution to the US economy: a closer look. *Family Business Review*, 16: 211–21.

Bachrach, P., and M. S. Baratz 1975. Power and its two faces revisited: a reply to Geoffrey Debnam. *American Political Science Review*, 69: 900–4.

Barney J. 1991. Firm resources and sustained competitive advantage. *Journal of Management*, 17: 99–120.

Barney, J., M. Wright and D. Ketchen 2001. The RBV of the firm: ten years after 1991. *Journal of Management*, 27: 625–41.

Baumol, W. J. 2004. Entrepreneurial enterprises, large established firms and other components of the free-market growth machine. *Small Business Economics*, 23 (1): 9–21.

Baysinger, B. D., and H. N. Butler 1985. Corporate governance and the board of directors: performance effects of changes in board composition. *Journal of Law, Economics and Organization*, 1 (1): 101–24.

Baysinger, B. D., and R. E. Hoskisson 1990. The composition of boards of directors and strategic control: effects on corporate strategy. *Academy of Management Review*, 15: 72–87.

Berle, A. A., and G. C. Means 1932. *The Modern Corporation and Private Property*. New York: Macmillan.

Bilimoria, D., and M. Huse 1997. A qualitative comparison of the boardroom experiences of U.S. and Norwegian women corporate directors. *International Review of Women and Leadership*, 3 (2): 63–77.

Björkman, I. 1994. Managing Swedish and Finnish multinational corporations: the role of the board of directors in French and Norwegian subsidiaries. *International Business Review*, 3 (1): 47–69.

Blair, M. M. 1995. *Ownership and Control: Rethinking Corporate Governance for the Twenty-First Century*. Washington: Brookings Institute.

Blair, M. M., and L. A. Stout 2001. Corporate accountability: director accountability and the mediating role of the corporate board. *Washington University Law Review*, 79: 403–47.

Bloch, S. 2005. What makes a great board chair? *Corporate Board*, 26: 6–12.

Borch, O. J., and M. Huse 1993. Informal strategic networks and boards of directors. *Entrepreneurship Theory and Practice*, 18 (1): 23–36.

Borch, O. J., M. Huse and K. Senneseth 1999. Resource configuration, competitive strategies and corporate entrepreneurship: an empirical examination of small firms. *Entrepreneurship Theory and Practice*, 24 (1): 49–70.

Bradach, J. L., and R. G. Eccles 1989. Price, authority and trust: from ideal types to plural forms. *Annual Review of Sociology*, 15: 97–118.

Bromiley, P., and L. L. Cummings 1995. Transactions costs in organizations with trust. In R. J. Bies, R. J. Lewicki and B. L. Sheppard (eds.), *Research on Negotiations in Organizations*. Greenwich, CT: JAI Press.

Browning, L. D., J. M. Beyer and J. C. Shetler 1995. Building cooperation in a competitive industry: SEMATECH and the semiconductor industry. *Academy of Management Journal*, 38: 113–52.

Brundin, E. 2002. *Emotions in Motion: The Strategic Leader in a Radical Change Process*. Dissertation Series no. 12, Jönköping International Business School, Jönköping, Sweden.

Brundin, E., and M. Nordqvist 2004. *Emotions in the boardroom: the role of emotions as power energizers in strategizing*. Unpublished revised version of paper presented at the European Group for Organizational Studies conference 'Organizational Politics and the Politics of Organizations', Barcelona, 4–6 July 2002.

Burt, R. S. 1980. Models of network structure. *Annual Review of Sociology*, 6: 79–141.

1992. *Structural Holes: The Social Structure of Competition*. Cambridge, MA: Harvard University Press.

1997. The contingent value of social capital. *Administrative Science Quarterly*, 42: 339–65.

Business Roundtable 2002. *Principles of Corporate Governance*. Business Roundtable: available at www.businessroundtable.org.

Cable, D. M., and S. Shane 1997. A prisoner's dilemma approach to entrepreneur–venture capitalist relationships. *Academy of Management Review*, 22: 142–76.

Cadbury, A. 1992. *Report of the Committee on the Financial Aspects of Corporate Governance*. London: Gee Publishing.

2002. *Corporate Governance and Chairmanship*. Oxford: Oxford University Press.

Carpenter, M. A., and J. D. Westphal 2001. The strategic content of external network ties: examining the impact of director appointment on board involvement in strategic decision-making. *Academy of Management Journal*, 44: 639–60.

Certo, S. T. 2003. Influencing initial public offering investors with prestige: signaling with board structures. *Academy of Management Review*, 28: 432–46.

Certo, S. T., C. M. Daily and D. R. Dalton 2001. Signalling firm value through board structure: an investigation of initial public offerings. *Entrepreneurship Theory and Practice*, 26: 33–50.

Charkham, J. 1994. *Keeping Good Company: A Study of Corporate Governance in Five Countries*. Oxford: Oxford University Press.

Child, J. 1972. Organization structure, environment and performance. *Sociology*, 6: 1–22.

Child, J., and S. B. Rodriguez 2003. The international crisis in confidence in corporations. *Journal of Management and Governance*, 7: 233–40.

2004. Repairing the breach of trust in corporate governance. *Corporate Governance: An International Review*, 12: 143–52.

Clarkson, M. B. E. 1995. A stakeholder framework for analyzing and evaluating corporate social performance. *Academy of Management Review*, 20: 92–117.

Coleman, J. S. 1990. *Foundations of Social Theory*. Cambridge, MA: Belknapp Press of Harvard University Press.

Collin, S.-O. 1990. *Aktiebolagets kontroll*. Lund, Sweden: Lund University Press.

2004. *The mastering of the corporation: an integrated view of corporate governance*. Unpublished manuscript.

Committee on Corporate Governance 2003. *The Combined Code of Practice (Revised)*. London: Gee Publishing.

Conger, J. A., D. Finegold and E. E. Lawler 1998. Appraising boardroom performance. *Harvard Business Review*, 76 (1): 136–48.

Cook, K. S., and R. M. Emerson 1978. Power, equity and commitment in exchange networks. *American Sociological Review*, 43: 721–39.

Corbetta, G., and D. Montemerlo 1999. Ownership, governance and management issues in small and medium sized family businesses: a comparison of Italy and the United States. *Family Business Review*, 12, 361–74.

Corbetta, G., and S. Tomaselli 1996. Boards of directors in Italian family businesses. *Family Business Review*, 9: 403–21.

Covin, J. G., and D. P. Slevin 1991. A conceptual model of entrepreneurship as firm behavior. *Entrepreneurship: Theory and Practice*, 16 (1): 7–25.

Cromie, S., B. Stephenson and D. Monteith 1995. The management of family firms: an empirical investigation. *International Small Business Journal*, 13 (4): 11–34.

Cuervo-Cazurra, A., and R. V. Aguilera 2004. The worldwide diffusion of codes of good governance. In A. Grandori (ed.), *Corporate Governance and Firm Organization: Microfoundations and Structural Forms*. Oxford: Oxford University Press.

Cyert, R. M., and J. G. March 1963. *A Behavioral Theory of the Firm*. Englewood Cliffs, NJ: Prentice-Hall.

Daft, R. L. 1989. *Organization Theory and Design*. St Paul, MN: West Publishing.

Dahl, R. A. 1957. The concept of power. *Behavioral Science*, 2: 201–5.

Daily, C. M., and D. R. Dalton 1992a. The relationship between governance structure and corporate performance in entrepreneurial firms. *Journal of Business Venturing*, 7: 375–86.

1992b. Financial performance of founder-managed versus professionally managed small corporations. *Journal of Small Business Management*, 30 (2): 25–34.

2003. Women in the boardroom: a business imperative. *Journal of Business Strategy*, 24 (5): 8–9.

Daily, C. M., D. R. Dalton and A. A. Cannella Jr. 2003. Corporate governance: decades of dialogue and data. *Academy of Management Review*, 28: 371–82.

Dalton, D. R., C. M. Daily, A. E. Ellstrand and J. L. Johnson 1998. Meta-analytic reviews of board composition, leadership structure, and financial performance. *Strategic Management Journal*, 19: 269–90.

Dalton, D. R., C. M. Daily, J. L. Johnson and A. E. Ellstrand 1999. Number of directors and financial performance: a meta-analysis. *Academy of Management Journal*, 42: 674–86.

Davis, G. F. 1991. Agents without principals? The spread of the poison pill through the intercorporate network. *Administrative Science Quarterly*, 36: 583–613.

Davis, G. F., and T. Thompson 1994. A social movement perspective on corporate control. *Administrative Science Quarterly*, 39: 141–73.

Davis, J. H., D. F. Schoorman and L. Donaldson 1997. Toward a stewardship theory of management. *Academy of Management Review*, 22: 20–47.

Deakins, D., E. O'Neill and P. Mileham 2000. Insiders vs outsiders: director relationships in small, entrepreneurial companies. *Enterprise and Innovation Management Studies*, 1: 175–86.

Demb, A., and F. F. Neubauer 1992. *The Corporate Board: Confronting the Paradoxes*. New York: Oxford University Press.

DiMaggio, P. J., and W. W. Powell 1983. The iron cage revisited: institutional isomorphism and collective rationality in organizational fields. *American Sociological Review*, 48: 147–60.

Donaldson, L. 1990. The ethereal hand: organization and management theory. *Academy of Management Review*, 15: 369–81.

Donaldson, L., and J. H. Davis 1991. Stewardship theory or agency theory: CEO governance and shareholder returns. *Australian Journal of Management*, 16: 49–64.

Donaldson, T., and L. E. Preston 1995. The stakeholder theory of the corporation: concepts, evidence, and implications. *Academy of Management Review*, 20: 65–91.

Dwyer, F. R., P. H. Schurr and S. Oh 1987. Developing buyer–seller relationships. *Journal of Marketing*, 51: 11–27.

Eisenhardt, K. M. 1989. Agency theory: an assessment and review. *Academy of Management Review*, 14: 57–74.

Eisenhardt, K. M., and J. A. Martin 2000. Dynamic capabilities: what are they? *Strategic Management Journal*, 21: 1105–21.

Etzioni, A. 1988. *The Moral Dimension*. New York: Free Press.

Fama, E. F. 1980. Agency problems and the theory of the firm. *Journal of Political Economics*, 88: 288–307.

Fama, E. F., and M. C. Jensen 1983a. Separation of ownership and control. *Journal of Law and Economics*, 26: 301–26.

1983b. Agency problems and residual claims. *Journal of Law and Economics*, 26: 327–50.

1985. Organizational forms and investment decisions. *Journal of Financial Economics*, 14: 101–19.

Fiet, J. O. 1995. Risk avoidance strategies in venture capital markets. *Journal of Management Studies*, 32: 551–74.

Filatotchev, I., and S. Toms 2003. Corporate governance, strategy and survival in a declining industry: a study of UK cotton textile companies. *Journal of Management Studies*, 40 (4): 895–920.

Finkelstein, S. 1992. Power in top management teams: dimensions, measurements and validation. *Academy of Management Journal*, 35: 505–36.

Finkelstein, S., and A. C. Mooney 2003. Not the usual suspects: how to use board process to make boards better. *Academy of Management Executive*, 17 (2): 101–13.

Firstenberg, P. B., and B. G. Malkiel 1994. The twenty-first-century boardroom: who will be in charge? *Sloan Management Review*, 36 (1): 27–35.

Fiss, P. C., and E. Zajac 2004. The diffusion of ideas over contested terrain: the (non)adoption of a shareholder value orientation among German firms. *Administrative Science Quarterly*, 49: 501–34.

Floyd, S. W., and P. J. Lane 2000. Strategizing throughout the organization: managing role conflict in strategic renewal. *Academy of Management Review*, 25: 154–77.

Fombrun, C. J. 1996. *Reputation*. Boston: Harvard Business School Press.

Fombrun, C. J., and V. Rindova 1994. *Reputational rankings: institutional social audits of corporate performance*. Paper presented to fifth annual conference of International Association of Business and Society, Hilton Head Island, SC, 17–20 March.

Forbes, D. P., and F. J. Milliken 1999. Cognition and corporate governance: understanding boards of directors as strategic decision-making groups. *Academy of Management Review*, 24: 489–505.

Foss, N. J. 2001. Bounded rationality in the economics of organization: present use and (some) future possibilities. *Journal of Management and Governance*, 5: 401–25.

Foucault, M. 1982. Afterword: the subject and power. In H. L. Dreyfus and P. Rabinow (eds.), *Beyond Structualism and Hermeneutics*, Chicago: University of Chicago Press.

Frank, R. H. 1988. *Passion within Reason: The Strategic Role of the Emotions*. New York: Norton.

Freeman, L. C. 1977. A set of measures of centrality based on betweenness. *Sociometry*, 40: 35–41.

Freeman, R. E. 1984. *Strategic Management: A Stakeholder Approach*. Boston: Pitman.

Freeman, R. E., and D. L. Reed 1983. Stockholders and stakeholders: a new perspective on corporate governance. *California Management Review*, 25 (3): 88–106.

Frey, B. S. 1997. *Not Just for the Money: An Economic Theory of Personal Motivation*. Cheltenham: Edward Elgar.

Fried, V. H., G. D. Bruton and R. D. Hisrich 1998. Strategy and the board of directors in venture capital backed firms. *Journal of Business Venturing*, 13: 493–503.

Fried, V. H., and R. D. Hisrich 1995. The venture capitalist: a relationship investor. *California Management Review*, 37 (2): 101–13.

Fukayama, F. 1995. *Trust: The Social Virtues and the Creation of Prosperity*. New York: Free Press.

Furr, R. M., and L. J. Furr 2005. Is your chairman a leader? *Corporate Board*, 26: 11–15.

Gabrielsson, J. 2003. *Boards and Governance in SMEs: An Inquiry into Boards' Contribution to Firm Performance*. Lund, Sweden: Lund University Press.

Gabrielsson, J., and M. Huse 2002. The venture capitalist and the board of directors in SMEs: roles and processes. *Venture Capital*, 4 (2): 125–46.

2004. Context, behavior, and evolution: challenges in research on boards and governance. *International Studies of Management and Organizations*, 34 (2): 11–36.

2005, 'Outside' directors in SME boards: a call for theoretical reflections. *Corporate Board: Roles, Duties and Responsibilities*, 1 (1): 28–37.

Gabrielsson, J., and H. Winlund 2000. Boards of directors in small and medium-sized industrial firms: examining the effects of the board's working style on board task performance. *Entrepreneurship and Regional Development*, 12 (4): 311–30.

Galaskiewicz, J., and S. Wasserman 1989. Mimetic processes within an interorganizational field: an empirical test. *Administrative Science Quarterly*, 34: 454–79.

Gedajlovic, E., M. Lubatkin and W. Schulze 2004. Crossing the threshold from founder management to professional management: a governance perspective. *Journal of Management Studies*, 41: 899–912.

Gedaljovic, E. R., and D. M. Shapiro 1998. Management and ownership effects: evidence from five countries. *Strategic Management Journal*, 19: 533–53.

Gersick, K. E., J. A. Davis, M. McCollon Hampton and I. Lansberg 1997. *Generation to Generation: Life Cycles of the Family Business.* Boston: Harvard Business School Press.

Ghoshal, S. 2005. Bad management theories are destroying good management practices. *Academy of Management Learning and Education*, 4: 75–91.

Gioia, D. E. 2003. Teaching teachers to teach corporate governance differently. *Journal of Management and Governance*, 7: 255–62.

Giddens, A. 1984. *The Constitution of Society: Outline of the Theory of Structuration.* Berkeley, CA: University of California Press.

Gnan, L., M. Huse and D. Montemerlo 2005. *Family councils and the governance of family businesses: agency theory or a paternalistic logic.* Paper presented at the Academy of Management Meeting, Honolulu, 5–10 August.

Goel, S., and L. Erakovic 2005. *Collaboration in the boardroom: resolving the paradox of monitoring and mentoring.* Unpublished manuscript.

Golden, B. R., and E. Zajac 2001. When will boards influence strategy? Inclination × power = strategic change. *Strategic Management Journal*, 22: 1087–111.

Gomez, P.-Y. 2004. On the discretionary power of top executives. *International Studies of Management and Organization*, 34 (2): 37–62.

Gomez, P.-Y., and H. Korine 2005. Democracy and the evolution of corporate governance. *Corporate Governance: An International Review*, 13: 739–52.

Goodall, K., and M. Warner 2002. Corporate governance in Sino-foreign joint ventures in the PRC: the view of Chinese directors. *Journal of General Management*, 27 (3): 77–92.

Goodstein, J., K. Gautam and W. Boeker 1994. The effects of board size and diversity on strategic change. *Strategic Management Journal*, 15: 241–50.

Grandori, A. 2004. Introduction. Reframing corporate governance: behavioral assumptions, governance mechanisms, institutional dynamics. In A. Grandori (ed.), *Corporate Governance and Firm Organization: Microfoundations and Structural Forms.* Oxford: Oxford University Press.

Grandori, A., and G. Soda 2004. Governing with multiple principals: an empirically based analysis of capital providers' preferences and superior governance structures. In A. Grandori (ed.), *Corporate Governance and Firm Organization: Microfoundations and Structural Forms.* Oxford: Oxford University Press.

Granovetter, M. S. 1973. The strength of weak ties. *American Journal of Sociology*, 78: 1360–80.

1985. Economic action and social structure: the problem of embeddedness. *American Journal of Sociology*, 9: 481–510.

Graves, S. B., and S. A. Waddock 1994. Institutional owners and corporate social performance. *Academy of Management Journal*, 37: 1034–46.

Green, P. G., C. G. Brush and T. E. Brown 1997. Resource configurations in new ventures: relationships to owner and company characteristics. *Journal of Small Business Strategy*, 8 (2): 25–40.

Greenbury, R. 1995. *Directors' Remuneration: Report of a Study Group*. London: Gee Publishing.

Grossman, S. J., and O. D. Hart 1986. The cost and benefits of ownership: a theory of vertical and lateral integration. *Journal of Political Economy*, 94: 691–719.

Gulati, R., and M. Gargiulo 1999. Where do interorganizational networks come from? *American Journal of Sociology*, 104: 1439–93.

Gulati, R., and J. D. Westphal 1999. Cooperative or controlling? The effect of CEO board relation and the content of interlocks on the formation of joint ventures. *Administrative Science Quarterly*, 44: 473–506.

Haalien, L., and M. Huse 2005. *Boards of Directors in Norwegian Family Businesses: Results from the Value Creating Board Survey*, Research Report no. 7-2005, Norwegian School of Management BI, Oslo.

Hagen, I. M., and M. Huse 2006. *Do employee representatives make a difference on corporate boards? Examples from Norway employee directors.* Paper presented at the European Academy of Management annual conference, Oslo, 17–20 May.

Halme, M., and M. Huse 1997. The influence of corporate governance, industry and country factors on environmental reporting. *Scandinavian Journal of Management*, 13 (2): 137–57.

Hambrick, D. C., and P. A. Mason 1984. Upper echelons: the organisation as a reflection of its top managers. *Academy of Management Review*, 9: 193–206.

Hannan, M. T., and J. Freeman 1977. The population ecology of organizations. *American Journal of Sociology*, 82: 929–64.

1984. Structural inertia and organizational change. *American Sociological Review*, 49: 149–64.

Harriman, A. 1985. *Women/Men/Management*. New York: Praeger.

Hendry, J. 2002. The principal's other problems: honest incompetence and management contracts. *Academy of Management Review*, 27: 98–113.

2005. Beyond self-interest: agency theory and the board in a satisficing world. *British Journal of Management*, 16 (Supplement 1): 55–64.

Hermalin, B. E., and M. S. Weisbach 1988. The determinants of board composition. *Rand Journal of Economics*, 19: 589–606.

1991. The effects of board composition and direct incentives on firm performance. *Financial Management*, 20 (4): 101–12.

Herman, E. S. 1981. *Corporate Control, Corporate Power*. Cambridge: Cambridge University Press.

Higashide, H., and S. Birley 2002. The consequences of conflict between the venture capitalist and the entrepreneurial team in the United Kingdom from the perspective of the venture capitalist. *Journal of Business Venturing*, 17: 59–82.

Higgs, D. 2003. *Review of the Role and Effectiveness of Non-Executive Directors*. London: Department of Trade and Industry.

Hill, C. W. L., and T. M. Jones 1992. Stakeholder-agency theory. *Journal of Management Studies*, 29: 132–54.

Hillman, A. J., A. A. Cannella Jr. and R. L. Paetzold 2000. The resource dependence role of corporate directors: strategic adaptation of board composition in response to environmental change. *Journal of Management Studies*, 37: 235–55.

Hillman, A. J., and T. Dalziel 2003. Board of directors and firm performance: integrating agency and resource dependence perspectives. *Academy of Management Review*, 28: 383–96.

Hitt, M. A., R. E. Hoskisson, R. D. Ireland and J. S. Harrison 1991. Effects of acquisitions on R & D inputs and outputs. *Academy of Management Journal*, 34: 693–706.

Hitt, M. A., R. E. Hoskisson, R. Johnson and D. Moesel 1996. The market for corporate control and firm innovation: effects of participation, strategy, size, and internal controls. *Academy of Management Journal*, 39: 1084–119.

Hoskisson, R. E., and T. A. Turk 1990. Corporate restructuring: governance and control limits of the internal capital market. *Academy of Management Review*, 15: 459–77.

Hosmer, L. T. 1995. Trust: the connecting link between organizational theory and philosophical ethics. *Academy of Management Review*, 20: 379–403.

Hung, H. 1998. A typology of the theories of the roles of governing boards. *Corporate Governance: An International Review*, 6: 101–11.

Huse, M. 1990. Board composition in small enterprises. *Entrepreneurship and Regional Development*, 2: 363–73.

1993a. Relational norms as a supplement to neo-classical understanding of directorates: an empirical study of boards of directors. *Journal of Socio-Economics*, 22: 219–40.

1993b. *The board's strategic involvement*. Paper presented at the 53rd Annual Meeting of the Academy of Management, Atlanta, 8–11 August 1993.

1993c. To be or not to be: on boards and bankruptcy. *Abhigyan*, 10 (winter): 43–52.

1994a. Board–management relations in small firms: the paradox of simultaneous independence and interdependence. *Small Business Economics Journal*, 6: 55–72.

1994b. Stakeholder analyses and boards of directors. *Abhigyan*, 10 (spring): 9–23.

1994c. *Distansert nærhet.* Bodø: Nordland Research Institute.

1996. *The role of trust in empowering boards of directors in small firms: researching unresearchable issues.* Paper presented at the Annual Meeting of the Academy of Management, Cincinnati, 9–11 August.

1998. Researching the dynamics of board–stakeholder relations. *Long-Range Planning*, 31: 218–26.

2000. Boards of directors in SMEs: a review and research agenda. *Entrepreneurship and Regional Development*, 12: 271–90.

2003a. *Styret: Tante, barbar eller klan* (2nd edn.). Bergen: Fagbokforlaget.

2003b. Renewing management and governance: new paradigms of governance? *Journal of Management and Governance*, 7: 211–21.

2005. Accountability and creating accountability: a framework for exploring behavioural perspectives of corporate governance. *British Journal of Management*; 16 (special issue): 65–79.

Huse, M., and D. Eide 1996. Stakeholder management and the avoidance of corporate control. *Business and Society*, 35: 211–43.

Huse, M., and J. Gabrielsson 2004. The effects of entrepreneurial posture on international activities in the lights of emerging globalization. In G. Corbetta, M. Huse and D. Ravasi (eds.), *Crossroads of Entrepreneurship*. Boston, New York and Dordrecht: Kluwer.

Huse, M., and H. Halvorsen 1995. *Styrearbeid i små og mellomstore bedrifter.* Bergen: Fagbokforlaget.

Huse, M., A. Minichilli and J. Gabrielsson (forthcoming). Knowledge and accountability: outside directors' contribution in the corporate value chain. In P.-Y. Gomez and R. Moore (eds.), *Board Members and Management Consulting: Redefining Boundaries*, Management Consulting Book Series. Charlotte, NC: Information Age Publishing.

Huse, M., A. Minichilli and M. Schøning 2005. Corporate boards as assets in the new Europe: the value of process-oriented boardroom dynamics. *Organizational Dynamics*, 34: 285–97.

Huse, M., D. O. Neubaum and J. Gabrielsson 2005. Corporate innovation and competitive environment. *International Entrepreneurship and Management Journal*, 1: 313–33.

Huse, M., and V. Rindova 2001. Stakeholders' expectation of board roles: the case of subsidiary boards. *Journal of Management and Governance*, 5: 153–78.

Huse, M., and A. G. Solberg 2006. Gender-related boardroom dynamics: how women make and can make contributions on corporate boards. *Women in Management Review*, 21: 113–30.

Institute of Chartered Accountants in England and Wales 1999. *Internal Control: Guidance for Directors on the Combined Code*. London: Institute of Chartered Accountants in England and Wales.

Janssens, M., and C. Steyart 1999. The world in two and a third way out? The concept of duality in organization theory and practice. *Scandinavian Journal of Management*, 15: 121–39.

Jarillo, J.-C. 1988. On strategic networks. *Strategic Management Journal*, 9: 31–41.

Jensen, M. C. 1983. Organization theory and methodology. *Accounting Review*, 58: 319–39.

1986. The agency costs of free cash flows, corporate finance and takeovers. *American Economic Review*, 76: 323–9.

1993. The modern industrial revolution, exit, and the failure of internal control systems. *Journal of Finance*, 48: 831–80.

Jensen, M. C., and W. H. Meckling 1976. Theory of the firm: managerial behaviour, agency costs and ownership structure. *Journal of Financial Economics*, 3: 305–60.

1979. Rights and production functions: an application to labor-managed firms and codetermination. *Journal of Business*, 52: 469–506.

Jensen, M. C., and R. S. Ruback 1983. The market for corporate control. *Journal of Financial Economics*, 11: 5–50.

Johannisson, B., and M. Huse 2000. Recruiting outside board members in the small family business: an ideological challenge. *Entrepreneurship and Regional Development*, 12: 353–78.

Johnson, G., L. Melin and R. Whittington 2003. Micro strategy and strategizing: towards an activity-based view. *Journal of Management Studies*, 40: 3–22.

Johnson, J. L., C. M. Daily and A. E. Ellstrand 1996. Boards of directors: a review and research agenda. *Journal of Management*, 22: 409–38.

Johnson, R. A., R. E. Hoskisson and M. A. Hitt 1993. Board of director involvement in restructuring: the effects of board versus managerial control and characteristics. *Strategic Management Journal*, 14: 33–50.

Jones, T. 1995. Instrumental stakeholder theory: a synthesis of ethics and economics. *Academy of Management Review*, 20: 404–37.

Jonnergård, K., M. Kärreman and C. Svensson 2004. The impact of changes in the corporate governance system on the boards of directors:

experiences from Swedish listed companies. *International Studies of Management and Organization*, 34 (2): 114–53.

Joskow, P. 1985. Vertical integration and long-term contracts: the case of coal-burning electric generating plants. *Journal of Law, Economics and Organization*, 1: 33–80.

1988. Asset specificity and the structure of vertical relationships. *Journal of Law, Economics and Organization*, 4: 95–117.

Judge, W. Q. Jr., and C. P. Zeithaml 1992. Institutional and strategic choice perspectives on board involvement in the strategic decision process. *Academy of Management Journal*, 35: 766–94.

Kaufman, A., and E. Englander 2005. A team production model of corporate governance. *Academy of Management Executive*, 19(3): 9–22.

Klein, B. 1980. Transaction cost determinants of 'unfair' contractual arrangements. *American Economic Review*, 70: 356–62.

1988. Vertical integration as organizational ownership: the Fisher Body–General Motors relationship revisited. *Journal of Law, Economics and Organization*, 4: 199–213.

Klein, B., R. A. Crawford and A. A. Alchian 1978. Vertical integration, appropriable rents, and the competitive contracting process. *Journal of Law and Economics*, 21: 297–326.

Klein, B., and K. B. Leffler 1981. The role of market forces in assuring contractual performance. *Journal of Political Economy*, 89: 615–41.

Kochan, T. 2003. Restoring trust in American corporations: addressing the root causes. *Journal of Management and Governance*, 7: 223–31.

Korsgaard, M. A., D. M. Schweiger and H. J. Sapienza 1995. Building commitment, attachment, and trust in strategic decision-making teams: the role of procedural justice. *Academy of Management Journal*, 38: 60–85.

Kosnik, R. D. 1987. Greenmail: a study of board performance in corporate governance. *Administrative Science Quarterly*, 32: 163–85.

1990. Effects of board demography and directors' incentives on corporate greenmail decisions. *Academy of Management Journal*, 33: 129–50.

La Porta, R., F. Lopez-de-Silanes and A. Shleifer 1999. Corporate ownership around the world. *Journal of Finance*, 54: 471–517.

Lansberg, I. 1999. *Succeeding Generations*. Boston: Harvard Business School Press.

Larson, A. 1992. Network dyads in entrepreneurial settings: a study of the governance of exchange relationships. *Administrative Science Quarterly*, 37: 76–104.

Lawrence, P. R., and J. W. Lorsch 1967. *Organization and Environment: Managing Differentiations and Integration*. Cambridge, MA: Harvard University Press.

Lazonick, W., and M. O'Sullivan 2000. Maximizing shareholder value: a new ideology for corporate governance. *Economy and Society*, 29 (1): 13–35.

Leblanc, R., and J. Gillies 2005. *Inside the Boardroom: How Boards Really Work and the Coming Revolution in Corporate Governance*. Hoboken, NJ: John Wiley.

Letendre, L. 2004. The dynamics of the boardroom. *Academy of Management Executive*, 18 (1): 101–4.

Levinthal, D. A., and J. G. March 1993. The myopia of learning. *Strategic Management Journal*, 14: 94–112.

Lewis, K. D. 2003. Board independence or interdependence? *Corporate Board*, 24: 1–4.

Lorsch, J. W., and E. MacIver 1989. *Pawns or Potentates: The Reality of America's Corporate Boards*. Boston: Harvard Business School Press.

Luhmann, N. 1988. Familiarity, confidence, trust: problems and alternatives. In D. Gambetta (ed.), *Trust: Making and Breaking Cooperative Relations*. Oxford: Basil Blackwell.

Lukes, S. 1974. *Power: A Radical View*. London: Macmillan.

Lynall, M. D., B. R. Golden and A. J. Hillman 2003. Board composition from adolescence to maturity: a multitheoretic view. *Academy of Management Review*, 28: 416–31.

MacAvoy, P., and I. Millstein 2003. *The Recurrent Crisis in Corporate Governance*. New York: Palgrave Macmillan.

Mace, M. L. 1971. *Directors: Myth and Reality*. Boston: Harvard Business School Press.

1972. The president and the board of directors. *Harvard Business Review*, 50 (2): 37–49.

Macneil, I. R. 1980. *The New Social Contract: An Inquiry into Modern Contractual Relations*. New Haven, CT, and London: Yale University Press.

Macus, M. 2002. *Towards a comprehensive theory of boards: conceptual development and empirical exploration*. Unpublished doctoral dissertation, University of St Gallen, Bamberg.

Manigart, S., and H. Sapienza 2000. Venture capital and growth. In D. Sexton and H. Landström (eds.), *Handbook of Entrepreneurship*, Oxford: Basil Blackwell.

March, J. G. 1962. The business firm as a political coalition. *Journal of Politics*, 24: 662–78.

March, J. G., and J. P. Olsen 1976. *Ambiguity and Choice in Organizations*. Bergen: Universitetsforlaget.

1989. *Rediscovering Institutions: The Organizational Basis of Politics*. New York: Free Press.

References

March, J. G., and H. A. Simon 1958. *Organizations*. New York: John Wiley.

Markman, G. D., D. B. Balkin and L. Schjoedt 2001. Governing the innovation process in entrepreneurial firms. *Journal of High Technology Management Research*, 12: 273–93.

Mattson, G. L. 2002. The effective lead director. *Corporate Board*, 23: 1–6.

McAllister, D. J. 1995. Affect- and cognitive-based trust as foundation for interpersonal cooperation in organizations. *Academy of Management Journal*, 38: 24–59.

McNulty, T., and A. Pettigrew 1999. Strategists on the board. *Organisation Studies*, 20: 47–74.

McNulty, T., J. Roberts and P. Stiles 2005. Undertaking governance reform and research: further reflections on the Higgs review. *British Journal of Management*, 16 (special issue): 99–107.

Melin, L. 1998. Strategisk förändring: om dess drivkrafter och inneboende logik. In B. Czarniawska (ed.), *Organisationsteori på svenska*. Malmö: Liber Ekonomi.

Meyer, J., and B. Rowan 1977. Institutionalized organizations: formal structures as myth and ceremony. *American Journal of Sociology*, 83: 333–63.

Michels, R. 1962. *Political Parties: A Sociological Study of the Oligarchical Tendencies of Modern Democracy*. New York: Collier.

Milliken, F. J., and L. L. Martins 1996. Searching for common threads: understanding the multiple effects of diversity in organizational groups. *Academy of Management Review*, 21: 402–33.

Mintzberg, H. 1983. *Power in and around Organization*. Englewood Cliffs, NJ: Prentice-Hall.

Mitchell, R. K., B. R. Agle and D. J. Wood 1997. Toward a theory of stakeholder identification and salience: defining the principle of who and what really counts. *Academy of Management Review*, 22: 853–86.

Mizruchi, M. S. 1996. What do interlocks do? An analysis, critique, and assessment of research on interlocking directorates. *Annual Review of Sociology*, 22: 271–98.

Mizruchi, M. S., and B. L. Stearns 1988. A longitudinal study of the formation of interlocking directorates. *Administrative Science Quarterly*, 33: 194–210.

Monks, R. A. G., and N. Minow 2004. *Corporate Governance* (3rd edn.). Oxford: Basil Blackwell.

Mustakallio, M. A. 2002. *Contractual and relational governance in family firms: effects on strategic decision-making quality and firm performance*. Doctoral dissertation, Helsinki University of Technology.

Nahapiet, J., and S. Ghoshal 1998. Social capital, intellectual capital and the organizational advantage. *Academy of Management Review*, 23: 242–66.

Näsi, J. (ed.) 1995. *Understanding Stakeholder Thinking*. Helsinki: LSR-Publications.

Nelson, R. R., and S. G. Winter 2002. Evolutionary theorizing in economics. *Journal of Economic Perspectives*, 16 (2): 23–46.

Neubauer, F., and A. G. Lank 1998. *The Family Business: Its Governance for Sustainability*. London: Macmillan Business.

Ng, W., and C. DeCock 2002. Battle in the boardroom: a discursive perspective. *Journal of Management Studies*, 39: 23–50.

Nordqvist, M. 2005. *Understanding the Role of Ownership in Strategizing: A Study of Family Firms*. Dissertation Series no. 29, Jönköping International Business School, Jönköping, Sweden.

Ocasio, W. 1994. Political dynamics and the circulation of power: CEO succession in US industrial corporations 1960–1990. *Administrative Science Quarterly*, 39: 285–312.

1999. Institutionalised action and corporate governance: the reliance on rules of CEO succession. *Administrative Science Quarterly*, 44: 384–416.

OECD 2004. *Principles of Corporate Governance*. Paris: Organisation for Economic Co-operation and Development.

Oliver, C. 1991. Strategic responses to institutional processes. *Academy of Management Review*, 16: 145–79.

Osterloh, M., and B. S. Frey 2004. Corporate governance for crooks? The case for corporate virtue. In A. Grandori (ed.), *Corporate Governance and Firm Organization: Microfoundations and Structural Forms*. Oxford: Oxford University Press.

Osterloh, M., B. S. Frey and J. Frost 2001. Managing motivation, organization and governance. *Journal of Management and Governance*, 5: 231–9.

Ouchi, W. G. 1980. Markets, bureaucracies, and clans. *Administrative Science Quarterly*, 25: 129–41.

Palmer, D. A. 1983. Broken ties: interlocking directorates and intercorporate coordination. *Administrative Science Quarterly*, 28: 40–55.

Palmer, D. A., and B. Barber 2001. Challenges, elites, and owning families: a social class theory of corporate acquisitions in the 1960s. *Administrative Science Quarterly*, 46: 87–120.

Patton, A., and J. C. Baker 1987. Why won't directors rock the boat? *Harvard Business Review*, 65 (6): 10–18.

Pearce, J. A. 1983. The relationship of internal versus external orientations to financial measures of strategic performance. *Strategic Management Journal*, 4: 297–306.

Pearce, J. A., and S. A. Zahra 1991. The relative power of CEOs and boards of directors: associations with corporate performance. *Strategic Management Journal*, 12: 135–53.

Pedersen, T., and S. Thomsen 2003. Ownership structure and value of the largest European firms: the importance of owner identity. *Journal of Management and Governance*, 7: 27–55.

Pennings, J. M. 1980. *Interlocking Directorates*. San Francisco: Jossey Bass.

1981. Strategically interdependent organizations. In P. C. Nystrom and W. H. Starbuck (eds.), *Handbook of Organizational Design*. New York: Oxford University Press.

Penrose, E. 1959. *The Theory of the Growth of the Firm*. New York: Oxford University Press.

Perrow, C. 1986. *Complex Organizations*. New York: Random House.

Pettigrew, A. M. 1992. On studying managerial elites. *Strategic Management Journal*, 13 (special issue): 163–82.

Pettigrew, A. M., and T. McNulty 1995. Power and influences in and around the boardroom. *Human Relations*, 48: 845–73.

1998. Sources and uses of power in the boardroom. *European Journal of Work and Organizational Psychology*, 7: 197–214.

Pettit, R. R., and R. F. Singer 1985. Small business finance: a research agenda. *Financial Management*, 14 (3): 47–60.

Pfeffer, J. 1972. Size and composition of corporate boards of directors: the organization and its environment. *Administrative Science Quarterly*, 17: 218–28.

Pfeffer, J., and G. R. Salancik 1978. *The External Control of Organizations: A Resource Dependence Perspective*. New York: Harper and Row.

Pierce, J. L., T. Kostova and K. T. Dirks 2001. Towards a theory of psychological ownership in organizations. *Academy of Management Review*, 26: 298–310.

Politis, D., and J. Gabrielsson 2005. Informal investors and the entrepreneurial process: an empirical study of opportunity, motivation and ability. In D. Politis, *Entrepreneurship, career experience and learning: developing our understanding of entrepreneurship as an experiential learning process*. Doctoral dissertation, School of Economics and Management, Lund University, Sweden.

Politis, D., and H. Landström 2002. Informal investors as entrepreneurs: the development of an entrepreneurial career. *Venture Capital*, 4 (2): 78–101.

Porter, M. E. 1985. *Competitive Advantage: Creating and Sustaining Superior Performance*. New York and London: Press Ganey Associates.

Powell, W. W., and P. J. DiMaggio 1991. *The New Institutionalism in Organizational Analysis*. Chicago: University of Chicago Press.

Preston, L. E. 1990. Stakeholder management and corporate performance. *Journal of Behavioral Economics*, 19: 361–75.

Pye, A. 2004. The importance of context and time for understanding board behavior. *International Studies of Management and Organization*, 34 (2): 63–89.

Quinn, R. E., and K. Cameron 1983. Organizational lifecycles and shifting criteria of effectiveness: some preliminary evidence. *Management Science*, 29: 33–51.

Radner, R. 1996. Bounded rationality, indeterminacy and the theory of the firm. *Economic Journal*, 106: 1360–73.

Ravasi, D., and A. Zattoni 2006. Exploring the political side of board involvement in strategy: a study of mixed-ownership institutions. *Journal of Management Studies*, 43: 1673–703.

Richardson, R. J. 1987. Directorship interlock and corporate profitability. *Administrative Science Quarterly*, 32: 367–86.

Rindova, V. 1999. What corporate boards have to do with strategy: a contingency perspective. *Journal of Management Studies*, 36: 953–75.

Ring, P. S. 1993. *Processes facilitating reliance on trust in interorganizational networks*. Paper presented at the European Science Foundation conference 'Forms of Inter-organizational Networks: Structures and Processes', Berlin, 6–7 September.

1996. Fragile and resilient trust and their roles in economic exchange. *Business and Society*, 35: 148–75.

Ring, P. S., and A. Van den Ven 1992. Structuring cooperative relationships between organizations. *Strategic Management Journal*, 13: 483–98.

1994. Developmental processes of cooperative interorganizational relationships. *Academy of Management Review*, 19: 90–118.

Roberts, J., T. McNulty and P. Stiles 2005. Beyond agency conceptions of the work of the non-executive director: creating accountability in the boardroom. *British Journal of Management* 16 (Special Issue): 5–26.

Roberts, J., and P. Stiles 1999. The relationship between chairman and chief executives: competitive and complementary roles? *Long-Range Planning*, 32 (1): 36–48.

Rosenstein, J. 1988. The board and strategy: venture capital and high technology. *Journal of Business Venturing*, 3: 159–70.

Rosenstein, J., A. V. Bruno, W. Bygrave and N. T. Taylor 1993. The CEO, venture capitalist, and the board. *Journal of Business Venturing*, 8: 99–113.

Sapienza, H. J., M. A. Korsgaard, P. K. Goulet and J. P. Hoogendam 2000. Effects of agency risks and procedural justice on board processes in venture capital-backed firms. *Entrepreneurship and Regional Development*, 12: 331–51.

Schulze, W. S., M. H. Lubatkin, R. N. Dino and A. K. Buchholtz 2001. Agency relationships in family firms: theory and evidence. *Organization Science*, 12 (2): 99–116.

Scott, R. W. 1995. *Institutions and Organizations*. London: Sage.

Selznick, P. 1949. *TVA and the Grass Roots: A Study in the Sociology of Formal Organization*. New York: Harper and Row.

1957. *Leadership in Administration*. Evanston, IL: Row, Peterson.

Shen, W. 2003. The dynamics of the CEO–board relationship: an evolutionary perspective. *Academy of Management Review*, 28: 466–76.

Simmel, G. 1950. The stranger. In K. Wolff (ed.), *The Sociology of Georg Simmel*. New York: Free Press.

Simon, H. A. 1945. *Administrative Behavior: A Study of Decision-Making Processes in Administrative Organizations*. New York: Macmillan.

1955. A behavioral model of rational choice. *Quarterly Journal of Economics*, 69 (1): 99–118.

Sjöstrand, S.-E. 1985. *Samhällsorganisation*. Lund, Sweden: Doxa Ekonomi.

1997. *The Two Faces of Management: The Janus Factor*. London: Thomson.

Sjöstrand, S.-E., and M. Tyrstrup 2001. Recognized and unrecognized managerial leadership. In S.-E. Sjöstrand, J. Sandberg and M. Tyrstrup (eds.), *Invisible Management: The Social Construction of Leadership*. London: Thomson Learning.

Smith, K. G., K. A. Smith, J. D. Olian, H. P. Sims, D. P. O'Bannen and J. A. Scully 1994. Top management team demography and processes: the role of integration and communication. *Administrative Science Quarterly*, 37: 412–38.

Sonnenfeld, J. A. 2002. What makes great boards great. *Harvard Business Review*, 80 (9): 106–13.

Stearns, B. L., and M. S. Mizruchi 1993. Board composition and corporate financing: the impact of financial institution representation on borrowing. *Academy of Management Journal*, 36: 603–18.

Stiles, P., and B. Taylor 2001. *Boards at Work: How Directors View Their Roles and Responsibilities*. Oxford: Oxford University Press.

Stone, C. D. 1975. *Where the Law Ends*. New York: Harper and Row.

Sundaramurthy, C., and M. Lewis 2003. Control and collaboration: paradoxes of governance. *Academy of Management Review*, 28: 397–415.

Swedish Government 2004. *Code of Corporate Governance*. Swedish Government Official Report SOU 2004/130. Stockholm: Swedish Government.

Swiss Business Federation 2002. *Code of Best Practice for Corporate Governance*. Zurich: Economiesuisse.

Taylor, B. 2001. From corporate governance to corporate entrepreneurship. *Journal of Change Management*, 2 (2): 128–47.

Teece, D. J. 1980. Economies of scope and the scope of the enterprise. *Journal of Economic Behavior and Organization*, 1: 223–47.

Thomsen, S. 2004. Convergence of corporate governance during the stock market bubble: towards Anglo-American or European standards? In A. Grandori (ed.), *Corporate Governance and Firm Organization: Microfoundations and Structural Forms*. Oxford: Oxford University Press.

Timmons, J. A., and W. D. Bygrave 1986. Venture capital's role in financing innovation for economic growth. *Journal of Business Venturing*, 1: 161–76.

Tricker, B. 1984. *Corporate Governance*. Aldershot: Gower Publishing.

Tyler, T. R. 1989. The quality of dispute resolution processes and outcomes: measurement problems and possibilities. *Denver University Law Review*, 66: 419–36.

Tyler, T. R., and E. A. Lind 1992. A relational model of authority in groups. *Advances in Experimental Social Psychology*, 25: 115–91.

Useem, M. 1982. Classwide rationality in the politics of managers and directors of large corporations in the United States and Great Britain. *Administrative Science Quarterly*, 27: 199–226.

1984. *Inner Circle: Large Corporations and the Rise of Business Political Activity in the US and UK*. Oxford: Oxford University Press.

1993. *Executive Defence: Shareholder Power and Corporate Reorganization*. Cambridge, MA: Harvard University Press.

Van Ees, H., J. Gabrielsson and M. Huse 2005. *For a behavioral theory on boards and governance*. Unpublished paper.

Van Ees, H., and T. J. B. M. Postma 2004. Dutch boards and governance: a comparative institutional analysis of board roles and member (s)election procedures. *International Studies of Management and Organization*, 34 (2): 90–112.

Vance, S. C. 1983. *Corporate Leadership*. New York: McGraw-Hill.

Walsh, J. P., and J. K. Seward 1990. On the efficiency of internal and external corporate control mechanisms. *Academy of Management Review*, 15: 421–58.

Ward, J. L. 1991. *Creating Effective Boards for Private Enterprises*. San Francisco: Jossey Bass.

Ward, J. L., and J. L. Handy 1988. A survey of board practices. *Family Business Review*, 1: 289–308.

Weber, M. 1956. *Wirtschaft und Gesellschaft: Grundriss der verstehenden soziologie*. Tübingen: Mohr.

Wenstøp, P. Z. 2005. *Power of action: applying the concept of board power to understand corporate boards.* Pre-doc-defence, Norwegian School of Management BI, Oslo.

Wernerfelt, B. 1984. A resource-based view of the firm. *Strategic Management Journal,* 5: 171–80.

Westhead, P., and P. Cowling 1998. Family firm research: the need for a methodological rethink. *Entrepreneurship Theory and Practice,* 28 (fall): 31–56.

Westphal, J. D. 1999. Collaboration in the boardroom: behavioral and performance consequences of CEO social ties. *Academy of Management Journal,* 42: 7–24.

2002. Second thoughts on board independence. *Corporate Board,* 23: 6–10.

Westphal, J. D., and J. W. Fredrickson 2001. Who directs strategic change? Director experience, the selection of new CEOs, and change in corporate strategy. *Strategic Management Journal,* 22: 1113–37.

Westphal, J. D., and P. Khanna 2003. Keeping directors in line: social distancing as a control mechanism in the corporate elite. *Administrative Science Quarterly,* 48: 361–98.

Westphal, J. D, M. D. L. Seidel and K. J. Stewart 2001. Second-order imitation: uncovering latent effects of board network ties. *Administrative Science Quarterly,* 46: 717–47.

Westphal, J. D., and E. J. Zajac 1994. Substance and symbolism in CEOs' long-term incentive plans. *Administrative Science Quarterly,* 39: 367–90.

1995. Who shall govern? CEO/board power, demographic similarity, and new director selection. *Administrative Science Quarterly,* 40: 60–83.

1998. The symbolic management of stockholders: corporate governance reforms and shareholder reactions. *Administrative Science Quarterly,* 43: 127–53.

2001. Decoupling policy from practice: the case of stock repurchase programs. *Administrative Science Quarterly,* 46: 202–28.

Whisler, T. L. 1984. *Rules of the Game: Inside the Boardroom.* New York: Dow Jones–Irwin.

Williamson, O. E. 1975. *Markets and Hierarchies.* New York: Free Press.

1979. Transaction-cost economics: the governance of contractual relations. *Journal of Law and Economics,* 22: 233–61.

1985. *The Economic Institutions of Capitalism.* New York: Free Press.

1988. The logic of economic organization. *Journal of Law, Economics and Organization,* 4: 65–93.

1996. *The Mechanisms of Governance.* New York: Oxford University Press.

Windolf, P. 2004. Corruption, fraud and corporate governance: a report on Enron. In A. Grandori (ed.), *Corporate Governance and Firm Organization: Microfoundations and Structural Forms*. Oxford: Oxford University Press.

Wright, M., I. Filatotchev, T. Buck and K. Bishop 2003. Is stakeholder corporate governance appropriate in Russia? *Journal of Management and Governance*, 7: 263–90.

Yermack, D. 1996. Higher market valuation of companies with a small board of directors. *Journal of Financial Economics*, 40: 185–211.

Yukl, G. A. 1998. *Leadership in Organizations*. Englewood Cliffs, NJ: Prentice-Hall.

Zadek, S. 2001. *The Civil Corporation: The New Economy of Corporate Citizenship*. London: Earthscan.

Zahra, S. A. 1991. Predictors and outcomes of corporate entrepreneurship: an exploratory study. *Journal of Business Venturing*, 5: 259–85.

1996. Governance, ownership, and corporate entrepreneurship: the moderating impact of industry technological opportunities. *Academy of Management Journal*, 39: 1713–35.

Zahra, S. A., and I. Filatotchev 2004. Governance of the entrepreneurial threshold firm: a knowledge based perspective. *Journal of Management Studies*, 41: 885–97.

Zahra, S. A., D. O. Neubaum and M. Huse 1997. The effect of the environment on export performance among telecommunication new ventures. *Entrepreneurship Theory and Practice*, 22 (1): 25–46.

2000. Entrepreneurship in medium-size companies: exploring the effects of ownership and governance systems. *Journal of Management*, 26: 947–76.

Zahra, S. A., and J. A. Pearce 1989. Boards of directors and corporate performance: a review and integrative model. *Journal of Management*, 15: 291–334.

1990. Determinants of board directors' strategic involvement. *European Management Journal*, 8: 164–73.

Zajac, E. J., and J. D. Westphal 1995. Accounting for the explanations of CEO compensation: substance and symbolism. *Administrative Science Quarterly*, 40: 283–308.

1996. Who shall succeed? How CEO/board preferences and power affect the choice of new CEOs. *Academy of Management Journal*, 39 (1): 64–90.

Zald, M. N. 1969. The power and functions of boards of directors: a theoretical synthesis. *American Journal of Sociology*, 75 (1): 97–111.

Index